Laughing Matters

Laughing Matters

FARCE AND THE MAKING
OF ABSOLUTISM IN FRANCE

SARA BEAM

Cornell University Press   *Ithaca & London*

First published 2007 by Cornell University Press

Printed in the United States of America

Library of Congress Cataloging-in-Publication Data
Beam, Sara.
   Laughing matters : farce and the making of absolutism in France / Sara Beam.
      p. cm.
   Includes bibliographical references and index.
   ISBN 978-0-8014-4560-6 (cloth : alk. paper)
      1. French farces—History and criticism.   2. French drama—16th century—History and criticism.   3. French drama—17th century—History and criticism.   4. Theater—Political aspects—France—History—16th century.   5. Theater—Political aspects—France—History—17th century.   I. Title.
   PQ584.B43 2007
   842'.409358—dc22   2006101254

Cornell University Press strives to use environmentally responsible suppliers and materials to the fullest extent possible in the publishing of its books. Such materials include vegetable-based, low-VOC inks and acid-free papers that are recycled, totally chlorine-free, or partly composed of nonwood fibers. For further information, visit our website at www.cornellpress.cornell.edu.

Cloth printing   10 9 8 7 6 5 4 3 2 1

Contents

Illustrations

Acknowledgments

This work could never have been completed without the support—financial, intellectual and emotional—I have received along the way. Many thanks to the Institut Français de Washington, Victoria University at the University of Toronto, the History Department at the University of California, Berkeley, the Mellon Foundation, and the Social Sciences and Humanities Research Council of Canada whose generous financial support made possible the research, thinking, and writing (not to mention rethinking and rewriting) that made this book what it is.

Many friends, colleagues, and teachers have contributed to this project. It was thanks to Nancy Partner at McGill University that I decided to pursue graduate studies and to focus on laughter as a historical category. In France, I owe a particular debt of gratitude to Madeleine de la Conté, chief archivist at the Archives Départementales Seine-Maritime, who led me to important documents that I would have otherwise overlooked. Robert Descimon and Roger Chartier at the École des Hautes Études very kindly allowed me to attend their seminars during the 1995–96 academic year and have encouraged me in my research since then. In North America, my colleagues at the Baltimore-Washington Old Regime Group, the Centre for Reformation and Renaissance Studies at the University of Toronto, the Centre for Studies in Religion and Society at the University of Victoria, and the Early Modern Discussion Group at the University of Victoria provided lively intellectual communities in which to develop many of the ideas that became central to this study. David Bell, Michael Breen, Gregory Brown, Paul Cohen, Julie Crawford, Mitch Lewis-Hammond, Mack Holt, Andrea McKenzie, Jacob Melish, André Lambelet, Ed Pechter, Jeffrey Ravel, and Sydney Watts generously took the time to read parts of the manuscript and to offer their thoughts and criticisms. Megan Armstrong and Carina Johnson went further, reading and rereading the book in its entirety at moments when I needed both critical engagement and encouragement. I would particularly like to thank John Ackerman, director of Cornell University Press, for his early enthusiasm for the manuscript as well as the anonymous readers for the Press whose comments were ever-so-helpful during the final editing process. Jim Collins and Barbara Diefendorf have been wonderful mentors, providing me with the kind of support that normally would be reserved for their own graduate students. This project was decisively shaped by my many teachers at the University of California at Berkeley, in particular Randy Starn, whose enthusiasm for my varied historical interests led me to the theater; Peter Sahlins, whose insistence that I keep the big picture in mind kept me from straying too far; and Carla Hesse, whose incisive criticism—coupled with confidence in my success—sustained me along the way. Finally, I thank Natalie Zemon Davis, whose work inspired me to become a French historian in the first place, and whose intellectual advice and personal example I always hold before me.

I owe my greatest thanks to those whose emotional support made this book possible, my family. Thanks to Irene Fairley for her endless enthusiasm for babysitting and her tactful editing; to Jordan Richards for his computer expertise and generous goodwill; to Robert Beam and Karen Takenaka for understanding completely when the book interfered with family holidays; to Matt Beam and Marjorie Garson for reading the entire manuscript with enthusiasm, love, and painstaking attention to style; to Iris and Emile Fairley-Beam for reminding me everyday of the importance of laughter; and to Peter Fairley, my life partner and best friend, who helped me in more ways than he can know.

Abbreviations

ADG	Archives Départementales de Gironde (Bordeaux)
ADHG	Archives Départementales de la Haute-Garonne (Toulouse)
ADSM	Archives Départementales Seine-Maritime (Rouen)
AMD	Archives Municipales Dijon
AN	Archives Nationales
AN MC	Archives Nationales Minutier Central
BM Bordeaux	Bibliothèque de Bordeaux
BNF	Bibliothèque Nationale de France

Until the late sixteenth century, the new calendar year began in late March or at Easter, depending on the jurisdiction. To avoid confusion, all dates have been converted to the new style, with the year presuming to have begun on 1 January.

Introduction

> What we see that is ugly, deformed, improper,
> indecent, unfitting, and indecorous excites
> laughter in us, provided we are not moved to
> compassion.
>
> LAURENT JOUBERT,
> *Treatise on Laughter* (1579)

In the French farce *The Fart*, a husband and wife bicker over who has just
let out a fragrant, resounding fart.[1] Unable to resolve the dispute, they turn
to a passing lawyer and then to a judge to ask for legal advice. The judge's
answer is simple: since, according to canon law, a married couple owns everything in common, the fart is theirs to share. The play ends happily, with
the husband and wife reconciled and the judge satisfied with his fatuous ruling that all couples share a common asshole. The play works on several levels: it renders comic the awkward situation caused by the fart, the couple's
inability to agree, and the inane application of canon law to a ridiculous
case. It exposes the tension in human society between what our bodies do
of their own accord and the social imperative to manage the body and its
products in what are often ridiculous ways. By mocking both the squabbling
couple and the judge, its satire does not render judgment on either—after all
the ending is happy—but it does destabilize the nature of power in human
relationships. It asks us to laugh at social conventions and traditional hierarchies, and to laugh at ourselves. As such, farces like *The Fart*, like much
modern comedy, reveal how we see ourselves and our relationships with
others. We may recognize the predicament faced by the fifteenth-century
couple in *The Fart*, though the way that we would solve this problem would
of course be different because our society has different structures of power
and distinct systems of bodily constraints.

1. "Farce nouvelle et fort joyeuse du pect," in *Recueil de farces (1450–1550)*, ed. André Tissier (Geneva: Droz, 1996), 10:23–63.

Because it is both universal and, paradoxically, culturally specific, humor can be a useful subject for historical investigation.[2] In most societies, there are things you can joke about and things you cannot—at least not in public. Some jokes are forbidden by law, and many others are deemed inappropriate in mixed company. Moreover, the rules about what can be joked about change through time. Take workplace culture in professional America: it is no longer acceptable to joke about race, to demean homosexuals, or to make rape a thing of laughter. Such jokes can lead to lawsuits, monetary compensation, and dismissal.[3] In a democratic society, changes in the culture of laughter sometimes advance the social and political status of groups relatively excluded from the locus of power. But this is not always the case. In authoritarian societies, changing norms about joking and laughter often limit what can be said in public and thereby inhibit political and social dialogue. Such was the case in early modern France: when common French men and women lost the freedom to joke about farts and to mock judges in public, their political freedoms were compromised as well.

Laughter is often a political act. As a result, where one can document humor's shifting context and impact over time, laughter can function as a litmus test of shifts in people's ideas about themselves and the political culture in which they live. It is a particularly useful entry into people's worldview when considering societies in which other reliable evidence is lacking, in which most people are illiterate, or in which crucial texts have been lost over time. This study examines humor, more particularly the changing fortunes of satirical theater, as a means to understand the political culture of early modern France, a society in which even the literate left relatively few records.

During the French Renaissance, young bourgeois men regularly made demeaning jokes in public. They performed short plays called farces in which

2. Sigmund Freud, *Jokes and Their Relation to the Unconscious*, trans. James Strachey (New York: Norton, 1960); Christopher P. Wilson, *Jokes: Form, Content, Use and Function* (London: Academic Press, 1979); Henri Bergson, *Le rire: Essai sur la signification du comique* (Paris: Presses Universitaires de France, 1969); Laurent Joubert, *Traité du ris: Contenant son essance, ses causes, et mervelheus effais* (Paris: Nicolas Chesneau, 1579); Dominique Bertrand, *Dire le rire à l'âge classique: Représenter pour mieux contrôler* (Aix-en-Provence: Publications de l'Université de Provence, 1995); William Ian Miller, *The Anatomy of Disgust* (Cambridge, Mass.: Harvard University Press, 1997).

3. Masoud Hemmasi, Lee A. Graf, and Gail S. Russ, "Gender-Related Jokes in the Workplace: Sexual Humor or Sexual Harassment?" *Journal of Applied Social Psychology* 24 (1994): 1114–28; Janice D. Yoder and Patricia Aniakudo, "When Pranks Become Harassment: The Case of African American Women Firefighters," *Sex Roles* 35 (1996): 253–70; Elizabeth Walker Mechling and Jay Mechling, "Shock Talk: From Consensual to Contractual Joking Relationships in the Bureaucratic Workplace," *Human Organization* 44 (1985): 339–43; Larry Smeltzer and Terry L. Leap, "An Analysis of Individual Reactions to Potentially Offensive Jokes in Work Settings," *Human Relations* 41 (1988): 295–304; Vicki Shultz, "The Sanitized Workplace," *Yale Law Journal* 112 (2003): 2061–90.

no one was exempt from being called a whore or a fool. They mocked those on the margins of society, mostly women, whom they portrayed as licentious shrews, and peasants, whom they portrayed as fools. Yet many of their jokes skewered their social superiors—clergy and royal officials—and they regularly accused these men of misusing their positions of authority. Because France was ruled by kings who considered direct criticism of royal officials to be treasonous, the laughter of the farce allowed both actors and audience a rare opportunity to express their opinions in a public context. Performing farce was thus a political act that helped shape public opinion and let the clergy, royal officials, and even the king know that the common people expected them to behave responsibly and rule in the interest of the public good. Being able to laugh out loud about those who ruled them was experienced as a moment of freedom in an otherwise rigidly hierarchical society.[4] Over time, however, this liberating culture of laughter was marginalized. Young bourgeois men ceased to perform satirical plays in the city streets, gradually submitting to a more closed cultural regime in which political and religious satire was pushed underground. This transformation took place in France between 1550 and 1650, and it marked the advent of a new political order—absolutism.

Farcical theater, and more particularly its regulation and later censorship, allows us to examine what role cultural change had in the establishment of absolutism, a form of governance that led to the modern European state. I argue that this transformation of farce from a ubiquitous to a marginal practice and its suppression was a two-stage process: the first stage occurred during the Wars of Religion (1562–98), when the urban elites who had until then been important patrons of farce first turned against the genre; the second began after peace was reestablished under Henry IV (1589–1610). I have found that urban officials, now eager to ingratiate themselves with a centralizing monarchy, decided that the teasing humor of the farce was too rude and crude to be performed during important civic events (especially when the king was present). Urban officials hungry for royal patronage turned instead to theatrical genres that flattered rather than mocked political power.

Seen in this light, the rise of absolutism in France—often presented as the strong arm bearing down on popular culture—becomes at least partly a *consequence* of censorship. Censorship is not simply imposed on subjects by a government but usually requires collusion at many levels of society and

---

4. Mikhail Bakhtin, *Rabelais and His World*, trans. Hélène Iswolsky (Bloomington: Indiana University Press, 1984). For critical readings of his interpretation of laughter, see Jan Bremmer and Herman Roodenburg, eds., *A Cultural History of Humour: From Antiquity to the Present Day* (Cambridge, Mass.: Polity Press, 1997); Aron Gurevich, *Medieval Popular Culture: Problems of Belief and Perception*, trans. János M. Bak and Paul A. Hollingsworth (New York: Cambridge University Press, 1988).

can itself transform political culture. The gradual demise of satirical farce was not the product of absolutism but one of its central constituents. Farce finally disappeared as an important political force at the moment when French urban officials decided they had more to gain from cooperating with the monarchy than from resisting its growing authority. This new intolerance for open religious and political debate took place between 1550 and 1650, the period *before* Louis XIV, the quintessential absolutist king, came to the throne.

My efforts to understand why farce was marginalized intersect with several strands of historical interpretation, including a well-established body of scholarship on the history of popular culture. Most historians agree that a relatively new distinction between popular and elite culture emerged in western Europe during the seventeenth century.[5] Before 1550, nobles and educated elites happily participated in festive entertainments designed for the common city folk. The king, nobles, clergy, and urban magistrates all commissioned farce players to perform and enjoyed their bawdy humor. At a certain point, however, educated elites and nobles started to withdraw from popular festivities, holding themselves above such spectacles. In documenting the role of satirical theater in this process, this volume revises our current understanding of how this marginalization of popular culture was tied to the rise of absolutist power in France.

Since Norbert Elias's *The Civilizing Process* was assimilated into early modern historiography in the 1980s, historians have linked the growing divergence between popular and elite culture to the development of the modern European state. In France, state centralization occurred under the auspices of absolutism. Absolutism, it is generally agreed, did not mean

---

5. Peter Burke, *Popular Culture in Early Modern Europe* (New York: Harper and Row, 1978); Robert Mandrou, *De la culture populaire aux XVIIe et XVIIIe siècles: La Bibliothèque bleue de Troyes* (Paris: Stock, 1964); Carlo Ginzburg, *The Night Battles: Witchcraft and Agrarian Cults in the Sixteenth and Seventeenth Centuries*, trans. John Tedeschi and Anne Tedeschi (Baltimore: Johns Hopkins University Press, 1983); Natalie Zemon Davis, "The Reasons of Misrule: Youth-Groups and Charivaris in Sixteenth-Century France," *Past and Present* 50 (1971): 41–75; Natalie Zemon Davis, "The Rites of Violence: Religious Riots in Sixteenth-Century France," *Past and Present* 59 (1973): 51–91; Robert Muchembled, *Culture populaire et culture des élites dans la France moderne, XVe–XVIIIe siècles: Essai* (Paris: Flammarion, 1977); Emmanuel Le Roy Ladurie, *Le Carnaval de Romans: De la Chandeleur au mercredi des Cendres, 1579–1580* (Paris: Gallimard, 1979); Roger Chartier, "Discipline et invention: La fête," in *Lectures et lecteurs dans la France d'ancien régime* (Paris: Seuil, 1987), 23–43; Nicole Pellegrin, *Les bachelleries: Organisations et fêtes de la jeunesse dans le Centre-Ouest, XVe–XVIIIe siècles* (Poitiers: Société des Antiquaires de l'Ouest, 1982); Michel Vovelle, *Les métamorphoses de la fête en Provence de 1750 à 1820* (Paris: Flammarion, 1976). See also two general collections of articles, Jacques Beauroy, Marc Bertrand, and Edward Gargan, eds., *The Wolf and the Lamb: Popular Culture in France from the Old Régime to the Twentieth Century* (Saratoga, Calif.: Anma Libri, 1977); Stephen L. Kaplan, ed., *Understanding Popular Culture: Europe from the Middle Ages to the Nineteenth Century* (Berlin: Mouton, 1984).

that French monarchs truly exercised absolute power.[6] Nevertheless, the kings of Bourbon France in the seventeenth and eighteenth centuries claimed to rule by divine right and in principle rejected the idea that any individual or corporate body could challenge their authority. In making these claims, French monarchs reinvented the traditional understanding of the body politic. In place of a medieval vision of the body politic, which mandated some measure of consultation between the king and his subjects, they substituted, by the seventeenth century, an absolutist body centered squarely on the king. According to Louis XIV, the king alone could act in the public good because God deemed it to be his right and duty to do so.

Norbert Elias saw a reciprocal connection between the absolutist body politic and the withdrawal of French elites from popular culture. For Elias, Louis XIV's construction of Versailles in the 1680s and his insistence that the aristocracy reside at court symbolized the changed political relationship between king and noble, in which the noble became a mere courtier under the ever-expanding authority of the monarch. Because the noble now depended on the king for a royal pension and could no longer live off his own estates, he was forced to participate in elaborate court rituals during which he debased himself before the king.[7] At Versailles, nobles adhered to a new code of manners called *civilité*, which demanded that courtiers avoid offending (at least directly) their social superiors and encouraged them to control their bodily urges, even if that meant tempering their usual habits of spitting in public and urinating in the halls. This new standard of public comportment similarly repudiated farce as crass and scandalous. For French elites increasingly controlled by a centralizing monarchy, adopting this new set of manners distinguished them from the rabble, and allowed them to assert cultural superiority during a period when their political autonomy was shrinking. Although Elias's relentless focus on Versailles as the locus of cultural change in France has been modified by historians who identify several sites in which increasing bodily constraints and political power intersect, for most historians of early

6. William Beik, *Absolutism and Society in Seventeenth-Century France: State Power and Provincial Aristocracy in Languedoc* (New York: Cambridge University Press, 1985); Fanny Cosandey and Robert Descimon, *L'absolutisme en France: Histoire et historiographie* (Paris: Seuil, 2002); Louis Marin, *Le portrait du roi* (Paris: Minuit, 1981). For a fuller discussion of absolutism, see chapter 6.

7. Norbert Elias, *The Civilizing Process: Sociogenetic and Psychogenetic Investigations*, trans. Edmund Jephcott, ed. Eric Dunning, Johan Goudsblom, and Stephen Mennell (Oxford: Blackwell, 2000), 109–28, 188–204, 365–403; Pierre Bourdieu, *La distinction: Critique sociale du jugement* (Paris: Minuit, 1979); Jorge Arditi, *A Genealogy of Manners: Transformations of Social Relations in France and England from the Fourteenth to the Eighteenth Century* (Chicago: University of Chicago Press, 1998); Jan A. Bremmer and Herman Roodenburg, eds., *A Cultural History of Gesture* (Ithaca: Cornell University Press, 1992).

modern Europe the withdrawal of elites from popular culture still signals an accommodation to the absolutist, hence modernizing, state.[8]

I argue in this book that farcical performance and its marginalization need to be taken into account to explain the development of this new sense of decorum and reorientation of political relationships in France. The suppression of farce was a process that began much earlier than the developments discussed by Elias, and it proceeded not from the centralized court at Versailles but from the direction of municipal officials in cities all over the country. Until recently, the role of urban elites in seventeenth-century French political developments has been elusive. Historians have focused on the role of the French provincial nobility as active partners in the development of absolute rule under Louis XIV but have assumed rather than explored the acquiescence of urban officials.[9] Recent studies of provincial cities, which focus on municipal politics and how urban officials interacted with the crown, have begun to correct this understanding of urban elites as passive recipients of absolutism.[10] This book broadens our understanding of urban officials' motivations by demonstrating the ways in which they were responding not only to new political pressures but also to religious influences—the threat of religious violence, the religious pressures of Catholic reform—deliberately underplayed by Elias. By the seventeenth century, urban officials increasingly identified with the nobility. Repudiating farce and embracing civility were important ways for them to distinguish

8. Muchembled, *Invention*, 135–201; Roger Chartier, "Distinction et divulgation: La civilité et ses livres," in *Lectures et lecteurs*, 45–86; Jacques Revel, "The Uses of Civility," in *Passions of the Renaissance*, ed. Roger Chartier, vol. 3 of *A History of Private Life*, trans. Arthur Goldhammer (Cambridge, Mass.: Harvard University Press, 1989), 167–205; Jay M. Smith, "'Our Sovereign's Gaze': Kings, Nobles, and State Formation in Seventeenth-Century France," *French Historical Studies* 18 (1993): 396–415; Orest Ranum, "Courtesy, Absolutism and the Rise of the French State, 1630–1660," *Journal of Modern History* 52 (1980): 426–51; Anna Bryson, *From Courtesy to Civility: Changing Codes of Conduct in Early Modern England* (Oxford: Clarendon Press, 1998). Also see studies of individual French cities, Philip T. Hoffman, *Church and Community in the Diocese of Lyon, 1500–1789* (New Haven: Yale University Press, 1984), 87–97; Robert A. Schneider, *Public Life in Toulouse, 1463–1789: From Municipal Republic to Cosmopolitan City* (Ithaca: Cornell University Press, 1989), 82–89, 255–75; Gregory Hanlon, *L'univers des gens de bien: Culture et comportements des élites urbaines en Agenais-Condomois au XVIIe siècle* (Talence: Presses Universitaires de Bordeaux, 1989).

9. Beik, *Absolutism*; James B. Collins, *Fiscal Limits of Absolutism: Direct Taxation in Early Seventeenth-Century France* (Berkeley: University of California Press, 1988); Albert N. Hamscher, *The Conseil Privé and the Parlements in the Age of Louis XIV: A Study of French Absolutism* (Philadelphia: American Philosophical Society, 1987); Sharon Kettering, *Patrons, Brokers and Clients in Seventeenth-Century France* (New York: Oxford University Press, 1986).

10. Michael P. Breen, "Legal Culture, Municipal Politics and Royal Absolutism in Seventeenth-Century France: The 'Avocats' of Dijon (1595–1715)," Ph.D. diss., Brown University, 2000; Hilary J. Bernstein, *Between Crown and Community: Politics and Civic Culture in Sixteenth-Century Poitiers* (Ithaca: Cornell University Press, 2004); Guy Saupin, *Nantes au XVIIe siècle: Vie politique et société urbaine* (Rennes: Presses Universitaires de Rennes, 1996); Yann Lignereux, *Lyon et le roi: De la "bonne ville" à l'absolutisme municipal (1594–1654)* (Seyssel: Champ Vallon, 2003).

themselves from their social inferiors and thereby constitute their identity as members of the French ruling elite.

Farce, and the theater more generally, is an effective window for viewing changes in political culture because of its predominance as a public venue. In a time before film, newspapers, and even widespread literacy, theater was a central medium for the dissemination of information and ideas. Townspeople and farmers bringing goods to market gathered to watch plays in the city square not just to be entertained but also to catch the latest news. Members of the local nobility and important city officials sat on raised platforms to watch these public shows unfold. Many of the actors were respectable members of the community, such as law clerks working at the royal courts or university students. The actors were educated enough to be in the know regarding political and religious questions, and their relatively secure social status meant that they could take some risks in mocking those who administered their town and its diocese. These amateur performers usually belonged to long-standing festive societies, associations of predominately young men who traditionally performed farces at religious festivals such as Carnival as well as other civic celebrations. During the Renaissance, festive societies were a regular and celebrated element of urban society; their performances were applauded by all social classes, even the men in positions of authority whom they sometimes mocked.

During the French Renaissance, theater was accessible to all, yet it was also controlled by the urban oligarchy that ruled the city. Generally speaking, city officials recognized that the theater was a primary medium for shaping public opinion and thus sought to regulate its performance. Groups that wanted to perform a play were limited to a specific location in the city and consulted with local authorities about the timing and content of their performance. Despite concern that actors would perform slanderous plays that might result in street fights and libel suits, city councils and nobles enjoyed farcical theater enough to help finance its performance on a regular basis. Happily for the historian, there was some disagreement about who had the authority to permit plays to be performed, leaving us a rich source of city council and royal court documentation to tell us why a particular local church might want a farce to be performed and why a particular city council might not. This evidence—sometimes of censorship, sometimes of patronage—tells us what local authorities thought to be worthy of performance. Theatrical regulation clarifies when it became unacceptable to make lewd and satirical jokes in public, and how the new ideal of civility eventually found its way onto the public stage.

Farces were inherently satirical plays, and their jokes directly challenged the authority that religious and royal officials enjoyed in Renaissance France. Their satire was informed by Christian morals: the players held everyone in society—from the peasant to the king—to the standards of modesty, charity, and submissiveness found in Christian teaching, and then laughed out loud when it became clear that no one but saints could possibly hope to achieve them. Laughing about bodies also had direct political ramifications in Renaissance Europe. Jokes about defecation and sex were particularly resonant because political power was imagined in terms of a spiritual body. All subjects of the king, including the king himself, were thought to belong to a single body politic rendered whole by God's sanction.[11] Usually characterized as the head of the body politic, the king was nevertheless also expected to consult with and consider the needs of the whole. As a result, when early modern Europeans wanted to make fun of political power, they often did so by reversing the hierarchy of the body politic: at Carnival and during other traditional festivals, the anus directed the head, the belly led the clergy, and lust for violence drove the nobility to war.

We know the farce was an inherently satirical genre thanks to the actions of judges and city councilors, who often imprisoned actors when they made the authority figures they mocked a little too recognizable. During the Renaissance, bawdy humor, social satire, and political commentary mixed, if not freely, at least with a certain license. Urban magistrates and city councilors patronized farce, even though it often resulted in slander, because they believed that a measure of open political and religious discussion was legitimate in order for the king to know how best to serve the public good. Acknowledging the political engagement of the theater and its role in shaping public opinion helps us to understand why festivals like Carnival were so closely regulated throughout the early modern period.

In France, a relatively open and tolerant period of theatrical performance came to an end during the sixteenth century. The general trend between 1550 and 1650 was toward increasing constraint: fewer people were allowed to perform farces in fewer places, and those who did so had less freedom to talk explicitly about the human body or about power relations. The reasons for this contraction are both religious and political. Initially, during the Wars of Religion, religious concerns predominated. Catholic urban officials, fearful of the threat of Protestantism, sought to reform lay Catholic practice in their cities. Increasingly, they deemed satirical farce to be a profane corruption of legitimate Catholic festivals such as saints' day celebrations and, as a result, censored its performance. The explicit references to the human body and sexuality found in many farces were thought to be dangerously provocative in cities riven by rival religious communities of Catholics and Protestants who often came to blows.

Once war ended, farce returned to the public stage but in a modified form. Theater audiences still chuckled at fart jokes and limp penises, but they no

---

11. Michel Foucault, *Surveiller et punir: Naissance de la prison* (Paris: Gallimard, 1975); M. S. Kempshall, *The Common Good in Late Medieval Political Thought* (Oxford: Clarendon Press, 1999); Ernst H. Kantorowicz, *The King's Two Bodies: A Study in Mediaeval Political Theology* (Princeton: Princeton University Press, 1957).

longer expected biting satire and political slander from the actors who performed these comic plays, largely because the social class of the farceurs had changed. The relatively high-status bourgeois and noble actors of the Renaissance were replaced by professional actors. Such men and women—those who made their living by performing—were socially marginal; they were usually itinerants, and their trade was frowned upon by the Catholic Church. They sought to entertain the crowds but had little interest in risking a prison sentence in order to articulate political concerns about the public good. By 1600, amateur festive societies no longer performed farce publicly, and pointed political and religious satire had largely exited the stage.

Political change also influenced the performance of farce. After the Wars of Religion, during which so many French cities rebelled against the crown, Henry IV (1598–1610) and his successors sought to limit the traditional political freedoms enjoyed by urban officials. Without immediately abrogating their political privileges, Henry IV, Louis XIII, and Louis XIV put increasing pressure on municipal elites to conform to royal policies and directives during the first half of the seventeenth century. Urban officials responded to this pressure in a variety of ways, one of which was to avoid antagonizing the king with bawdy jokes made at his expense. In this context, most urban officials chose not to resuscitate the groups of amateurs who had traditionally performed farces, favoring Jesuit students who performed quiescent Christian tragedies after royal entry ceremonies and at other important civic events. The Jesuits explicitly refused to perform farce, which they considered unruly and immoral, and instead used student theater to cement their patronage relationship with the monarchy and to express their theological conservatism. Jesuit students were taught to embody the new ideal of civility. In ballets and neoclassical plays performed not only in Paris but in most provincial cities throughout the seventeenth century, the Jesuits displayed their students' physical grace, Christian piety, and political deference for the pleasure of the king and for the local urban elite. Supporting the reinvention of the French body politic advanced by the king, the Jesuits employed what I call the discourse of absolutism to enhance the status of their order and to pressure the French monarchy to pursue particular political ends.

And who were the students of this conservative Catholic religious order? They were in fact the sons of the city officials, youth who were thus naturally inclined to identify with the messages articulated in the Jesuit student theater. These officials learned from the Jesuits that the best way to get ahead politically under the Bourbon monarchy was to adopt civility, flatter the monarchy, and thereby secure themselves a position in royal service. In fact, urban elites throughout France adopted the discourse of absolutism decades before the traditionally independent French nobility, signaling their willingness to set aside a measure of local autonomy in order to profit from the extending reach of royal patronage. In the process, farce with its bawdy satire and its ability to express political discontent was sacrificed.

I have examined theater and political culture in France in part because an unusually rich set of printed and archival sources remains to tell the French story. Yet the changes I describe are not unique to France. Farce flourished all over western Europe during the Renaissance. By the eighteenth century, its prestige had waned, and in many Catholic regions from Bavaria to southern Italy, Jesuit students came to dominate the civic stage.[12] Indeed, further research may establish that a similar combination of changing religious values and political centralization contributed to the rise of civility elsewhere. Throughout western Europe, there was clearly a link between changes in elite manners and elite identification with the modernizing state. Relative elites, from the nobility to urban officials, chose to participate in the censorship of political and religious criticism in order to cement their own positions of power in the emerging state. This was not a universal or an inevitable process, but it was a defining element of becoming modern in the West. How this cultural transformation came about and at what political cost are the subjects of the chapters that follow.

12. Joël Lefebvre, *Les fols et la folie: Étude sur les genres du comique et la création littéraire en Allemagne pendant la Renaissance* (Paris: Klincksieck, 1968); Barbara I. Gusick and Edelgard E. DuBruck, eds., *New Approaches to European Theater of the Middle Ages: An Ontology* (New York: Peter Lang, 2004); Jean-Marie Valentin, *L'école, la ville, la cour: Pratiques sociales, enjeux poétologiques et répertoires du théâtre dans l'Empire au XVIIe siècle* (Paris: Klincksieck, 2004); Jennifer D. Selwyn, *A Paradise Inhabited by Devils: The Jesuits' Civilizing Mission in Early Modern Naples* (Aldershot: Ashgate, 2004).

I   Farce, Honor, and the Bounds of Satire

At the break of dawn on October 29, 1447, Dijon awakens to a clear day, a good day for theater going. Just inside the city walls, at a place called Morimont's Field near the Carmelite monastery, several dozen people hurry about in the early morning light. Priests, monks, and city folk prepare for the day's performance. Pierre Montbeliard, a priest and the local organizer of the event, consults with the amateur actors, making sure each one knows where to stand during the play and when to say his or her lines.[1] Today is the Sunday before the Christian holiday of Toussaint (All Saints' Day) and to celebrate the community has decided to perform a play recounting the life of a local patron saint. In preparation, carpenters finish assembling the raised platforms that are to be the stage, which are about two meters off the ground and open to the sky. At the eastern end of these platforms hang curtains depicting heaven, complete with illustrations of the sky and angels, while the other end is darkened with images of fiery hell. These theatrical platforms stand alongside another, more sinister, platform: Dijon's public execution site. Morimont's Field is the place where the Dijon executioner burns heretics and hangs those condemned to death for murder. In other cities, theatrical performances often took place in cemeteries, where the souls of

1. James R. Farr, *Hands of Honor: Artisans and Their World in Dijon, 1550–1650* (Ithaca: Cornell University Press, 1988), 77, 89; Grace Frank, *The Medieval French Drama* (Oxford: Clarendon, 1954), 161–73; Jean Richard, "Le Dijon des ducs et de la commune (XIe–XIVe siècles)," in *Histoire de Dijon*, ed. Pierre Gras (Toulouse: Privat, 1981), 44; Élie Konigson, *L'espace théâtral médiéval* (Paris: CNRS, 1975), 77–79, 93–94; Louis Petit de Julleville, *Histoire du théâtre en France: Les mystères* (Paris: Hachette, 1880; reprint, Geneva: Slatkine, 1968), 2:19, 23; Charles Mazouer, *Le théâtre français de la Renaissance* (Paris: Champion, 2002), 43–52; Michel Rousse, "Fonction du dispositif théâtral dans la genèse de la farce," in *Atti del IV Colloquio della Société Internationale pour l'Étude du Théâtre Médiéval*, ed. M. Chiabò, F. Doglio, and M. Maymone (Viterbo: Centro Studi sul Teatro Medioevale e Rinascimentale, 1984), 388.

those waiting in purgatory were thought to be lingering. This juxtaposition of death with a theatrical performance does not disturb the good citizens of Dijon. They are accustomed to the close proximity of sanctity, violence, and death. Today's performance, a mystery play depicting the life and death of Saint Eloi, will, like the executions, seek to entertain as well as to inspire the spectators with fear of God's wrath and wonder at his good works.[2]

Slowly, as the sky brightens, the first spectators arrive. They are probably artisans and working poor who live in the nearby urban parishes of Saint Philibert and Saint Jean. They come early to stake out a good viewing spot on the ground near the stage, and they look forward to a free and what they hope will be an amusing performance. Some artisans chat with their friends already dressed in costume and ready to take part in the ceremonial procession that will announce the beginning of the performance.[3] The wealthier city dwellers—retail merchants, lawyers, city councilors, local nobility—arrive a bit later. They station themselves on some raised seating, perhaps a window or a balcony of a nearby house, or a cart mounted with benches. They are also looking forward to the show, which the city council probably helped to fund and which may feature notable and wealthy Dijon citizens in prominent roles.[4] The field is large and can accommodate hundreds of spectators. Since the expense involved in mounting a mystery play is considerable and the planning likely a project of several months, the performance is a major civic event.[5]

But events do not enfold entirely as planned. In the middle of the mystery play three men, hoping to keep "the audience awake and amused," perform a short farce.[6] This intermission, likely fifteen minutes to an hour long, begins with a song followed by a short play. The farce players perform on a portion of the stage, and it is possible that the actors portraying the saint and other characters in the mystery are still sitting or standing nearby, visible to the audience.[7] The farce players are distinguished from the other actors by

---

2. Michel-Hilaire Clément-Janin, *Le Morimont de Dijon: Bourreaux et suppliciés* (Dijon: Darantière, 1889), 20–21; Konigson, *Espace*, 96; Dominique Viaux, *La vie paroissiale à Dijon à la fin du moyen âge* (Dijon: Éditions Universitaires de Dijon, 1988), 199–201; Jelle Koopmans, *Le théâtre des exclus au moyen âge: Hérétiques, sorcières et marginaux* (Paris: Imago, 1997), 11–40.

3. Farr, *Hands*, 83–85; Konigson, *Espace*, 69; Michel Rousse, "L'espace scénique des farces," in *Le théâtre au moyen âge*, ed. Gari R. Muller (Montreal: Aurore/Univers, 1981), 137–46.

4. Louis de Gouvenain, *Le théâtre à Dijon, 1422–1790* (Dijon: E. Joubard, 1888), 33; Konigson, *Espace*, 72, 101–3; Louis Petit de Julleville, *Histoire du théâtre en France: Répertoire du théâtre comique en France au moyen âge* (Paris: Le Cerf, 1886), 330–35.

5. Konigson, *Espace*, 74; Danielle Quéruel, "Fêtes et théâtre à Reims à la fin du XVe siècle," in *Et c'est la fin pour quoi sommes ensemble: Hommage à Jean Dufournet*, ed. Jean-Claude Aubailly (Paris: Champion, 1993), 1182; Viaux, *Vie*, 166.

6. Gouvenain, *Théâtre*, 32.

7. Ibid., 32–34; Barbara C. Bowen, *Les caractéristiques essentielles de la farce française et leur survivance dans les années 1550–1620* (Urbana: University of Illinois Press, 1964), 62; Konigson, *Espace*, 96; Geneviève de Chambure, "La musique dans les farces," *Cahiers de l'Association Internationale des Études Françaises* 26 (1974): 49–59.

their more down-to-earth costumes, which represent immediately recogniz-able social roles: the priest, the judge, the wife, the peasant. The farce play-ers are men, probably young men, who perform both male and female roles by exaggerating stereotypes to comic effect. Unlike the mystery play, which deals with historic and divine events, the farce represents everyday life, or at least a particular version of it, in which men and women never seem to get along and authority figures always seem to make bad decisions.[8] On this day, two of the actors dressed as commoners named Robin and Jacquin jest in rhyme about current events. Speaking in the regional dialect, they joke at length about a particular military expedition near the town of Montbéliard that certain inept people, who remain nameless, recently made. Their humor is coarse, and they rely on broad physical gestures to make sure that the audience gets all the jokes. Amid general laughter, a commotion starts up in the audience. Several of the more prominent citizens of Dijon watching the performance suddenly get up and leave Morimont's Field without even waiting for the farce to end.[9]

A few days later, after Toussaint, the city council heard a formal complaint brought against the farce players. Several "notable persons" who had attended the performance alleged that the farce players spoke foolish and outrageous words that day and should be brought to justice. These honorable citizens claimed that some jokes went so far as to mock the king, his son the dauphin, and their attendants. The chief prosecutor for the city, listening carefully to these allegations, decided that this matter challenged the very "honor and functioning of the city" and determined that the city council should investi-gate further.[10] The judicial inquiry quickly focused on the farce and the man who played Robin, the character who spoke the offending lines.

The role of Robin had been performed by a man named Savenot, who worked in Dijon's textile industry, the backbone of the city's economy. As an artisan in another's shop, Savenot was a member of the working poor, who made up about half of Dijon's population. It is possible that he was a young man, still hoping to open a shop of his own someday when he married and settled down. We know he was literate, which suggests that he came from a family secure enough in its finances to send him to a local priest for instruction before he began to apprentice in his early teens. Savenot was thus of a decidedly lower social status than the "notable persons" who brought the complaint against him and the members of the city council who judged his case.[11] Once the investigation got under way,

---

8. André Tissier, "Le rôle du costume dans les farces médiévales," in *Le théâtre et la cité dans l'Europe médiévale*, ed. Jean-Claude Aubailly and Edelgard E. Dubruck (Stuttgart: H.-D. Heinz, 1988), 373, 377.
9. Gouvenain, *Théâtre*, 33.
10. Ibid., 34.
11. Farr, *Hands*, 80, 239–40; Bernard Chevalier, *Les bonnes villes de France du XIVe au XVIe siècle* (Paris: Aubier-Montaigne, 1982), 83–88, 204–9.

Savenot, who took responsibility for having performed the role of Robin and for being the owner of the farcical play in question, agreed to be imprisoned in the city jail as a way of making amends for his transgression.

After a brief imprisonment of a few days, the mayor interrogated Savenot about his involvement in the farce. Savenot willingly admitted that he had referred to the dauphin's military campaigns, but he also defended his actions. Savenot claimed that he had meant no harm in performing the farce, which he had first seen performed two years earlier, in 1445, in the nearby town of Beaune. At that time, Savenot had so enjoyed the performance that he had paid to have the farce copied down so that he could take it home and perform it himself. When the residents of Dijon began to prepare for the mystery play performance, the actors together decided that Savenot's copied farce would provide an appropriate intermission. Savenot insisted that none of the actors thought the play contained "words referring to or disrespectful of the honor of anyone, and likewise the king our majesty's and the dauphin's men."[12] Nevertheless, at the urging of one performer, they all agreed to remove the word *escorcheurs* (flayers) from the text of the play, replacing it with the more neutral *estradeurs* (travelers) in a crucial scene of the play. Savenot also tried to ingratiate himself with the mayor, claiming that his own intentions had been innocent but that his judgment may have been clouded by the fact that he was "no cleric and could not read well."[13] Despite Savenot's claims of naiveté, the farce players' decision to replace the word *escorcheurs* with *estradeurs* signals that they were aware of the satirical potential of the farce and that they understood how easy it was for stereotypical jokes to become topical and pointed.

Reconstructing the political context of mid-fifteenth-century Dijon is crucial for understanding why local authorities understood this farcical performance to be slanderous satire. At first glance, it seems surprising that the Dijon city council would have been concerned about jokes made at the expense of the king of France. Dijon, a city of 6,000 to 8,000 inhabitants in eastern France, was the capital of the duchy of Burgundy, a province that had long had a turbulent relationship with the French monarchy. Since the mid-fourteenth century when King Charles V (1364–80) gave the duchy to his youngest son Philip, the duchy had been ruled by the French king in name only. In practice, the dukes of Burgundy, who also acquired adjacent lands in Flanders through marriage, began ruling Burgundy as their own, including waging wars and conducting diplomacy as if they were independent territorial rulers. It was the duke rather than the king of France who affirmed Dijon's legal and fiscal privileges during the first half of the fifteenth century, and it was to the duke that Burgundian taxes were

---

12. Gouvenain, *Théâtre*, 34–35.
13. Ibid., 35.

paid.[14] During the devastating Hundred Years' War (1337–1453) between France and England, a war fought to determine who would control the area that is now France, the Duke of Burgundy sided with the English, a decision that inevitably weakened the French king's authority. Under these circumstances, jokes about the military weakness of the French crown might have seemed apropos, or at least inoffensive. Yet by the mid-1440s, the political balance of power was again shifting, and the Dijon city council had begun playing a delicate game of splitting its loyalties between the duke and the king. Technically, as subjects of the French monarch, all Dijon residents owed allegiance to the king. Although the duke might have laughed out loud at the farce players' barbs, the small oligarchy that controlled Dijon's city council and law courts was concerned how the king would react if he heard of the Dijon performance.

By referring to the town of Montbéliard and the *estradeurs*, the farce players raised delicate issues that the city council preferred not be aired in public. Although King Charles VII (1422–61) of France and Philip of Burgundy had settled their differences at the 1435 Peace of Arras, in actuality this treaty only marked the beginning of a prolonged cold war between the two rulers. Charles VII wanted the duchy of Burgundy back under his direct control, and, short of going to war, did his best to undermine the duke's authority in the region. With his aim in mind, Charles allowed decommissioned French troops to roam Burgundy. He also launched several military campaigns through Burgundy, including an offensive led by the dauphin on Montbéliard, the campaign mentioned in the farce. Although these military operations were directed against the Swiss and took place some 120 kilometers east of Dijon, the troops marched through Burgundy in order to reach their target. In between military campaigns, the king's troops lived off the land, requisitioning grain, harassing travelers, and looting farmhouses. Their actions threatened the public peace and the prosperity of the whole region throughout the decade between 1435 and 1445, that is to say, up to two years before Savenot performed his farce in Dijon. The French king's soldiers were known to everyone, even referred to in public documents, as the *escorcheurs*, a pejorative term that referred to their marauding and thievery.[15] In the political context of 1447, the mere changing of the word *escorcheurs* to *estradeurs* (travelers) would have done little to hide the true object of the farce players' jokes. Everyone in the Dijon audience would have known that Robin was referring to the dauphin's military actions: puns, wordplay, and allusions were part of the fun of watching a farce; audiences

14. Joseph Garnier, *Chartes de communes et d'affranchissements en Bourgogne* (Dijon: J.-E. Rabutot, 1867), 1:87–111; Richard Vaughan, *Valois Burgundy* (Hamden, Conn.: Archon Books, 1975), 70, 110.
15. Joseph de Fréminville, *Les écorcheurs en Bourgogne, 1435–1445: Étude sur les compagnies franches au XVe siècle* (Dijon: Darantière, 1888), 194–97; Richard Vaughan, *Philip the Good: The Apogee of Burgundy* (London: Longmans, 1970), 94–97, 114–19.

were trained to be on the lookout for hidden meanings.[16] Laughing about the French king's marauding troops was probably a useful way of coping with an unstable and potentially dangerous military situation.

The Dijon city council saw the situation rather differently. The *escorcheurs* had so destabilized political authority in Burgundy that the urban elite had reacted by renewing its bonds of loyalty to Charles VII.[17] By the mid-1440s, the chief law court of Burgundy was regularly sending appeal cases to the king of France rather than to the duke. The council probably worried that news of the farce might reach the king's ears and make him doubt the city's loyalty. By investigating the matter diligently, the council cleared itself of any responsibility for the offending jokes. Such was often the motivation of authorities who investigated accusations of slander against farce players.

The 1447 Dijon performance was not unusual. Farces often referred to contemporary political events, usually local ones; it was one of the elements that made these plays interesting to fifteenth- and sixteenth-century audiences.[18] Sometimes such performances led to complaints and even to violence. In Dijon alone, we know of at least two more incidents of farce players getting into trouble within a decade of the *escorcheurs* incident. Six years earlier, a man named Colas Malart, pleading on his knees, apologized to the mayor of Dijon for having mocked him during a farce. A few years later, in 1452, several people, including a monk from Cîteaux, broke into the home of a Dijon schoolteacher and threatened him with violence because of a farce he had written and had had his students perform.[19] Though by no means an everyday event, the disciplining of rowdy and satirical farce players was an expected element of civic life during the fifteenth and early sixteenth centuries. Obviously, only the most sensational of these incidents found their way into the archives or personal memoirs. Yet the language that local magistrates regularly used when granting permission to farce players to perform gives a clear sense of how commonplace it was for their performances to result in complaints of slander. Magistrates often warned the players to avoid "scandal" or disorder even as they helped to pay for the costumes needed for the performance.[20]

---

16. *Journal d'un bourgeois de Paris sous le règne de François 1er, 1515–1536*, ed. Ludovic Lalanne (Paris: Jules Renouard, 1854), 13–14.

17. Garnier, *Chartes*, 1:103n11; Vaughan, *Valois*, 196; André Leguai, "The Relations between the Towns of Burgundy and the French Crown in the Fifteenth Century," in *The Crown and Local Communities in England and France in the Fifteenth Century*, ed. J. R. L. Highfield and Robin Jeffs (Gloucester: Alan Sutton, 1981), 131–36.

18. Michel Rousse, "Angers et le théâtre profane médiéval," *Revue d'Histoire du Théâtre* 43 (1991): 53–67.

19. Gouvenain, *Théâtre*, 35–36; Archives Municipales (AM) Dijon 1 B 159, fol. 27 (19 Oct. 1450).

20. Archives Nationales (AN) x1a 4906, fol. 589, 6 Aug. 1538; AN x1a 1545, fol. 336, 7 May 1540; AN x1a 1584, fol. 75, 5 Feb. 1557; Archives Départementales (AD) Haute-Garonne (HG) 2 Mi 165, fol. 421, 27–29 May 1478; ADHG B 57, fol. 793, 17 Aug. 1564; ADHG B

FIGURE 1. Farceurs on stage, 1542. (Source: Bibliothèque Municipale Cambrai MS 126, fol. 53r)

It was not only in border cities like Dijon that farce was often satirical; throughout France, farce players regularly entertained audiences in public marketplaces and were chastised for being too pointed in their criticisms. So why did authorities allow such performances to continue? Why did they not insist on rigorously censoring every farce performed within their jurisdiction? By the 1560s, a hundred years later, this is in fact what happened. Farce became too dangerous to encourage or to tolerate any longer. But in the cities and towns of France until the mid-sixteenth century, city authorities did not make the choice to suppress farce. Their tolerance

485, fol. 291, 18 May 1628; AD Seine-Maritime (SM) 1 B 447, 20 May 1536; AD Gironde (ADG) 1 B 84, fol. 82, 7 Feb. 1534; ADG 1 B 277, fol. 33, 5 Jan. 1565; Michel Félibien, *Histoire de la ville de Paris* (Paris: G. Desprez et J. Desessartz, 1725), 4:674b (27 Dec. 1523), 4:702b (27 Jan. 1542); Michel Rousse, *La scène et les tréteaux: Le théâtre de la farce au moyen âge* (Orleans: Paradigme, 2004), 248–49. In contrast, see Yves-Marie Bercé, *Fête et révolte: Des mentalités populaires du XVIe au XVIIIe siècle* (Paris: Hachette, 1976), 31–36.

and indeed patronage of farce reveal a relatively open environment in which criticism of the political and religious elite could take place publicly as long as it was made in jest.

Farce experienced a heyday in France between 1450 and 1560, a period that some historians and literary theorists define as the Renaissance.[21] Although the performance of farce was not new in the fifteenth century, the cultural prominence of festive societies intensified during this period. The conclusion of the Hundred Years' War, the subsiding of the plague, and an invigorated monarchy all contributed to a cultural flowering after 1450, a phenomenon that lasted over a century until the onset of the Wars of Religion. Farce was performed throughout France, usually by amateur theatrical groups made up of respectable city residents. Amateur actors mounted shows in a wide variety of urban venues: at religious festivals, in the marketplace, and even at the king's court. Farce playing was thus a public form of entertainment enjoyed by a wide segment of French society, from the common people of the cities to the noble elite.[22] Despite the ever-present possibility that playful satire could become pointed political or religious critique, the urban officials who had authority over the theater only rarely banned farcical performances during the Renaissance. They tolerated the actors' disrespectful jests because their plays reflected values held dear by all urban residents, most important among them being Christian morality and the need to maintain one's personal honor. Rather than being an inherently transgressive practice, farce upheld central social values and as a result the sometimes vicious jokes made during these plays were usually met with laughter rather than violence. Yet farce was also supervised: local authorities did not hesitate to chastise farce players whose jokes caused unwanted trouble. Actors were certainly given more license to joke and to be outrageous than were everyday folk, but contemporary French political culture also established distinct limits on that freedom. Farce players were sometimes punished when they mocked a particular, identifiable individual who held power in the community. Because of its public visibility and its regulation, farce playing provides a precise picture of the bounds of acceptable political discourse and public behavior during the Renaissance.

French cities had of course experienced an earlier "renaissance" in the thirteenth century, when many of the urban centers of Roman Gaul reemerged as hubs for manufacture, trade, and cultural exchange. It was at this time that lay religious associations first began performing plays on stage and that the comic forbears of the farce, such as the medieval

---

21. J. Russell Major, *From Renaissance Monarchy to Absolute Monarchy: French Kings, Nobles and Estates* (Baltimore: Johns Hopkins University Press, 1994); Mikhail Bakhtin, *Rabelais and His World*, trans. Hélène Iswolsky (Bloomington: Indiana University Press, 1984).
22. Charles Mazouer, *Le théâtre français du moyen âge* (Paris: SEDES, 1998), 271–72; André Tissier, *Recueil de farces, 1450–1550* (Geneva: Droz, 1986), 1:53–54.

fabliaux, were first aired. This period of prosperity and development was cut short, however, by the twin setbacks of the Black Death and warfare. The Black Death, traditionally thought to be the bubonic plague, ravaged western Europe repeatedly after 1348, killing over one-third of the population of France in the short term and preventing a demographic recovery for over a century. Not long after the first arrival of the Black Death, the Hundred Years' War burdened French subjects with military exactions, loss of manpower, and in some cases, the ravages of siege warfare. Although farces were performed during this period, as indicated by the 1447 performance in Dijon, wartime conditions inhibited the development of comic theater.

Farcical performance expanded on a large scale only when the French monarchy was able to eliminate the English threat. Finally, under Charles VII the last of the English armies were driven off French soil. Over the next century, French cities experienced a period of newfound prosperity, political confidence, and economic growth that justifies the use of the term *Renaissance* to describe this period. Many cities expanded their tax base, rebuilt their physical infrastructure, and attracted waves of rural immigrants. Paris was the giant of French—indeed of European—cities, with a population of approximately 250,000 by 1550. Its cultural diversity could never be matched by any other French urban center, and it held the favored place as the king's capital. Nevertheless, after 1500 several other cities, including Rouen, Lyon, and Toulouse, passed the 50,000 benchmark, becoming hubs of diversified manufacture, regional governance, and higher education. Until the middle of the sixteenth century, French cities grew rapidly, and their residents were optimistic about their future prospects.[23]

French cities participated in the monarch's expansion of political power after the Hundred Years' War. Because the cities' loyalty had been essential to the victory over the English, their representatives became important members of the regional estates, the provincial institutions with which the king consulted before settling peace treaties and setting tax rates. Many cities confirmed or established special relationships with the king that exempted their residents from the land tax and granted local officials the privilege of self-rule. This is not to suggest that French cities sought or obtained anything approaching autonomy, merely that their prestige and prosperity mirrored that of the French monarchy. As the monarchy grew stronger after 1450, so did the cities. This newfound confidence manifested itself in a renewal of cultural and artistic production: new maps of cities

23. Philip Benedict, introduction to *Cities and Social Change in Early Modern France* (London: Unwin Hyman, 1989), 24–25; Jean-Pierre Babelon, *Nouvelle histoire de Paris: Paris au XVIe siècle* (Paris: Hachette, 1986), 271–76; Michel Cassan, "Villes et cultures au XVI et XVIIe siècles," in *Société, culture, vie religieuse au XVIe et XVIIe siècles*, ed. Yves-Marie Bercé (Paris: Presses de l'Université de Paris-Sorbonne, 1995), 29.

were commissioned, and new histories extolling the virtues of urban life were written during the last decades of the fifteenth century. French urban subjects were beginning to enjoy life again and to renew festive traditions that had been put aside during the disruptive decades of warfare and uncertain political leadership. Farce playing in particular profited from this time of renewal.[24]

One of the manifestations of this newfound wealth and confidence was the establishment of publishing houses in many French cities. Beginning in Paris and Lyon but soon spreading to relatively small regional centers such as Dijon, men who called themselves *imprimeurs* set up shop around 1500. For the next fifty years, these regional printers published the more than two hundred and fifty farces, *sotties*, and comic morality plays that are still extant today. Although the large number of printed farces reflects the rapid expansion of the French printing industry, this output of comic literature is still remarkable. The French Renaissance, a period normally associated with renewed interest in classical Greek and Roman literature, was also a time when farce flourished.[25] At a time when the vast majority of books published in France were Latin theological or legal treatises, the growing number of published farces suggests that its humor could be appreciated by the literate minority of the French population. Published plays circulated more widely than hand-copied ones, thereby contributing to the proliferation of theatrical productions at the turn of the sixteenth century.[26]

Most farces were performed by amateur rather than professional actors. Like the Dijon cloth worker Savenot, most farce players did not make their living from acting and probably donned the fool's cap but a handful of times each year. They were male city residents who spent most of their time working at respectable professions. Many, though not all, were also young. These three qualities—their social status, gender, and youth—granted amateur farce players special license to make jokes at the expense of their social betters.

24. Chevalier, *Bonnes villes*, 43–63, 101–3; Graeme Small, "The Crown and the Provinces in the Fifteenth Century," in *France in the Later Middle Ages*, ed. David Potter (Oxford: Oxford University Press, 2003), 142–49.
25. Barbara C. Bowen, "'Honneste' et sens de l'humour au XVIe siècle," in *Humour and Humanism in the Renaissance* (Ashgate: Variorum, 2004).
26. *Vers composés pour les enfants de la Mère-Folle de Dijon vers la fin du XVIe siècle*, ed. Luc Verhaeghe (Dijon: Bibliothèque Municipale, 1995); Heather Arden, *Fools' Plays: A Study of Satire in the "Sottie"* (Cambridge: Cambridge University Press, 1980), 71; Elizabeth Armstrong, *Before Copyright: The French Book-Privilege System, 1498–1526* (Cambridge: Cambridge University Press, 1990), 182–83; Graham A. Runnalls, *Les mystères français imprimés: Une étude sur les rapports entre le théâtre religieux et l'imprimerie à la fin du moyen âge français* (Paris: Champion, 1999), 55–60; *Recueil d'actes notariés relatifs à l'histoire de Paris et ses environs*, ed. Ernest Coyecque (Paris: Imprimerie Nationale, 1905), 1:222 (9 Aug. 1529); Julie Stone Peters, *Theatre of the Book, 1480–1880* (Oxford: Oxford University Press, 2000), 15–27.

Professional actors were not completely unheard of in late fifteenth- and sixteenth-century France. Like other European cultures, the French had a venerable tradition of jongleurs, and their kings had long employed fools at court. Nevertheless, until the late sixteenth century, professional actors were not the norm in most French cities and towns, in part because city councils were quick to send itinerant professional acting troupes packing if they caused any trouble.[27] As a result, theatrical performances were usually organized by local associations composed of amateur actors whose social status ranged from the urban elite to the humble artisan. One association that performed in Dijon in the sixteenth and seventeenth centuries, the Mère Folle, drew its members from the "the flower and elite of the city's young men."[28] Sometimes, particularly in the fifteenth century, the actors were priests or priests-in-training.[29] More often, however, the actors were drawn from the *couche moyenne*—the middle layer of the lay urban population—the perhaps 30 percent of the population that neither lived in poverty nor held the reins of power. Farce players were usually tradesmen, artisans, notaries, and petty merchants. As such, they were often self-employed and might even own a house or two. Some of them were responsible heads of households who could be called by the city to serve in the urban militia or night watch in times of trouble. These men were often wealthy enough that they paid taxes but they had no direct say in how those taxes were collected or spent. Many of them enjoyed the legal status of bourgeois, which exempted them from some taxes and, in some cities, gave them the right to vote in local elections (although they were unlikely to sit on the city council itself, a body that was increasingly the preserve of a narrow oligarchic elite). In short, amateur farce players were men who had a stake in the community and could not easily be dislodged. They were not beggars to be kicked out of town or itinerant actors whose very profession rendered them illegitimate in the eyes of the Catholic

27. Rousse, *Scène*, 145–65; Jean-Claude Aubailly, *Théâtre médiéval profane et comique* (Paris: Larousse, 1975), 49–58; Mazouer, *Théâtre du moyen âge*, 269–71; Tissier, *Recueil*, 1:50; *Recueil d'actes*, 1:580–98; Henri Clouzot, *L'ancien théâtre en Poitou* (Niort: L. Clouzot, 1901), 7–8; Achille Durieux, *Le théâtre à Cambrai avant et depuis 1789* (Cambrai: J. Renaut, 1883), 39, 168; Charles Mazouer, *La vie théâtrale à Bordeaux des origines à nos jours*, vol. 1, *Des origines à 1789*, ed. Henri Lagrave (Paris: CNRS, 1985), 59–61; Kathy Stuart, *Defiled Trades and Social Outcasts: Honor and Ritual Pollution in Early Modern Germany* (Cambridge: Cambridge University Press, 1999), 24–25.
28. *Genethliaque autrement triomphe sur la naissance de Monseigneur le Daufin, par l'Infanterie Dijonnoise le 27 décembre 1601: Dedié à Monseigneur le duc de Biron* (Cisteaux: Jean Savine pour Pierre Grangier, 1602). In some cities, the leader of the festive society was the son of a prominent official. See Maurice Agulhon, *Pénitents et francs-maçons de l'ancienne Provence* (Paris: Fayard, 1968), 59–60; Aristide Joly, *Note sur Benoet du Lac: Ou le théâtre et la Bazoche à Aix, à la fin du XVIe siècle* (Lyon: Scheuring, 1862; reprint, Geneva: Slatkine, 1971), 80.
29. Petit de Julleville, *Répertoire*, 348, 358, 365; J.B.L. Du Tilliot, *Mémoires pour servir à l'histoire de la fête des fous qui se faisait autrefois dans plusieurs églises* (Lausanne: Marc-Michel Bousquet, 1751), 97–117.

Church. They were respectable city residents who happened to enjoy a privilege to perform farce on the public stage.[30]

Most farce players performed under the auspices of associations loosely termed festive societies.[31] These associations performed farce in public at particular moments during the calendar year, most often at Carnival or in early May. The privilege of performing was usually based on long-standing practice or legal statutes: when challenged about their rights to perform, the leaders of the Basoche, an association of law clerks who worked at the Parlement of Paris, argued that they had been permitted to perform each May "for so long that there is no memory of it being otherwise."[32] In general, until the 1550s, local authorities found such claims persuasive and allowed festive societies to continue to perform even when the group had a reputation for mounting satirical plays. Some of these associations were ad hoc groups of neighbors or coworkers who pulled together a farcical performance at the last minute, sometimes at the request of the city council.[33] Often, however, festive societies survived for generations and gained a prominent role in urban life. In Cambrai, the Abbey of Lescache performed farces regularly throughout the fifteenth and sixteenth centuries; in Paris and in Amiens, groups called the Enfants-sans-Souci (Carefree Youth), led by a Prince des Sots (Prince of Fools), entertained the urban populace and nobles at the king's court; in Lyon, the Enfants de la Ville performed farces and marched in civic processions from the late fifteenth century until 1622.[34] In most French cities and towns, such associations were a regular part of civic life.

Festive societies were embedded in civic life not only through their performances but also through day-to-day religious or professional activities. Some festive societies were lay religious associations called confraternities. These groups, which began to multiply in France during the thirteenth

30. Chevalier, *Bonnes villes*, 76–84; Farr, *Hands*, 34–75; Mack P. Holt, "Popular Political Culture and Mayoral Elections in Sixteenth-Century Dijon," in *Society and Institutions in Early Modern France* (Athens: University of Georgia Press, 1991), 98–116; S. Annette Finley-Croswhite, *Henry IV and the Towns: The Pursuit of Legitimacy in French Urban Society, 1589–1610* (Cambridge: Cambridge University Press, 1999), 122–26.
31. There is no single sixteenth-century term to describe these amateur associations of farce players. Louis Petit de Julleville, who has written the most comprehensive history of late medieval comic performance in France, invented the general term *sociétés joyeuses*, which I have translated as "festive societies." Louis Petit de Julleville, *Histoire du théâtre en France: Les comédiens en France au moyen âge* (Paris: Le Cerf, 1885), 192–93.
32. AN x1a 8345, fol. 256, 14 July 1528.
33. Georges Lecocq, *Histoire du théâtre en Picardie, depuis son origine jusqu'à la fin du XVIe siècle* (Paris: Menu, 1880; reprint, Geneva: Slatkine, 1971), 138–42.
34. Ibid., 153–54; Durieux, *Théâtre*, 13–15; Hyacinthe Dusevel, *Notice et documents sur la fête du prince des sots à Amiens* (Amiens: Lenoël-Hérouart, 1859), 8–13; Jean Tricou, "Les confréries joyeuses de Lyon au XVIe siècle et leur numismatique," *Revue Numismatique* 40 (1937): 294; Petit de Julleville, *Répertoire*, 345, 349.

century, were designed to enrich the spiritual life of their members through self-help and spiritual activities, including performing plays. Many late medieval confraternities were affiliated with a local chapel but were led by laypersons and enjoyed a mixed membership of men and women drawn from a variety of social classes. These organizations served important extrafamilial functions, providing a sense of community and financial aid for their members. Confraternities often arranged for a burial mass when a member died and at least once a year gathered together to celebrate their patron saint's day with a feast and a procession through the city streets. Theatrical performance was an extension of these annual processions and, until the mid-sixteenth century, was considered compatible with Catholic piety.[35] Some confraternities in fact specialized in performing theater. The Confrérie de la Passion of Paris is the best known of these groups, but similar organizations existed in many cities and towns; all of them regularly mounted tableaux vivants and mystery plays. Other confraternities, such as the Conards of Rouen and the Mère Folle of Dijon, instead specialized in comic theater.[36]

Other festive societies were occupational associations called *corps* or corporations.[37] Analogous to English and German guilds though less powerful, French corps nevertheless impressed themselves on the political life of the city. By the fifteenth century, French kings recognized trade-related corporations, granting their members certain financial privileges and the right to manage their own affairs. Corps became accustomed to fighting for their legal privileges in the law courts if they felt a royal official was

35. Catherine Vincent, *Les confréries médiévales dans le royaume de France: XIIIe–XVe siècle* (Paris: A. Michel, 1994), 17–29, 53–66, 74–79, 159–60; Robert L.A. Clark, "Charity and Drama: The Response of the Confraternity to the Problem of Urban Poverty in Fourteenth-Century France," *Fifteenth-Century Studies* 13 (1988): 370; Christopher F. Black, *Italian Confraternities in the Sixteenth Century* (Cambridge: Cambridge University Press, 1989), 109–16; Benjamin R. McRee, "Unity or Division? The Social Meaning of Guild Ceremony in Urban Communities," in *City and Spectacle in Medieval Europe*, ed. Barbara A. Hanawalt and Kathryn L. Reyerson (Minneapolis: University of Minnesota Press, 1994), 189–207.
36. Alphonse-Honoré Taillandier, *Notice sur les Confrères de la Passion* (Paris: Fournier, 1834); Célestin Doais, *La Confrérie de l'Assomption à Saint-Etienne de Toulouse* (Paris: A. Picard, 1892); P. Le Verdier, *Documents relatifs à la Confrérie de la Passion de Rouen* (Rouen: Cagniard, 1891); *Deux chroniques de Rouen: 1er des origines à 1544; 2ème de 1559 à 1569*, ed. A. Héron (Rouen: Lestringant, 1900), 151; Joachim Durandeau, *La Mère-Folle de la Sainte-Chapelle de Dijon* (Dijon, 1910); Du Tilliot, *Mémoires*, 117–43; ADHG B 82, fol. 326, 27 Aug. 1580.
37. Léon Lefebvre, *Fêtes lilloises du XIVe au XVIe siècle* (Lille: Lefebvre-Ducrocq, 1902), 19; Tricou, "Confréries," 295–96; Émile Coornaert, *Les corporations en France avant 1789* (Paris: Gallimard, 1941), 86–104, 231–33; Farr, *Hands*, 16–23; Marc Venard, "La fraternité des banquets," in *Pratiques et discours alimentaires à la Renaissance*, ed. Jean-Claude Margolin and Robert Sauzet (Paris: G.-P. Maisonneuve et Larose, 1982), 137–45. Regarding the institutional and terminological fluidity between corporations and confraternities, see Marc Venard, "Les confréries en France au XVIe siècle et dans la première moitié du XVIIe siècle," in Bercé, *Société, culture, vie religieuse*, 49; Vincent, *Confréries*, 27–31.

overstepping its authority or compromising the guild's monopoly.[38] Farce playing for these associations would be just a small part of their activities, but it was an important one since it allowed members to make their concerns known to a wider public. Whereas guildsmen would turn to the royal tax courts to complain of an extortionist tax collector, farce playing enabled members of the couche moyenne to universalize their complaints. In early 1492, arts students at the University of Caen, a fiercely independent regional university, did just that when they performed a farce titled *The Farce of Pates-Ouaintes*, which questioned the king's right to levy the *décime* tax on the university. The play referred in explicit terms to the hated levy and mocked Hugues Bureau, the official who was to collect the tax, as a corrupt man who greased his palms with cash at every opportunity.[39] Even though most residents of Caen were not subject to this tax, the students tried to garner sympathy for their cause by portraying Bureau as an immoral and rapacious outsider. Similarly, in 1583, the Mère Folle of Dijon performed a series of short plays that mocked Élie du Tillet, the royal official in charge of managing the king's forests in Burgundy. Du Tillet was mocked for his personal foibles, specifically for having beaten his wife while residing in Dijon.[40] In both these performances, farce players tried to turn public opinion against a royal official by discrediting him as an immoral individual out to fleece the poor. Far from subverting conventional Christian morality, farceurs tried to universalize a group's particular gripes with royal power through appeals to well-worn moral imperatives.[41]

Most farces were written by the men who performed them, usually a bourgeois who enjoyed a certain level of education. Notorious farcical playwrights include men such as Pierre Gringore, who was born into a family of lawyers in Normandy, and Roger de Collerye, who also studied law before

38. Coornaert, *Corporations*, 95–105; Chevalier, *Bonnes villes*, 76–83; Farr, *Hands*, 35–59; Vincent, *Confréries*, 159–60.

39. Pierre Lemonnier de Lesnauderie, *La farce de Pates-Ouaintes: Pièce satyrique représentée par les écoliers de l'Université de Caen, au carnaval de 1492*, ed. T. Bonnin (Evreux: Jules Ancelle, 1843); Paul de Longuemare, *Le théâtre à Caen* (Paris: A. Picard, 1895), 4–6; Petit de Julleville, *Répertoire*, 206–8; A. Bigot and H. Prentout, *L'Université de Caen: Son passé, son présent* (Caen: Malherbe de Caen, 1932), 57–61; Lyse Roy, "Histoire d'une université régionale: L'Université de Caen au XVe siècle," *Paedagogica Historica* 34 (1998): 408–10.

40. *Vers composés;* Juliette Valcke, "La satire sociale dans le répertoire de la Mère Folle de Dijon," in *Carnival and the Carnivalesque: The Fool, the Reformer, the Wildman and Others in Early Modern Theatre*, ed. Konrad Eisenbichler and Wim Hüsken (Amsterdam: Rodopi, 1999), 150–54; Joachim Durandeau, *La grande asnerie de Dijon, étude sur la menée et chevauchée de l'âne au mois de mai* (Dijon: Darantière, 1887), 39–43.

41. Jean-Claude Aubailly, *Le monologue, le dialogue et la sottie: Essai sur quelques genres dramatiques de la fin du moyen âge et du début du XVIe siècle* (Paris: Champion, 1976), 437–38; Juliette Valcke, "Théâtre et spectacle chez la Mère Folle de Dijon (XVe–XVIe)," in *Les arts du spectacle dans la ville (1404–1721)*, ed. Marie France Wagner and Claire Le Brun-Gouanvic (Paris: Champion, 2001), 72–76.

turning to comic writing and performance.[42] Although some scholars have assumed that a mere handful of well-known playwrights were responsible for most of the farcical repertoire, the evidence suggests otherwise.[43] First of all, most farces were published anonymously: since playwriting, particularly comic playwriting, was not a prestigious literary venture, writers did not want to advertise their authorship.[44] So the question of exactly who wrote which play will always be speculative. Nevertheless, we know that farces were often commissioned for local civic celebrations and that many of them were never published at all, circulating only in manuscript form. As a result, it was very easy for performers to add a timely joke or excise satirical references when necessary. In addition to men of the law, schoolmasters, secretaries, priests, and merchants continued to pen new farces until the middle of the sixteenth century. Playwriting, it seems, was ubiquitous, undertaken with some ease by literate urban residents who would have been steeped in performance culture all their lives.[45] Although these plays are by no means an unfiltered reflection of the mentality of the couche moyenne, the recurrent concerns about royal and clerical abuses of power are consistent with what we know about this social class during the Renaissance.

The fact that most of the farce players were youths—sometimes mere teenagers—tempered the plays' reception as slander or satire. In medieval and early modern Europe, being a youth meant that one was old enough to be an apprentice but too young to own a shop. In practice, this meant that most farce players were probably somewhere between twelve and thirty years of age.[46] Male youths were supposed to be more rowdy and more

---

42. Sylvie Lécuyer, *Roger de Collerye: Un héritier de Villon* (Paris: Champion, 1997), 9–18; Charles Oulmont, *Pierre Gringore: La poésie morale, politique et dramatique à la veille de la Renaissance* (Paris: Champion, 1911), 4–7; Jennifer Britnell, *Jean Bouchet* (Edinburgh: Edinburgh University Press, 1986), 1; Marie Bouhaïk-Gironès, "La Basoche et le théâtre comique: Identité sociale, pratiques et culture des clercs de justice (Paris, 1420–1550)," Ph.D. diss., University of Paris 7, 2004, 213–33.

43. Gustave Cohen, "Clément Marot et le théâtre," *Marche Romane* 2 (1952): 14–19; Gérard Defaux, introduction to *Oeuvres poétiques de Clément Marot* (Paris: Classiques Garnier, 1990), 1:xxxi–xxxii; M.J. Freeman, introduction to *Oeuvres suivies d'oeuvres attribuées à l'auteur* (Geneva: Droz, 1975), xxxviii–xl; Howard Graham Harvey, *The Theatre of the Basoche: The Contribution of the Law Societies to French Mediaeval Comedy* (Cambridge, Mass.: Harvard University Press, 1941), 72, 83–102.

44. Armstrong, *Before Copyright*, 182, 187; Cynthia Jane Brown, *Poets, Patrons and Printers: Crisis of Authority in Late Medieval France* (Ithaca: Cornell University Press, 1995), 146–51.

45. André Bossuat, "Le théâtre à Clermont-Ferrand," *Revue d'Histoire du Théâtre* 13 (1961): 109; Durieux, *Théâtre*, 159; Lefebvre, *Fêtes*, 10–11; Petit de Julleville, *Répertoire*, 372; Clouzot, *Ancien théâtre*, 52–53.

46. Giovanni Levi and Jean-Claude Schmitt, introduction to *A History of Young People in the West*, vol. 1, *Ancient and Medieval Rites of Passage*, trans. Camille Nash (Cambridge, Mass.: Harvard University Press, 1997), 1–11; Robert Muchembled, *L'invention de l'homme moderne: Sensibilités, moeurs et comportements collectifs sous l'ancien régime* (Paris: Fayard, 1988), 291–302; Maria Boes, "The Treatment of Juvenile Delinquents in Early Modern Germany," *Continuity and Change* 11 (1996): 43–60.

audacious than the rest of the urban population. People expected youths to grow out of such behavior, so, as a result, French judicial officials during this period were willing to tolerate young men roaming through the city streets making noise, disturbing the peace, and performing farces.[47] This tolerance meant that farce players, if they were young, were unlikely to be punished very harshly for performing a farce that slandered a local bishop or city official. A few days in prison, a small fine, or public shaming was the usual punishment meted out to rowdy farce players.[48] Women sometimes performed sacred theater, but they did not perform farce. Instead, men played the female roles, often dipping their head in flour to depict the fair complexion of the opposite sex. This cross-dressing obviously added to the humor of many farces and probably neutralized their critical commentary. After all, complaining women did not need to be taken seriously. Men could exploit the stereotype of the shrewish, deceitful woman in order to speak more freely than usual.[49]

These often rowdy young actors performed a variety of comic genres during the period between 1450 and 1560. We know this from two main sets of evidence: the more than 250 comic plays that have survived, and the records of city councils and judicial courts that either permitted or forbade particular festive societies' performances. Judicial archives record hundreds of performances by informal or long-standing groups of farce players. Usually the plays were referred to as "jeux" (games), but sometimes the records are more specific, noting that the men were allowed to perform "farces et moralités," and occasionally "sotises."[50] This archival evidence corroborates the literary evidence, since most extant printed plays fall into one or more of the genres referred to by city officials. Only rarely, however, is it possible

---

47. Jacques Rossiaud, "Fraternités de jeunesse et niveaux de culture dans les villes du sud-est à la fin du moyen âge," *Cahiers d'Histoire* 21 (1976): 68–102; Merry E. Wiesner, "'Wandervogels' and Women: Journeymen's Concepts of Masculinity in Early Modern Germany," *Journal of Social History* 24 (1991): 767–82.

48. Michel Rousse, "Le pouvoir royal et le théâtre des farces," in *Le pouvoir monarchique et ses supports idéologiques*, ed. Jean Dufournet, Adeline Fiorato, and Augustin Redondo (Paris: Sorbonne Nouvelle, 1990), 186–87; Petit de Julleville, *Répertoire*, 358.

49. Natalie Zemon Davis, *Society and Culture in Early Modern France: Eight Essays* (Stanford: Stanford University Press, 1975), 136–42; Jean Howard, "Cross-Dressing, the Theater and Gender Trouble in Early Modern England," *Shakespeare Quarterly* 39 (1988): 418–40; Claire Sponsler, "Outlaw Masculinities: Drag, Blackface and Late Medieval Laboring-Class Festivities," in *Becoming Male in the Middle Ages*, ed. Jeffrey Jerome Cohen and Bonnie Wheeler (New York: Garland, 1997), 321–47.

50. That *jeux* was a common term to describe comic theater in fifteenth- and sixteenth-century France, see Alan E. Knight, *Aspects of Genre in Late Medieval French Drama* (Manchester: Manchester University Press, 1983), 44–45. Examples of different terms used to describe the Basoche of the Paris Parlement's performances include "jeux" in AN x1a 1511, fol. 148a, 24 May 1508; AN x1a 1525, 13 May 1523; AN x1a 1585, fol. 520a, 15 June 1557; "farces et moralités" in AN x1a 1486, fol. 163, 2 May 1474; AN x1a 4906, fols. 589–90a, 6 Aug. 1538; AN x1a 4947, fol. 413, 12 Jan. 1552; "cris" in AN x1a 1540, fol. 121, 23 Jan. 1538; "sotises" in AN x1a 1529, fol. 279, 16 June 1526; x1a 1530, fol. 266, 5 June 1527.

to link particular performances with a play that still exists today. Obviously, the extant plays are just a fragment of what was performed during farce's heyday; many farces were probably never written down or existed in only a single handwritten copy.[51] So, for example, both the farce and the mystery play that were performed in October 1447 in Dijon have long since been lost. Frustratingly, we know how the authorities reacted to the Dijon play, but we cannot compare their reaction to the text itself. Conversely, literary scholars must interpret a play without knowing, in most cases, the context of its performance. As a result, their discussion of theatrical satire usually focuses on questions of genre that were of little relevance to Renaissance authors and audiences.

In fact, late medieval and Renaissance comic theater resists convenient labeling by genre. Modern typology of drama, which at its most basic distinguishes between comedy and tragedy, did not apply to people for whom the general term *comedy* encompassed all theatrical performances. Until the mid-sixteenth century, tragedies were not performed on the French stage; mystery plays and historical romances were instead the more somber fare presented to city residents. Even as late as the sixteenth century, Frenchmen were not particularly interested in drawing distinctions among different theatrical genres, a tendency that can be seen both in literary and judicial documents. Apart from the generic term *jeux*, the most common term they used to describe comic theater was *farce*. Sixteenth-century publishers and booksellers usually labeled as farces plays that modern literary scholars have convincingly argued represent distinct late medieval comic genres.[52] I am using the term *farce* in the same loose way they did: except in this section, in which I discuss some of the structural qualities of different kinds of comic plays, I employ *farce* as an umbrella term for all French comic theater of the fifteenth and early sixteenth centuries.

All farces performed in Renaissance France shared some basic characteristics: most of the plays were short (usually approximately five hundred lines long), most of the characters were stereotypical or fixed types, and all of them were, at their core, depictions of good and evil underpinned by basic

51. For a list of modern editions of these plays, see Mazouer, *Théâtre du moyen âge*, 273; Graham A. Runnalls, "The Catalogue of the Book-Seller and Late Medieval French Drama," in *André de la Vigne*, ed. Anna Slerca (Montreal: Ceres, 1982), 125.
52. Runnalls, *André*, 125; André Tissier, "Sur la notion de 'genre' dans les pièces comiques de la farce de 'Pathelin' à la comédie de 'L'Eugène' de Jodelle," *Littératures Classiques* 27 (1996): 20; Jelle Koopmans, "Genres théâtraux et 'choses vues': Le cas du théâtre profane de la fin du moyen âge," *Fifteenth-Century Studies* 16 (1990): 131–42; Jonathan Beck, *Théâtre et propagande aux débuts de la Réforme: Six pièces polémiques du Recueil La Vallière* (Geneva: Slatkine, 1986), 35; Arden, *Fools' Plays*, 8–9; Halina Lewicka, *Études sur l'ancienne farce française* (Paris: Klincksieck, 1974), 9; Grace Frank, "The Beginnings of Comedy in France," *Modern Language Review* 31 (1936): 377–84; *Deux moralités de la fin du moyen âge et du temps des Guerres de Religion*, ed. Jean-Claude Aubailly and Bruno Roy (Geneva: Droz, 1990), 7–9.

Christian values.[53] These plays asked the audience to laugh at characters who were selfish, greedy, arrogant, or gluttonous and sometimes to judge them as well. The use of stereotypical characters kept the plays humorous: stereotypes are recognized by the audience as types, not representations of actual people, a quality that helps the audience to disassociate from the people presented and laugh at rather than sympathize with their plight.[54] Yet at the same time, the use of stereotypes and allegorical figures also made the concerns of the farce players universal and intelligible to a broad urban audience. The three main comic genres or modes to be found in these plays are the farce, the *sottie*, and the morality play. Often these different genres were combined in a single play, which is part of the reason categorizing them is so problematic.

Of these three, farces were the most earthy comic mode or genre. Full of scenes of fighting, trickery, and verbal sparring between the sexes, farces portray stereotypical men and women going about their daily lives sinning and otherwise demonstrating human fallibility.[55] Specifically religious themes are rare in the farce, though it is shared Christian values—a belief in the importance of fidelity, honesty, chastity, and charity—that give the plays their comic bite: it is the tension between human selfishness and these implicit moral standards that makes the plays funny rather than just cruel. Farces teach by bad example: they show how ridiculous humanity's selfishness is and so point the audience in the direction of Christian morality. Some farces underline the importance of ethics by ending the play with a brief "moral," a few lines of verse that clarify the lesson to be learnt from the play. In the *New Farce of a Jealous Husband who Wanted to Test his Wife*, the husband tries to trick his wife into revealing her lover. He fails to do so and admits at the conclusion of the play that it was the sin of jealousy that drove him to deception.[56] Yet because moral assumptions, though they underlie the humor of the farce, are not usually made explicit, many literary critics argue that farce was the least satirical of these comic genres.[57]

---

53. Some morality plays were longer, running several thousand lines. Other related genres include the *sermon joyeux*, the *monologue*, and the *fabliaux*. Mazouer, *Théâtre du moyen âge*, 276–82; Aubailly, *Monologue*, 9–198; Bernadette Rey-Flaud, *La farce ou la machine à rire: Théorie d'un genre dramatique*, 1450–1550 (Geneva: Droz, 1984), 114–43.

54. Henri Bergson, *Le rire: Essai sur la signification du comique* (Paris: Felix Alcan, 1931), 1–22.

55. Bernard Faivre, *Répertoire des farces françaises: Des origines à Tabarin* (Paris: Imprimerie Nationale, 1993), 21–22, 480–96; Madeleine Lazard, *Le théâtre en France au XVIe siècle* (Paris: Presses Universitaires de France, 1980), 66–76; Lewicka, *Études*, 9–17.

56. "Farce nouvelle d'ung mary jaloux qui veult esprouver sa femme," in *Recueil*, ed. André Tissier, 9:124–26; Jorge Arditi, *A Genealogy of Manners: Transformations of Social Relations in France and England from the Fourteenth to the Eighteenth Century* (Chicago: University of Chicago Press, 1998), 45–46; Bowen, *Caractéristiques*, 64–66; Aron Gurevich, *Medieval Popular Culture: Problems of Belief and Perception*, trans. Janos M. Bak and Paul A. Hollingsworth (Cambridge: Cambridge University Press, 1988), 193–94. For an opposing view, see Mazouer, *Théâtre du moyen âge*, 268, 347–48.

57. Mazouer, *Théâtre du moyen âge*, 287, 352–58; Rey-Flaud, *Farce*, 37–40; Bowen, *Caractéristiques*, 32–35.

Most literary scholars agree that the sottie and the morality play have more scope for satire because these plays are populated with characters who judge the flaws of others.[58] A sottie was usually distinguished by extensive dialogue between *sots*, fool characters wearing the traditional dunce cap and bells. These fools often commented on the sexual lives of local authority figures and criticized contemporary mores as corrupt. The sots usually presented themselves as outsiders, which allowed them to judge society's flaws, usually on the basis of straightforward Christian definitions of good and evil. Tax collectors and financiers were accused of fleecing their own pockets, and the nouveaux riches were criticized for flaunting their wealth. The sots' comments were nevertheless always ambivalent, since the characters were, after all, fools. The sots' authority to judge society drew on a long-standing tradition of linking wisdom with folly. Their playful wisdom can be found not only in comic theater but also in sixteenth-century humanist texts such as Erasmus's *Praise of Folly*.

Morality plays, often populated with allegorical figures who mock local officials, priests, or the pope, and representing virtues and vices, commented most explicitly on questions of Christian salvation and damnation. A young sinner might encounter Vice, Reason, and Virtue in turn, characters that tempted him to do evil and then encouraged him to return to the fold of the church by the end of the play. Other morality plays eschewed allegory for explicit religious propaganda and advocated for or against the reform of the church, particularly during the sixteenth century, once the threat of Protestant reform became a real challenge to the Catholic tradition.[59] In the latter plays, satire was integral to the humor of the text. In practice, because censors and judicial officials almost always referred to all three of these comic genres as farces, it is impossible to know which of them was seen to be the most satirical at that time, but all were clearly received as satire. Audiences responded to the Christian context in which the farces were performed and to the particular jokes in the plays rather than to their structural and generic qualities.[60]

In short, all the comic genres were saturated with Christian values. The distinction between the satirical aspect of farce and its orthodox Christian aspect is not as sharp as some scholars suggest. Mikhail Bakhtin, a literary theorist whose work on François Rabelais has inspired a generation of scholars interested in Carnival and social protest, has argued that the fluidity of individual identity in sixteenth-century French comic genres implied a rejection of conventional Christianity and of any notion of self-contained

58. Aubailly, *Monologue*, 413–42; Arden, *Fools' Plays*, 5–14; Knight, *Aspects*, 41–67, 78–91; Mazouer, *Théâtre français de la Renaissance*, 85–86.
59. Beck, *Théâtre*, 17–18, 28–34.
60. Jelle Koopmans, "Du texte à la diffusion; de la diffusion au texte: L'exemple des farces et des sotties," *Moyen Français* 46–47 (2000): 309–26.

individuality. Farcical humor, for Bakhtin, was a vibrant popular culture that he calls the "carnivalesque," which functioned in large measure in opposition to the dominant social, religious, and political hierarchy.[61] While I agree with Bakhtin that during the Renaissance the human body was imagined in less restrictive ways than during the seventeenth century, my sense is that he and some who follow his example distort the historical narrative by exaggerating the anti-authoritarian potential of Carnival. Both the license of farceurs to mock and the limits on their freedom of expression were shaped by the religious conventions of Christianity and the social conventions of honor. Despite some tensions between these two systems of social regulation, together Christianity and honor provided both the farceurs and their censors with the means to justify their actions.

It is true that farces were often performed at Carnival, the late winter celebration that marked the beginning of Lent. During Carnival, and in particular on Mardi Gras (Fat Tuesday), people in fifteenth- and sixteenth-century European cities exploded onto the city streets to celebrate excess and physical pleasure for one last glorious day before submitting to the six-week penitential regime of Lent. Lent ended with Easter, the annual remembrance of Jesus' execution and resurrection that was the sacred culmination of the Christian calendar year. At Carnival, and other analogous festivals, including the Feast of Fools after Christmas, the Feast of Saint Nicholas in early May, and Corpus Christi celebrations in June, city dwellers throughout Europe dressed in humorous costumes, drank heavily, ate as much as they could, and danced in the streets.[62] Masked and anonymous, commoners could mock authority figures, poke fun at their neighbors, and otherwise turn the world upside down for a day.[63] Amateur actors participated in this carnivalesque popular culture by performing satirical farces that questioned authority in a way that was taboo during the rest of the year. Farce playing took place in a highly charged ritual context, a time outside of time that

---

61. Bakhtin, *Rabelais*, 220. For a different approach, see Dylan Reid, "The Triumph of the Abbey of the Conards: Spectacle and Sophistication in a Rouen Carnival," in *Medieval and Early Modern Rituals: Formalized Behaviour in the East and West*, ed. Joëlle Rollo-Koster (Leiden: Brill, 2001), 148–73.

62. AN x1a 1512, fol. 65, 23 Feb. 1509; AN x1a 1517, fol. 58, 1 Feb. 1515; AN x1a 1540, fol. 121, 23 Jan. 1538; AN x1a 4947, fol. 413, 12 Jan. 1552; Claude Gaignebet, "Le cycle annuel des fêtes à Rouen au milieu du XVIe siècle," in *Les fêtes de la Renaissance*, ed. Jean Jacquot and Élie Konigson (Paris: CNRS, 1975), 3:569–78; Lecocq, *Histoire*, 138–40; J. Lestrade, "Les gâteaux de la basoche," *Revue Historique de Toulouse* 2 (1915–19): 147–48; Tricou, "Confréries," 303; Lefebvre, *Fêtes*, 5; Louis Paris, *Le théâtre à Reims, depuis les Romains jusqu'à nos jours* (Reims: Michaud, 1885), 29–31; Nicole Pellegrin, *Les bachelleries: Organisations et fêtes de la jeunesse dans le centre-ouest, XVe–XVIIIe siècles* (Poitiers: Société des Antiquaires de l'Ouest, 1982), 185–94.

63. Jacques Heers, *Fêtes des fous et carnaval* (Paris: Fayard, 1983); Davis, *Society*, 98–123; Peter Burke, *Popular Culture in Early Modern Europe* (New York: Harper and Row, 1978); Peter Stallybrass and Allon White, *The Politics and Poetics of Transgression* (London: Methuen, 1986).

allowed Europeans to leave everyday social and political hierarchy behind them for a brief moment of release. As such, argues Bakhtin, Carnival was a time of resistance and a moment when a more equitable future could be imagined.[64] In contrast, some historians emphasize the degree to which clerical and secular authorities controlled or manipulated Carnival celebrations in order that they function as a social safety valve.[65] By allowing the populace free reign for a few short hours, authorities found it easier to reestablish and maintain the status quo throughout the rest of the year. Neither of these characterizations does full justice to the realities of farce playing. Although it is true that the power to jest lasted only a fleeting moment, the sting of the farce players' jokes often lingered. Fighting, law suits, and complaints of slander attest to fears that jokes made at festival time impacted the ability of the clergy and secular officials to rule with impunity.

At the heart of Bakhtin's analysis is his insight that the laughter of Carnival was generated by a particular vision of the human body. Farces and other carnivalesque texts explore the porous nature of the human body and its interdependence with the wider world. Priests, kings, royal officials, and wealthy merchants are mocked and debased with reference to the physical imperatives of the organic body that no one can transcend: its need to eat, drink, and excrete. Bakhtin calls this humorous vision of the body the "grotesque" and contrasts it to a more self-contained individualized body idealized by bourgeois and neoclassical culture after 1600.[66] For Bakhtin, the Renaissance was a period in which the grotesque body attained a particular prominence. Both European elites and commoners shared an appreciation for grotesque humor as expressed in the great vernacular writers of the period such as Rabelais, Shakespeare, and Cervantes.

Evidence concerning the performance of farce in many ways supports Bakhtin's characterization of the Renaissance as a period of cultural openness. Indeed, through the early sixteenth century, there are numerous instances of cross-fertilization between erudite classical genres and traditional farcical content. The well-known rector of the University of Paris, Ravisius Textor, wrote both Latin and French plays for the student stage and reveled in the satirical nature of student performance.[67] Similarly, in 1512 a Latin "comedy" titled *Verterator, alias Pathelinus* was published in Paris. In fact, it was not a new play at all but a translation from the French into Latin of the most famous fifteenth-century French farce, *The Farce of Master*

64. Bakhtin, *Rabelais*, 89, 274; Davis, *Society*, 122–23, 131; Victor Turner, *The Ritual Process: Structure and Anti-Structure* (Chicago: Aldine, 1969), 94–130; Edward Muir, *Ritual in Early Modern Europe* (Cambridge: Cambridge University Press, 1997), 85–104.
65. Bercé, *Fête*, 18–23; Emmanuel Le Roy Ladurie, *Le carnaval de Romans: De la Chandeleur au mercredi des Cendres, 1579–1580* (Paris: Gallimard, 1979), 337–59.
66. Bakhtin, *Rabelais*, 26, 318–20.
67. Ibid., 299.

Pathelin.[68] The play was probably translated so that university students could demonstrate their facility in the Latin language while at the same time amusing themselves in very much the same way as they might with Erasmus's often scatological colloquies; such fare was not by any means considered inappropriate for even university students to perform in this period.

Nevertheless, the "grotesque" body expressed in farces was not incompatible with Christianity as practiced and understood during the French Renaissance. Although much has been made of the traditional Western privileging of the soul over the body, during the fifteenth and sixteenth centuries Catholicism was very much a religion of the body. The human body was considered to be a pathway to the sacred: physical practices such as sexual abstinence, fasting, and flagellation were means to achieve a closer relationship with God and to purge the soul of impurities. These practices were not merely cruel punishments inflicted on a body held in contempt but also efforts to harness physicality to help the individual to find his or her path to God.[69] This emphasis on physical experience manifested itself in a number of beliefs and practices. The fifteenth- and sixteenth-century cult of the Host, in which crowds gathered to see Christ's "body" made manifest during the Eucharist, demonstrates how accessible such metaphors were to both the literate and illiterate. Europeans also celebrated the miracle of transubstantiation during the Corpus Christi festival, a relatively new celebration that first became popular in the fourteenth century and focused explicitly on the physical suffering of Christ. Many sixteenth-century Europeans believed that the Devil roamed the earth in physical form, tempting errant Christians from the true path; many kept prayers copied on pieces of paper as talismans to protect them from disease. Although saving the soul was the aim of the sacraments from baptism to last rites, the way that many Christians experienced the sacred was primarily physical and literal. Their religious experience was made manifest by actions: praying to the Virgin, going on a pilgrimage, touching a relic, or even purchasing an indulgence.[70]

Religious instruction also encouraged Christians to understand their situation in concrete, physical terms. When sixteenth-century Europeans saw

68. Raymond Lebègue, "La Pléiade et le théâtre," in *Études sur le théâtre français* (Paris: Nizet, 1977), 1:207–9.

69. Peter Brown, *The Body and Society: Men, Women and Sexual Renunciation in Early Christianity* (New York: Columbia University Press, 1988), 442–47; Lisa Silverman, *Tortured Subjects: Pain, Truth, and the Body in Early Modern France* (Chicago: University of Chicago Press, 2001), 112–30; Michael P. Carroll, *Madonnas That Maim: Popular Catholicism in Italy since the Fifteenth Century* (Baltimore: Johns Hopkins University Press, 1992), 123–37.

70. John Bossy, *Christianity in the West, 1400–1700* (Oxford: Oxford University Press, 1985), 1–56; Eamon Duffy, *The Stripping of the Altars: Traditional Religion in England, c. 1400–c. 1580* (New Haven: Yale University Press, 1992), 266–98; Miri Rubin, *Corpus Christi: The Eucharist in Late Medieval Culture* (Cambridge: Cambridge University Press, 1991); Muir, *Ritual*, 158–65.

a morality play in which the Devil was portrayed tempting an individual to sin, they did not experience the performance as allegory but as a representation of a real and dangerous situation. For someone who believed that the Devil could indeed walk the earth, the physical performance of the morality play was a purgative ritual that sought to purify the community and the individual alike. Similarly, in many sermons, stories that played on the grotesque body were often introduced to illustrate the more general religious message of the sermon. These stories were often humorous and explicitly physical in their representations of good and evil: a simple priest gives his pants away to a beggar and walks around naked but is forgiven because of his generosity; a miserly layman is punished by Saint Nicetas of Lyon, who returns from the dead to beat the man in his sleep. These stories of physical intervention and humiliation, whose comic elements are very similar to the humor of the farce, were not told to subvert Catholic teaching but to bring the listener face to face with the challenges of living as a good Christian in a corrupt world. The grotesque body, far from being antithetical to Renaissance Christianity, operated very much within a religious worldview that understood evil as a physical and corporeal as well as spiritual threat.[71]

This concrete understanding of Christianity is reflected in the popular entertainment of the day. Individual farces, though remaining essentially comic in tone, often taught pointed lessons of obedience, piety, and resignation through bawdy dialogue and grotesque metaphors. In the comic morality play *The Church, Nobility and Poverty Doing the Laundry*, these themes are worked through in the mundane setting of the common washhouse. The scene opens as three characters, Church, Nobility, and Poverty, wash their dirty laundry together. Church's laundry is stinky, polluted by simony and ill-begotten wealth; Nobility rushes through the task of washing his filthy finery so that he can continue fighting destructive wars at the expense of the poor. In case the audience has not yet understood that their motives are reprehensible, the third character, Poverty, takes both Church and Nobility to task by reminding them that his closest companions are Famine and Death. Poverty's last line—"have pity on Poverty"—reminds the wealthy and powerful of their obligation to consider their responsibilities to the wider community.[72] Full of light-hearted songs and witty repartee, the overall tone of the play remains comic, despite the underlying moral message: at the play's conclusion, Church and Nobility are unrepentant. After all their talk, they end up leaving Poverty to finish up the laundry on his own. This play combines elements of grotesque humor with a critique of the balance of power in French society. Yet far from envisioning a more equitable future, it

71. Natalie Zemon Davis, "The Sacred and the Body Social in Sixteenth-Century Lyon," *Past and Present* 90 (1981): 40–70; Gurevich, *Medieval*, 195–210; Pellegrin, *Bachelleries*, 234–58.
72. Beck, *Théâtre*, 121.

shows Poverty at the end shrugging his shoulders and grudgingly accepting his Christian burden.

Reaction to a 1541 performance of *Doing the Laundry* supports this reading: a festive society famous for its satirical theater, the Conards of Rouen, performed the play without mishap.[73] Although the Conards were satirists, they were also exemplars of Christian piety. Their association, composed of artisans and minor legal officials, played an important role in the urban community as a pious confraternity. Both in February 1535 and June 1542, the seventy-six members of the "association devoted to the worship of the Virgin Mary founded at the Bonnes Nouvelles convent, commonly known as the association of the Conards," participated in religious processions dictated by the king to purge French society of Lutheran heresies.[74] Marching in sequence after the confraternities affiliated with the Rouen cathedral and the prominent Church Saint-Ouen, the Conards took their place in the urban community as devout Christians eager to celebrate the divine nature of the Blessed Sacrament. Even though the Conards regularly spoofed religious authority in Carnival performances, and in vulgarly physical ways, their broad humor did not suggest that they were anything but devout Catholics. The satirical play they performed in 1541 was a thoroughly conventional rendering of Christian themes. This combination of comic critique and Christian submission colors many farces; for the most part, these plays did not counsel rebellion but reminded those who held power to use it wisely and for the public good. The prestige and influence of Bakhtin's analysis of Carnival have sharpened a distinction between soul and body, decorum and vulgarity, transgressiveness and orthodoxy that was in fact blurred in Renaissance French farce.

To be sure, despite the overall message of reform and Christian piety, audiences took pleasure in the deceptive, irreverent, and grotesque interpretation of human relations presented in the farce. As with any theatrical performance, French men and women exhibited a range of reactions to satirical farces, which often played off social tensions as well as contradictory definitions of honor. Hostility to farce was most apparent when performances left the realm of allegory to malign the personal honor of a leading citizen. The Conards' festive society, with its portrayal of the Church as an exploitative and corrupt institution, did not raise eyebrows in 1541; nevertheless it was disciplined on several other occasions when the group's jokes attacked specific clerics. In 1547, one of their members, Jacques Sireulde, was fined heavily and suspended from his post at the Rouen Parlement for having

---

73. *Triomphe de l'abbaye des Conards avec une notice sur la fête des fous* (Rouen, 1587; reprint, Paris: Librairie des Bibliophiles, 1874), 47–51.
74. *Deux chroniques*, 151, 165; David Nicholls, "Inertia and Reform in the Pre-Tridentine French Church: The Response to Protestantism in the Diocese of Rouen, 1520–1562," *Journal of Ecclesiastical History* 32 (1981): 192–94; Petit de Julleville, *Répertoire*, 385. For an opposing interpretation, see Beck, *Théâtre*, 55–60.

APPOLOGIE
faicte par le grant abbe des Conards

Sur les Inuectiues Sagõ, Marot, La Hu
terie, Pages, Valetz, Braquetz, &c.

On la vend Deuant le College de Reims.

FIGURE 2. The Conards of Rouen, ca. 1537. Frontpiece of *Appologie faicte par le grant abbe des Conards*. (By permission of the Houghton Library, Harvard University *FP8. So135R v. 68)

accused a superior magistrate of being a cuckold.[75] The Christian imperative to expose sin often came into conflict with the pride and honor of the city's elite.

The distinction between laughing satire and malicious slander was often in the eyes of the beholder. For Jean de Gaufreteau, a judge who lived in Bordeaux during the middle of the sixteenth century, farcical performances were almost always reprehensible. Gaufreteau made his prejudices clear when he wrote a history of his home city, Bordeaux. On a number of occasions, Gaufreteau decried the performances of local farce players, whose "insolent" jokes he claims regularly resulted in violent fighting in the city streets. Gaufreteau was particularly critical of a Basoche performance of 1550, when the law clerks attacked a specific individual, a magistrate at the court who was well known for being a particularly strict taskmaster.

One day, writes Gaufreteau, when a judge working at the court passed through the courtyard of the parlement, he happened upon some clerks performing a farce. This courtyard was open to the public and usually filled with booksellers and hawkers selling their wares, so the audience for the clerks' performance probably included men working at the court as well as common city residents. The Basochiens were dressed in the costumes of Italian commedia dell'arte, a new comic genre that was just beginning to penetrate southern France in the mid-sixteenth century. Commedia dell'arte plays were similar to traditional French farces: they usually involved a romantic plot combined with acrobatics, singing, plenty of physical humor, and comic improvisation. Gaufreteau describes one scene of the play in which two clerks were dressed up as stock commedia dell'arte characters. One clerk was dressed as Pantalon, a fool character who usually wore bright red pants and a long cape. Like fools in other farcical genres, in this performance Pantalon was the character who stood back and judged society, dispensing witticisms and social critique. His foil, Zani, was a servant dressed in the simple white outfit of the sixteenth-century Italian laborer. Zani, as the social inferior of Pantalon, asked the leading questions and egged his master on to ever more daring feats of linguistic and acrobatic heroism. The object of their satire in this case was a judge who happened to be passing by, a magistrate named Sevin.[76]

75. ADSM 1 B 447, 20 May 1536; Jacques Sireulde, *Le trésor immortel: Tiré de l'Écriture sainte*, ed. Charles de Beaurepaire (Rouen: Leon Gy, 1899), xlii–xlv; Édouard Gosselin, *Recherches sur les origines et l'histoire du théâtre à Rouen avant Corneille* (Rouen: Cagniard, 1868), 45, 50; A. Floquet, "Histoire des Conards de Rouen," *Bibliothèque de l'École des Chartes* 1 (1839–40): 117; Dylan Reid, "Carnival in Rouen: A History of the Abbaye des Conards," *Sixteenth Century Journal* 32 (2001): 1040–41.
76. Elena Polovedo, "Le bouffon et la 'Commedia dell'arte' dans la fête vénitienne au XVIe siècle," in Jacquot and Konigson, *Fêtes de la Renaissance*, 3:253–66; Gustave Attinger, *L'esprit de la commedia dell'arte dans le théâtre français* (Paris: Librarie Théâtrale, 1950), 13–59; Claude Bourqui, *La commedia dell'arte: Introduction au théâtre professionnel italien entre le XVIe et le XVIIIe siècle* (Paris: SEDES, 1999), 11–20.

The Zani held in his hand a large cup of wine, and while drinking it, or while seeming to do so, asked of Pantalon what he thought of this wine, of which he had also drunk and tasted. The Pantalon character immediately answered: this wine is worth nothing. In saying this wine [ce vin], he made a pun on the chief magistrate's name, who was, as has been noted, named Sevin, and in doing so was understood to be speaking about him and not about the wine in the cup, and, finally, saying and repeating at every opportunity this phrase "ce vin" he said a thousand wrongs and insults of the chief magistrate and mocked him with a thousand intolerable and insolent legalisms and jokes, to the great dishonor of this great personage, who, nevertheless, made no complaint; on the contrary, he even laughed first, since, concerning this pun on his name, he had no idea that he had been taken in by these mockers and farce players.[77]

For Gaufreteau, this incident, which he probably narrated long after the Bordeaux Basoche had been abolished, stuck in his memory for showing the license of the clerks during the Basoche's heyday. Gaufreteau is appalled that the Basoche made these jokes at the expense of a senior magistrate: the clerks were the social inferiors of the magistrate Sevin and should have shown him deference. At the same time, Gaufreteau's account shows some contempt for his colleague Sevin, who did not even have the sense to know that he was being mocked. It does not seem to occur to Gaufreteau that Sevin might well have understood the jokes at his own expense but thought them funny nevertheless.

There is some reason to believe that Gaufreteau is referring to an actual event since many other incidents in his memoirs can be corroborated by external sources.[78] In this case, there was indeed a magistrate by the name of Pierre Sevin working at the Bordeaux Parlement during the 1550s. Sevin's career at the parlement was unremarkable until, some twenty years later, in 1572, he was murdered for being a member of the Reformed Calvinist church. His murder took place during the Saint Bartholomew's Day massacres, in which French Catholics went on a killing spree and murdered thousands of French Calvinists throughout France.[79] Could Gaufreteau's contempt for Sevin and his supposed reputation for being a particularly strict taskmaster have anything to do with his Calvinist faith? We cannot know. What we can know is that Sevin did not complain to the parlement about any jokes performed by the Basoche. Nor did any of his fellow magistrates complain on his behalf. Normally, such complaints were brought before the

---

77. Jean de Gaufreteau, *Chronique bordeloise* (Bordeaux: Charles Lefebvre, 1877), 1:83.
78. Christian Jouhaud, "La construction de l'image de l'autre chez Jean de Gaufreteau," *XVIIe Siècle* 134 (1982): 51–62.
79. Jean de Métivier, *Chronique du Parlement de Bordeaux, 1462–1566* (Bordeaux: Arthur de Brezetz et Jules Delpit, 1886–87), 2:70 (3 Aug. 1554), 2:222–23 (12 Nov. 1558); C.-B.-F. Boscheron des Portes, *Histoire du Parlement de Bordeaux, 1462–1640* (Bordeaux: Charles Lefebvre, 1877), 226–27, 245; Ernest Gaullieur, *Histoire du Collége de Guyenne, d'après un grand nombre de documents inédits* (Paris: Sandoz et Fischbacher, 1874), 257.

magistrates in the parlement and were recorded in its minutes. Although other groups were reprimanded for performing scandalous farces during the 1550s, the parlement records contain no complaints against the Basoche regarding the "ce vin" performance.[80] In other words, Gaufreteau's distaste for the Basochiens' performance did not seem to have been shared by most of his contemporaries. Evidence from the parlement records suggests that most magistrates found the clerks' jokes harmless fun. In this case, satire was diffused through laughter, and the clerks emerged unscathed.

As in so many cases of known farcical performances, we cannot know exactly what jokes the clerks made about the magistrate Sevin when they characterized him as a bottle of bad wine. But knowing other comic plays of the period, we can make an informed guess. We know that their jokes compromised the honor of the magistrate, so no doubt they sought to debase him in as broad terms as possible. During this period, such debasement usually involved references to bodily functions, sexuality, and reversals of authority. This wine, "ce vin," probably caused digestive trouble, either producing horrible gas which Pantalon would have released audibly with great satisfaction or caused an overwhelming urge to urinate, which the actor would probably have done on stage, possibly into a bottle while commenting on the quality of the urine. The wine bottle, a phallic symbol, would be mocked for being limp and flaccid, the lifeless wine inside incapable of satisfying the appetite, either gastronomical or sexual. Perhaps "ce vin" would be accused of having tried but failed to find himself a lover. The two clerks might even have acted out the attempted seduction: in many farces, two lovers enjoy a brief meal before their love tryst. In this case, after drinking "ce vin," the woman might be disgusted and refuse to go on, or the man might be rendered impotent. When it was drunk, "ce vin" may have produced a horrible hangover, which felt like one had been hit over the head (Pantalon, tricking Zani, might in fact have hit him over the head in order to demonstrate). "Ce vin" also almost inevitably impaired the reason of the drinker, who would begin spouting doggerel Latin and ridiculous judicial pronouncements. Such were the kinds of jokes regularly performed on the farcical stage during the sixteenth century.[81]

People expected bawdy jokes, puns, and double entendres when they attended the theater and were inclined to grant farce players special license.

80. Mazouer, *Vie*, 59; Métivier, *Chronique*, 1:427 (26 Jan. 1545); BM Bordeaux MS 369, Savignac, "Extraits des registres secrets du parlement de Bordeaux," 1:365 (16 Jan. 1545).
81. "La farce du poulier," in *Recueil*, ed. André Tissier, 11:183–234; "Le nouveau marié qui ne peut fournir à l'appointement de sa femme," in Ibid., 1:67–104; *L'ouverture des jours gras, ou l'entretien du Carnaval*, ed. J. Lough (Oxford: Blackwell, 1957); André Tissier, "L'évocation et représentation scénique de l'acte sexuel dans l'ancienne farce française," in Chiabò, Doglio, and Maymone, *Atti*, 521–47; Jelle Koopmans, "Les mots et la chose, ou la métaphore comme spectacle," *Versants: Revue Suisse des Littératures Romanes* 38 (2000): 31–51; Mazouer, *Théâtre du moyen âge*, 296, 316, 341; Muchembled, *Invention*, 43–56.

The ritual setting, the costumes, and the membership of the clerks in a festive society like the Basoche all granted the young men a temporary privilege to challenge social norms. In this case, the fact that the Basochiens were mocking a man of the law could have mitigated the severity of the response. In any hierarchy, inferiors tend to feel ambivalent about their superiors. The freedom to express hostility publicly is not always forthcoming but was granted by French society during farce's heyday. Other groups were also allowed to ritually mock their elders. During the Feast of Kings at Epiphany, young novices at some of the most important cathedrals of France performed mock sermons and ritually demeaned their superiors by dressing up as bishops and riding around backward on asses. Clerks at the parlements, who were themselves the butt of many jokes in contemporary farces, took the opportunity once or twice a year to dish out similar abuse against their betters.[82] As long as the overall political situation was stable, such jokes and antics did not fundamentally threaten local authorities. The Basochiens who made fun of Sevin were not questioning the authority of the magistrates, nor could they surely have intended to undermine the power of the parlement, since they too hoped to profit from its power later in their careers.

Not all parlement magistrates were, of course, as naive or as good-humored as Pierre Sevin, even during the relatively open period of the Renaissance. In 1553, another Bordeaux Parlement magistrate named Odet Mathieu complained that the king of the Basoche, Jean Puchabilier, had insulted him, and he sought a formal apology.[83] A decade earlier, Paris Basochiens who mocked two solicitors and a fellow clerk during their May performance were threatened with being barred from the court. In general, these complaints were couched in terms of loss of honor. In 1538, the chastised Basochiens were warned that "the honor, reverence and obedience that they owe to these solicitors" prohibits them from "chastising" (literally "spanking," *baculer*) and "slandering" their employers. Gaufreteau notes that, in his opinion, the Basochiens "dishonored" Sevin by having him witness their play. Similarly, after the 1447 performance in Dijon, the prosecutor general complained that the "honor . . . of the city" had been compromised by Savenot's jokes about the king's son.[84] Indeed, the notion of honor is as important as an awareness of the Christian sense of the body for an appreciation of the social function of farce. Farce players not only challenged the honor of their social superiors but also earned it for themselves during their performances.

---

82. Marguerite de Navarre, *Heptaméron*, ed. Renja Salminen (Geneva: Droz, 1999), 318–24 (nouvelle 36).
83. AN x1a 4906, fols. 589–90, 6 Aug. 1538; Métivier, *Chronique*, 1:427 (26 Jan. 1545), 2:55 (8 Aug. 1553); BMB MS 369, Savignac, "Extraits," 1:365 (16 Jan. 1545), 1:556 (8 Aug. 1553).
84. AN x1a 4906, fols. 589–90, 6 Aug. 1538; Gaufreteau, *Chronique*, 1:83; Gouvenain, *Théâtre*, 34.

Traditionally honor was considered to be primarily the preserve of the social elites, most obviously the military nobility. The brave and virtuous knight going to battle to fight out of loyalty to his king or his faith was the epitome of honorable behavior in the sixteenth century, just as he had been for hundreds of years.[85] By definition, nobles were considered to be honorable in the sense of possessing a natural propensity for virtue and deserving of social deference in a way that peasants, artisans, and merchants were not. Honor was, however, an attribute also claimed by groups lower on the social scale. A person's honor was defined by a combination of social status and personal reputation in the community. As an artisan, a person behaved honorably if he produced high-quality goods, paid off debts in a timely fashion, and took responsibility for caring for his family. Such tangible evidence of right living could result in an honorable reputation, which in turn might be transformed into "honors," symbols of social preeminence, usually in the form of public office. Becoming the local leader of a confraternity, of an occupational corporation, or even of a festive society was an honor that men of the couche moyenne might acquire.[86] Royal officials, including judges at the parlements such as the memoir writer Jean Gaufreteau and the mocked judge Pierre Sevin, were also honorable men whose relatively high social status was signaled by the long black robes they wore to court and their education in Latin and the law. Some French magistrates during the sixteenth century tried to argue that their learning and their role as public officials granted them honor equal to that of the nobility. Not everyone was convinced by these pretensions to grandeur, which may help to explain why there are more legal officials satirized in farces than nobles. Yet although almost all members of French society could behave with honor by fulfilling their profession competently and living virtuously, honor was also a cultural construct that reenforced hierarchy and social deference. According to this system of honor, men of the couche moyenne, whatever their personal honorable status among their peers, owed deference to those more socially elevated than themselves. The system of honor thus made manifest and justified the social hierarchy of French society.[87]

The men of the couche moyenne who performed farces in French cities certainly understood their lives in terms of honor. Paradoxically, performing farce was one way of gaining honor in this system. Festive societies often

85. Kristen B. Neuschel, *Word of Honor: Interpreting Noble Culture in Sixteenth-Century France* (Ithaca: Cornell University Press, 1989), 38–58.

86. Arlette Jouanna, "Recherches sur la notion d'honneur au XVIe siècle," *Revue d'Histoire Moderne et Contemporaine* 15 (1968): 597–623; Julie Hardwick, *The Practice of Patriarchy: Gender and the Politics of Household Authority in Early Modern France* (University Park: Pennsylvania State University Press, 1998), 195–218.

87. Jouanna, "Recherches," 610–23; Julian Pitt-Rivers, "Honour and Social Status," in *Honour and Shame: The Values of Mediterranean Society*, ed. J. G. Peristiany (Chicago: University of Chicago Press, 1966), 38; Aubailly, *Monologue*, 426.

spent large sums, sometimes from their own coffers and sometimes donated by local patrons, to produce their farces on the public stage. Although their processions were often undertaken in mock-serious tone, sometimes making fun of figures of authority, the young men's elaborate accoutrements signaled that these performances were rituals that also integrated them into the urban community.[88] Published accounts of these events abound with descriptions of the rich colors of the silks worn by the performers and the elaborate decorations on chariots and horses. Some festive societies invested considerable resources in their processions: professional musicians were hired to accompany them, and metal coins depicting the festive society's king were distributed to spectators. One of the wealthiest festive societies, the Mère Folle of Dijon, had scepters and crowns made that remain in a municipal museum to this day.[89] Performing on the public stage gave the actors a chance to show off their wealth as honorable members of the community. Although their actual status was humble in comparison with that of the urban elite who administered the city, their silks and bright banners were designed to impress the majority of city residents who were much poorer still. Farce playing was after all a privilege enjoyed only by a minority of urban residents.

For sixteenth-century French men and women, honor was one of the most valued attributes. Yet because honor depended on the opinion of others, perhaps in one's neighborhood or the king's court, it was inherently fragile. Loss of reputation might mean loss of tangible honors, including royal office, lucrative pensions, or access to credit. It might become impossible to marry off one's daughters or to maintain a customer base for one's product.[90] Defending one's honor was a just cause in a society in which a good reputation could be crucial for maintaining harmony within a neighborhood or for asserting political authority over others.[91] Members of the nobility never hesitated to

---

88. Martine Grinberg, "Carnaval et société urbaine à la fin du XVe siècle," in Jacquot and Konigson, *Fêtes de la Renaissance*, 3:551–53; Sharon Collingwood, *Market Pledge and Gender Bargain: Commercial Relations in French Farce, 1450–1550* (New York: Peter Lang, 1996), 1–8; Adrian Blanchet, "Les écus du palais et la monnaie de Basoche," *Revue Numismatique* 30 (1927): 88–89.
89. Du Tilliot, *Mémoires*, xx–1; Maurice Lambert, *Le sceau d'un roi de basoche conservé à la bibliothèque de Besançon* (Besançon: Dodivers, 1909); Tricou, "Confréries," 309–13.
90. Jouanna, "Recherches," 598; Stuart, *Defiled*, 189–221; Thierry Dutour, *Une société de l'honneur: Les notables et leur monde à Dijon à la fin du moyen âge* (Paris: Champion, 1998), 221–34.
91. Natalie Zemon Davis, *Fiction in the Archives: Pardon Tales and Their Tellers in Sixteenth-Century France* (Stanford: Stanford University Press, 1987), 38–40; Pitt-Rivers, "Honour," 24; Farr, *Hands*, 177–86; Muchembled, *Invention*, 37–41, 218–27; Isabelle Paresys, *Aux marges du royaume: Violence, justice et société en Picardie sous François 1er* (Paris: Publications de la Sorbonne, 1998), 90–109; Sandra Cavallo and Simona Cerutti, "Female Honor and the Social Control of Reproduction in Piedmont between 1600 and 1800," in *Sex and Gender in Historical Perspective*, ed. Edward Muir and Guido Ruggiero, trans. Margaret A. Gallucci, Mary M. Gallucci, and Carole C. Gallucci (Baltimore: Johns Hopkins University Press, 1990), 80–81; Garthine Walker, "Expanding the Boundaries of Female Honour in Early Modern England," *Transactions of the Royal Historical Society* 6 (1996): 235–45.

lash out physically at men who insulted their family name or questioned their military prowess, and nobles could be forgiven for such acts, even for murder, if they could justify them as necessary to defend their honor.

The physicality of honor during the medieval and early modern periods is no doubt another reason why farce players' jokes so often focused on bodily functions and desires. Indeed, the body was an important site for the acquisition and loss of honor, not only for elites but also for French commoners, who also justified the physical assaults they committed in the same terms. Although many of the assaults brought before magistrates in French law courts involved conventional punches, kicks, and knife wounds, the common people of French cities also engaged in ritual assaults on the bodies of others. Since hats, caps, helmets, women's bonnets, or head scarves, always worn in public, denoted the wearer's honorable status, a common kind of assault was to knock or rip off the headdress of the offending party. Usually such conflicts started with a verbal insult: artisans accused one another, and sometimes their social superiors, of being worthless, of being dishonest, or of being cuckolds. Women's honor usually hinged on their sexual behavior: in most contexts they were expected to be, or to appear to be, virgins until marriage and then monogamous forever afterward. Insulting a woman's modesty thus often caused fights between men or sometimes fights between women in the city streets. Such cases often came before the local law courts and city councils of France during the fifteenth and sixteenth centuries. Defending one's honor was a just cause in a society in which a good reputation could be crucial for maintaining harmony within a neighborhood or for asserting political authority over others.[92]

When they performed farces, members of festive societies entered this competitive arena of honor acquisition. Their performances could enhance their honor, but they usually did so by compromising the honor of another, sometimes a social superior. Farce playing was thus often a zero-sum game in which the honor of the player was only enhanced as much as the honor of another was compromised. The possibility of losing face on the public stage was also an ever-present danger to the farce players, who as amateurs were not always very skilled actors. The players hoped to win the laughter of the audience, but they did not always succeed. The competitive element of farcical performance was openly acknowledged by northern French and Flemish cities, where groups from different locales performed and competed together during the months of May or July. City councilors sometimes awarded a prize for the best performance, but even when no prize was distributed, festive societies sought to outdo one another whenever they performed or processed together. Particularly in the north,

92. Davis, *Fiction*, 38–40; Pitt-Rivers, "Honour," 24; Farr, *Hands*, 177–86; Muchembled, *Invention*, 37–41, 218–27; Paresys, *Marges*, 90–109; Cavallo and Cerutti, "Female Honor," 80–81; Walker, "Expanding," 235–45.

companies of farceurs traveled from city to city competing for a prize, and the group that returned home with a trophy in hand was thought to have enhanced the honor of the city as a whole.[93] Even when only one group performed, the competitive element, though less overt, was still present. An incident in Dijon in 1511 demonstrates the extent to which a young man's honor was at stake when he performed on the stage.[94] That July, a woman in the audience thought that one of the actors was doing a poor job and began to laugh *at* his performance so audibly and rudely that the actor's wife, who was also present, became enraged and challenged her; eventually the two came to blows. By his incompetence as a farceur, the young man compromised rather than enhanced his honor.

When farce players succeeded in making the audience laugh, they often did so by attacking their social betters. This kind of disrespect, which could result in physical blows when it occurred during an everyday encounter, was licensed by the social ritual of farce. Verbal play also protected the farce players from prosecution and censorship. Although they regularly mocked authority figures, they often did so by hinting at the victim's identity rather than declaring it openly. When brought before city judges and accused of having slandered an important citizen or royal official, actors usually defended their actions by claiming that they were only trying to make people laugh, a defense that usually convinced the judges to be lenient.[95]

During the French Renaissance, an unprecedented number of festive societies mounted farces that both joked about the failure of Christians to live as they should and mocked the honor of people of all social castes. Their satire was no more biting than earlier medieval comic genres, but the frequency and the elaborateness of the farceurs' performances during the 1450 to 1560 period is remarkable. Amateur actors used farce to express their concerns, their complaints, and their joie de vivre. Most of the time, their performances were applauded, but sometimes political tensions hampered their ability to laugh out loud about morality and power in their communities.

93. John Huizinga, *Homo Ludens: A Study of the Play-Element in Culture* (London: Temple Smith, 1970), 70, 100, 108; Lecocq, *Histoire*, 139–41; Lefebvre, *Fêtes*, 18–23; Petit de Julleville, *Répertoire*, 336, 344.
94. Gouvenain, *Théâtre*, 39.
95. Tricou, "Confréries," 299–300; AN x1a 4906, fols. 589–90, 6 Aug. 1538; Pitt-Rivers, "Honour," 26.

2 The Politics of Farcical Performance in Renaissance France

Farce flourished in France between 1450 and 1560 because the elite allowed it to. From the king, who enjoyed ultimate authority over all his subjects, to the city officials who usually regulated the theater, farce was constantly overseen, patronized, and, to some extent, censored during this period. Overall, those in authority were tolerant and often enthusiastic appreciators of farce, but they were also wary of its potential to sow dissent, promote violence, and undermine authority. Satire in the farc e kept the authorities watchful of the fine line between humor and slander. During times of prosperity and peace, this tension was kept within acceptable bounds. Jokes about the clergy and royal officials could more easily be forgiven when royal power was strong and the clergy secure in its pastoral role. Farce could even be used by the king or his officials to mock those out of favor or, at the very least, to keep the city's youth occupied at Carnival.

No group was exempt from the enjoyment of farce; everyone laughed at the sight of cuckolded husbands, fights on the stage, and sexually explicit dialogue.[1] The pleasure that French men and women found in the farce stemmed in part from its role in shaping public opinion. In a society in which most people were not literate and in which there were no newspapers, farcical theater satisfied many functions: it was entertaining, it could inform people of new political and religious developments, and it sometimes presented critical commentary about current events. Audiences were eager to decipher the actors' puns and to hear the latest scandal about men who held power in their communities. Elites assumed that farce could shape public opinion in such a way as to bolster or undermine the authority of officials,

---

1. Regarding the presence of the urban poor at farcical performances, see Archives Nationales (AN) x1a 4914, fols. 80–82, 9 Dec. 1541; Michel Félibien, *Histoire de la ville de Paris* (Paris: G. Desprez et J. Desessartz, 1725), 4:833b–834a (15 Sept. 1571).

from the local tax collector to the king. Farce playing reveals that public opinion mattered in sixteenth-century France. Comic theater was a central means for urban commoners to make their political and religious concerns heard—concerns that were sometimes shared by the social superiors who claimed the right to license and censor farce.

Royal enjoyment of farce, though hardly new, was also crucial to the genre's success and its cultural prominence during the Renaissance.[2] French kings, most notably Louis XII (1498–1515) and Francis I (1515–47), were important patrons of farce. Throughout their lives, they commissioned performances by both amateur festive societies and professional actors, who often resided at the court for long periods of time. Louis in particular enjoyed the biting satire of farcical performance. In 1505, he had the law clerks of the Basoche and university students perform several "satirical comedies" at court, one of which mocked the pope and the marshal of Gié, a powerful member of Louis's court who was being tried for treason at the time. Louis was also somewhat tolerant of satire directed at himself and on a number of occasions refrained from punishing comic actors who questioned his policies or his virility.[3] His tolerance can be in large measure explained by his popularity: despite some misgivings about the continuation of the Italian Wars and his negotiations with the pope, Louis was generally well-respected by his subjects, particularly during the last years of his reign.[4] When in 1514, at the age of fifty-three, Louis married the young princess of England, Mary Tudor, the Basochiens of Paris performed a play in which they implied that the king's new bride would exhaust him in bed. In a public performance in the capital, they claimed that "the king of England has sent an ass to the king to bring him very soon and very sweetly to hell or to heaven."[5] Since usually only a man who had been cuckolded by his wife rode an ass, the Basochiens were suggesting that Mary Tudor would soon be looking elsewhere to satisfy her sexual needs (as indeed turned out to be the case). Although we cannot be sure that Louis was aware of this performance, he might have guffawed in appreciation.

2. Michel Rousse, "Le pouvoir royal et le théâtre des farces," in *Le pouvoir monarchique et ses supports idéologiques*, ed. Jean Dufournet, Adeline Fiorato, and Augustin Redondo (Paris: Sorbonne Nouvelle, 1990), 185.
3. Ibid., 188–89; Frederic J. Baumgartner, *Louis XII* (New York: St. Martin's Press, 1994), 136–39; Jean d'Auton, *Chroniques de Louis XII*, ed. René de Maulde La Clavière (Paris: Renouard, 1893), 3:352–54; Louis Petit de Julleville, *Histoire du théâtre en France: Répertoire du théâtre comique en France au moyen âge* (Paris: Le Cerf, 1886), 345; Charles Oulmont, "Pierre Gringore et l'entrée de la reine Anne en 1504," in *Mélanges offerts à M. Émile Picot* (Paris: Rakir, 1913; reprint, Geneva: Slatkine, 1969), 389; Adolphe Fabre, *Les clercs du palais: Recherches historiques sur les Bazoches des Parlements et sociétés dramatiques des Bazochiens et Enfants-sans-Souci* (Lyon: Scheuring, 1875), 142–43; Ronald S. Love, "Contemporary and Near-Contemporary Opinion of Louis XII, 'Père du Peuple,'" *Renaissance and Reformation* 8 (1984): 241.
4. Love, "Contemporary," passim; Baumgartner, *Louis XII*, 208.
5. *Mémoires du maréchal de Florange dit le Jeune Adventureux*, ed. Robert Goubaux and P.-André Lemoisne (Paris: Renouard, 1913), 1:162–63.

Francis I, his young successor, was much less willing to allow farce players to joke about politics.[6] Yet Francis's sensitivity to slander should not be interpreted as a repudiation of farce. He merely resented having its barbs directed at himself, particularly during the first few years of his reign when he was establishing his authority and reputation.[7] In 1516, for example, Francis lashed out at three farce players who were accused of saying that "Mother Folly ruled at the king's court and that she taxed, plundered and stole everything."[8] Francis had the three guilty players, one of them a well-known actor named Jean de Pont-Alais, imprisoned at his château at Amboise. Yet this clash did not mark a turning point in royal attitude to farce or a sudden transformation of farce playing in the capital.[9] Festive societies such as the Enfants-sans-Souci and the Basoche continued to perform in Paris throughout the first half of the sixteenth century. Their performances continued to be appreciated by the king, as long as they avoided discussions of royal authority and religious reform. Francis often commissioned the performance of farcical plays, including one that, in 1523, made satirical allusions to his own mother, Louise of Savoy.[10] By the early 1530s, Francis had even established Jean de Pont-Alais, the farceur he had imprisoned in 1516, as one of his regular court entertainers. Disbursements of several hundred livres to Pont-Alais continued throughout the 1530s, along with payments to other farce players.[11] Lewd farcical jokes that mocked one's political enemies continued to be a part of French court culture throughout the sixteenth century and

---

6. *Journal d'un bourgeois de Paris sous le règne de François 1er, 1515–1536*, ed. Ludovic Lalanne (Paris: Renouard, 1854), 13–14; Félibien, *Histoire*, 4:634a (5 Jan. 1516), 4:645a (27 Dec. 1523).

7. A poor sense of humor was not unusual for recently crowned kings. In 1486, Charles VIII lashed out at the Basoche, and in 1594, soon after the conversion of Henry IV, a rector at the University of Paris was reprimanded for having written a satirical play. Félibien, *Histoire*, 5:25b (23 Aug. 1594); Henri Baude, *Les vers de maître Henri Baude, poète du XVe siècle*, ed. M. J. Quicherat (Paris: Aubry, 1856), 110–11.

8. *Journal d'un bourgeois*, 44; Jean Frappier, "Sur Jean du Pont-Alais," in *Mélanges d'histoire du théâtre du Moyen-Age et de la Renaissance, offerts à Gustave Cohen, professeur honoraire en Sorbonne* (Paris: Nizet, 1950), 135–36.

9. Many historians argue or imply that Francis was personally hostile to farce. Howard Graham Harvey, *The Theatre of the Basoche: The Contribution of the Law Societies to French Mediaeval Comedy* (Cambridge, Mass.: Harvard University Press, 1941), 228; Louis Petit de Julleville, *Histoire du théâtre en France: Les comédiens en France au moyen âge* (Paris: Le Cerf, 1885), 113–14; Rousse, "Pouvoir royal," 188–89; R. J. Knecht, "Popular Theatre and the Court in Sixteenth-Century France," *Renaissance Studies* 9 (1995): 367–68.

10. AN x1a 1524, fol. 251, 31 May 1522; AN x1a 1529, fol. 279, 16 June 1526; *Recueil d'actes notariés relatifs à l'histoire de Paris et ses environs*, ed. Ernest Coyecque (Paris: Imprimerie Nationale, 1905), 1:580 (22 Apr. 1544), 1:598 (23 Sept. 1544); Charles Mazouer, *Le théâtre français de la Renaissance* (Paris: Champion, 2002), 87; *Journal d'un bourgeois*, 268; Frappier, "Pont-Alais," 140–41.

11. Frappier, "Pont-Alais," 136, 140–41; *Journal d'un bourgeois*, 414; *Collection des ordonnances des rois de France: Catalogue des actes de François 1er* (Paris: Imprimerie Nationale, 1887), 4:203, 7:792, 8:303; AN x1a 1524, fol. 251, 31 May 1522; AN x1a 1529, fol. 279, 16 June 1526; Petit de Julleville, *Répertoire*, 376, 379, 383.

well into the seventeenth, long after the urban notables, who regulated farce at the local level, had repudiated the genre.

Patronage of farce was not limited to the king. Other members of the high nobility, many of whom had spent some time at the royal court or were educated in its ways, also commissioned farce players to perform during the late fifteenth and early sixteenth centuries.[12] Such performances were also commissioned by noble clergy. The cardinal of Bourbon, who in addition to being a man of the cloth was also one of the highest-ranking peers of France, commissioned farce players to perform at his personal residence in Paris in 1482 to mark the Peace of Arras. Other clerics, such as the abbot of Saint-Omer, regularly paid comic actors to perform at traditional festivals such as the Feast of Kings and the Feast of Innocents.[13] The violence and sexuality depicted in farces were not considered too risqué to entertain a high-ranking cleric during the heyday of the French Renaissance.

The nobility's enthusiasm for farcical humor, coupled with wariness of its potential for satire, was reflected in the poetry of the time. Aspiring poets interested in maintaining or obtaining a court post wrote poems that celebrated the audacity of farce players. Roger de Collerye, a poet who worked for the bishop of Auxerre, wrote verse on behalf of the Basoche of the Paris Parlement, rivals at that point with another group of clerks, those who worked at the Châtelet, a court of first instance also located on the Ile de la Cité in the heart of Paris.[14]

> Basochiens, that we will not be disappointed,
> For it is said, without making a great commotion,
> That you will play this fine month of May.
>
> Let military men and their attendants come running
> Guards, heralds, if it happens that they are prevented
> From stepping out, so the wind blows
> But that your antics never be suppressed![15]

Collerye's verses, first published in 1530, suggest that the performances of the Basoche were impatiently awaited by the people of Paris, who would rush to come see the clerks perform at a moment's notice. The audience

---

12. Petit de Julleville, *Répertoire*, 345, 349, 360, 364, 381.
13. Ibid., 343, 345, 359, 381.
14. Sylvie Lécuyer, *Roger de Collerye: Un heritier de Villon* (Paris: Champion, 1997), 10; Marie Bouhaïk-Gironès, "La Basoche et le théâtre comique: Identité sociale, pratiques et culture des clercs de justice (Paris, 1420–1550)," Ph.D. diss., University of Paris 7, 2004, 72–73.
15. Roger de Collerye, *Oeuvres*, ed. Charles d'Héricault (Paris: P. Jannet, 1855), 271–72; André de la Vigne, "Les complaintes et epitaphes du roi de la Bazoche," in *Recueil des poésies françoises des XVe et XVIe siècles*, ed. Anatole de Montaiglon (Paris: Daffis, 1878), 13:383–413; Clément Marot, "Des Enfans Sans Soucy," "Le cry du jeu de l'Empire d'Orleans," and "Au roy. Pour la Bazoche," in *Oeuvres poétiques*, ed. Gérard Defaux (Paris: Classiques Garnier, 1990), 1:107–11, 2:175–76.

Collerye imagines is public and diverse, composed of noble youths and their lackeys, as well as local officials working near the parlement compound. These are not merely skits to amuse fellow clerks during a day off of work but events that might disturb the public peace. Because of this potential to sow dissension, Collerye is concerned that the Basoche might not be allowed to perform any longer, a fear that was in fact not realized for several more decades. Similar poems, in which appreciation for the bright colors and playful nature of farcical performance was mixed with an awareness of an ever-present possibility of censorship, were written by well-known poets and playwrights such as André de la Vigne and Clément Marot. Such poems were not expressions of a popular culture at odds with elite tastes but took for granted that farcical humor would be appreciated by a wide variety of audiences, including their patrons, the nobles and clerics who frequented the king's court.

Although the popularity of farce at the king's court certainly added to its cultural prominence, farce players also needed the support of the local urban elite if they were to survive. This was because on a day-to-day level, theatrical regulation was a local affair. In the normal course of things, authority figures made decisions about local performances with no expectation that their rulings would have any impact outside of the town or city in which they were issued. Only occasionally did the king himself issue an order concerning the theater. When he did so, it was usually to punish a particular group of performers whose plays had affronted him and had come dangerously close to treason. Until the mid-sixteenth century, when the threat of Protestant heresy raised the stakes of theatrical performance, French kings made no systematic effort to regulate the theater. Nevertheless, sixteenth-century French subjects harbored no illusions about their freedom to speak their mind outside of the ritualized and comic performance of farce. Freedom of speech did not exist in this period, and common city residents who insulted even minor city officials could often find themselves imprisoned as a result.[16]

The local context of theatrical regulation reflected the fundamentally decentralized nature of royal authority. Even after having won back much land from the English at the end of the Hundred Years' War, French monarchs were still faced with the challenge of imposing their will over all their subjects. One way French kings managed to do so was by expanding the royal judicial system: they founded new royal law courts to defend the king's law, and they granted royal sanction to existing law courts in newly acquired lands. In this way, Charles VII and his successors attempted to enforce the French crown's claim to be the supreme judge of the land, a conception of

16. Alfred Soman, "Press, Pulpit and Censorship in France before Richelieu," *Proceedings of the American Philosophical Society* 120 (1976): 439–63; Hilary J. Bernstein, *Between Crown and Community: Politics and Civic Culture in Sixteenth-Century Poitiers* (Ithaca: Cornell University Press, 2004), 38.

the monarchy that had long been expressed in late-medieval royal iconography.[17] As supreme judges, French kings were nevertheless limited by the law—either Roman or customary law, depending on the region—and by the extent of their control over the royal judges acting in the provinces. So although the king's judicial authority was in theory supreme, it was in practice compromised by his reliance on local institutions staffed with local men who had their own regional, familial, and individual interests to think of. Although the king could unilaterally promulgate new legislation, these royal edicts needed to be ratified by the local parlement before they became law. Enforcement of royal edicts thus required a degree of cooperation from local elites, who often sought to protect their own authority from royal hegemony. Although theatrical regulation was rarely the subject of political negotiations between king and provincial elites, the ways that farce was deployed by these elites reveal the contested nature of political power at this time. Theater was one element of a ritual vocabulary that allowed provincial elites to articulate their expectations of the monarch, and for authorities within the city itself to compete with one another for power.

The men who controlled theatrical regulation in French provincial cities belonged to a fairly stable oligarchy, a small number of families among whom positions of authority regularly rotated. Socioeconomically, this urban elite was mixed: some of these families were rural nobility with long-standing ties to the land whereas others had built up wealth in the city as wholesale merchants or local moneylenders. Increasingly, by 1500 or so, some of these men were trained lawyers, educated at university in the hopes of obtaining a post at the royal law courts. These families intermarried during the late fifteenth and sixteenth centuries, gradually cementing family ties and accumulating capital at the local level. Political office and religious office were an expected component of these families' status as the city's elite, its *hommes notables*. Elected to the city council, appointed as head of the urban militia, delegated to collect taxes in the city, or appointed as judges at the regional parlement, these men collectively kept order in the city. Second sons often became priests in the city's most wealthy parishes or canons of the city's cathedral.[18]

17. John Russell Major, *From Renaissance Monarchy to Absolute Monarchy: French Kings, Nobles and Estates* (Baltimore: Johns Hopkins University Press, 1994), 16–22, 44–47; Jean Barbey, *Être roi: Le roi et son gouvernement en France de Clovis à Louis XVI* (Paris: Fayard, 1992), 165–83; Robert Descimon, "La royauté française entre féodalité et sacerdoce: Roi seigneur ou roi magistrat?" *Revue de Synthèse* 112 (1991): 455–73.
18. Bernard Chevalier, *Les bonnes villes de France du XIVe au XVIe siècle* (Paris: Aubier-Montaigne, 1982), 66–76, 137–43; Jonathan Dewald, *The Formation of a Provincial Nobility: The Magistrates of the Parlement of Rouen, 1499–1610* (Princeton: Princeton University Press, 1980), 109–12; Barbara B. Diefendorf, *Paris City Councillors in the Sixteenth Century: The Politics of Patrimony* (Princeton: Princeton University Press, 1983), 42–59; Roger Doucet, *Les institutions de la France au XVIe siècle* (Paris: A. Picard, 1948), 368–75; Philip T. Hoffman, *Church and Community in the Diocese of Lyon, 1500–1789* (New Haven: Yale University Press, 1984), 13; George Huppert, *Les Bourgeois Gentilhommes: An Essay on the Definition of Elites in Renaissance France* (Chicago: University of Chicago Press, 1977), 16–23.

Jean Guéraud, a cloth merchant who lived in Lyon during the first half of the sixteenth century, typifies this urban *notable* class and illustrates their tolerant and even enthusiastic attitude toward farcical humor. Descended from artisans who had lived in Lyon for at least a hundred years, Guéraud was born around 1500 to a family that had accumulated sufficient capital to own two houses in the city and some farmland nearby. He probably attended school from the age of about seven until his midteens, when he was brought into the family business. As a result of this schooling, he was comfortable reading and writing French and likely knew a smattering of Latin grammar as well. By his thirties, Guéraud had established himself as a prominent cloth merchant, an important man in his neighborhood. In his forties, he began to attend meetings of the Lyon city council, to act as a tax assessor, and eventually, as a city administrator to oversee trade. In the 1550s, Guéraud was sent on a number of missions to Burgundy to obtain provisions for the city during a time of famine, a commission of considerable responsibility.[19]

Guéraud's role in Lyon public life was not particularly remarkable—he was never at the heart of city politics—but he is exceptional in that he left behind a memoir. In it Guéraud reveals himself to be a fervent Catholic, a man of deep faith who ultimately left the city when Protestants took over the city government during the Wars of Religion. His descriptions of Lyon religious and festive life are vivid: he depicts with pleasure the various festivals that enlivened street life, and he clearly enjoyed the farcical performances he attended. In July 1552 he describes how city officials commissioned the local Basoche festive society to perform farces on the riverbank until late into the night, accompanied by "tambourines, fifes, oboes, violins and trumpets."[20] Like others of his time and education level, Guéraud takes these performances for granted; they are a legitimate, enjoyable part of urban cultural life.[21]

Guéraud was also fiercely loyal to his home, the city of Lyon, and as a result was willing to applaud farce players who defended the city's honor against outsiders. Although he praises the king in his memoir, he also writes of resenting royal financial impositions and is wary of the Church as an institution. Guéraud's worldview is thus framed by fundamentally local concerns: although obedience and homage to the king are assumed, his priorities were the pride and prosperity of his native city.[22] In 1540, Guéraud

---

19. Jean Guéraud, *La chronique lyonnaise de Jean Guéraud, 1536–1562*, ed. Jean Tricou (Lyon: Audin, 1929), 1–15.
20. Ibid., 63.
21. Gilles de Gouberville, *Le journal du sire de Gouberville*, ed. Alexandre Tollemer, Eugène Robillard de Beaurepaire, Auguste de Blangy, and Madeleine Foisil (Bricqueboscq: Éditions des Champs, 1993), 1:134 (Feb. 1551); Petit de Julleville, *Répertoire*, 346.
22. Major, *Renaissance Monarchy*, 19–20; Timothy Watson, "Friends at Court: The Correspondence of the Lyon City Council, c. 1525–1575," *French History* 13 (1999): 281–302.

notes with some satisfaction that the Enfants de la Ville, an elite youth group that performed farces and accompanied nobility when they arrived in the city, had dishonored the cardinal of Ferraro, archbishop of Lyon. The cardinal was an Italian noble recently appointed to the post by the king of France. During the cardinal's first ceremonial entry into Lyon, the Enfants insulted the cardinal by appearing at this important occasion in everyday dress, in notable contrast to the silks worn by the city councilors and the elaborate costumes the Enfants usually wore on such occasions. Guéraud's tacit approval of the young men's misbehavior probably resulted from the cardinal's foreign birth and the unlikelihood that he would reside in Lyon for long. Indeed, after a brief three-day visit, the archbishop left Lyon, only to return once more during his long tenure over the archdiocese.[23] For men of Guéraud's station in life, the festive antics of the young men were a safe way of acknowledging the ambivalence felt about those in authority, particularly outsiders who might undermine urban autonomy in some way.

During the Renaissance, the urban elite to which Guéraud belonged not only appreciated farce but also organized and financed its performance. In mid-sixteenth-century Lille, the leader of a well-established festive society, known as the Prince d'Amour, was a nail merchant and city councilor named Allard Dubosquiel. In 1548, Dubosquiel persuaded the city council to contribute two hundred livres—a considerable sum—toward his association's participation in a nearby festival. Such funds went toward outfitting the young performers in elaborate costumes and hiring musicians to accompany them.[24] In Cambrai at the end of the fifteenth century, some members of a similar amateur theatrical group, the notorious Abbey of Lescache, were prominent men of the city who had been involved in peace negotiations with the king of France. Besides allowing festive societies to perform on traditional religious holidays, sixteenth-century magistrates began commissioning groups to perform farce during secular civic events, such as celebrations after peace treaties and the dedications of civic buildings. Far from merely allowing farce players to perform, they requested their services, dined with the players before their performances, and sometimes paid them in wine as a means of showing their appreciation. What could be more appropriate to celebrate the victory of King Charles VII over the far-flung province of Guyenne in 1451 than to commission a local group to perform?[25] To

23. Jean Tricou, "Les confréries joyeuses de Lyon au XVIe siècle et leur numismatique," *Revue Numismatique* 40 (1937): 294; Jean Tricou, "Un archevêque de Lyon au XVIe siècle, Hippolyte d'Este," *Revue des Études Italiennes* 5 (1958): 147–54; Guéraud, *Chronique*, 18, 31, 51, 63, 117–18.

24. Achille Durieux, *Le théâtre à Cambrai avant et depuis 1789* (Cambrai: J. Renaut, 1883), 30–31; Léon Lefebvre, *Fêtes lilloises du XIVe au XVIe siècle* (Lille: Lefebvre-Ducrocq, 1902), 21–25; Adrien Blanchet, "Les écus du palais et la monnaie de Basoche," *Revue Numismatique* 30 (1927): 77–91; Petit de Julleville, *Répertoire*, 344.

25. Georges Lecocq, *Histoire du théâtre en Picardie, depuis son origine jusqu'à la fin du XVIe siècle* (Paris: Menu, 1880; reprint, Geneva: Slatkine, 1971), 138–40; Petit de Julleville,

the fifteenth- and early sixteenth-century urban oligarchy, the answer was obvious. For them farce was not something done by social marginals who needed to be controlled but a practice that they supported because they felt it reflected favorably on the honor of the city.

Farce also played a role in the provincial cities' public interaction with the monarchy, most notably during royal entry ceremonies. Although French cities could not have survived as independent political entities, their loyalty to the Valois monarchy was not taken for granted but formally renewed at the ascension of each king. The willingness of each city to accept the protection of the king and a reciprocal affirmation of the city's legal privileges normally took place during a ritual called the royal entry, held at the beginning of each reign. French cities had hosted royal entry ceremonies since the fourteenth century, but the elaborateness and political significance of these events became more marked during the Renaissance. Normally, the king arrived at the city's gates with a large entourage. He was greeted by a select group of the city's notables and usually presented with an elaborate gift and the keys to the city's gates. The king was then ushered through the city streets under ceremonial arches decorated with royal colors, past floats on which city commoners dressed up in allegorical costumes. Finally, the ceremony culminated in a mass held at the city's cathedral. Royal entries were opportunities for the urban elite to demonstrate their power and wealth, for the clergy to flaunt its spiritual supremacy, and for the king to confirm his authority over local governing bodies.[26] Because these events were important in cementing a good working relationship between the king and the city, urban authorities went to great lengths to ensure that the performance was sufficiently "solemn" and "as honorable and magnificent as possible."[27] Well-known groups that performed religious plays were often barred from performing or had their plays censored for fear that they might bring scandal and dishonor to the city.[28]

Répertoire, 336, 344; Tricou, "Confréries," 296; F. H. Dusevel, *Notice et documents sur la fête du prince des sots à Amiens* (Amiens: Lenoël-Hérouart, 1859), 9.

26. Lawrence M. Bryant, *The King and the City in the Parisian Royal Entry Ceremony: Politics, Ritual, and Art in the Renaissance* (Geneva: Droz, 1986), 207–24; Edward Muir, *Civic Ritual in Renaissance Venice* (Princeton: Princeton University Press, 1981), 299–305; Robert A. Schneider, *Public Life in Toulouse, 1463–1789: From Municipal Republic to Cosmopolitan City* (Ithaca: Cornell University Press, 1989), 74–81. See also *Les entrées royales françaises de 1328 à 1515*, ed. Bernard Guenée and François Lehoux (Paris: CNRS, 1968); *The Royal Tour of France by Charles IX and Catherine de'Medici: Festivals and Entries 1564–6*, ed. Victor E. Graham and W. McAllister Johnson (Toronto: University of Toronto, 1979); Roy Strong, *Art and Power: Renaissance Festivals, 1450–1650* (Berkeley: University of California Press, 1984).

27. *Inventaire sommaire des Archives Communales antérieure à 1790, Rouen*, ed. Charles de Robillard de Beaurepaire (Rouen: Lecerf, 1887), 1:66; *Registres des délibérations du bureau de la ville de Paris*, ed. François Bonnardot, Alexandre Tuetey, Paul Guérin, and Louis Le Grand (Paris: Imprimerie Nationale, 1886), 3:7.

28. *Registres des délibérations*, 2:81; *Inventaire sommaire*, 1:171 (17 July 1550); Claudius Brouchoud, *Les origines du théâtre à Lyon* (Lyon: Scheuring, 1865), 19.

Royal entry ceremonies gave local elites the opportunity to signal to the new king both their willingness to obey as well as their hopes and expectations for his reign. There were also opportunities to impress the king with the skills of local craftspeople and the sophistication of local culture. The entry of Henry II (1547–59) into the northern city of Rouen in 1550 demonstrates the way that humanist interests in the classical, the vernacular, and even the exotic were combined to great rhetorical effect. The ceremony began outside the city walls, where the king witnessed a mock battle featuring Brazilian "savages," whose noble bravery in warfare was applauded. As the procession entered the city, the king was confronted with numerous tableaux vivants extolling a classical ideal of the scholar-king, a coded allegorical message encouraging Henry to promote the arts and diplomacy over the military aggression that had characterized his father's reign.[29] City leaders thus both offered homage to the king by flattering him with references to his noble personal qualities and at the same time made clear that they hoped he would promote peace and prosperity throughout the land.

Despite the urban notables' concerns about scandal and their eagerness to honor the king, farces were often performed during and after French royal entry ceremonies. Sometimes it was the king who asked for a particular group, such as the law clerks of the Basoche, to perform after the royal entry; at other times, local city leaders chose the entertainment they thought would best suit the king's tastes.[30] In 1559, when the queen of Spain visited Bordeaux, she was treated with the respect befitting a French princess and the wife of France's recent enemy turned ally. The Basoche, dressed in full military regalia, accompanied her majesty during her entry into the city and later performed plays in her honor.[31] In Paris, the parlement magistrates arranged for the Basoche to perform at several royal celebrations, including the royal entries of Queen Anne in 1504 and King Henry II in 1549. In Dijon, this honor was usually fulfilled by a local group called the Mère Folle; in Lyon, several groups, including the Enfants de la Ville, performed various "diversions" during sixteenth-century royal entry ceremonies.[32] At these events, festive societies performed as the local elite's "court fools": city notables offered the festive societies for the pleasure of the king, whom they hoped to entertain with the vitality of provincial humor. Entertaining the king successfully, though not as crucial as presenting the city's keys to his

---

29. Michael Wintroub, "Civilizing the Savage and Making a King: The Royal Entry Festival of Henry II (Rouen, 1550)," *Sixteenth Century Journal* 29 (1998): 471, 480.
30. *Registres des délibérations*, 2:80, 87; Petit de Julleville, *Répertoire*, 345.
31. Archives Départementales Gironde (ADG) 1 B 210, fol. 40, 29 Nov. 1559; Jean de Métivier, *Chronique du Parlement de Bordeaux, 1462–1566* (Bordeaux: Arthur de Brezetz et Jules Delpit, 1886), 2:275–77 (5 Dec. 1559); Bibliothèque Municipale (BM) Bordeaux (B) MS 369, Savignac, "Extraits des registres secrets du Parlement de Bordeaux," 2:194–95.
32. AN x1a 1565, fol. 18, 9 May 1549; Auton, *Chroniques*, 3:353–54; *Journal d'un bourgeois*, 414; Guéraud, *Chronique*, 52, 62–63; Tricou, "Confréries," 296; *Entrées royales et fêtes populaires à Lyon du XVe au XVIIIe siècle* (Lyon: Bibliothèque de la ville de Lyon, 1970), 111–15.

majesty when he entered the city gates, was nevertheless an important element of his visit. Through a bounteous feast and lighthearted entertainment, local magistrates demonstrated their hospitality and good will.

Often farce players undermined or mocked the solemn allegories presented during the king's entry into the city. In 1550, it was Henry II who requested that the most famous farce-playing group in Rouen, the Conards, perform before him. Several days after the royal entry, Henry II visited the Rouen Parlement to conduct official business, including the registration of several royal edicts. At that time, Henry, "having had the pleasant entertainments that the Youth of Rouen were accustomed to perform once a year brought to his attention, [decided that] he wanted to see the next day the triumphant and joyous procession of the Conards."[33] The Conards accordingly paraded before the king and performed several plays for his pleasure, including a short sottie titled the *Farce of the Calves*. This play inverted many of the allusions to his courage, generosity, and wisdom that had been presented in the royal entry pageant held a few days earlier.[34] Under the pretense that the abbey of the Conards was owed tithes by all ranks of French society, the Conards discuss the quality of the contributions, which were presented to them in the form of live calves. This scenario allows them to mock various groups: the magistrates of the parlement, whose calf is intelligent but lacking in courage; the city councilors, whose thin calf reflects their ineffective complaints; and the local Basoche, whose calf is fat with the labor of profit-seeking clerks. As in so much comic theater of this period, the Conards make a point through self-deprecating humor and negative examples. In the world-turned-upside-down context of the sottie, the elite of Rouen owe obedience to the Conards only because the farce players are lacking in the good qualities of leadership: bravery, decisiveness, and selfless labor. Implicitly, the Conards suggest that a proper king, as they hope Henry will be, would inspire enthusiastic obedience from his subjects. The Conards' traditional humor infused the celebration with an earthy reminder of human foibles that, for sixteenth-century audiences, did not undermine the solemnity of the royal entry or offend the king's sensibilities. Classical allegory and bawdy farce, deployed in succession—a combination of genres unique to the Renaissance—conveyed a rich civic message of comic vitality and allegiance to the king. It is remarkable to realize that less than a century later, performing satirical farce before the king after a royal entry ceremony was considered so scandalous that on at least one occasion it resulted in the outlawing of the festive society.

Farce also reveals the contested and fluid nature of political power within the city walls during the Renaissance. Local authorities sometimes fought

33. *Cest la deduction du sumptueux ordre plaisantz spectacles et magnifiques theatres dressés, et exhibes par les Citoiens de Rouen* (Rouen: Robert le Hoy Robert, 1551).
34. "Farce des veaulx," in *Recueil de farces, moralités et sermons joyeux*, ed. Antoine-Jean-Victor Le Roux de Lincy (Paris: Techener, 1837), vol. 2, no. 33.

over farce: who had the right to control it, and what should or should not be censored. Everyone agreed that allowing farce players to perform whatever they wanted was not acceptable, but that was about all they could agree on. For all their power and wealth, the urban oligarchy that ran the city council and the royal law courts did not have a monopoly on power within the city walls. In matters of public order, the city council often had to compete with direct emissaries of the king or the military governor of the region, all of whom could overrule the authority of the city council. In matters of taxation, the city was often dictated to by the regional estates, an elected body that, in some provinces, determined how much the city would contribute in taxes to the king each year and prevented the city from negotiating directly with the king. Even in the realm of spiritual authority, the local oligarchy was often thwarted. Although the lower positions of cathedral canon and parish priest were usually occupied by local men who were either related to or could be dominated by the city's notables, those in the highest ranks such as bishop and archbishop were appointed by the king and were usually of high noble blood. City politics was dominated by clashes among these different groups: the local oligarchy, royal appointees, and the high nobility. Often areas of authority overlapped and disputes were frequent.[35] Farce was sometimes a means by which these corporate rivalries were articulated. It was both a weapon in this heated environment and an object over which different bodies competed to control. All of these groups enjoyed farce on principle and commissioned farce players to perform, but they wanted to be sure that the performers were mocking their rivals rather than themselves.

Because theatrical regulation was considered relatively important, the power to censor plays usually devolved on the most powerful corporate entity in the city. In some cities, it quickly became clear which institution would take responsibility for regulating the theater, and conflict over such matters rarely arose. In theory, the clergy had ultimate authority over farce players since they had the power to excommunicate Christians: such was the decision made by the bishop of Reims after the city's law clerks processed through the city streets to challenge the clergy's exemption from the land tax in 1490. But apart from excommunication, which was not a weapon to be

---

35. Chevalier, *Bonnes villes,* 101–12, 202–10, 219–24; P. S. Lewis, "The Centre, the Periphery, and the Problem of Power Distribution in Later Medieval France," in *The Crown and Local Communities in England and France in the Fifteenth Century,* ed. J. R. L. Highfield and Robin Jeffs (Gloucester: Alan Sutton, 1981), 34–47; Mack P. Holt, "Popular Political Culture and Mayoral Elections in Sixteenth-Century Dijon," in *Society and Institutions in Early Modern France* (Athens: University of Georgia Press, 1991), 98–116; Robert Schneider, "Crown and Capitoulat: Municipal Government in Toulouse, 1500–1789," in *Cities and Social Change in Early Modern France,* ed. Philip Benedict (London: Unwin Hyman, 1989), 24, 195–220; Frederick M. Irvine, "From Renaissance City to Ancien Régime Capital: Montpellier, c. 1500–c. 1600," in Benedict, *Cities and Social Change,* 105–33; Bernstein, *Between Crown,* 87–89, 103–26.

used lightly, clerics had no direct authority to police laypersons. As a result, they often tried to bully or convince the local city council to act on their behalf.[36] In Rouen, where both the cathedral and the city council were relatively weak, the most important royal law court, the Parlement of Rouen, took over responsibility for regulating the theater; it both granted permission to acting troops to perform and disciplined them when they breached acceptable norms of respectability. In sixteenth-century Bordeaux, the city council handled questions about the theater on a case-by-case basis, but it sometimes appealed to the Parlement of Bordeaux to issue systematic censorship rulings.[37] In other cities, the ability to control the theater shifted depending on the personal dynamism of individuals as well as on the waxing and waning of institutions over time. On rare occasions, questions of theatrical regulation were referred to the highest level of royal appeals court, the Parlement of Paris.[38] These conflicts demonstrate how crucial local authorities felt it was to control public performances and manipulate public opinion. Often urban notables expressed concern that theatrical performances could spread disease, cause riots, and undermine the authority of public officials. Yet internal disputes between local authorities often rendered their efforts to control the theater ineffective.

Clermont was the site of one such dispute at the turn of the sixteenth century. A small community of five hundred to a thousand inhabitants, it nevertheless had a cathedral and was the largest urban center in the province of Auvergne. Politically, the city was in flux. Traditionally, Clermont was under the direct authority of the bishop of Clermont, usually a member of the Bourbon noble family. It was the bishop who controlled local affairs, from the assessment of local taxes to the construction of new fortifications during the Hundred Years' War. Yet in actuality the bishop was rarely present in Clermont; instead his underlings undertook most of his affairs in the town. This hegemony was challenged in 1481 when the king decided to thank the city of Clermont for its loyalty during a recent civil rebellion. In reward, the city was declared an independent political entity, with its own city council and an exemption from the land tax for city residents. The king also appointed a military governor to supervise the governance of the province. Only four years later, however, the king reversed his decision: in 1485, in an effort to placate the bishop of Clermont, Cardinal Charles II de Bourbon, he

---

36. Louis Paris, *Le théâtre à Reims depuis les Romains jusqu'à nos jours* (Reims: Michaud, 1885), 30–31; Petit de Julleville, *Répertoire*, 337, 355.

37. Archives Départementales Seine-Maritime (ADSM) 1 B 447, 20 May 1536; 1 B 534, 5 May 1550; 1 B 567, 25 Oct. 1556; Philip Benedict, *Rouen during the Wars of Religion* (Cambridge: Cambridge University Press, 1981), 32–36; Archives Municipales (AM) Bordeaux, GG 1005, April 1558; ADG 1 B 229, 330, 24 May 1561; BM Bordeaux, MS 369, Savignac, "Extraits," 2:13 (7 Mar. 1557); "Arrêts du Parlement de Bordeaux," *Archives Historiques de la Gironde* 3 (1896–97): 467.

38. Petit de Julleville, *Répertoire*, 355.

rescinded Clermont's newly acquired privileges. The city council protested this change of policy, and by the early 1490s it was once again functioning, though uncertain of its future authority.[39]

It was in this context of political flux that the city council of Clermont and the canons of the cathedral came to blows over the theater. In 1492, the cathedral canons proposed performing a morality play and requested that the city council help defray the cost. The city council refused to contribute to the performance, arguing that there was a real danger of the plague and that the time was not ripe for such a public celebration. A few years later, in 1495, it was the canons' turn to protest a theatrical performance. When local inhabitants performed an anticlerical morality play in the public square, the canons were scandalized and demanded that the city councilors prosecute the players. The city council was reluctant to do so. Undeterred, the canons appealed to the bishop for help. The bishop not surprisingly supported his canons' request, pressuring the military governor of Clermont to do something to settle these questions of theatrical regulation once and for all. The governor issued a unilateral decree stating that "no inhabitant nor others were to perform farces or morality plays in this city without the leave and permission of the governor of Clermont or one of his officers and without having informed them before the performance, in order to prevent public disturbances that might follow."[40] Like many rulings of the early modern period, the governor's proclamation was probably more a wishful statement of policy than a strictly enforceable law. Because the governor was often absent from the city, it was not practical to appeal to his authority before each theatrical performance. Meanwhile, the city councilors resented the governor's heavy-handed interference in local policing, a responsibility they thought of as their own. In the months that followed, a compromise was reached: the city council agreed to organize a board of two clerics and two lay residents that would in theory examine each farce before it was performed.[41] On paper at least, a balance of power between the cathedral and the city council had been achieved.

In the meantime, of course, the people of Clermont carried on with their traditional festivities oblivious to the infighting among their betters. Each year they continued to dress up in masks and run through the city streets at Christmas, harassing passersby and making fun of authority figures, without clearance from either the bishop or the city council.[42] The practical inefficacy of the Clermont censorship board became apparent in 1517 when a group of players performed a farce that mocked "the councilors, magistrates, and

39. André Bossuat, "Le théâtre à Clermont-Ferrand," *Revue d'Histoire du Théâtre* 13 (1961): 108–9; André-Georges Manry, *Histoire de Clermont-Ferrand* (Clermont-Ferrand: Volcans, 1975), 114–18.
40. Bossuat, "Théâtre," 110.
41. Ibid., 109–10.
42. Ibid., 113.

tax-collectors" themselves.[43] Now that its members and associates were the targets of scorn and slander, the council decided that the very honor of the city had been compromised and prosecuted the farce players to the fullest extent of the law. These disciplinary measures probably did not deter the city's festive societies from continuing to perform in the years that followed, but these conflicts illustrate the importance that both lay and clerical authorities gave to theatrical regulation. Although neither group sought to ban farcical theater altogether, they hoped to control the direction of its satire.

French city councils or local magistrates thus tended to take action against satire only when their corporate interests were at stake. Indeed, on the whole, competition between authorities enhanced rather than compromised the success of farce in fifteenth- and sixteenth-century France. Because no one institution and individual held absolute control over the city and competing authorities might have had an interest in allowing lighthearted mockery some room for expression, farce players more often than not got away with their jokes. Farce profited from the divided authority and limited police power of city officials. Only when all of the urban elite—the clergy, the city council, the courts, and the military officials—decided that farce was dangerous in principle, a phenomenon that occurred during the Wars of Religion of the late sixteenth century, did local people lose their freedom to mock local authority figures when they performed farces.

When they were not fighting among themselves over the performance of a particular play, urban authorities often found it useful to promote farce playing, in part because it satisfied practical considerations: the need to maintain public order and limit youth violence in the city streets. By the sixteenth century, such violence was an endemic problem, and farce playing was often a useful way for urban officials to focus young men's rowdy energies.

It was no accident that the majority of farce players were young men between the ages of fifteen and thirty. Farce playing evolved out of long-standing traditions of youth festivals that had long existed in Europe. These rituals, which varied from region to region, established young men as sexually potent quasi-adults and as active members of their communities. In early May, French youths went out into the forest, cut down a tree, and returned to plant it in the village square in preparation for a courtship dance or procession. Girls would be teased with gifts of flowers and sometimes forced to dance with young men who had raised the maypole. In many villages, young men donned costumes to fight or to play competitive sporting games with other youths from nearby communities during the summer months. These competitions allowed them to show off their physical skills and to defend their village turf against the sexual competition of their male neighbors. Young men also mocked the sexual practices of their elders: during rituals that contemporaries referred to either as charivari or as *chevauchée d'asne*,

43. Ibid., 114.

costumed youths marched in processions singing derisive songs and banging on pots to humiliate newlyweds and cuckolded men.[44] Sometimes, when the object of the abuse refused to be shamed, these rituals could turn violent, resulting in destruction of private property and even physical assault. All of these activities involved a combination of dressing up in costume, engaging in verbal harassment, and threatening physical violence. As well, they allowed the youths to affirm, in their own rowdy way, the sexual norms of the community.[45] These rituals were for the most part tolerated because they were inherently liminal. Not only were the participants mere youths, but also these activities usually occurred during transformative rituals such as marriages or festivals when normal social strictures were temporarily suspended.[46]

Like most male youths, farce players often fought among themselves, made fun of their elders, and acted as informal judges of sexual norms. In the north of France, festive societies were sent off to summer fairs to compete with youths from neighboring communities. In many cases, theatrical performances occurred alongside athletic, archery, and harquebus

44. Natalie Zemon Davis, *Society and Culture in Early Modern France* (Stanford: Stanford University Press, 1975), 97–123; Roger Vaultier, *Le folklore pendant la Guerre de cent ans d'après les lettres de rémission du Trésor des chartes* (Paris: Guénégaud, 1965), 11–12, 30–42; Nicole Pellegrin, *Les bachelleries: Organisations et fêtes de la jeunesse dans le Centre-Ouest XVe–XVIIIe siècles* (Poitiers: Société des Antiquaires de l'Ouest, 1982); Jacques Le Goff and Jean-Claude Schmitt, eds., *Le charivari: Actes de la Table ronde organisée à Paris, 25–27 avril 1977* (Paris: École des Hautes Études en Sciences Sociales, 1981); Jacques Rossiaud, "Fraternités de jeunesse et niveaux de culture dans les villes du sud-est à la fin du moyen âge," *Cahiers d'Histoire* 21 (1976): 67–102; Jacques Rossiaud, "Prostitution, jeunesse et société dans les villes du sud-est au XVe siècle," *Annales: Économies, Sociétés, Civilisations* 31 (1976): 289–326; Chevalier, *Bonnes villes*, 264–69; Robert Muchembled, *L'invention de l'homme moderne: Culture et sensibilités en France du XVe au XVIIIe siècle* (Paris: Fayard, 1988), 21–33, 241; Norbert Schindler, "Guardians of Disorder: Rituals of Youthful Culture at the Dawn of the Modern Age," in *A History of Young People in the West*, vol. 1, *Ancient and Medieval Rites of Passage*, ed. Giovanni Levi and Jean-Claude Schmitt (Cambridge, Mass.: Harvard University Press, 1997), 240–82.
45. Regarding the relationship of these rituals to violence, see François Billacois, *The Duel: Its Rise and Fall in Early Modern Europe*, ed. and trans. Trista Selous (New Haven: Yale University Press, 1990), 205–8, 240–42; James R. Farr, *Hands of Honor: Artisans and Their World in Dijon, 1550–1650* (Ithaca: Cornell University Press, 1988), 177–95; David D. Gilmore, *Manhood in the Making: Cultural Concepts of Masculinity* (New Haven: Yale University Press, 1990), 12–20, 89–91, 114–16; Kristen B. Neuschel, *Word of Honor: Interpreting Noble Culture in Sixteenth-Century France* (Ithaca: Cornell University Press, 1989), 204–8; Petrus Cornelis Spierenburg, "Masculinity, Violence and Honor: An Introduction," in *Men and Violence: Gender, Honor, and Rituals in Modern Europe and America* (Columbus: Ohio State University Press, 1998), 12–18.
46. Jean-Christophe Agnew, *Worlds Apart: The Market and the Theater in Anglo-American Thought, 1550–1750* (Cambridge: Cambridge University Press, 1986), 17–56; Mikhail Bakhtin, *Rabelais and His World*, trans. Hélène Iswolsky (Bloomington: Indiana University Press, 1984), 81, 89–91, 274; Claude Gaignebet, *Le carnaval: Essais de mythologie populaire* (Paris: Payot, 1974), 157–58; Robert W. Scribner, *Popular Culture and Popular Movements in Reformation Germany* (London: Hambledon Press, 1987), 1–47; Victor W. Turner, *The Ritual Process: Structure and Anti-Structure* (Chicago: Aldine, 1969), 94–130.

competitions.[47] Almost all festive societies performed in the context of a religious or civic festival or of a procession in which the young men dressed up, carried arms, and made loud music. The Basoche associations explicitly linked their theatrical performances to the traditional youth festivities of early May. Each year, they went into the forest and cut a tree to mount in the courtyard of the parlement. But instead of dancing with local girls, the Basoche turned to the audience and performed comic plays that mocked authority and derided community members who had transgressed sexual mores. Their maypoles represented male sexual potency, and the Basochiens protected their poles from abuse, sometimes fining or imprisoning men who sought to desecrate or to remove the maypole from its rightful place.[48]

Like other youth groups, farce players were quick to ridicule the foibles of their elders. Although virtually all sotties and comic morality plays contain characters who judge society, in a handful of plays the actors make direct reference to rituals such as charivari.[49] Other performances, several of which occurred in Lyon during the sixteenth century, transformed a shaming ritual into theater. These entertainments were called *chevauchées d'asne,* but these performances were not classic *chevauchées,* a ritual in which a single individual is lampooned by his neighbors, but civic celebrations involving hundreds of men that were mounted to entertain visiting peers or dignitaries.[50] In a 1578 account of such a performance, the author notes the quality of the silk costumes, the numbers of harquebusiers and lances carried by the men, and the beauty of the music performed by the musicians who accompanied each neighborhood festive society.[51] Each company in the procession carried a banner proclaiming with pride the name of its neighborhood and presented a float that conformed to the overall theme of the march. One float bore a group of women fighting one another; another depicted a man in the process of being beaten by his wife; a third, which the author calls "the real chevauchée," showed a man who was riding an ass backward and covered in foul-smelling plants. Alongside these satirical floats, in a manner that might seem incongruous to us but is consistent with a Renaissance sensibility in which humor and piety could be sustained simultaneously, many companies also displayed an effigy of the patron saint of their local parish. In the middle of the procession,

47. Lecocq, *Histoire,* 139–40; Durieux, *Théâtre,* 142.
48. AN x1a 1558, 2 June 1546; ADSM 1 B 2151, 30 Sept. 1588; Nicole Belmont, "Le joli mois de mai," *Histoire* 1 (1978): 20; John Bossy, *Christianity in the West, 1400–1700* (Oxford: Oxford University Press, 1985), 70; Lefebvre, *Fêtes,* 24, 27; Pellegrin, *Bachelleries,* 185–94.
49. Jean-Marie Privat, "Sots, sotties, charivari," in *Atti del IV Colloquio della Société Internationale pour l'Étude du Théâtre Médiéval,* ed. M. Chiabò, F. Doglio, and M. Maymone (Viterbo: Centro Studi sul Teatro Medioevale e Rinascimentale, 1984), 339–42.
50. Ibid., 341; Guéraud, *Chronique,* 53; Vaultier, *Folklore,* 40–42.
51. "Recueil de la chevauchee faicte en la ville de Lyon, le dix septiesme de novembre 1578," in *Collection des meilleurs dissertations, notices et traités particuliers relatifs à l'histoire de France,* ed. J. M. C. Leber (Paris: Dentu, 1838), 9:148–68; *Entrées royales et fêtes populaires,* 46–59.

three men performed a play that depicted all the ways that a wife might abuse her husband. One wife, for example, reputedly kept her husband confined in the attic of their house on a diet of bread and water; another wife, while spitting and farting in her husband's face, called him a "bastard" and kicked him out of the house. At the procession's end, a great banner announced the motto of the performance, that being beaten by one's wife is against nature. Those who allowed their wives to subjugate them deserve only contempt. Like a traditional *chevauchée d'asne* in its articulation of sexual norms, this more theatrical version performed by the festive societies of Lyon was carefully choreographed to maximize comic effect and to display the wealth and honor of the festive societies. The hostility of the traditional ritual was muted by the pageantry of the performance and the jokes' lack of specificity.

Farce players not only judged their elders but also turned their wit and their limited authority against their own members, a practice that sometimes helped to ingratiate them with local authorities. To do so, they created elaborate mock hierarchies within their organizations. Not only did they appoint a king or a prince to lead their processions, but some groups even appointed sergeants, magistrates, and bishops. These elections were themselves performances, with hundreds of spectators gathering to witness the burlesque appointment of the group's highest officials.[52] In 1541, the Conards festive society, which called itself an abbey, elected and then proclaimed in a mock papal bull that a large fat man had been appointed cardinal of Montalinas. Delighted by his appointment, the new cardinal proudly received his flour-encrusted cardinal's hat and took his place on an ass, solemnly vowing to "eat cooked beans three times a week."[53] The clerks of the Paris Basoche often participated in similar festivities, marching to celebrate the recent election of their new "king" and performing a comic play on the third Thursday of January. By the end of the sixteenth century, the officialdom of the Paris Basoche organization had extended to some fifty young men, all of them formally elected each year.[54] These elections both parodied and affirmed the social hierarchy of French society. By dressing up as their betters—as kings and abbots—the young men were inverting social norms. Nevertheless, the men who were chosen to lead these organizations were often, in actual fact, the wealthier or older members of the group, partly because the leader was expected to help pay for or solicit funds for the festive society's annual procession.[55] Some kings of youth groups, such as the Mère Folle of Dijon and

---

52. Métivier, *Chronique*, 1:304–5 (30 Dec. 1533); Tricou, "Confréries," 303.
53. *Triomphe de l'abbaye des Conards avec une notice sur les fêtes des fous* (Rouen, 1587; reprint, Paris: Libraire des Bibliophiles, 1874), 7–8. Broad beans—*fèves*—were a favorite holiday dish, and the *roi de la fève* was a familiar term for the king of Twelfth Night.
54. AN x1a 8345, fols. 256–58, 14 July 1528; AN x1a 1674, fol. 343, 10 Feb. 1582.
55. Aristide Joly, *Note sur Benoet du Lac: Ou le théâtre et la Bazoche à Aix, à la fin du XVIe siècle* (Lyon: Scheuring, 1862; reprint, Geneva: Slatkine, 1971), 78; Métivier, *Chronique*, 1:287 (16 Dec. 1559).

Es cõplain-
tes et Epita
phes du roy de la Bazoche.

FIGURE 3. King of the Basoche, 1520. Frontpiece to *Les cõplaintes et Epitaphes du roy de la Bazoche*. (Source: British Library c.39.a.58)

the Basoche associations, also had the right to punish their own members when they fought among themselves or neglected to pay their annual dues to the association.[56] Thus many festive societies replicated on a small scale the very hierarchical system of social control that they parodied in their performances. Indeed, despite their transgressive elements, festive societies on the whole actually helped to train the sons of the couche moyenne to obey their elders and act as a group. The urban notables who ruled French cities were thus able to exploit the disciplinary function that festive societies could have and use it to their advantage.

Until the sixteenth century, there was no clear-cut distinction between youth groups that performed plays and those that engaged in other kinds of festive activities. During the course of the century, however, behaviors as varied as soliciting prostitutes in the local tavern, loitering in the city streets, and dressing in costume at Carnival were increasingly considered at odds with the maintenance of public order.[57] Although in principle many festivities were tolerated and even patronized, the king and local officials sought to curb public behavior considered most conducive to violence. One obvious target was the wearing of masks, a practice often employed by criminals as well as by festival goers. A 1514 royal edict noted that not only were many of these masks "impudent" but, more importantly, they were associated with "scandal and inconvenience," disruptions, in other words, to public order. The law banned all shops in Paris from selling masks and required that all masks be gathered by the authorities and burnt in a public bonfire.[58] During the same period, secular officials began to criminalize the traditional mocking ritual of charivari. Whereas in previous centuries city officials had tolerated the harassment of young newlyweds, increasingly those who engaged in charivari were brought to court and punished for their behavior, particularly when the ritual resulted in violence.[59] During the sixteenth century, local officials also made increasing attempts to control the notoriously

56. ADG 1 B 359, fol. 2, 2 June 1572; AN x1a 1545, fols. 148–49, 23 June 1540.
57. E. William Monter, *Judging the French Reformation: Heresy Trials by Sixteenth-Century Parlements* (Cambridge, MA: Harvard University Press, 1999), 22–24; Muchembled, *Invention*, 156–70.
58. AN x1a 1516, fols. 148–49, 27 Apr. 1514; Antoine Fontanon, *Les édicts et ordonnances des Roys de France depuis S. Loys jusques à present* (Paris: Du Puys, 1580), 1:508 (9 May 1539), 1:526 (1558), 1:865 (July 1559); Félibien, *Histoire*, 4:752b (21 July 1551); Archives Municipales Dijon (AMD) B 197, fol. 100v, 28 Nov. 1559; AMD B 197, fol. 117r–v, 9 Jan. 1560; AMD B 198, fol. 103v, 13 Feb. 1561; AMD B 210, fol. 108, 9 Jan. 1573; Isabelle Paresys, *Aux marges du royaume: Violence, justice et société en Picardie sous François Ier* (Paris: Publications de la Sorbonne, 1998), 175.
59. Yves-Marie Bercé, *Fête et révolte: Des mentalités populaires du XVIe au XVIIIe siècle* (Paris: Hachette, 1976), 40–44; Edward Muir, *Ritual in Early Modern Europe* (Cambridge: Cambridge University Press, 1997), 98–104; Rossiaud, "Fraternités," 85–87; AMD B 231 fol. 134v, 15 Feb. 1594; Martine Grinberg, "Charivaris au moyen âge et à la Renaissance," in *Charivari*, 144; Davis, *Society*, 117; Vaultier, *Folklore*, 30–35; *Inventaire des archives communales de la ville de Toulouse antérieures à 1790, série AA*, ed. E. Roschach (Toulouse: E. Privat, 1891), 5:228.

undisciplined student life of the cities. Although these efforts to control festivals and limit violence were rarely successful, they mark a significant shift in elite attitudes toward policing in the city. Royal judicial officials were starting, in the name of the king, to claim a monopoly on violence, a tendency that would intensify in the seventeenth century with the rise of an absolutist conception of monarchical power.[60] In curbing traditional festive practice, local authorities were defining a more disciplined and orderly ideal of public conduct for French city residents. Urban elites began to insist that young men behave with civility when they spent time in the city streets.

In this atmosphere of tightening control over public rowdiness, farce playing nevertheless continued to flourish. Increasingly, however, festive societies were able to win city officials' approval only if their performances eschewed violence. By the 1470s, the two Basoche organizations of Toulouse often attracted unwanted attention from local authorities because their irreverent farces sparked fighting between the performers and rival youth groups. These performances were in effect ritualized games of insults that often escalated into physical conflict. In 1480, the parlement magistrates prohibited both the Basoche and another group known as the Mondains from referring to one another in the farces they performed or the songs they sang.[61] The Basochiens disregarded this warning and, as a result, were chastised again in 1484, 1491, and 1502 for performing farces without permission and for fighting among themselves.[62] Although the magistrates were for several decades unable to contain the Basochiens' fighting, they were finally able to do so in 1524 when they stripped the clerks of the right to perform comic theater in the city. The Toulouse Basochiens were still allowed to hold an annual parade, but their farces were considered to be too inflammatory to be conducive to public order.[63] All evidence suggests that the Basochiens followed the directive of the parlement, shifting their activities away from performing farce during the decades that followed.

In contrast, the Basoche of the Paris Parlement, also known for farces and street fighting, were able to gain the support of the parlement magistrates for their performances. Whereas throughout the mid-fifteenth century the magistrates frequently outlawed them and punished the clerks by sending them to jail, the king's unprecedented decision to interfere directly in the

---

60. Norbert Elias, *The Civilizing Process: Sociogenetic and Psychogenetic Investigations*, trans. Edmund Jephcott, ed. Eric Dunning, Johan Goudsblom, and Stephen Mennell (Oxford: Blackwell, 2000), 157–60, 290–317.
61. Archives Départementales de la Haute-Garonne (ADHG) 2 Mi 166, fol. 320, 2 May 1480.
62. ADHG 2 Mi 165, fol. 421, 27–29 May 1478; ADHG 2 Mi 166, fol. 462, 5 Jan. 1481; ADHG 2 Mi 167, fol. 199, 13 Jan. 1484; ADHG 2 Mi 167, fol. 221, 22 March 1484; ADHG 2 Mi 169, fol. 340, 13 May 1491; ADHG 2 Mi 172, fols. 574–75, 22 March 1502. See also Michel Cassan, "Basoche et basochiens à Toulouse à l'époque moderne," *Annales du Midi* 94 (1982): 263–76.
63. ADHG 2 Mi 328, fol. 73, 8 Feb. 1524; ADHG 2 Mi 206, fol. 189, 5 May 1526.

disciplining of the Basoche in 1486 caused the magistrates to switch sides and offer the clerks some measure of fiscal and moral support. In return, the clerks showed themselves willing to limit the violence associated with their performances.

The performance that sparked the king's intervention occurred as part of the Basoche May Day festivities in 1486 when some law clerks performed a satirical play that explicitly mocked the king and his court. The king Charles VIII (1483–98) lashed out in response. Asserting that "certain morality plays and farces . . . publicly said or had said several seditious speeches that caused a commotion, principally referring to us and to our reign," he ordered the author of the play and the Basoche performers to be imprisoned indefinitely in the Paris city jail at the Châtelet.[64] Surprisingly, far from supporting the king's effort to punish the Basoche, the magistrates stepped in to free the clerks as quickly as was legally possible.

The play performed by the Basoche that pivotal day has been lost, but we know it was written by a Parisian poet and former fiscal official named Henri Baude. Baude had written other plays that criticized royal authority: in 1485, he penned a morality play that complained in very specific terms about high taxes, the venality of offices, and the weak leadership provided by the king's court.[65] We know thus that Baude was a man able to speak directly to the political concerns of the day and it seems that the play he wrote for the Basoche was equally unabashed in its criticism of royal policy. In a letter written by Baude to the Duke of Bourbon to elicit Baude's own release from prison, he defended the May 1486 performance. Baude admits that his play was critical but claims that it was not treasonous. According to Baude, the play presents the parlement as the defender of "public good," and describes in some detail how the parlement's efforts were being blocked by the "plants, roots, boulders, rocks, mud, and gravel" that collected around the fountain of France.[66] The parlement sought to but could not remove these blockages that were causing the public good to suffer. Baude's defense thus hinged on the fact that the king himself, "the fountain of France," had not been personally slandered. Criticizing the king's ministers and councilors was a much less grave crime that maligning his majesty. Baude also claims that the parlement magistrates had explicitly permitted the Basochiens to perform this play. Although one should always remain skeptical about the details of a letter written by an accused party in the hopes of a pardon, Baude's letter reveals much of what was at stake in the Basochiens' performance.

In 1486, Charles VIII had been king for three years. During that time considerable dissatisfaction was brewing, particularly among the nobility and urban elites. Because at the time of his father's death in 1483 Charles

---

64. Quoted in Baude, *Vers*, 113–14 (10 May 1486).
65. Ibid., 62–68.
66. Ibid., 75.

had been only twelve, too young to take on the full responsibility of ruling, a powerful council dominated by his sister Anne de Beaujeu and her husband, Pierre de Beaujeu, the Duke of Bourbon, the noble to whom Baude addressed his plea for clemency, in effect directed royal policy. In 1484, Charles's council convoked a meeting of the Estates General, a national assembly of elected delegates from the three estates and the embodiment of the late medieval French body politic. At this meeting, the delegates tried to establish the precedent that taxes like the taille, a relatively new tax on land, would be subject to the Estates General's regular approval. Although the king's council reduced the taille in the coming years, it provocatively set the amount slightly higher than the Estates General's recommendation in an effort to demonstrate royal autonomy. Charles and his council also failed to implement most of the administrative and judicial reforms requested by the Estates General, including an end to venality and currency manipulation.[67] The parlement was not normally a party to the Estates General, hence the magistrates had been excluded from the 1484 debates. Nevertheless, they no doubt shared some of these concerns, possibly seeing Baude's 1486 play as a means of expressing their frustration with the direction of royal policy. Certainly, there is no evidence that the magistrates protested the Basochiens' performance, which had taken place in the courtyard in front of the Grand' Chambre and had probably been witnessed by some members of the court. Indeed, the magistrates' actions in the weeks after the Basochiens' imprisonment suggest that they had a measure of sympathy for Baude and the Basochiens.

After having imprisoned Baude and four clerk performers, Châtelet officials were directed to send the prisoners to the king, currently residing at Melun, forty kilometers from Paris. But quick action on the part of the parlement magistrates, who raised questions about which court should try the accused, kept the prisoners in Paris. During the next two weeks, the magistrates held several audiences relating to the Basochiens' plight. They insisted that Châtelet officials release the text of the offending play and also considered a request by the bishop of Paris that the case be turned over to his jurisdiction. On May 23, having heard a recitation of the play, the magistrates dismissed the bishop's claim, concluding that the case was serious enough to warrant being considered by the parlement alone.[68] The next day, the magistrates ordered that Châtelet officials transfer Baude and the clerks to the parlement's prison. Once they had the prisoners under their control, the magistrates' attitude toward the crime of satirical performance rapidly softened. Although the magistrates would not admit that they had sanctioned the Basoche performance, they concluded that the performers'

67. C. de Cherrier, *Histoire de Charles VIII, d'après des documents diplomatiques inédits ou nouvellement publiés* (Paris: Didier, 1868), 1:113–40.
68. Baude, *Vers*, 117 (23 May 1486).

actions did not warrant further punishment. Baude and the four clerks were soon released on the condition that they promised to remain within Paris and to reside with named relatives in good standing with the court. In short, within two weeks of the king's order, the parlement magistrates had taken the matter into their own hands and effectively dismissed the case.[69] Even if they were not willing to approve the use of farce as a means for public consultation, their actions suggest that they took the Basochiens' jokes far less seriously than did the king and his councilors.

Although the parlement magistrates were on this occasion not precisely defying the authority of the king, they nevertheless were asserting their institutional privilege to discipline their own members, even though, technically speaking, the Basochiens were not employees of the court. The 1486 incident speaks of a perhaps oversensitive and weak royal court and a parlement confident enough to intervene to mitigate the sentences of those who spoke out directly against the king. Interestingly, the king's court made no effort to overrule the parlement magistrates. Implicitly, Charles VIII seemed to acknowledge that it was within the magistrates' authority to discipline their own, even when the slander concerned the king and his court.

The 1486 incident marked an important turning point in the history of the Basoche in Paris. On the one hand, it signaled the magistrates' willingness to take responsibly for the clerks' behavior: in the future, only the magistrates regulated and censored Basoche performances. On the other hand, having been freed from prison by the magistrates, the leaders of the Basoche were now somewhat in their debt. A peaceful renegotiation of the Basoche's responsibilities and freedoms resulted, and benefited both parties.[70] The clerks certainly responded to the magistrates' long-standing concerns about disturbances to public order, but they also profited from the new arrangement. Almost every year during the first half of the sixteenth century, the Basoche treasurers requested the magistrates' financial support to help pay for the group's farcical performances. The magistrates usually granted these requests, and over the years the amount allotted for Basoche performances gradually increased: from 30 livres in 1505, to 60 livres in 1512, to 120 livres by 1528.[71] These amounts, though not exorbitant, were sufficient to pay for the clerks' costumes and props, and were equivalent to the sums that kings of France paid professional farce players for a short stay at court. The Basochiens also gained the intangible reward of cultural prominence. Having agreed to cooperate with the magistrates, the clerks

69. Ibid., 113–19.
70. In contrast, Bercé argues that 1486 marks the end to Basoche satire. Bercé, *Fête et révolte*, 28.
71. AN x1a 1510, 18 July 1505; AN x1a 1514, fol. 157, 26 May 1512; AN x1a 1531, fol. 280, 18 June 1528. King Francis I paid similar sums to commercial actors who performed at court. See *Collection des ordonnances*, 4:203 (22 May 1541), 8:303 (Dec. 1538); Pellegrin, *Bachelleries*, 81–92.

were permitted to participate in important civic celebrations such as royal entry ceremonies.[72] By offering the clerks a measure of support, the magistrates were able to temper some of the most disruptive elements of Basoche performance. Although the Basoche of Paris continued to perform satirical farces during the first half of the sixteenth century, their restless energies were directed to inventing clever puns and sly insults rather than engaging in fisticuffs in the city streets.

Of course, neither the king nor local authorities were always pleased with the way that farcical theater worked out in practice. Young men often deviated from texts that had been approved by city magistrates and neglected to seek permission for their performances. In 1518, the city council of Lyon was dismayed to discover that a local bourgeois had, of his own accord, constructed a stage outside his home on which he planned to perform plays publicly mocking members of the community during the royal entry of Francis I and his wife Claude into the city.[73] Only the quick action of the council and the intervention of royal officials to dismantle the stage prevented this mishap from occurring. In 1515, Francis I took even more drastic measures when he heard that a cleric named Mr. Cruche had mocked him during a play he had recently performed in Paris. Cruche had had the audacity to accuse the king of having an affair with the daughter of a prominent magistrate at the Paris Parlement. In retaliation, Francis had some of his lackeys round up Cruche and throw him into the Seine.[74] On the flipside, the king and local city officials sometimes employed farce players to broadcast satirical jokes that served their political interests. Being patrons of farce also meant engaging in manipulation of public opinion, most of the time at the local level but sometimes concerning matters of royal policy. Indeed, those who regulated and patronized farce, as well as the performers who eluded their censorship efforts, were creating a political public sphere in Renaissance France.

Whether or not such a sphere existed in early modern France before the mid-eighteenth century has been much debated.[75] Discussions of public opinion in sixteenth- and seventeenth-century Europe examine two interlocking networks of power and political communication during this period: the social and political influence of the traditional military nobility and the power

72. *Journal d'un bourgeois*, 413; AN x1a 1565, fol. 18, 9 May 1549; Auton, *Chroniques*, 3:352–54. Regarding the continuing satirical element of Basoche performance, see Jean Bouchet, *Épistres morales et familières du Traverseur*, ed. M. A. Screech (London: Jonson Reprint, 1969), XLII.
73. Brouchoud, *Origines*, 19; AN x1a 4906, fols. 589–90, 6 Aug. 1538.
74. *Journal d'un bourgeois*, 13–14.
75. Jürgen Habermas, *The Structural Transformation of the Public Sphere: An Inquiry into a Category of Bourgeois Society*, trans. Thomas Burger and Frederick Lawrence (Cambridge, Mass.: MIT Press, 1991), 38–43; Roger Chartier, *Les origines culturelles de la Révolution française* (Paris: Seuil, 1990), 37–56; Jeffrey K. Sawyer, *Printed Poison: Pamphlet Propaganda, Faction Politics, and the Public Sphere in Early Seventeenth-Century France* (Berkeley: University

of the printed word. Historians argue that politics during the Renaissance centered on the actions of the king's most powerful subjects, the traditional military nobility who had the wealth and power to shape politics at court or to threaten rebellion. Wealthy members of the peerage could often harness the support of minor nobility to raise armies in the countryside and ensure the political cooperation of urban officials in the cities, including Paris.[76] This class was of course amenable to new political ideas circulated in print. Many political pamphlets published during the sixteenth century were written by clients of the great nobility with the intent of shaping their patrons' opinions. Although some historians argue that commoners occasionally wrote political tracts independent of patronage connections, the limits of literacy—less than 50 percent of urban residents would have felt comfortable reading through an entire pamphlet—could keep printed propaganda from reaching the working poor of the cities.[77] Certainly most sixteenth-century political pamphlets were not directed at an illiterate audience unaware of the machinations of court politics. The importance of the type of theater I am discussing is that it addresses this illiterate commonor audience directly.

Traditionally, historians have underplayed the role of the theater in the shaping of public opinion or the creation of a public sphere during the Renaissance. Most historians emphasize the relative passivity of theater audiences and playwrights' limited freedom of expression until the mid-eighteenth century, when, like the coffeehouse and the salon, theaters became a site for the expression of new social and political ideas.[78] Yet the theater, particularly

---

of California Press, 1990), 10–13, 133–45; Harold Mah, "Phantasies of the Public Sphere: Rethinking the Habermas of Historians," *Journal of Modern History* 72 (2000): 153–82; Alain Viala, *Naissance de l'écrivain: Sociologie de la littérature à l'âge classique* (Paris: Minuit, 1985), 124, 143–47; Hélène Merlin, *Public et littérature en France au XVIIe siècle* (Paris: Belles Lettres, 1994), 35–87.

76. Stuart Carroll, "The Guise Affinity and Popular Protest during the Wars of Religion," *French History* 9 (1995): 139–41; Sharon Kettering, "Clientage during the French Wars of Religion," in *Patronage in Sixteenth- and Seventeenth-Century France* (Aldershot: Ashgate, 2002), IX; Robert R. Harding, *Anatomy of a Power Elite: The Provincial Governors of Early Modern France* (New Haven: Yale University Press, 1978), 21–37.

77. Hubert Carrier, "Pour une définition du pamphlet: Constantes du genre et caractéristiques originales des textes polémiques du XVIe siècle," in *Le pamphlet en France au XVIe siècle* (Paris: École Normale Supérieure des Jeunes Filles, 1983), 133–36; Viala, *Naissance*, 60–68; Jennifer Britnell, "Anti-Papal Writing in the Reign of Louis XII: Propaganda and Self-Promotion," in *Vernacular Literature and Current Affairs in the Early Sixteenth Century: France, England and Scotland*, ed. Jennifer Britnell and Richard Britnell (Aldershot: Ashgate, 2000), 45, 50–51; Sawyer, *Printed Poison*, 52–54, 67–72; Pauline Croft, "Libels, Popular Literacy and Public Opinion in Early Modern England," in *Historical Research* 68 (1995): 284–85; Natalie Mears, "Counsel, Public Debate, and Queenship: John Stubbs's 'The Discoverie of a Gaping Gulf,'" *Historical Journal* 44 (2001): 634.

78. Jeffrey S. Ravel, *The Contested Parterre: Public Theater and French Political Culture, 1680–1791* (Ithaca: Cornell University Press, 1999), 1–11; Jean-Marie Apostolidès, *Le prince sacrifié: Théâtre et politique au temps de Louis XIV* (Paris: Minuit, 1985), 28–38; Maurice Descotes, *Histoire de la critique dramatique en France* (Tubingen: Narr, 1980), 13–16. In contrast, see Jean-Claude Aubailly, *Le monologue, le dialogue et la sottie: Essai sur quelques genres dramatiques de la fin du moyen âge et du début du XVIe siècle* (Paris: Champion, 1976), 413–38.

performances by amateur actors before the rise of absolutism in the seventeenth century, was a potent medium for shaping public opinion. As relatively high-status members of the urban community, amateur actors spoke with more authority than did the professional actors of later periods. The performances of festive societies were not generally directed at a narrow public. Although they did at times perform in a private setting, most festive societies performed in the city streets, where they drew attention to their antics with an elaborate procession. Farce players addressed a broad public, including the nonliterate working poor, who made up the majority of French city residents. Nor was this popular audience passive. Authorities in French cities knew that farce could shape public opinion in unexpected ways, causing riots and undermining the authority of local officials. This fear of public disorder was their primary motive for trying to control its performance, albeit not always with great success.

Not only were farces performed before a broad urban public but they also articulated a broadly held notion of the public good, a standard of political behavior by which royal officials and the clergy could be measured. Although often the vision of the public good was articulated negatively through the criticism of government officials or clerics, in some farces the public good was personified in a character called Chose Publicque (Public Matters), Commun (Commoner), or Peuple Français (French People).[79] These characters represented the interests of poor working commoners when they complained of being abused by the nobility, taxed by royal officials, and treated as fools by a corrupt clergy. Sometimes Sotte Commune (Common Fool) was portrayed as a foolish female character who need not be taken entirely seriously: humor was often created by emphasizing her whining tones or her obsessive concern with filling her belly with food and wine; in the plays themselves, other characters minimized or dismissed her complaints.[80] Nevertheless, such characters sometimes defined the moral high ground and convinced others of the validity of their concerns, articulating a morally inflected understanding of the public good for the audience. Nobles and priests protested that Commun was wrong, but their only defense was to claim that they too were acting out of a concern for the community as a whole.[81] Even though farces were usually performed by relatively prosperous young men of the couche moyenne and sometimes even noble university students, their plays articulated a concept of the public good that embraced the traditional Christian virtues of poverty. Indeed, the Renaissance idea of public good was somewhat different from the eighteenth-century notion of the public sphere, which, as Jürgen Habermas and others have argued,

79. For depictions of characters that represent the public good or the interests of the laboring poor, see *L'Eglise et le Commun; Jeu du Capifol; Jeu du Prince des Sotz.*
80. Rousse, "Pouvoir royal," 193–94.
81. "Sotie nouvelle a cinq personnages de sots fourrez de malice," *Recueil Trepperel*, ed. Eugénie Droz (Geneva: Slatkine, 1966).

claimed authority for objective, rational, and increasingly secular, public debate of political issues. In the sixteenth century, the vision of the public good was very much grounded in the traditional Christian obligation of the wealthy to care for the poor.[82] Grievances were aired in the expectation that those in power would take responsibility for their obligations to society as a whole. If they did not, then they ran the risk of being publicly dishonored with accusations of lechery, impotence, or incontinence.

The ability of characters in farces to articulate a concept of public good before a diverse theater-going public was in part due to the loose nature of theatrical censorship. During the fifteenth and sixteenth centuries, there were real institutional constraints on the king's political power. Because he was often absent from Paris, his authority was episodic even in the capital, and he did not have firm-enough control over royal officials in the provinces to impose an effective censorship regime on festive societies. Within urban communities, local authorities, not all of them supportive of the monarchy, competed to control the city and to censor farce. Specific institutional constraints, however, are only part of the reason why farce players mocked their betters. Political culture was equally important. Farce players had a degree of license not only because of the powerful rivalries I have been discussing but also because of the particular way that political relationships were imagined during the Renaissance.

Farceurs could draw on the body as a ready metaphor for their political grievances, in part because authority was understood in somatic terms. By the late medieval period, the predominant analogy for describing political and spiritual relationships, both within the Catholic Church and within secular political units, was the metaphor of the body politic. In their sermons and writings, clergy commonly asserted that Jesus Christ was the head of the body of the Church, a body that was composed of all believers. Jurists and clergy, interested in justifying the growing power of secular princes, adapted this analogy to the secular context: the prince was, like Christ, head of a body composed of all his subjects.[83] In such secular constructions of the body politic, the prince is accorded a place equivalent to Christ himself, and the body politic as a whole is blessed by God. The king's primary responsibilities, as head, were to protect his subjects and to rule according to law; in return, the limbs and torso owed him obedience. By the fourteenth century, this corporeal metaphor became a key concept in French political theory and practice. The supreme manifestation of the body politic was considered to be composed of the king and the three estates—representatives of the

---

82. Davis, *Society*, 117–19; E. P. Thompson, "The Moral Economy of the English Crowd in the Eighteenth Century," *Past and Present* 50 (1971): 76–136; William Beik, *Urban Protest in Seventeenth-Century France: The Culture of Retribution* (Cambridge: Cambridge University Press, 1997), 49–72.
83. John of Salisbury, *The Statesman's Book of John of Salisbury*, trans. John Dickinson (New York: Russell and Russell, 1963), 3–31, 173, 243.

clergy, the nobility, and nonnoble representatives of the towns—when they consulted together on matters of state. Faced with a need to raise taxes to fight wars and otherwise maintain the court, French kings frequently met with representatives of the three estates at both the local and the national levels after 1300. At these meetings, the king sought obedience through consultation with the estates, but in practice he often faced intransigence and resistance.[84]

The French king did not stand alone as ruler or as sole representative of the polity during the late medieval and Renaissance periods but existed, both in the minds of political theorists and the French political elite at large, in an organic relationship of dependence with the body politic as a whole. This corporeal metaphor was sometimes used to explain or to justify political resistance against monarchical authority. As Christine de Pisan notes in her early fifteenth-century *The Book of the Body Politic*, the head is dependent on the limbs and on the belly. Should the limbs rebel against a tyrannical ruler, warned Christine, then the whole body will weaken and eventually die. When referring to the belly, she concludes that "likewise, when a prince requires more than a people can bear, then the people complain against their prince and rebel by disobedience."[85] Without counseling rebellion, Christine nevertheless articulates in a treatise dedicated to the heir of the French throne the importance of consent and consultation in the healthy working of the French polity.[86] The body politic metaphor was further exploited during the late sixteenth century when both Catholics and Calvinists used it to justify rebellion against the Valois kings, whom they considered heretical and tyrannical in their rule over the French body politic.[87] This con cern with a generalized notion of the public good was not limited to rebels: political treatises and debates at the Estates General called by the kings of France also drew on the same concept, though usually in the context of defending noble privilege only.[88] Although the sacred authority of the monarchy carried great

---

84. Ernst Kantorowicz, *The King's Two Bodies: A Study in Mediaeval Political Theology* (Princeton: Princeton University Press, 1957), 193–223; John Russell Major, *Representative Government in Early Modern France* (New Haven: Yale University Press, 1980), 10–26; M. S. Kempshall, *The Common Good in Late Medieval Political Thought* (Oxford: Clarendon Press, 1999), 104–5, 147–48.

85. Christine de Pisan, *Le livre du corps de policie*, ed. Angus J. Kennedy (Paris: Champion, 1998), 92.

86. Bakhtin, *Rabelais*, 378.

87. Frederic J. Baumgartner, *Radical Reactionaries: The Political Thought of the French Catholic League* (Geneva: Droz, 1975), 145–60; Donald R. Kelley, *The Beginning of Ideology: Consciousness and Society in the French Reformation* (Cambridge: Cambridge University Press, 1981), 301–22.

88. James B. Collins, "Noble Political Ideology and the Estates General of Orléans and Pontoise: French Republicanism," *Historical Reflections/Réflexions Historiques* 27 (2001): 224–27; Paul Solon, "Tax Commissions and Public Opinion: Languedoc, 1438–1561," *Renaissance Quarterly* 43 (1990): 485–87; Robert Descimon, "Les fonctions de la métaphore du mariage politique du roi et de la république France, XVe–XVIIIe siècles," *Annales: Économies, Sociétés, Civilisations* 47 (1992): 1136–38.

weight with French Renaissance nobles and urban notability, the metaphor of the body politic allowed provincial elites to understand their relationship with the monarchy as a reciprocal one in which loyalty and financial gifts to the royal coffers should result in tangible gains and honors.[89]

Farce, though far from counseling rebellion, played with this ambiguous metaphor in comic and concrete ways. Many farces sought to slander or satirize particular religious or political leaders, even the king, with bawdy jokes about the grotesque body. Farces sought to debase those who ruled and to remind the king that the head and soul cannot rule without the more humble contributions of the belly. Patrons of farce permitted the performance of plays that exposed the decentralized and competitive nature of political power or even challenged the king's actions and plans. Farcical theater was thus a tangible manifestation of a widely held belief in the consultative nature of the French polity. Its raucous laughter reminded everyone—players and audience alike—that people should be good Christians but also that a good king (or for that matter, mayor) heard and responded to the complaints of his subjects. Although French kings often resisted this interpretation of the body politic, it remained a commonplace means of justifying resistance to royal power throughout the Renaissance.[90]

The consultative nature of farcical performance and its role in shaping public opinion are illustrated by two performances that took place in 1512 and 1513, both of which focused on important political developments and sought to garner public support for particular policies. These policies were a response to the turbulent relationship between the French king, Louis XII, and the controversial, aggressive leader of Western Christendom, Pope Julius II, who resented Louis's ambitions in Milan and Naples. Although Louis had been allied with the papacy earlier in his reign, by 1509 Julius II had made it clear that he aimed to oust the French from the Italian peninsula. By late 1510, he began sending his troops into battle against the French, a situation that demanded a response. Louis did so on many fronts: he engaged papal troops in military conflict, and he also convoked an international ecclesiastical council in Pisa in the hopes of galvanizing clerical opposition to Julius. By early 1512, Louis's aim was to discredit Julius as pope and to have him formally removed from office.

---

89. Ralph Giesey, "The Juristic Basis of Dynastic Right to the French Throne," *Transactions of the American Philosophical Society* 51 (1961): 3–42; Major, *Renaissance Monarchy*, 47–56; Merlin, *Public et littérature*, 59–73; Éric Gojosso, *Le concept de république en France, XVIe–XVIIIe siècle* (Aix-en-Provence: Presses Universitaires d'Aix-Marseille, 1998), 45–60; Paul Kléber Monod, *The Power of Kings: Monarchy and Religion in Europe, 1589–1715* (New Haven: Yale University Press, 1999), 33–42.
90. Monod, *Power of Kings*, 40–41; David Potter, "King and Government under the Valois," in *France in the Later Middle Ages*, ed. David Potter (Oxford: Oxford University Press, 2003), 156.

Knowing that pursuing war against the pope was likely to be objected to on both theological and fiscal grounds, Louis sought the support of French public opinion. Court writers penned tracts damning Julius as the leader of Christendom, and satirical placards portraying Julius as having abandoned his role as spiritual leader circulated in Paris.[91] But Louis also took advantage of the power of the theater. For the Mardi Gras celebrations of 1512, Louis allowed and quite possibly commissioned the well-known playwright Pierre Gringore to compose and direct a special theatrical event for the Parisian public that addressed his political dilemma directly. The resulting *Play of the Prince of Fools*, a collection of plays including a *cri*, a sottie, a morality play, and a farce, characterized Pope Julius as a ridiculous, power-hungry schemer and presented the king's efforts to combat him in a noble light.[92] In the sottie, Louis is represented by a character called the Prince des Sots (Prince of Fools), who has been betrayed by his mother, Mère Sotte (Mother Folly), representing Pope Julius. Mère Sotte is presented as a vain and greedy queen who wants control over not only spiritual but also temporal affairs. During the play, she is able to gain support from corrupt abbots of the Church, but the nobles loyal to the prince refuse to join her camp. Frustrated by her inability to convince the nobles to abandon their prince, Mère Sotte strips down on stage to military garb and launches a spontaneous military assault against the prince's supporters, as indeed commentators noted with some dismay that Pope Julius II had done when he led his troops into battle at Mirandola in January 1511. The prince, ostensibly surprised by Mère Sotte's aggression, asks his fools what to do. Though they lament the perils and costs of war, they advise him that he must defend himself. Sotte Commune, who represents the common folk, regrets the need for the war but concludes that it is not "Mère Sainte Église" who wages this war against the prince but merely Mère Sotte, a statement that, set in the context of earlier references in the play to Louis's schismatic Council of Pisa, reveals that Gringore's aim is to discredit Julius as the rightful ruler of Christendom.[93] In an effort to whitewash Louis's position, the sottie makes no mention of the Italian context of the fighting—indeed, the order of the

---

91. Frederic J. Baumgartner, "Louis XII's Gallican Crisis of 1510–1513," in *Politics, Ideology, and the Law in Early Modern Europe*, ed. Adrianna E. Bakos (Rochester: University of Rochester Press, 1994), 60–67. In doing so, these writers were following the lead of Erasmus in his satire *Julius Excluded from Heaven*.

92. Pierre Gringore, "Jeu du Prince des Sotz," in *Oeuvres complètes de Gringore*, ed. Charles d'Héricault and A. Montaiglon (Paris: P. Jannet, 1858), 1:243; Cynthia Jane Brown, *The Shaping of History and Poetry in Late Medieval France: Propaganda and Artistic Expression in the Works of the Rhétoriqueurs* (Birmingham, Ala.: Summa Publications, 1985), 111–21; Oulmont, "Pierre Gringore," 389; Nicole Hochner, "Pierre Gringore: Une satire à la solde du pouvoir?" *Fifteenth-Century Studies* 26 (2001): 102–20.

93. Jody L. H. McQuillan, "Dangerous Dialogues: The *Sottie* as a Threat to Authority," in *Bakhtin and Medieval Voices*, ed. Thomas J. Farrell (Gainesville: University Press of Florida, 1995), 74.

stage entrances suggests that Mère Sotte has invaded France rather than the other way around—or the broader context of French military aggression in Italy since 1494. Gringore, though not an official propagandist of the king's court, makes a strongly polemical claim in the play in support of the king's military actions. Published in the months that followed, Gringore's plays were also probably read by bourgeois urban readers.

Yet the Mardi Gras performance of 1512 did not end political debate on this issue. The following year, in 1513, some prominent Florentine residents of the city of Lyon paid farce players to perform "certain plays and farces in favor of and in praise of the pope."[94] Although the city council did not finance this performance, it sanctioned the Florentines' actions and did nothing to stop the airing of the pro-papal views, even at a time when awareness of the king's position would have been widespread. Of course by early 1513 Julius II was dead, the French had lost their military advantage in Italy, and the new pope Leo X was open to negotiations. Nevertheless, Louis XII would not admit that his plan to depose the pope at the Pisa council had been schismatic, and he did not reestablish formal working relations with the papacy until December 1513, months after the Lyon performance. The Florentine bankers, whose loans underwrote the French military effort, likely sought to hurry the king along a path of reconciliation.[95] The fact that the Italian merchants had this point of view comes as no surprise, but what is interesting is that they decided to air those views publicly in a well-publicized theatrical performance. Whereas a century later powerful financial brokers preferred to air their differences with the king by sending a messenger to court, during the Renaissance it was still acceptable to offer the king public counsel through the medium of the farce.

The traditions surrounding farcical performance thus allowed both nobles and commoners to contribute to public political debate during the Renaissance. Whether questioning the king's policies toward the papacy or, as was more often the case, mocking the foibles of the local city council, farce was a concrete expression of the commonly held understanding of the reciprocal nature of political power. The relative freedom of farce players to speak their minds was also made possible by the divided nature of political power. The conflict among local authorities over who had the right to censor the theater meant that farceurs could evade their control most of the time. As long as the youth of the festive societies avoided violence in favor of verbal play, most people laughed with appreciation.

Through the performance of political satire, farce players participated in the creation of public opinion, a phenomenon that elites assumed existed in the sixteenth century and which they sought to shape and control. Louis

94. Brouchoud, *Origines*, 19.
95. Baumgartner, "Louis XII," 70–71; Martin Wolfe, *Fiscal System of Renaissance France* (New Haven: Yale University Press, 1972), 61–64; Watson, "Friends," 291–92.

XII's approach was to be proactive: to shape debate through the comic portrayal of papal abuses and to tolerate some satirical portrayals of his policies. His successor, Francis I, though by no means opposed in principle to
farcical humor, was nevertheless quick to act when his own actions were
mocked in public. Indeed, the impulse to clamp down on farce intensified on
several fronts as anxiety about religious reform mounted during the 1520s.

3   *The Growing Cost of Laughter*

BASOCHE AND STUDENT PERFORMANCE

By the middle of the sixteenth century, even before the outbreak of the Wars of Religion in 1562, the opportunities for satirical theater began to contract. Although festive societies continued to perform farces in the city streets, they were subject to more regulation and sometimes to outright censorship. This transformation of comic theater was linked to two interrelated phenomena: the growing assertiveness of royal political institutions, notably the parlements, and the rising tide of religious reform.

These phenomena had a particularly visible impact on two groups of farce players: law clerks of the Basoche and university students. During the fifteenth century, both Basochiens and students were well known for their satirical performances. Secular and clerical authorities often noted with dismay the audacity of the plays performed by these two groups, although they did little to curb them. Often sons of respectable bourgeoisie and sometimes of the nobility, law clerks and students were of a higher social status than most youths who performed farce. In a society in which the law almost always judged the poor more harshly than the rich, their relatively high social status granted them some immunity from severe punishments at the hands of royal officials. On the other hand, their junior membership at the universities and the parlements also rendered them more vulnerable to censorship at the hands of their institutional superiors. Often they could perform satirical farces only if their masters, the magistrates or the university rectors, permitted them to do so.

The Basochiens and students were the canaries in the coal mine in that they illustrate the rising political and religious tensions in French society during the last decades of the Renaissance. Their satirical audacity and their association with powerful institutions resulted in more stringent censorship by the 1530s, a fate that other festive societies, especially in the provinces, were spared for a few more decades.

The origins of the Basoche in Paris are lost in the past. During the seventeenth and eighteenth centuries, some members claimed that the association was founded in the early fourteenth century, when the Paris Parlement became a permanent institution.[1] Such an early inception is certainly possible, but the association shows up in the historical record only in 1420. By the middle of the fifteenth century, the Basoche had emerged as an association that sought to defend the interests of one particular group of petty legal officials: clerks working at royal law courts. Most of these clerks, young men in their teens and early twenties, worked for solicitors (*procureurs*), but they could also be employed by barristers (*avocats*), registrars, and magistrates.[2] They were, in effect, young journeymen who sought to become masters of the pen rather than creators of commercial goods. During the time of their clerkship, these young men held no formal posts at the parlement but were employed by individual solicitors or barristers. Despite this lack of official status or perhaps because of it, the Basochiens banded together to feast on Saint Nicholas's Day in May and began acting like a corporation or guild as early as the mid-fifteenth century. By the 1460s, the Basochiens insisted that all their members participate in the association's annual procession and claimed the right to charge all clerks annual dues whether or not they wanted to be a part of the festivities. Like other youth groups, each year after its burlesque procession the Basochiens elected themselves a king. Soon

1. *Recueil des statuts, ordonnances, reiglements, antiquitez, prérogatives, et prééminences du royaume de la Bazoche* (Paris: C. Besongne, 1654), postscript; David Avrom Bell, "Lawyers and Politics in Eighteenth-Century Paris (1700–1790)," Ph.D. diss., Princeton University, 1991, 62–63; Charles Desmaze, *Le Châtelet de Paris* (Paris: Didier, 1870), 380; Adolphe Fabre, *Les clercs du palais: Recherches historiques sur les bazoches des parlements et sociétés dramatiques des bazochiens et Enfants sans Souci* (Lyon: Scheuring, 1875), 127; Lucien Genty, *La Basoche notariale: Origines et histoire du XIVe siècle à nos jours* (Paris: Delamotte, 1888), 115; Pierre de Miraulmont, *Les mémoires de Pierre de Miraulmont sur l'origine et institution des cours souveraines* (Paris: Chevalier, 1612), 651; Françoise Autrand, *Naissance d'un grand corps de l'état: Les gens du Parlement de Paris*, 1345–1454 (Paris: Publications de la Sorbonne, 1981), 21; Marie Bouhaïk-Gironès, "La Basoche et le théâtre comique: Identité sociale, pratiques et culture des clercs de justice (Paris, 1420–1550)," Ph.D. diss., University of Paris 7, 2004, 25–26, 50–53.

2. Various definitions of Basoche membership found in the Paris Parlement records include the following: "clercs d'advocats et procureurs," Archives Nationales (AN) x1a 1482, fol. 252, 17 Aug. 1443; "tous les clercs et serviteurs tant du palais que du chastellet," AN x1a 1487, fol. 59, 13 May 1476; "les clercs de ceans autrement dit bazochiens," AN x1a 8345, fols. 256–58, 14 July 1528; "clercs du palais," AN x1a 1667, fol. 314, 24 Mar. 1580; AN x1a 1680, 14 May 1583. There is limited evidence to suggest that separate Basoche groups existed at different courts in Paris. AN x1a 4947, fol. 413, 12 Jan. 1552; Bell, "Lawyers and Politics," 64; Louis Petit de Julleville, *Histoire du théâtre en France: Les comédiens en France au moyen âge* (Paris: Le Cerf, 1885), 91; Louis Petit de Julleville, *Histoire du théâtre en France: Répertoire du théâtre comique en France au moyen âge* (Paris: L. Cerf, 1886), 378–79. I have translated various posts at parlement as follows: *procureurs*, "solicitors"; *avocats*, "barristers"; *greffiers*, "registrars"; *huissiers*, "process servers"; and *conseillers*, "magistrates." This terminology avoids some confusion but does not resolve all difficulties: solicitors (*procureurs*), for example, had a higher status at the parlement than did *praticiens* or *solliciteurs*.

the clerks established an elaborate hierarchy of posts in the organization—from king to chancellor to solicitor—thereby parodying the hierarchies of the law court. By 1500, the clerks at the parlement and the Châtelet together probably numbered at least five hundred, by far the largest association of employees working at the royal law courts in Paris.[3]

Although during the fifteenth century the parlement magistrates repeatedly denied the Basochiens formal corporate status and the right to perform farces, by 1500 the clerks and the magistrates had reached a mutually satisfactory compromise. As long as the Basochiens avoided disturbing public order with their festivities, the magistrates would tolerate and even help pay for them. Indeed, the magistrates were sometimes willing to release funds for performances they had not approved. When in early 1516, after the death of Louis XII, the Basochiens performed a series of plays during the official period of mourning, the magistrates chastised the clerks but nevertheless contributed sixty livres to the performance.[4]

Following the example of Paris, Basoche organizations were founded at several other parlements and seneschal courts. In Toulouse, where a parlement had sat since 1437, there are references to Basoche performances as early as the 1470s. In Rouen in 1499, the clerks at the newly founded royal court received letters patent from Louis XII authorizing them to perform farces.[5] In Aix, Avignon, Bordeaux, Dijon, Lyon, and many smaller cities, Basoche organizations enacted similar festivities.[6] Some of these

3. Charles Bataillard, *Histoire des procureurs et des avoués, 1483–1816* (Paris: Hachette, 1882), 1:102n3; Antoine Fontanon, *Les édicts et ordonnances des Roys de France depuis S. Loys jusques à present* (Paris: Du Puys, 1580), 1:235. Most solicitors employed at least two clerks. See Archives Départementales Gironde (ADG) 1 B 382, fol. 6, 9 Mar. 1574; Bibliothèque Municipale (BM) Bordeaux MS 369, Savignac, "Extraits des registres secrets du Parlement de Bordeaux," 2:663 (18 Apr. 1566).

4. AN x1a 1517, fol. 58a, 1 Feb. 1515.

5. Archives Départementales de la Haute-Garonne (ADHG) 2 Mi 165, fol. 421, 27 May 1478; ADHG 2 Mi 166, fol. 320, 2 May 1480; ADHG 2 Mi 169, fol. 340, 13 May 1491; ADHG 2 Mi 206, fol. 189, 5 May 1526; Archives Départementales Seine-Maritime (ADSM) 1 B 619, 3 Feb. 1571; Édouard-Hippolyte Gosselin, *Recherches sur les origines et l'histoire du théâtre à Rouen* (Rouen: Cagniard, 1868), 55–60; ADSM 1 B 534, 5 May 1550; ADSM 1 B 2151, 30 Sept. 1588; ADSM 1 B 870, 4 Apr. 1618.

6. Evidence of Basoche maypoles and springtime farce playing in other French cities include Marc Venard, *Réforme protestante, Réforme catholique dans la province d'Avignon au XVIe siècle* (Paris: Cerf, 1993), 977–79; ADG 1 B 81, fol. 196, 7 May 1532; ADG 1 B 357, 29 Apr. 1572; Jean Guéraud, *La chronique lyonnaise de Jean Guéraud, 1536–1562*, ed. Jean Tricou (Lyon: Audin, 1929), 43, 63; J. H. M. Salmon, *Society in Crisis: France in the Sixteenth Century* (London: Ernest Benn, 1975), 101; Kevin C. Robbins, *City on the Ocean Sea: La Rochelle, 1530–1650: Urban Society, Religion and Politics on the French Atlantic Frontier* (New York: Brill, 1997), 137–41; André Bossuat, "Le théâtre à Clermont-Ferrand," *Revue d'Histoire du Théâtre* 13 (1961): 113–14; Achille Durieux, *Le théâtre à Cambrai avant et depuis 1789* (Cambrai: J. Renaut, 1883), 13–15; Jean Tricou, "Les confréries joyeuses de Lyon au XVIe siècle et leur numismatique," *Revue Numismatique* 40 (1937): 300; Maurice Lambert, *Le sceau d'un roi de basoche conservé à la bibliothèque de Besançon* (Besançon: Dodivers, 1909); Archives Municipales (AM) Dijon G 39, basoche folio; Genty, *Bazoche*, 145–52, 162–74.

organizations claimed to be directly linked to the Parisian association: the Basoche of Poitiers claimed to be a subsidiary of the Paris Basoche, arguing that the Paris association heard appeals on all questions of Basoche jurisdiction.[7] Despite some regional variation, all these organizations were made up of young clerks who hoped someday to become legal officials. All of them were also known for performing farcical theater both privately for the magistrates' entertainment and publicly during civic events such as royal entry ceremonies.

Basoche processions and theatrical performances in Paris are particularly well documented. Their processions were bold. Armed with batons and muskets, festooned in their traditional blue and yellow garb or dressed in a costume decided by the marching company's captain, the Basoche strode triumphantly through the Paris city streets.[8] On some occasions, this brightly colored blur of marching men was accompanied by hired musicians who played the fife and sounded drums and by elaborately painted horse-drawn chariots. The king of the Basoche, carrying a scepter, marched among his subjects or was carried by his fellow revelers.[9] Such celebrations were not limited to Maytime. In Paris, the Basoche also performed in January and to mark important civic events such as the king's entry into his capital. The Basochiens mounted tableaux vivants and performed plays at the great Table du Marbre in the Grande Salle of the parlement as well as in front of the Palais du Justice. In the provinces, each Basoche association celebrated a different feast: in Rouen and Toulouse they usually performed in May, but in Bordeaux the Basoche performances were associated with Carnival and the Feast of Saint Ives. Nevertheless, all their processions and performances were characterized by broad, bawdy comedy that involved the satirical inversion of social hierarchy.[10]

The amusing nature of the clerks' performances, and the way in which they sought to parlay the right to perform into formal recognition of their

---

7. AN x1a 8345, fol. 256, 14 July 1528.

8. Miraulmont, *Mémoires*, 663; AN x1a 8345, fols. 256–258, 14 July 1528; AN x1a 1680, 14 May 1583. *Arrêts* that mention the location of the Basoche's performance include AN x1a 1487, fol. 59, 13 May 1476; AN x1a 1547, fol. 32, 1 June 1541; AN x1a 1596, fol. 162a, 8 Jan. 1561.

9. AN x1a 8345, fols. 256–58, 14 July 1528; AN x1a 1604, fol. 118, 31 Dec. 1562. For evidence of contracts between the Basoche and local musicians and chariot/horse owners, see *Recueil d'actes notariés relatifs à l'histoire de Paris et ses environs au XVIe siècle*, ed. Ernest Coyecque (Paris: Imprimerie Nationale, 1905), 1:300 (2 June 1540); *Histoire de l'art au XVIe siècle, 1540–1600*, ed. Catherine Grodecki (Paris: Archives Nationales, 1986), 2:155 (30 Apr. 1551).

10. AN x1a 1517, fol. 58a, 1 Feb. 1515; Durieux, *Théâtre*, 142; Claude Gaignebet, "Le cycle annuel des fêtes à Rouen au milieu du XVIe siècle," in *Les fêtes de la Renaissance*, ed. Jean Jacquot and Élie Konigson (Paris: CNRS, 1975), 3:569–78; Georges Lecocq, *Histoire du théâtre en Picardie, depuis son origine jusqu'à la fin du XVIe siècle* (Paris: Menu, 1880; reprint, Geneva: Slatkine, 1971), 138–40; J. Lestrade, "Les gateaux de la basoche," *Revue Historique de Toulouse* 2 (1915–19): 147–48; AN x1a 1565, fol. 18, 9 May 1549; Jean de Gaufreteau, *Chronique bordeloise* (Bordeaux: Charles Lefebvre, 1877), 1:82.

association as a corporation, can be seen from an account of a Basoche procession that occurred in July 1528. That summer the Basoche presented to the parlement a *cause grasse* (mock case) in which the Basoche justified its punishment of a young clerk. This case was based on a farcical situation in which a young clerk was humiliated for having refused to dress up like a woman. Brought before the magistrates as an appeal of the Basoche's decision to fine the clerk, this case both upheld and inverted the traditional hierarchies that dominated day-to-day court life.[11]

In preparation for that year's May parade, the clerks of the Basoche had divided into marching companies, each of which was to dress in a distinctive costume. The captain of each company drew a picture of its proposed costume, and clerks who intended to join that company were to sign their name under the appropriate picture. Should they fail to appear on the day of the march wearing the specified costume, they would be fined ten *escus*, a considerable sum of money that likely most would be unable to produce on demand.[12] Of his own free will, the young plaintiff apparently chose to sign up for a marching company that planned to dress up as women. Perhaps regretting his decision, the plaintiff was nowhere to be found on the day of the parade. Two Basoche officials, dispatched to search for him, found him at home dressed in a bed robe and cap claiming to be sick. He was also armed with a *baton*: apparently the visit of the Basoche officials was expected. Concluding that the clerk was in perfect health, the Basoche officials attempted to collect the requisite fine from him, but "because he did not want to go we got violent with him, [and] we took his coat from his shoulders."[13] Having stripped him of his clothes for refusing to dress like a woman, the Basoche left with his coat in hand.

The comedy of the incident would have been obvious to all involved in the case—Basochiens, lawyers, and magistrates—and it seems that the lengthy description of the clerk's humiliation was recounted with some relish. Dressing like a woman, particularly during a procession in which the clerks were likely to be carrying arms, would evidently have been ridiculously incongruous: it is an example of the kind of inversion of social norms characteristic of farce. The 1528 "company of women" case also uses another technique common in sixteenth-century plays: exposure of the victim's true identity. In many sotties, characters introduced as respectable members of society are later exposed as fools. In this case, the young clerk, fearful of appearing unmanly in women's costume, assumes instead the

11. Regarding the practice of pleading *causes grasses*, see Bouhaïk-Gironès, "Basoche," 174–90.
12. In 1519, one *escu* was the equivalent of two livres, so the fine assessed the clerk would have totaled twenty livres. See Martin Wolfe, *The Fiscal System of Renaissance France* (New Haven: Yale University Press, 1972), 293.
13. AN x1a 8345, fol. 257, 14 July 1528.

costume of an invalid only to be exposed as a coward unwilling to fulfill his manly obligations.[14]

This apparently silly comedy was played on an unexpectedly solemn and dignified "stage": the Grand' Chambre, the usually somber courtroom of the parlement, and the men who argued the case were not lowly clerks but well-respected barristers, some of whom would have long and illustrious careers at the court. Augustin de Thou, who defended the Basoche's authority to fine the clerk, was a member of a prominent Parisian elite family and was eventually promoted to the office of chief magistrate at the parlement. Another barrister who argued at length for the Basoche's privileges was Guillaume Poyet, later to become the chancellor of France, the highest judicial office in the country and one that conferred membership in the king's council.[15]

De Thou's testimony in particular linked the Basoche's privileges to the clerks' history of performance. Although he maintained that the Basoche officials had been abusive when they confiscated the clerk's only coat, de Thou nevertheless defended the Basoche's right to punish its members, arguing that

> the said Basochiens are accustomed every year to perform plays and march in parades and *in order to do so* elect a king, a chancellor, twelve masters of requests, four accountants and treasurers, ushers, captains, lieutenants, and standard-bearers. And since they have been established for so long that there is no memory otherwise, both affirmed by custom and by decrees of the court . . . the rulings of the king of the Basoche are to be enforced notwithstanding resistance and appeals.[16]

The privilege of the Basoche to elect its leaders and fine its members, argued de Thou, derived from the clerks' performance tradition rather than from the association's formal corporate status. Notably, de Thou did not refer to any letters patent or other evidence of the Basoche's formal incorporation: the earliest evidence of the Paris Basoche's letters patent dates from the 1560s. De Thou was being disingenuous, however, when he claimed that the right to perform had been "authorized for so long that there is no memory otherwise." Surely some at the court remembered the conflicts that plagued Basoche–magistrate relations as late as the 1470s. Nevertheless, de Thou

---

14. Heather Arden, *Fools' Plays: A Study of Satire in the "Sottie"* (Cambridge: Cambridge University Press, 1980), 44–52.

15. Both Poyet and de Thou are only referred to by their last names in the 1528 ruling, but are referred to in the 1539–41 Garnier case as "Messire Augustin de Thou president en Enquetes" and "Guillaume Poyet chevallier de France." See AN U*2220, Le Nain, fols. 71–75, 14 Jan. 1541. I thank Barbara B. Diefendorf for confirming that Augustin de Thou was most likely the only son of Jacques III de Thou, *avocat général* at the Cour des Aides. Augustin de Thou was already a member of the Paris city council in 1528 when he defended the Basoche.

16. AN x1a 8345, fol. 256, 14 July 1528 (emphasis mine).

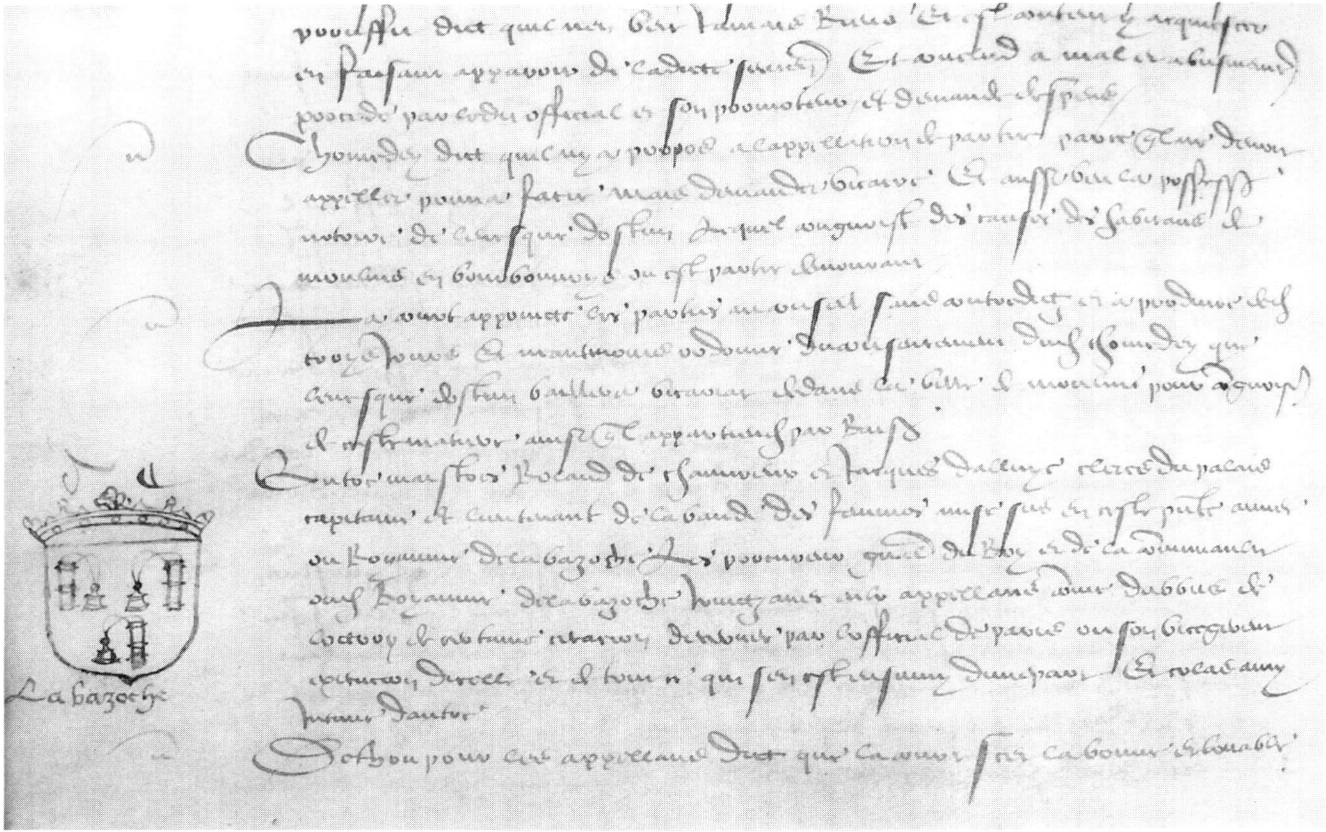

FIGURE 4. Basoche coat of arms, 1528. (Source: Archives Nationales x1a 8345, fol. 255)

was able to convince the magistrates, who decreed that as long as "the king of the Basoche rules his subjects with more courtesy" in the future, he and his officials could continue to fine these "subjects" for similar transgressions.[17] During debate of the "company of women" case, no one questioned the right of the Basochiens to hold their May processions or to perform satirical plays; all this was taken for granted. Indeed, their performance tradition allowed them to confirm other rights normally associated with formal corporations.

Poyet and de Thou, still young barristers in 1528, would not themselves have marched in the Basoche parades, but they apparently had no qualms defending the clerks at length in the Grand' Chambre. Although parlement magistrates strove for a public demeanor of professional sobriety and seriousness, sixteenth-century Frenchmen accepted that during certain ritual moments of the year, serious behavior could be temporarily thrown off without fundamentally challenging the social order. A note in the margins of the parlement records supports this interpretation. In the Plaidoiries records, the margins of most pages are left wide and blank, but beside the "company of women" case, the registrar drew in ink the Basoche coat of arms: a shield with three bells on sticks for ringing during the clerks' Carnival procession.[18] The existence of this image in the court register makes clear that even sober registrars knew and appreciated Basoche comedy. Despite the fact that the "company of women" case was probably argued tongue in cheek, the clerks frequently referred to the 1528 ruling throughout the sixteenth century to justify imprisoning their members and to uphold the validity of their election procedures.[19]

Both the 1528 case and the magistrates' willingness to pay for Basoche theatrics attest to the shared culture of laughter that tied the Basochiens and the magistrates together. Yet even during this heyday of the Basoche between 1500 and the mid-1530s, a wide gulf of wealth, expertise, and worldliness divided the clerks from their superiors at the court. This distance is illustrated by the nature of the physical space in which the drama of the courtroom unfolded each day. Throughout much of the compound where the parlement held its sessions—collectively known as the Palais de Justice—booksellers, hawkers, and men of court noisily went about their business. All such ruckus was to stop at the entrance to the Grand' Chambre, however. A raised dais at the northwest corner, reserved for the king's occasional visits to the parlement, dominated the courtroom. During a

---

17. AN x1a 8345, fol. 258, 14 July 1528. See also AN x1a 1506, fol. 121, 6 May 1501.
18. AN x1a 8345, fol. 256, 14 July 1528. Although coats of arms often included bells as an image, the inclusion of several bells attached to festive *batons* distinguishes the Basoche coat of arms from others.
19. AN x1a 1545, fol. 443, 23 June 1540; AN x1a 1557, fols. 206–7, 9 Feb. 1546; AN x1a 1558, 2 June 1546; x1a 1674, fol. 343, 10 Feb. 1582; *Recueil des statuts*, 56–64 (20 May 1546).

normal court session, the chief magistrates, dressed in their ceremonial red robes, and the magistrates, dressed in black, sat on benches that framed the dais.[20] Beyond a barrier that divided the royal and plebeian halves of the chamber sat the barristers who presented verbal pleading. The solicitors, dressed in their caps and long black robes, sat behind the barristers. Finally, behind the solicitors sat their clerks, whom the magistrates enjoined to remain silent, to refrain from sending messages, and to remain seated during the sessions.[21] Within the Grand' Chambre, the social and professional distance between the clerks of the Basoche and the magistrates could not have been more graphically illustrated.

Unlike the parlement magistrates, the solicitors and clerks usually worked outside the Grand' Chambre. Their days were spent next door in the Grande Salle, where solicitors and barristers established benches and dealt with clients in a busy, crowded, semipublic environment. Hired by plaintiffs or defendants in cases brought before the parlement, sixteenth-century solicitors worked to keep the paperwork flowing: in civil and criminal cases, solicitors recorded and copied testimonies, registered cases with the court registrar, and submitted documents to the legal representatives of the opposing party.[22] Because many cases brought before the parlement were handled entirely through written pleading, or were appeals of cases in which the client did not live in Paris, a competent solicitor could be crucial to a case's efficient conclusion. Being a solicitor at the parlement was not, however, a position of great prestige. Although barristers often earned little more than solicitors, their role as prosecutors provided some public visibility, and their formal legal training presented wider opportunities for advancement in royal service. Other officers of the king recognized barristers as professionals whose intellectual training marked them as members of an elite. In contrast, the work of solicitors—collecting documents, copying them, and dealing with matters of procedure—was perceived to be mechanical and base.[23] Most of the clerks of the Basoche would become mere solicitors and so were destined to remain in the lower echelons of the parlements, particularly

20. Sarah Hanley, *The "Lit de Justice" of the Kings of France: Constitutional Ideology in Legend, Ritual and Discourse* (Princeton: Princeton University Press, 1983), 63n28; Édouard Maugis, *Histoire du Parlement de Paris de l'avènement des rois Valois à la mort d'Henri IV* (Paris: A. Picard, 1913–16; reprint, New York: Burt Franklin, 1967), 1:285–86; J. H. Sheenan, *The Parlement of Paris* (Ithaca: Cornell University Press, 1968), 101–6.

21. Bataillard, *Histoire*, 1:221; Ferdinand Lot and Robert Fawtier, *Histoire des institutions françaises au moyen-âge* (Paris: Presses Universitaires de France, 1958), 2:394–98.

22. Bataillard, *Histoire*, 1:113–22, 218–30; Fontanon, *Édicts*, 1:57 (18 Dec. 1537); Timothy Watson, "Friends at Court: The Correspondence of the Lyon City Council, c. 1525–1575," *French History* 13 (1999): 281–302.

23. La Roche Flavin, in his defense of the *procureur* profession, confesses that it is at best a "petit art," contrasted to the "grands arts" of the *avocats*. Bernard de La Roche Flavin, *Treze livres des parlemens de France* (Bordeaux: Simon Millanges, 1617), 136. See also David Avrom Bell, *Lawyers and Citizens: The Making of a Political Elite in Old Regime France* (Oxford: Oxford University Press, 1994), 31–34, 132–34.

in Paris. Since they would never plead cases before the magistrates in the Grand' Chambre, as did the university-trained *avocats*, the theatrical antics of the Basoche were not practice pleading sessions. Nevertheless, the enactment of mock cases was an important way in which the oral legal traditions of the court were transmitted from generation to generation.[24]

As young men in training, the solicitors' clerks spent their time copying manuscripts, carrying heavy bags of documents to barristers' offices, and being scolded by their employer's wife.[25] This life of drudgery, however, would not last forever. In principle, a young man who had served ten years as a solicitor's clerk and was at least twenty-five years old was eligible to become a solicitor. Most clerks were probably between the ages of fifteen and twenty-five; if they had family in the business already, a clerk could hope to secure the post of solicitor before he finished the full ten-year apprenticeship.[26] No formal legal training was necessary for this job, though legible handwriting and a practical knowledge of legal procedure were essential. Solicitors' clerks probably were tutored at home or attended a few years of collège before going into service in their midteens. They were thus solidly entrenched in the couche moyenne of Paris and of the provincial cities in which Basoche organizations existed.[27]

The magistrates, in contrast, represented the pinnacle of the urban elite. Particularly at the prestigious Paris Parlement, but also at the other seven parlements located in provincial capitals throughout France, the magistrates

24. Bouhaïk-Gironès, "Basoche," 171–75, 206–8; Bell, *Lawyers and Citizens*; Sarah Maza, *Private Lives and Public Affairs: The Causes Célèbres of Prerevolutionary France* (Berkeley: University of California Press, 1993).
25. De Tournabons, *La misère des clercs des procureurs* (Paris: A. Robinot, 1627); *Le Pont-Breton des procureurs, dedié aux clercs du Palais* (1624).
26. AN x1a 1572, fol. 5, 30 Apr. 1552; AN x1a 1540, fol. 46a, 10 Dec. 1537; Bataillard, *Histoire*, 1:101–15, 208–9. Examples of clerks who became solicitors in Paris after more than ten years of service include AN x1a 1631, fol. 29, 27 Nov. 1570; AN x1a 1554, fol. 532, 23 Mar. 1545; AN x1a 1611, fol. 326, 30 Jan. 1565. At the Parlement of Bordeaux, clerks were only required to serve at the court for a maximum of seven years. Jean de Métivier, *Chronique du Parlement de Bordeaux, 1462–1566* (Bordeaux: Arthur de Brezetz et Jules Delpit, 1886–87), 1:287 (16 Nov. 1532), 1:317 (4 Dec. 1534); George Huppert, *Public Schools in Renaissance France* (Chicago: University of Illinois Press, 1984), 41–44.
27. Robert Descimon, "Paris on the Eve of Saint Bartholomew: Taxation, Privilege, and Social Geography," in *Cities and Social Change in Early Modern France*, ed. Philip Benedict (London: Unwin Hyman, 1989), 91–98; Sara Beam, "The 'Basoche' and the 'Bourgeoisie Seconde': Careerists at the Parlement of Paris during the League," *French History* 17 (2004): 372–74; Barbara B. Diefendorf, *Paris City Councillors in the Sixteenth Century: The Politics of Patrimony* (Princeton: Princeton University Press, 1983), 46–47; Robert Descimon, "Le corps de ville et les élections échevinales à Paris aux XVIe et XVIIe siècles," *Histoire, Économie, Société* 13 (1994): 507–30. Although it was virtually unheard of for a solicitor to become a parlement magistrate or city councilor in Paris by the mid-sixteenth century, in provincial cities like Dijon promotion to important civic political roles was still possible. Michael P. Breen, "Legal Culture, Municipal Politics and Royal Absolutism in Seventeenth-Century France: The 'Avocats' of Dijon (1595–1715)," Ph.D. diss., Brown University, 2000, 142; Robert A. Schneider, "Crown and Capitoulat: Municipal Government in Toulouse, 1500–1789," in Benedict, *Cities and Social Change*, 196.

brought to their work both the knowledge of the law and the confidence of a ruling elite. The magistrates were from families of the lower nobility or from the retail merchant class, that is, from the urban oligarchy. Unlike most urban officials, however, magistrates had to have attended university. Because civil law could only be studied at a handful of universities in France, some future magistrates would have traveled outside their native region for their studies, even if they ended up returning home to take up office at their local parlement.[28] Magistrates also enjoyed the possibility of geographical and social mobility: a *président* of a provincial parlement could, if he married into the right Parisian family, acquire or purchase an office at the Parlement of Paris. Many magistrates held other prestigious posts in the city and were descendants of families that had climbed the ranks through royal service during the late fifteenth century: families like those of Poyet and de Thou, the barristers who defended the Basoche in 1528.[29] For ambitious royal officials, acquiring the office of parlement magistrate (*conseiller*) or *président* was highly desirable because the post not only exempted them from most forms of taxation but also could confer nobility upon them.[30] Consequently, by the mid-sixteenth century, candidates were willing to pay the king considerable sums to acquire a *conseiller* office. Despite the fact that the post of magistrate was increasingly purchased rather than acquired by election or appointment, the parlements' leading magistrates seem to have been sincerely committed to their professional duties.[31]

The parlements had a unique role to play in sixteenth-century France, a role that had judicial, legislative, and executive elements. Founded as law courts to dispense the king's justice, the parlements served as appeal courts for the various regions of France. The largest of these jurisdictions, the Île-de-France, which covered about one-third of the French monarchy's

28. Jonathan Dewald, *The Formation of a Provincial Nobility: The Magistrates of the Parlement of Rouen, 1499–1610* (Princeton: Princeton University Press, 1980), 24–28; Nancy Lyman Roelker, *One King, One Faith: The Parlement of Paris and the Religious Reformations of the Sixteenth Century* (Berkeley: University of California Press, 1996), 96–98.

29. Autrand, *Naissance*, 108–32; Diefendorf, *Paris City Councillors*, 44–45, 52–56; Maugis, *Histoire*, 1:176, 3:159–76; Robert Descimon, "The 'Bourgeoisie Seconde': Social Differentiation in the Parisian Municipal Oligarchy in the Sixteenth Century, 1500–1610," *French History* 17 (2004): 388–424; Diefendorf, *Paris City Councillors*, 83–111.

30. For parlement magistrates, nobility was conferred only in the third generation. Robert Descimon, "The Birth of the Nobility of the Robe," in *Changing Identities in Early Modern France*, ed. Michael Wolfe (Durham, N.C.: Duke University Press, 1997), 95–121.

31. Christopher Stocker, "Public and Private Enterprise in the Administration of a Renaissance Monarchy," *Sixteenth Century Journal* 9 (1978): 4–25; Dewald, *Formation*, 28–30, 57–64; Roelker, *One King*, 134–37; Maugis, *Histoire*, 1:214–23; Christopher Stocker, "Office as Maintenance in Renaissance France," *Canadian Journal of History* 6 (1971): 38–41; Élie Barnavi and Robert Descimon, *La Sainte Ligue, le juge et la potence: L'assassinat du Président Brisson: 15 novembre 1591* (Paris: Hachette, 1985), 128–77; Mark Cummings, "The Social Impact of the 'Paulette': The Case of the Parlement of Paris," *Canadian Journal of History* 15 (1980): 329–54.

territory, was the responsibility of the Parlement of Paris. The fact that in their executive capacity the eight French parlements were responsible for maintaining the peace made the magistrates acutely aware of the dangers of scandal and of the need to protect the common people from religious and political sedition. As we have seen, the magistrates' sense of dignity and self-importance did not prevent them from laughing at the antics of the Basoche, but it certainly inhibited them from participating in farcical performance themselves. Finally, the parlements had a crucial legislative role to play: royal edicts could become law only when the parlements registered them. Although the magistrates were under an obligation to register the king's will, they had the right to delay registration and to present written complaints (*remonstrances*) concerning royal edicts they thought undermined traditional liberties. Magistrates often asserted this privilege during the turbulent early years of Francis I's reign. In this period the parlement clashed on a number of interrelated matters, including the interference of the king's council in judicial cases, the new religious settlement between the monarchy and the papacy called the Concordat of Bologna, and the persecution of heretics. Although it would be misleading to represent the parlement as fundamentally at odds with the monarchy during the first half of the sixteenth century, the magistrates were convinced that rule by law—specifically justice dispensed by the parlement—was a fundamental cornerstone of the French monarch's authority.[32] By appearing at court or by sending *lettres de jussion*, the king was usually able to impose his will on the parlement, but the magistrates had a number of lawful and effective means for bringing their concerns to the king's attention.[33] The parlements, though very much royal institutions, were by no means putty in the hands of the monarchy. Intense negotiation, persuasion, and sometimes a show of force were necessary to ensure the obedience of parlement magistrates, who often had their own agenda distinct from the king's.[34] The magistrates clearly saw themselves as a limb in a political body that was not solely directed by the monarchy. Their support for the Basochiens, whose jokes and audacity they appreciated, reflects this institutional confidence.

32. Ralph E. Giesey, "The Presidents of the Parlement at the Royal Funeral," *Sixteenth Century Journal* 7 (1976): 27–28; Robert J. Knecht, "Francis I and Paris," *History* 66 (1981): 21–27; Christopher W. Stocker, "The Politics of the Parlement of Paris in 1525," *French Historical Studies* 8 (1973): 199–200.
33. Hanley, *Lit de Justice*, 11–13, 48–85; Elizabeth A. R. Brown and Richard C. Famiglietti, *The "Lit de Justice": Semantics, Ceremonial and the Parlement of Paris, 1300–1600* (Sigmaringen: Thorbeckee, 1994), 11–18, 61–74; Mack P. Holt, "The King in Parlement: The Problem of the 'Lit de Justice' in Sixteenth-Century France," *Historical Journal* 31 (1988): 507–23; Robert J. Knecht, "France I and the 'Lit de Justice': A Legend Defended," *French History* 7 (1993): 53–83.
34. Lawrence M. Bryant, "Parlementaire Political Theory in the Parisian Royal Entry Ceremony," *Sixteenth Century Journal* 7 (1976): 15–24; Roger Doucet, *Les institutions de la France au XVIe siècle* (Paris: Picard, 1948), 1:220–23; Giesey, "Presidents," 27–28; Sheenan, *Parlement*, 188–221.

The growing assertiveness of the Parlement of Paris intensified during the rising tide of religious reform. News of theological debates, papal bills, and the religious agitation in Germany reached French magistrates' ears as early as the late 1510s and registered even more strongly after Martin Luther was excommunicated in late 1520. Reform of course did not begin with Luther. Erasmus had been urging a return to a simpler Catholic practice and emphasizing the authority of the Bible for almost a decade before Luther began publishing, and an indigenous reform movement had existed within the borders of France for several decades.[35] Convinced that true Christianity necessitated a direct engagement with the original Christian texts, humanists such as Jacques Lefèvre d'Étaples translated the Bible into French. Clergy such as Guillaume Briçonnet, bishop of Meaux, undertook a reform program in his diocese near Paris with the support of the king's sister, Marguerite of Angoulême, later of Navarre, a noblewoman known to be sympathetic to religious reform. By the early 1520s, Briçonnet and several young clerics began preaching the Bible directly to the people in a way that attracted the suspicions of both the parlement and the Sorbonne, the Faculty of Theology at the University of Paris. In 1523, an obscure hermit from Normandy was the first French subject to be executed for "Lutheran" heresy. Not long afterward, the Parlement of Paris forced Briçonnet and his followers to abjure their reformist beliefs or flee the country. Other executions followed, most notably that of Louis de Berquin, a noble member of the parlement who was executed for possessing Lutheran tracts in 1529. Although Francis I was concerned about heresy, during the 1520s he remained reluctant to condemn evangelical Catholics like Berquin to the stake. Indeed on a number of occasions, Francis attempted to block or mitigate the sentences rendered by the parlement. Instead, it was the Sorbonne and the parlement that led the initial wave of prosecutions against "Lutheran" beliefs in France.[36]

Not surprisingly then, the magistrates of the parlement rather than the king were those who first became concerned about the possibility of actors spreading heresy among the people.[37] The magistrates' wariness of theater, and religious theater in particular, came to a head in June 1541, when they objected to a theatrical performance already approved by Parisian authorities and by Francis I. The play in question was called the *Mystery of the*

35. Augustin Renaudet, *Préréforme et humanisme à Paris pendant les premières guerres d'Italie: 1494–1517* (Paris: d'Argences, 1953).
36. Roelker, *One King*, 189–205; E. William Monter, *Judging the French Reformation: Heresy Trials by Sixteenth-Century Parlements* (Cambridge, Mass.: Harvard University Press, 1999), 55–84; Linda L. Taber, "Religious Dissent within the Parlement of Paris in the Mid-Sixteenth Century: A Reassessment," *French Historical Studies* 16 (1990): 684–99.
37. AN x1a 1516, fols. 148a–49, 27 Apr. 1514; AN x1a 1521, fol. 314, 2 Sept. 1519; AN x1a 1522, fol. 44, 11 Jan. 1520; Alfred Soman, "The Theatre, Diplomacy and Censorship in the Reign of Henry IV," *Bibliothèque d'Humanisme et Renaissance* 35 (1973): 276.

Acts of the Apostles and was produced by a well-established confraternity known as the Confrérie de la Passion. This pious association had been performing religious plays in Paris since its foundation in 1402, and there was no obvious reason to doubt the orthodoxy of the organizers' religious sentiments. Indeed, the procedures by which the confrérie had gone about organizing the 1541 performance had been entirely above board. In December 1540, having received approval from the local Parisian police at the Châtelet and from the king, the organizers of the mystery play arranged a procession to announce the performance and to encourage inhabitants of Paris to participate.[38] Such a public announcement was common practice in French cities, where mystery plays recounting the life of Christ often continued for several weeks, involved hundreds of performers, and employed the services of local trades' people, who made the costumes, floats, and banners. In this case, the performance of *The Acts of the Apostles* was to take place during thirty-five separate performances between May and October 1541. Almost a month after its beginning, the parlement magistrates suddenly expressed misgivings about the project. Soon after, however, they relented, and the play went ahead as planned.[39]

The magistrates' reasons for objecting to such performances became clearer the following year when they blocked plans for another play, this time the *Mystery of the Old Testament*. They were concerned about several aspects of the proposed production. Parlement lawyers, who advocated that the play be suppressed, complained that the organizers were charging too much for admission and that the plays would distract the people of Paris from pious Corpus Christi celebrations. More importantly, they argued that the event's organizers are "ignorant men, and not learned . . . that they don't understand what they are doing."[40] Citing earlier plays organized by the Confrérie de la Passion, the lawyers accused the members of not being well versed in the Bible stories they proposed to reenact and alleged that they would add "mockeries" and inventions to the sacred text in order to prolong their performance. These included "farces and other impudent and divisive games, which are performed at the end or at the beginning" as well as statements that contradicted Catholic doctrine, such as the claim "that the Holy Spirit had not at all wanted to descend to earth."[41] Although none of the lawyers arguing the case mentions Lutheran heresy specifically, they are clearly concerned about possible irregularities in the theological content

38. Bibliothèque Historique de la Ville de Paris, MS C.P. 4338, Le cry et proclamation publicque: Pour jouer le mistere des Actes des Apostres en la ville de Paris: Faict le jeudy seiziesme jour de décembre l'an mil cinq cens quarante (Paris, 1541).
39. AN x1a 1547, fol. 12a, 23 May 1541; AN x1a 1547, fol. 47a, 10 June 1541; AN x1a 1547, fol. 68a, 21 June 1541; Graham A. Runnalls, "Theatre in Paris in the Late Middle Ages," in *Études sur les mystères* (Paris: Champion, 1998), 97–99.
40. AN x1a 4914, fol. 80, 9 Dec. 1541.
41. Ibid., fols. 80–81.

of the production.[42] Interestingly, all these concerns could be read as the fears of orthodox Catholics about dangerous reformist ideas or as the wariness of humanist Christians about the traditional beliefs of uninstructed laymen. The repeated references to the importance of the confraternity members knowing the texts of the Bible well seems an argument shaped by Renaissance humanism and an Erasmian concern for the return to authentic texts. Whatever the lawyers' motivations, their argument met with deaf ears outside of the parlement. Despite the parlement's misgivings, the Confrérie de la Passion sought and received renewed support from both the Châtelet and Francis I, thereby ensuring that the planned production took place.

This incident was one of many in which the Paris Parlement magistrates revealed themselves to be more cautious than the king about the impact of the theater on public order.[43] Far from always following the lead of the monarch, the parlement initiated censorship of farce and theater more generally, a new attitude that even affected its relationship with the Basoche.

As early as the mid-1520s, the magistrates in Paris began to have misgivings about the Basochiens' behavior at court. Even though they approved of the Basoche's performances in principle, often helping to pay for them through the 1550s, they were sometimes dismayed by the clerks' lack of civility and respect for decorum. Clerks were often reprimanded for entering the court wearing inappropriate clothes such as long Spanish-style capes, for carrying swords, or for sporting beards, all behaviors considered to be flamboyant and attention seeking in a way that was inappropriate to their station.[44] Occasionally the magistrates punished clerks who had been caught fighting on the courtyard grounds or behaving with disrespect toward their superiors. In the spring of 1553, the magistrates also protested while the clerks began playing tambourines in the courtyard of the Palais du Justice while the court was in session.[45] These rulings do not point to a complete rejection of Basoche high spirits, but they suggest a new sensitivity about courtroom civility. Whereas a hundred years earlier, the magistrates seemed content when the Basochiens were not actually fighting in the city streets, by the mid-sixteenth century their standards for public deportment had become more restrictive.

42. James K. Farge, "Early Censorship in Paris: A New Look at the Roles of the Parlement of Paris and of King Francis I," *Renaissance and Reformation* 13 (1989): 178–82; Roelker, *One King*, 189, 204, 213.
43. Michel Félibien, *Histoire de la ville de Paris* (Paris: G. Desprez et J. Desessartz, 1725), 4:702b (27 Jan. 1541), 3:623b (12 Nov. 1543), 4:114b (11 Mar. 1544).
44. AN x1a 1527, fol. 87, 11 Mar. 1525; AN x1a 1565, fol. 4, 27 April 1549; AN x1a 1616, fol. 188, 8 Mar. 1566; AN x1a 1690, fol. 318, 20 Mar. 1585; AN U*2220, Le Nain, "Registres du Parlement," fol. 40 (6 Feb. 1540); AN U*2194, Le Nain, fols. 98–100 (19 Nov. 1542). In 1535 Francis I outlawed the wearing of beards by anyone but the nobility. See Bataillard, *Histoire*, 1:116n1; Édouard-Hippolyte Gosselin, *Des usages et moeurs de MM. du Parlement de Normandie au palais de justice de Rouen* (Rouen: Cagniard, 1868), 24; Maugis, *Histoire*, 1:364–66.
45. AN x1a 4953, fol. 36a, 13 April 1553.

The parlement magistrates were also becoming more concerned about the content of the Basoche's plays. In May 1536, the Paris Basoche was prohibited from performing because the magistrates had not yet seen what the clerks wanted to perform; only after a private viewing would they allow a public performance to take place.[46] Two years later, in January 1538, the Basoche was allowed to perform during the upcoming Carnival season only on condition that the performers adhere to the written text and omit "the things that had been crossed out," a statement clearly indicating that a magistrate had read through the play with pen in hand.[47] Similar rulings can be found through the 1540s. Because in none of these cases do we know which plays the Basochiens sought to perform, we cannot know what was censored, yet context provides clues. Certainly, as an institution now very much concerned about religious heresy, the parlement would not have tolerated open discussion of religious reform. The parlement magistrates' new policy of direct censorship seems to have been effective and to have been sustained more or less consistently after the mid-1530s. By the 1550s, the magistrates repeatedly warned the clerks to keep their performances "modest" and lacking in "scandal."[48] Whereas previously regulation of the Basoche had been reactive and episodic, it seems that the magistrates were increasingly keeping a close eye on all Basoche activity, including its theatrical performances.

Parlement censorship did not, however, suppress all Basoche satire. In May of 1538, the Basoche performed a play that some members of the court thought should have been censored more aggressively. Later that summer, two solicitors working at the parlement filed a complaint against the Basochiens for slander. They accused eight young clerks—Anthoine Baulm, Louis Clochet, Guillaume Cappitaine, Armand Petit, Guillaume Le Gauffre, Anne Charenton, Florent Le Grand, and Estienne Descroux—of having shamed them during a performance. The solicitors claimed that they had tried to discipline the clerks themselves but had failed and so had to take their complaint to the magistrates. The accused clerks adamantly denied their

---

46. AN x1a 1539, fol. 281, 17 May 1536; AN U*2033, Le Nain, fol. 30, 24 Jan. 1536.

47. AN x1a 1540, fol. 121, 23 Jan. 1538. Other examples of the magistrates' censorship of the Basoche include AN x1a 1539, fol. 284, 20 May 1536; AN x1a 1545, fol. 336, 7 May 1540; AN x1a 1552, fol. 321, 19 Mar. 1544; AN x1a 1599, fol. 348a, 5 Jan. 1562; AN x1a 1604, fol. 136, 4 Jan. 1563; ADSM 1 B 534, 5 May 1550; BM Bordeaux MS 369, Savignac, "Extraits," 1:207 (30 Dec. 1533), 1:260 (27 Feb. 1538), 1:365 (16 Jan. 1545), 1:556 (8 Aug. 1553).

48. *Arrêts* that refer to the need of the Basoche to avoid scandal include AN x1a 1547, fol. 12a, 23 June 1540; AN x1a 1582, fol. 7, 8 Jan 1558; AN x1a 1604, fol. 118, 31 Dec. 1562. During the 1540s and 1550s, the magistrates prohibited the Basochiens from performing more often than previously. See AN x1a 1545, fol. 336, 7 May 1540; AN x1a 1552, fol. 321, 19 Mar. 1544; AN x1a 1554, 10 Mar. 1545; AN x1a 4947, fol. 413, 12 Jan. 1552; AN x1a 1572, fol. 147, 2 June 1552. Nevertheless, most years, they continued to pay for their plays and processions. See AN x1a 1549, 6 June 1542; AN x1a 1551, fol. 85a, 6 June 1543; AN x1a 1554, fol. 289a, 29 Jan. 1545; AN x1a 1557, fol. 310, 18 Mar. 1546; AN x1a 1565, fol. 18, 9 May 1549; AN x1a 1569, fol. 308, 2 July 1551; AN x1a 1582, fol. 7, 8 Jan 1556.

involvement in the slanderous skit. Although the magistrates were not convinced by the Basochiens' protestations of innocence, they nevertheless concluded that the accused clerks had "done this out of thoughtlessness rather than malice."[49] As a result, the magistrates merely chastised the wrongdoers, warning the young clerks that if they engaged in similar behavior in the future, they would forfeit the opportunity of ever being promoted to the solicitor's bench.

This case was exceptional not because the clerks slandered someone during a farcical performance but because they were referred to by name. In most sixteenth-century rulings concerning the Paris Basoche, the association's members were not named individually but were referred to en masse or according to their Basoche rank. This absence of individual names was not accidental. In fact, one of the threats the magistrates regularly used to discipline recalcitrant Basoche performers was to warn them that if they disobeyed the court's rulings, their "very own private names" would be exposed.[50] Public disclosure of the clerks' names and those of their employers was clearly undesirable. As a result, the slandered solicitors in the 1538 incident may have felt avenged by the magistrates' ruling, even though the clerks suffered no punishment other than public exposure. Notary records confirm that most of these young men did in fact go on to become solicitors at the parlement, so their satirical Maytime performances did not in the end compromise their careers at court.[51] Despite rising religious tensions, the 1538 case suggests that traditional concerns about honor and dishonor still predominated in the Basochiens' performance. Mere mockery of one's employer, which often took the form of sexual slander, was still considered an acceptable part of the Basoche repertoire. During the last decades of the French Renaissance, the magistrates were still willing to patronize Basoche theater as long as its satire remained social rather than religious or political in nature.

It is one thing to understand why the magistrates wanted to contain the satire of the Basochiens' festivities, but quite another to comprehend why the Basochiens complied with their demands. Of course the magistrates did have financial power over the clerks: the Basochiens were accustomed to receiving cash disbursements from the parlement to help pay for their lavish

49. AN x1a 4906, fol. 589b, 6 Aug. 1538.
50. AN x1a 1632, fol. 57, 8 May 1571. Similar warnings can be found in AN x1a 1539, fol. 284, 20 May 1536; AN x1a 1599, fol. 348a, 5 Jan. 1562; AN x1a 1628, fol. 249a, 11 Jan. 1570.
51. Anne Charenton, Archives Nationales Minutier Central (AN MC) VIII:73, 18 June 1546; Guillaume Le Gauffre, AN MC VIII:68, fol. 210, 13 Dec. 1540; AN MC VIII:70, fol. 497v, 13 Mar. 1543; Guillaume Cappitaine and Florent le Grand, in *Inventaire des registres des insinuations du Châtelet de Paris, règnes de François I et Henri II*, ed. Émile Campardon and Alexandre Tuetey (Paris: Imprimerie Nationale, 1906), 115n1063, 117n1094, 132n1231, 234n2071. Other examples of Basoche leaders being promoted to the post of parlement solicitor include AN x1a 1611, fol. 185a, 5 Jan. 1565; AN x1a 1613, fol. 11a, 4 May 1565.

processions and performances. Merely threatening to deprive them of their annual pension might have been sufficient incentive to encourage them to self-censor their plays. But the clerks had an additional reason for wanting to obey the magistrates: by the 1540s, they were increasingly dependent on the parlement magistrates for securing their jobs. Much more was at stake than a few laughs each January and May. As the sixteenth century continued, clerks at the parlements, not only in Paris but also in the provinces, found it more and more difficult to graduate from their long apprenticeship and to a secure post at the court. In Bordeaux, individual clerks tried to parlay their service as king of the Basoche into a permanent post as a solicitor; similarly, in Rouen, the Basochiens were willing to curb their traditional festivities in order to be able to secure the shrinking numbers of solicitor posts.[52] The Basochiens faced a job squeeze created by the regulatory assertiveness of the monarchy. Beginning with Francis I, French kings sought to transform the profession of solicitor into a venal office-holding class, and the Basochiens paid the price.

The profession of solicitor, like that of barrister, had traditionally been a liberal profession in France: these legal officials were self-employed entrepreneurs who sold their services to clients and received no wage from the courts in which they argued cases or prepared legal paperwork. As a result, unlike the parlement magistrates, who increasingly had to pay the king of France for the privilege of sitting as a judge on one of his benches, solicitors had not been making regular contributions to the king's coffers. Francis I and his successors decided to rectify this situation by regulating how many solicitors served at the parlements and demanding that each pay the king a sum of money to secure a permanent post. Although the king was moderately successful in imposing limits on the number of solicitors practicing at the various parlements, his broader aim—to make all solicitor posts venal offices—was not fully achieved until the middle of the seventeenth century. In the meantime, clerks who hoped to become solicitors found themselves in a difficult situation. The number of solicitors was now restricted to 250 at the Paris Parlement and to much smaller numbers at the provincial courts, for example to 50 at the Parlement of Bordeaux.[53] Technically, the magistrates of the parlement were now prohibited from accepting new solicitors until the older ones died or retired. In practice, however, the magistrates,

52. ADSM 1 B 619, 23 Feb. 1571; ADSM 1 B 663, 23 Dec. 1580; ADG 1 B 81, fol. 196, 7 May 1532; ADG 1 B 84, fol. 234, 30 May 1534; ADG 1 B 210, fol. 182, 12 Jan. 1560; ADG 1 B 210, fol. 345, 16 Feb. 1560; Métivier, *Chronique*, 2:287 (16 Dec. 1559), 2:330–31 (15 and 20 Nov. 1560). Unlike the Paris Parlement magistrates, the Bordeaux magistrates were wary of allowing clerks to serve in the name of other solicitors. See Métivier, *Chronique*, 2:7 (12 Feb. 1551), 2:83–84 (19 Jan. 1555), 2:218 (2 July 1558), 2:256–57 (23 June 1559); C.-B.-F. Boscheron Des Portes, *Histoire du Parlement de Bordeaux depuis sa créâtion jusqu'à sa suppression (1451–1790)* (Bordeaux: Lefebvre, 1877), 1:115–16.
53. Bataillard, *Histoire*, 1:102, 116–17.

who probably resented the king's heavy-handed interference in matters that traditionally had been under their control, surreptitiously defied the king's orders. Without actually admitting more solicitors to posts at the court, they allowed long-serving clerks to serve in the name of specific solicitors; in other words, they allowed them to practice fraudulently. In 1549, the king was dismayed to discover that over fifty clerks were practicing in this way at the Paris Parlement.[54] Without such collaboration, few Basochiens would have become solicitors in the 1530s and 1540s. Unless they wished to give up the possibility of secure employment at a time of economic contraction, the Basoche, both in Paris and the provinces, had every incentive to comply with the magistrates' requests.

The fact that the Basochiens continued to perform farces at all during these decades of rising religious tensions and intensified regulation is itself a testament to the enjoyment that their performances brought to the magistrates and to the wider Parisian public. The parlement magistrates, who year after year continued to pay for their celebrations, clearly did not find the clerks' jokes inherently scandalous and shocking as they would in the decades to come. Nevertheless, by the middle of the sixteenth century, the Basoche were increasingly being held in check: censorship had become a regular accompaniment of Basoche performance, and the clerks' rowdy antics during court sessions were now frowned upon.

During the French Renaissance, students at the universities were also well known for performing farce. In the third book of his satirical novel *Gargantua pantagruel*, Rabelais recalls his involvement in a farce at the University of Montpellier. We have plenty of evidence that such farces were a common occurrence.[55] Like the members of festive societies, student actors performed not only at traditional Catholic festivals, in particular the Feast of Kings after Christmas, but also at civic events and before the king.[56] Also like festive society members, students often spent large sums on elaborate costumes, and sometimes after slandering someone on the stage would fight with those insulted in the city streets. Of all the Renaissance farceurs, however, university students were of the highest social status and were, at least initially, best protected from the wrath of those

---

54. AN x1a 1554, fol. 465, 9 Mar. 1545; AN x1a 1554, fol. 546, 1 Apr. 1545; AN x1a 1555, fol. 42, 16 May 1545; AN x1a 1555, fol. 415, 24 July 1545; AN x1a 1556, fol. 160, 26 Aug. 1545; Bataillard, *Histoire*, 1:107–9, 238.

55. François Rabelais, *Le tiers livre des faicts et dicts héroiques du bon Pantagruel*, ed. Jean Plattard (Paris: Société des Belles Lettres, 1948), 137–38 (chap. 34). Studies of French Renaissance student theater are scarce. See Edmé Cougny, *Des représentations dramatiques et particulièrement de la comédie politique dans les collèges* (Paris: Imprimerie Impériale, 1868); L.-V. Gofflot, *Le théâtre au collège du moyen-âge à nos jours* (Paris: Champion, 1907), 14–87; Petit de Julleville, *Comédiens*, 291–323.

56. Durieux, *Théâtre*, 166–70; Gofflot, *Théâtre*, 28; Petit de Julleville, *Répertoire*, 382, 395–97; Jean d'Auton, *Chroniques de Louis XII*, ed. René de Maulde La Clavière (Paris: Renouard, 1893), 3:352–54.

they mocked. Confusion at the universities about jurisdiction over student behavior meant that students were sometimes allowed more leeway than were members of other festive associations. Yet conversely, because student actors so often touched on questions of religious policy, both university and secular officials were trying to censor their performances by the 1520s. These efforts, not always successful, delineate very clearly how the bounds of satire were changing during the last decades before the outbreak of the Wars of Religion. When they took on the topics of Catholic religious practice and the corruption of the Church, students pushed their right to consult with authorities—the right implied by the metaphor of the body politic—beyond its acceptable limits.

French universities, first established during the thirteenth century, had a long history of excellent scholarship and a tradition of intellectual independence that rendered them renowned throughout Europe. Traditionally, students in Paris and in the provinces were granted considerable leeway in the conduct of their affairs. The older universities at Paris, Montpellier, and Toulouse were founded under the auspices of the papacy rather than those of the French monarchy; they were independent "universes" that had their own statutes and regulations.[57] Universities claimed legal authority over all their members, including students. Petty student crime and infractions, short of physical violence, were usually dealt with by the university because the students claimed clerical immunity from secular prosecution.[58] During the late medieval period, students were notorious for taking advantage of this liberty. Contemporaries complained that they took decades to complete their degrees and were rarely seen at their studies. One way that students amused themselves was with amateur theater. Since at least the beginning of the fourteenth century, students, particularly those studying at the arts faculty, were well known for performing farces, sotties, and comic morality plays that were "indecent" and slanderous.[59] University rectors and the principals of the collèges did not necessarily approve of

57. Hastings Rashdall, *The Universities of Europe in the Middle Ages* (Oxford: Clarendon Press, 1895), 1:299–316; André Tuilier, *Histoire de l'Université de Paris et de la Sorbonne* (Paris: Nouvelle Librairie de France, 1994), 1:41–47; Roger Chartier, Marie-Madeleine Compère, and Dominique Julia, *L'éducation en France du XVIe au XVIIIe siècle* (Paris: SEDES, 1976), 249–52; Dewald, *Formation*, 22–24; Cyril Eugene Smith, *The University of Toulouse in the Middle Ages* (Milwaukee: Marquette University Press, 1958), 32–55; Jacques Verger, *Les universités françaises au moyen âge* (Leiden: Brill, 1995), 207–8; *L'Université de Caen: Son passé, son présent* (Caen: Imprimerie Artistique Malherbe de Caen, 1932), 19–61.
58. Pearl Kibre, *Scholarly Privileges in the Middle Ages* (Cambridge, Mass.: Mediaeval Academy of America, 1962), 85–131; Philippe Ariès, *Centuries of Childhood: A Social History of Family Life*, trans. Robert Baldick (New York: Vintage, 1965), 148–67; Pearl Kibre, *The Nations in the Mediaeval Universities* (Cambridge, Mass.: Mediaeval Academy of America, 1948), 112; Tuilier, *Histoire*, 1:244, 248–52.
59. Petit de Julleville, *Comédiens*, 296.

the students' antics, but their efforts to chastise them do not seem to have been very effective.[60]

By the end of the fifteenth century, however, the corporate autonomy of the universities and the freedom of students to speak their minds were increasingly undermined. After retaking Paris from the English in 1436, Charles VII sought, not surprisingly, to discipline the University of Paris, which had spoken out openly against his authority during the course of the conflict. During the next ten years, the king and the university clashed repeatedly: on six separate occasions, to protest royal infringements of university privileges, the university rector ordered a complete cessation of all lectures and sermons. In 1446, claiming that such petty disputes were taking up too much of his time, Charles delegated authority for all matters relating to the university to the Parlement of Paris. For the University of Paris, whose scholars had accompanied French kings on diplomatic missions in the early fifteenth century, the king's ruling undermined both the university's honor and its political power.[61] Under Charles VIII and Louis XII the privileges of the University of Paris came under further assault: these kings limited the number of years that students could claim tax-exempt status and narrowed the jurisdiction of the university's internal regulatory body.[62] Similar erosion of corporate autonomy occurred at several other French universities, where royal officials repeatedly ignored traditional tax exemptions and interfered with student discipline.[63]

One of the reasons that kings could justify violating the clerical immunity of university students by the end of the fifteenth century was that fewer and fewer students were studying to become priests. Most students, whose ages ranged widely from ten to twenty-five, were drawn from a relatively narrow swath of French society, and they aimed for secular careers after graduation.[64]

60. Robert Bossuat, "Le théâtre scolaire au Collège de Navarre," in *Mélanges d'histoire du théâtre du moyen âge et de la Renaissance, offerts à Gustave Cohen, professeur honoraire en Sorbonne* (Paris: Nizet, 1950), 171–72; André Bossuat and Robert Bossuat, *Deux moralités inédites composées et représentées en 1427 et 1428 au Collège de Navarre* (Paris: d'Argences, 1955); Verger, *Universités*, 203–7; Dorothy MacKay Quynn and Harold Sinclair Snellgrove, "Slanderous Comedies at the University of Orléans in 1447," *Modern Language Notes* 57 (1942): 185–88.

61. Kibre, *Privileges*, 206–13; Tuilier, *Histoire*, 1:238–41; Verger, *Universités*, 210–19.

62. Kibre, *Privileges*, 189–91, 213, 220–25.

63. Smith, *University*, 177–87; Jacques Verger, "Crise et mutation à la fin du moyen âge," in *Histoire des universités en France*, ed. Jacques Verger (Paris: Privat, 1986), 120–25.

64. At any given time during the sixteenth century, a few hundred University of Paris students were genuinely poor and were supported by scholarships. See Ariès, *Centuries*, 191–97, 238–40; L. W. B. Brockliss, "Patterns of Attendance at the University of Paris, 1400–1800," *Historical Journal* 21 (1978): 511, 530–34; Dominique Julia, "Les institutions et les hommes," in *Histoire des universités en France*, ed. Jacques Verger (Paris: Privat, 1986), 180–82; Jacques Verger, "Universités et société en France à la fin du moyen âge," in Verger, *Histoire des universités*, 89–100.

Approximately 15 percent of the 10,000 to 11,000 students were sons of the old nobility; most of the rest were the sons of financial and judicial officials. These young men usually completed the arts course since they required further degrees—usually in the law—to pursue careers in royal service. In time, they would become the financial officials or urban magistrates who patronized farcical theater during the first half of the sixteenth century. In contrast, other students—the sons of petty royal officials, prominent merchants, wealthy farmers, and successful artisans—probably studied at collège for only a few years and then supplemented their education with hands-on experience. The education of Oliver Lefèvre, the son of a registrar at the Paris Parlement, was typical. After learning to read at home, he attended the Collège de Navarre for three years before apprenticing with a solicitor at the Chambre des Comptes, where he presumably became a member of the Basoche.[65] By the middle of the century, many Basochiens and even members of some of the more prominent festive societies in the provinces, such as the Conards of Rouen and the Mère Folle of Dijon, would have at some point in their youth attended a French university, if only briefly. As they grew older and attained positions of some responsibility within their communities, many of these men retained links with festive performance. Thus, the prominence of satirical theatrical performance at the collèges of the Renaissance ensured its continuation as an honorable youthful pastime for decades afterward.

Despite efforts to reform the university, the lifestyle of most Renaissance students remained relatively unstructured. Both in Paris and in the provinces, most nonresident students lived in the homes of junior masters or with artisan families, where collège officials had little opportunity to regulate their behavior.[66] Overall, there is no evidence that student debauchery declined during the French Renaissance: throughout the sixteenth century, local officials and memoir writers complained that students continued to visit brothels, drink in taverns, and fight one another with illegal weapons.[67] What had changed, however, was royal officials' authority over these students. By the sixteenth century, the universities no longer defended students who broke laws or disturbed the peace but increasingly cooperated with secular officials who sought to contain their excesses.

Inevitably, these institutional changes had an effect on the censorship of student theater. By the mid-fifteenth century, at the same time that they began to curb Basoche performances, the Paris Parlement magistrates also

65. *Journal d'Olivier Lefèvre d'Ormesson et extraits des mémoires d'André Lefèvre d'Ormesson*, ed. M. Chéruel (Paris: Imprimerie Impériale, 1860), 1:iv–vii.
66. Ariès, *Centuries*, 164–70.
67. Sophie Cassagnes-Brouquet, "La violence des étudiants à Toulouse à la fin du XVe et au XVIe siècle," *Annales du Midi* 94 (1982): 245–62; Jean-Baptiste-Louis Crévier, *Histoire de l'Université de Paris, depuis son origine jusqu'en l'année 1600* (Paris: Desaint et Saillant, 1761), 6:29–50; Léon Roulland, "La Foire Saint-Germain sous les règnes de Charles IX, de Henri III et de Henri IV," *Mémoires de la Société de Paris et de l'Ile-de-France* 3 (1876): 192–218.

lost patience with student satire. The magistrates both insisted on their right to punish recalcitrant students and encouraged university officials to develop a more systematic approach to the censorship of student performance. As early as 1468, when parlement magistrates complained to the university that students had been roaming the Paris streets on the feast days of Saint Catherine, Saint Martin, and Saint Nicolas wearing masks, the university rector agreed that royal officials could imprison them.[68] The following year the rector announced that all student celebrations on those saints' days were prohibited indefinitely. In 1483, again at the insistence of the Parlement of Paris, which deemed that "the principals . . . allowed plays or comedies to be shown in their collèges containing insufficient academic dignity and honor," the rector Thomas Ruscher de Gamundia ruled that "it is not permitted to play any shameful games that dishonor honest people; in short, that no one can perform any play, unless it has been seen and examined by the Principals or by their masters."[69] The university now established a basic procedure for the censorship of student theater: collège principals and masters would be held accountable to the parlement for their students' behavior.

These new forms of control by no means reduced the mirth of students at the University of Paris at the turn of the sixteenth century. A farce probably written and performed around 1500 by students at the Collège de Navarre in Paris contains no contemporary political and religious references but remains full of social satire and bawdy humor.[70] In *The Tailor and Esopet*, the comedy hinges on a simple trick that Esopet, a tailor's apprentice, plays on his master. The scene opens with Esopet angry with his master for having eaten a meal of partridge without saving any for him. Deciding to take revenge, Esopet makes mischief during a visit to the home of a noble customer. By way of making general conversation, the nobleman asks whether Esopet's master is a good workman. Esopet replies that he is but that he is afflicted with a terrible malady. Suddenly solemn, the apprentice describes how his master sometimes enters a trancelike state in which he is overcome with a desire to attack anyone who happens to be in his presence. The nobleman, appropriately shocked, questions Esopet about the symptoms of his master's malady. Esopet replies that one always knows that a trance is starting when his master looks furtively from side to side and taps his workbench. Intrigued, the nobleman visits the tailor to see the manifestations of this dread disease for himself. Inevitably, when asked some question about the garment his client commissioned, the tailor begins looking furtively

68. Quoted in César-Égasse Du Boulay, *Historia Universitatis Parisiensis* (Paris: Pierre de Bresche, 1673), 5:656. For similar rulings, see ibid., 5:777, 783; Constantin Gérard, *Histoire du Châtelet et du Parlement de Paris* (Paris: Cognet, 1847), 61.
69. Quoted in Du Boulay, *Historia*, 5:761.
70. Petit de Julleville, *Comédiens*, 185; Emmanuel Philipot, *Trois farces du "Recueil de Londres": Recherches sur l'ancien théâtre français* (Rennes: Plihon, 1931), 15–19.

for his scissors and tapping on his workbench. The noble, fearing that the master is about to attack, launches a preemptive strike and gives the master a solid thrashing. Esopet's ruse is quickly exposed, but instead of repenting, the defiant apprentice argues that he was only repaying his master for his gluttony.[71] Like many farces, this play mocks all the characters, but particularly those of higher social class. The master is punished for his greed, and the nobleman is characterized as dull witted and inclined to violence.

It was not only farces that French students performed at the universities. Italian humanistic studies began to cross the Alps in the late fifteenth century, renewing French scholars' interest in classical historical texts and poetry, including the comedies of Plautus and Terence. Despite the Sorbonne's sometimes hostile attitude toward humanism, individual masters at the arts collèges began stressing the study of rhetoric in their classes during the first decades of the sixteenth century.[72] These pedagogical innovations gradually began to transform its students' rowdy *jeux* into refined neoclassical performances. Basing their pedagogy on that of the Italian academies that taught young men Latin rhetoric as training for public service, sixteenth-century French collège masters encouraged students to demonstrate their linguistic skills on the stage. In Paris, Ravisius Viater was writing humanist Latin comedies as early as the 1510s. By midcentury, even at provincial collèges, masters were expected to write and direct neoclassical tragedies and comedies in which the students could demonstrate, as Michel de Montaigne recalls later in life, "an assured countenance, a suppleness of voice and gesture."[73]

During the high Renaissance of the 1550s, the patronage of Henry II (1547–59) further encouraged students to turn away from rowdy and satirical farces. During this period, collèges affiliated with the University of Paris were the venue of choice for the rhetorical experiments of an ambitious group of poets known as the Pléiade. Pierre de Ronsard, student of the respected scholar Dorat, reputedly performed his own translation of Aristophanes' *Plutus* in 1549 at the Collège de Coquerat. A few years later, Henry II attended a performance at the Hôtel de Reims of another young

---

71. "Le Couturier et Esopet," in *Recueil de farces, 1450–1550*, ed. André Tissier (Paris: Droz, 1986), 2:131–85; Petit de Julleville, *Comédiens*, 292.
72. Gwendolyn Blotevogel, "Humanism and Church Reform in France: The Role of Parisian-Trained Provincial College Masters before 1562," in *In Laudem Caroli: Renaissance and Reformation Studies for Charles G. Nauert*, ed. James V. Mehl (Kirksville, Mo.: Thomas Jefferson University Press, 1998), 136; Anthony Grafton, "Teacher, Text and Pupil in the Renaissance Classroom: A Case Study from a Parisian College," *History of Universities* 1 (1981): 44–48.
73. Michel de Montaigne, *Les essais de Michel de Montaigne, publiés d'après l'exemplaire de Bordeaux*, ed. Fortunat Strowski (Bordeaux: F. Pech, 1906), 1:229 (essay 1:26); Petit de Julleville, *Comédiens*, 293, 303; Blotevogel, "Humanism," 136–40; Anthony Grafton and Lisa Jardine, *From Humanism to the Humanities: Education and the Liberal Arts in Fifteenth- and Sixteenth-Century Europe* (London: Duckworth, 1986), 161–200. For two collège master contracts that specify writing and directing plays as part of the job description, see Marie Madeleine Compère, *Du collège au lycée (1500–1850): Généalogie de l'enseignement secondaire français* (Paris: Gallimard, 1985), 22–23; *Recueil d'actes*, 1:499 (4 Sept. 1543).

poet's classical play: Étienne Jodelle's tragedy *Cleopatra captive*, based on Plutarch's history of the famous love affair, was hailed as the first original French-language comedy. A second performance of Jodelle's comedy occurred soon afterward at the Collège de Boncourt before a large audience, "where all the windows were decorated by innumerable persons of distinction and the courtyard so full of students that the doors of the collège were bursting."[74] Whereas French kings had long commissioned students to perform for their pleasure, it was only in the mid-sixteenth century that such performances began to shift from traditional to classical genres. This royal praise for more refined plays arguably had far more impact on the gradual transformation of university theater than did any royal edict or internal effort to censor student performance of farce.

Nevertheless, we should not draw too sharp a contrast between neoclassical plays and farce. French kings continued to enjoy farcical fare long after they began to appreciate the poetry of the Pléiade, and much collège theater of the Renaissance, such as Barthélemy Aneau's *Lyon Marchant*, was a hybrid colored by both farcical elements and classical allusions. Despite the fact that humanist scholars began to distance themselves in principle from the farce (and from the late medieval French language more generally), by the 1550s much sixteenth-century French comedy continued to mix the classical and the farcical with an equanimity that would become foreign to seventeenth-century French theatrical tastes.

University and collège students profited from the relative openness of theatrical tastes during the Renaissance to continue performing farces throughout the sixteenth century. As religious tensions intensified in the 1520s, some reform-minded students and rectors indeed found that the traditional farce was an apt medium through which to express their doubts about the church. Not surprisingly, their mockeries of Catholicism resulted in discipline at the hands of the Paris Parlement. The parlement, with the support of the Sorbonne, sought to keep reformist ideas off the Parisian stage, and as a result during the 1520s it began to take a more aggressive stance toward student theater. At least twice during the 1520s, the Paris Parlement magistrates, seemingly on their own initiative, warned University of Paris collège principals to prevent their students from performing scandalous plays.[75] They did not do so at the behest of the king. In December 1525, when the parlement issued the second of these warnings, Francis was absent from Paris,

74. Étienne Pasquier, *Les recherches de la France*, ed. Marie-Madeleine Fragonard and François Roudaut (Paris: Champion, 1996), 2:1416; Raymond Lebègue, "La Pléiade et le théâtre," in *Études sur le théâtre français* (Paris: Nizet, 1977), 1:208–9; Tuilier, *Histoire*, 1:369–72; *Ronsard et ses amis*, ed. Madeleine Jurgens (Paris: Archives Nationales, 1985), 59–67; Frances Amelia Yates, *The French Academies of the Sixteenth Century* (London, 1947; reprint, London: Routledge, 1988), 14–21, 236–74.
75. Félibien, *Histoire*, 4:645a (27 Dec. 1523), 4:674b (29 Dec. 1525); Petit de Julleville, *Comédiens*, 301; Knecht, "Francis I and the 'Lit de Justice,'" 57–72; Knecht, "Francis I and Paris," 25; Maugis, *Histoire*, 1:559–66.

imprisoned at Madrid after losing the battle of Pavia. Parisians' confidence in the regent, François's mother Louise of Savoy, was mixed, and the parlement sometimes challenged her authority directly. Only a few months earlier, a group of young men, thought to be members of the Basoche, had run through Paris claiming that the king was dead, which caused a ruckus until the rumors were squelched.[76] The magistrates of the parlement, clearly afraid of serious religious or civic conflict, ordered the principals "not to tolerate or permit to have performed in the said collèges or elsewhere by students and by members of the university any farces, masquerades, or sotties at the next Feast of Kings" and expressed concern that such a performance could undermine public order during this time of troubles.[77]

Although these *arrêts* do not complain explicitly about the dangers of religious satire in the students' performances, this question must have been on the magistrates' minds. We know that farce was being used to advocate evangelical reform and even a break with the Catholic Church during this period. Even before two French-language sotties advocating religious reform were performed in Geneva in 1523 and 1524, students at the University of Paris began to take issue with the Sorbonne's defensive approach to humanist critiques of contemporary Catholic religious practice. In 1521, students mocked Nicholas Bèda, the notoriously conservative syndic of the Sorbonne, and were severely chastised for having done so.[78] By the early 1530s, students in Clairac, at the University of Caen, and at the University of Toulouse took advantage of traditional Catholic festivals to stage farcical plays or to speak publicly about religious reform.[79] These performances were probably similar in content to the *Farce of the Théologastres*, a play perhaps written by the accused heretic Louis de Berquin in the mid-1520s.[80] Although in many ways similar to satirical morality plays of the fifteenth century, the *Farce of the Théologastres* not only condemns the corruption of the Church but also provides a radical new theological solution to the problem of reform: direct engagement by individual laypersons with the vernacular text of the Bible. The parlement, wary of religious reform in any shape, had reason to be concerned about the content of student theater during this early period of heated debate. Nevertheless, the magistrates continued to pay for Basoche performances throughout the 1520s.[81] The magistrates were clearly not hostile to all sotties and morality plays, only those that had

---

76. *Journal d'un bourgeois de Paris sous le règne de François 1er (1515–1536)*, ed. Ludovic Lalanne (Paris: Jules Renouard, 1854), 268–69.
77. Félibien, *Histoire*, 4:674b (29 Dec. 1525).
78. Du Boulay, *Historia*, 6:132.
79. Jonathan Beck, *Théâtre et propagande aux débuts de la Réforme: Six pièces polémiques du Recueil La Vallière* (Geneva: Slatkine, 1986), 39; Monter, *Judging*, 65.
80. *La farce de Théologastres*, ed. Claude Longeon (Geneva: Droz, 1989).
81. AN x1a 1524, fol. 251, 31 May 1522; AN x1a 1526, fol. 232, 25 May 1524; AN x1a 1529, fol. 279, 16 June 1526; AN x1a 1530, fol. 266, 5 June 1527; AN x1a 1531, fol. 280, 18 June 1528.

the potential to undermine public order or to exacerbate tensions within the Catholic Church.

Indeed, the magistrates may have encouraged or at least sanctioned satirical student theater that was explicitly antireform. Such a performance occurred on at least one occasion, and not surprisingly, neither the parlement nor the Sorbonne protested in the least. In October 1533, arts students at the university performed a play that satirized the evangelical leanings of the king's sister, Marguerite, Queen of Navarre. She was portrayed as a religious fanatic whose reading of the Bible drove her to heresy. Dismayed that his sister was being maligned publicly, the king sent the chief constable of Paris to imprison two masters at the collège who were responsible for the performance. None of the three contemporaries who provide an account of this performance—Johann Sturm, John Calvin, or Théodore Bèze—mentions the direct involvement of the parlement. This incident was soon eclipsed by the Sorbonne's banning of Marguerite's poem, *Mirror of a Sinful Soul*, a few months later. Francis again intervened directly on his sister's behalf, forcing the Sorbonne to rescind its ban.[82] Francis's aggressive measures against both student theater and the Sorbonne's ban indicate the degree to which the university's autonomy had been compromised by the mid-sixteenth century. Francis considered it within his rights not only to punish students who spoke out about religious heresy but also to prevent the Faculty of Theology from determining whether a treatise expressed orthodox Catholicism or not.

Despite his efforts to defend his sister against accusations of heresy, Francis I eventually began to cooperate closely with the parlement and the Sorbonne to combat the threat of Protestantism. Most historians see 1534 as a turning point in the king's attitude toward religious reform. Whereas previously he had been reluctant to label evangelicals as heretics, after this date he was more willing to condemn those with reformist leanings. The catalyst for this shift in policy was an audacious placard posted throughout Paris in October 1534. The placard claimed that the Catholic sacraments were shams born of the Devil and that they did not contribute to salvation. In particular, it mocked the Catholic conception of transubstantiation, the doctrine that the bread and wine were transformed into the body and blood of Christ during the Mass. The placard, which was also posted near the king's residence in Blois, expressed the ideas of

82. Théodore de Bèze, *Histoire ecclésiastique des églises réformées au royaume de France* (Lille: Leleux, 1841), 1:8; James K. Farge, *Orthodoxy and Reform in Early Modern France: The Faculty of Theology of Paris, 1500–1543* (Leiden: Brill, 1985), 203–4; *Correspondance des réformateurs dans les pays de langue française*, ed. A.-L. Herminjard (Geneva: H. Georg, 1866–97), 3:93–94, 107–8; Larissa Juliet Taylor, *Heresy and Orthodoxy in Sixteenth-Century Paris: François le Picart and the Beginnings of the Catholic Reformation* (Leiden: Brill, 1999), 45–46. These reformers' letters refute Petit de Julleville's and Cougny's claim that the 1533 performance took place at the Collège de Montaigu. See Petit de Julleville, *Comédiens*, 303; Cougny, *Représentations*, 44–45.

the Swiss reformation and insisted on a separation between the spiritual and the physical worlds that many sixteenth-century Catholics could not sanction. Francis was shocked and responded harshly. In Paris, more than two dozen individuals were tried and executed for heresy in the months that followed.[83] Soon afterward, Francis gave both the parlements and the Sorbonne enhanced authority to define heresy and purge it from France. He also turned to the Sorbonne to develop a list of doctrines that would define Catholic orthodoxy and began to uphold its efforts to censor any publications that leaned toward reform. Over the next decades, the royally sanctioned Index of Forbidden Books (1544) was used to justify the harassment and prosecution of many French printers suspected of heretical sympathies.[84] Wary of granting too much authority to the clergy, however, Francis also urged secular law courts, specifically the parlements, to prosecute heretics. During the mid-1530s, not only in Paris but also at the other parlements, the number of heresy cases increased as the French sought to suppress religious debate with the iron arm of the law.[85] Thus as a result of religious dissension, both the Sorbonne and the parlements actually gained authority and a voice in royal policy during this period.

It was not only at the universities that students performed satirical and religiously charged material. By the 1530s, the humanist reforms at the University of Paris inspired dozens of provincial cities to found new collèges. As knowledge of Latin culture and the law became a prerequisite for many royal offices, provincial city councilors needed local institutions that could provide their sons with the training required to climb the ladder of royal service.[86] From the outset, city councilors took an active role in the day-to-day administration of these collèges. In Lyon, the future principal of the Collège de la Madeleine proposed a collège charter to the city council in 1540, which was duly approved. The charter specified the educational qualifications of the four masters to be hired and made clear that the principal's authority in all educational matters was derived from the city council.[87] City leaders expected these new schools to teach their sons the skills necessary for civic leadership and to imbue them with virtue and "good morals."[88] Consequently, they insisted that instructors hold a university arts degree, swear to be good Catholics, and teach only the texts approved by the council. Sometimes,

83. Monter, *Judging*, 69–75.
84. Elizabeth Armstrong, *Before Copyright: The French Book-Privilege System, 1498–1526* (Cambridge: Cambridge University Press, 1990), 100–105; *Histoire de l'édition française*, vol. 1, *Le livre conquérant*, ed. Roger Chartier, Henri-Jean Martin, and Jean-Pierre Vivet (Paris: Promodis, 1982), 1:316–21; Francis Higman, *Censorship and the Sorbonne* (Geneva: Droz, 1979); James K. Farge, *Le parti conservateur au XVIe siècle: Université et Parlement de Paris à l'époque de la Renaissance et de la Réforme* (Paris: Collège de France, 1992).
85. Monter, *Judging*, 75–115.
86. Huppert, *Public Schools*, 4–11, 16–20, 33–38; Compère, *Collège au lycée*, 31–35.
87. De Gröer, *Réforme*, 29–35; Huppert, *Public Schools*, 21–23, 40–46.
88. Huppert, *Public Schools*, 57–60; Compère, *Collège au lycée*, 22.

however, things did not work quite the way they planned. In Dijon, where the Collège de Martins was founded in the 1530s, the councilors appointed a doctor of theology to be collège principal and sent him to Paris to recruit four masters of arts. He returned with four promising candidates to teach grammar and rhetoric to the boys of Dijon, but a few months later Dijon councilors were dismayed to discover all four teachers soliciting services at a local brothel. Although two of them were allowed to continue at their posts, the other two were prohibited from teaching anywhere in Dijon. Since at that period Dijon's brothels were legal and an accepted component of many unmarried men's public life, the councilors' harsh judgment of the masters demonstrates that they held these men to much higher standards of public decorum than they did other city residents.[89] Unlike the universities, which could still sometimes defend themselves against secular officials, provincial collèges were explicitly municipal institutions under the thumb of the local city council and royal law courts.

By midcentury, collège masters were increasingly dismissed for doctrinal rather than sexual misadventures. Collèges and universities were thought to be infested with "Lutheran vermin," and later with adherents of the even more dangerous Reformed or Calvinist faith.[90] Calvinism arrived on a large scale in France in 1555 when John Calvin, a French theologian who led the Reformation in Geneva, began sending out pastors to convert the French. Unlike Luther, whose ideas were disseminated in France by the printed word, Calvin realized that conversion of the French would require charismatic preachers with a clear message of action. In addition to his stress on the theological doctrine of double predestination, one of Calvin's most important innovations was his reform of the church as an institution. Realizing that secular authorities often co-opted religious reform movements to strengthen their political control over city residents, Calvin made the Reformed Church in Geneva as autonomous and self-regulating as possible. The consistory, a form of church court composed of lay elders and pastors, was invented to regulate the faithful. When Calvin and later Bèze sent pastors to France, they encouraged them to found congregations and establish local consistories as quickly as possible. The first of these congregations was established in Paris in 1555, and within a few years, hundreds more sprouted up all over France, each of them a highly integrated and disciplined flock operating independently of both the Roman Catholic and secular hierarchy. All the parlements were put on alert in order to prevent more of these congregations of Huguenots, the term that French Catholics used to describe

89. Charles François Muteau, *Les écoles et collèges en province depuis les temps les plus reculés jusqu'en 1789* (Dijon: Darantière, 1882), 182–85; Jacques Rossiaud, "Prostitution, jeunesse et société dans les villes du Sud-Est au XVe siècle," *Annales: Économies, Sociétés, Civilisations* 31 (1976): 312.
90. Compère, *Collège au lycée*, 36–41; Blotevogel, "Humanism," 143–44.

the Calvinists, from forming. Well aware that judicial repression was no longer stemming the tide of Protestantism, Henry II vowed to confront the rising crisis more directly. It was in this context that religious reform and satirical farce came into conflict in the provincial city of Bordeaux.

Bordeaux students and faculty were particularly suspect for their heretical tendencies. Although the city had had a university since the mid-fifteenth century, most students studying in the city attended the relatively new Collège de Guyenne. Founded in 1533 by municipal edict, the collège had flourished, attracting prominent humanists as teachers and instructing thousands of students.[91] Almost immediately, it also developed a reputation for religious reform.[92] By the mid-1550s, the Collège de Guyenne was a hotbed of reform theology and activism. As a result, in 1555 the Parlement of Bordeaux banned the collège from publishing anything and required the students to attend mass each morning. Bordeaux city councilors were also increasingly unwilling to pay for physical repairs to the school building because of their fear that the institution might be harboring heretics.[93] Although the collège had the support of powerful nobles, within Bordeaux itself the students faced growing hostility from authorities eager to keep the city Catholic.

Although as late as 1557 there was no formal Calvinist congregation in Bordeaux, nevertheless growing numbers of city residents were sympathetic to reform. In nearby Agen, Bourg, and Libourne, heretics had recently been executed. City officials were aware that just outside the Bordeaux city walls, Calvinists lay in wait. One of the ways in which authorities attacked heresy was by regulating comic theater. Concerned about the spread of Calvinist ideas among the local population, the Parlement of Bordeaux repeatedly issued edicts prohibiting the performance of farce both in Bordeaux and in the surrounding region. These rulings were directed at a number of different groups, including the students at the Collège de

91. Ernest Gaullieur, *Histoire du Collège de Guyenne* (Paris: Sandoz et Fischbacher, 1874), 159. The Parlement of Bordeaux insisted on ratifying the collège charter in 1533. Métivier, *Chronique*, 1:299 (26 Aug. 1533).

92. Boscheron des Portes, *Histoire*, 1:46–51; L. Desgraves and F. Loirette, *Histoire de Bordeaux*, vol. 4, *Bordeaux de 1453 à 1715*, ed. Robert Boutruche (Bordeaux: Fédération Historique du Sud-Ouest, 1966), 4:89–91, 235–39; ADG 1 B 187, fol. 209, 27 Jan. 1558; BM Bordeaux MS 369, Savignac, "Extraits," 1:634 (16 Mar. 1556), 2:203 (14 Feb. 1560), 2:273 (14 Apr. 1561); Marie-Madeleine Compère and Dominique Julia, *Les collèges français: XVIe–XVIIIe siècles* (Paris: CNRS, 1984), 1:143–44; Gaullieur, *Histoire*, 151–62, 238–40; Métivier, *Chronique*, 1:335 (27 July 1537); Anne-Marie Cocula, "Crises et tensions d'un parlement au temps des guerres civiles: Le Parlement de Bordeaux dans la seconde moitié du XVIe siècle," in *Les parlements de province*, ed. Jacques Poumarède and Jack Thomas (Toulouse: FRAMESPA, 1996), 724–27.

93. Boscheron des Portes, *Histoire*, 1:54–59; Desgraves and Loirette, *Histoire*, 4:236–38, 240–41; Jonathan Powis, "Guyenne 1548: The Crown, the Province and Social Order," *European Studies Review* 12 (1982): 1–15. ADG 1 B 187, fol. 209, 27 Jan. 1558; ADG 1 B 186, fol. 241v, 1 Feb. 1558; BM Bordeaux MS 369, Savignac, "Extraits," 1:634 (16 Mar. 1556), 2:203 (14 Feb. 1560), 2:273 (14 Apr. 1561); Compère and Julia, *Collèges français*, 1:143–44; Gaullieur, *Histoire*, 151–62, 238–40; Métivier, *Chronique*, 1:335 (27 July 1537).

Guyenne, the Catholic-leaning Basoche association, a local branch of the Enfants-sans-Souci, and itinerant actors.[94] Although not all theater being performed in Bordeaux engaged directly with questions of religious reform, the magistrates were well aware that theater performances could be propaganda opportunities for both Huguenots and radical Catholics and sought to avoid them at all costs.

In open defiance of these rulings against the theater, students at the Collège de Guyenne chose in early March 1557 to perform a satirical farce. Processing through the city streets, the students allegedly tried to humiliate the city council, the institution that had not only brought the collège into being but also funded most of its activities. The parlement magistrates soon got wind of the student performance, which they considered to be slanderous and disrespectful. "On the fifth of March, 1556, the city councilors complained in the Grand' Chambre that on the previous Sunday at the city's collège, of which they are the founders, were performed several defamatory plays [in which the students] attached to the end of *batons*, that everyone carried, depictions of rats, shouting 'skinned rats!' and then throwing them on the ground, saying 'You are skinned rats' [jus/rats pelées]."[95] The students, presumably resentful of the city council's recently expressed doubts about the quality of education being offered at the collège, attacked the city councilors (*jurats)* with traditional punning humor. By splitting the word *jurat* into *jus* and *rat*, they implied that *jus*, or justice, had been skinned or stripped bare—at once debasing the councilors as grotesque vermin and undermining their temporal authority as upholders of the law. The students had flouted earlier censorship rulings, and at this pointed attack the magistrates no longer hesitated to intervene. Not only did they prohibit the students from referring either directly or indirectly to the city councilors in future performances, but more importantly, they concluded that from then on no "farces, comedies or tragedies could be performed at the said collège except by permission of the court."[96] Considering the students' history of transgression, the parlement's ruling was relatively moderate: no students were imprisoned, nor did magistrates completely rule out future student theater.

We should not read the parlement's censorship as hostility to theater per se, just to performances that touched on delicate and dangerous matters. In 1558, the Bordeaux city council granted permission for a troupe of

94. Desgraves and Loirette, *Histoire*, 4:241; ADG 1 B 129, fol. 201, 16 Sept. 1553; ADG 1 B 158, fol. 96, 14 May 1555; "Arrêts du Parlement de Bordeaux," *Archives Historiques de la Gironde* 3 (1896–97): 466 (Apr. 1556); BM Bordeaux MS 369, Savignac, "Extraits," 2:13 (5 Mar. 1557); AM Bordeaux MS 764, François Martial de Verthamon d'Ambloy, "Registres secrets du Parlement de Bordeaux," 801–15 (27 Jan. 1558); BM Bordeaux MS 369, "Extrait des registres secrets de la cour de parlement de Bordeaux, de 1462 au 6 septembre 1582," 8 Feb. 1558.
95. BM Bordeaux MS 369, Savignac, "Extraits," 2:13 (5 Mar. 1557); Métivier, *Chronique*, 2:138.
96. BM Bordeaux MS 369, Savignac, "Extraits," 2:13 (5 Mar. 1557).

commercial actors to perform for a few days in the city. Even as late as the Carnival season of 1560, the parlement allowed collège instructor Jacques Martin, well known for his Protestant leanings, to perform certain "tragedies, morality plays, farces, and comedies, both in Latin and in French, for the exercise of the students and the pleasure of the people."[97] Presumably these plays were neither satires nor overtly religious polemics or permission would not have been granted. Nevertheless, the magistrate's authorization is notably tolerant, given national political and religious developments. Henry II had been unexpectedly killed in a joust the summer before and was succeeded by his teenage and often-ill son Francis II (1559–60). By February 1560, the noble family of Guise, who advocated the active suppression of heresy, became dominant at court. In this context, one might have expected the Bordeaux magistrates to have been even more wary of allowing reform-minded students to perform in the city streets.

Over the next year, the religious situation deteriorated in France, and the politics of theatrical performance once again required the intervention of the Bordeaux Parlement. Francis II died in December 1560, leaving the throne in the hands of Catherine de Medici, mother of and regent for the nine-year-old Charles IX (1560–74). In early 1561, Catherine tried to alleviate the mounting religious violence between Catholics and the Reformed congregations with an edict of toleration that placated neither group. Realizing that immediate action was needed to keep matters under control, Charles IX wrote to the magistrates of Bordeaux urging them to keep the peace at all costs.[98] Meanwhile, the number of Calvinists in Bordeaux was quickly mushrooming: two pastors now directed a congregation of perhaps as many as one thousand city residents.[99] This was the height of the Calvinist movement, a time when it seemed possible that the whole of France—even the king—might be converted to the Reformed faith. By 1561, there were over two thousand Reformed congregations in France, and between 10 and 15 percent of the population considered themselves to be members of the Reformed faith. Nobles and urban residents in particular were flocking to the Reformed cause in large numbers. Huguenots all over France were meeting in large fields and marching together through city streets, hoping to convert through their example. In Bordeaux, Huguenot students gathered in armed groups, openly proselytized, and sang psalms in the streets with hundreds of their coreligionists.[100] Not surprisingly, student theater that year became a lightening rod for growing religious tensions.

97. *Archives Historiques*, 3:465; ADG, "Registre de Loirette," 1650n264 (3 Feb. 1560). Ernest Gaullieur conflates this ruling of 1560 with rulings against student and Basoche gatherings of the following year. Gaullieur, *Histoire*, 259.
98. Desgraves and Loirette, *Histoire*, 4:242.
99. Ibid., 4:243.
100. ADG 1 B 214, fol. 23, 3 May 1560; ADG 1 B 226, fol. 321, 26 Feb. 1561; ADG 1 B 226, fol. 320, 26 Feb. 1561; BM Bordeaux MS 369, Savignac, "Extraits," 2:273 (14 Apr. 1561); Métivier, *Chronique*, 2:301–2 (3 May 1560).

Unfortunately, we do not know what the Collège de Guyenne students performed that February 1561. Whatever it was, it sparked the ire of the local Basoche, by then an association probably over two hundred strong. Charles Amussat, king of the Basoche, decided to retaliate by mounting a rival farcical performance. Such competitive theatrics were not uncommon among local festive societies, even before religious reform became an issue, and the Basochiens advertised their intention of mocking the students by posting a placard to that effect.[101] The students, thus challenged, decided to attack the Basoche physically. When Jacques Martin and other instructors got wind of these plans, they rushed to warn the city councilors and parlement magistrates. No one in a position of authority could have felt that a violent encounter between the now openly Huguenot students and the Basochiens would be desirable. In the meantime, the Basochiens massed at the collège doors, and the students sounded the *tocsin*, the city's alarm bell. Only the direct intervention of the city council, reinforced by the city guard, prevented the two groups from coming to blows.[102] A few days later the parlement magistrates ruled that both the Basoche and the students would be severely punished should they attempt to gather illegally or bear arms in the city.[103] Classes at the collège were shut down, and the Basochiens were refused permission to gather again that year.[104] Later that spring, the parlement issued a ruling that made the link between religious reform and farce more explicit. Stating that no residents of the city were permitted to gather together for any reason, even "under the pretext of religion," the magistrates prohibited anyone from performing "morality plays, farces or other genres" anywhere in the city, even in private.[105] Whereas rivalries and even fighting among festive societies had been a normal part of urban life during the Renaissance, the development of a large Huguenot community within the French body politic rendered the performance of satirical farce increasingly dangerous. Even before the outbreak of the first civil war in 1562, tensions between Huguenots and Catholics in many French cities were so high that jokes and mockery more often led to violence than to laughter.

101. For earlier incidents of Basoche associations fighting with other youth groups, including students, see ADG 1 B 84, fol. 234, 30 May 1534; AD Haute-Garonne 2 Mi 166, fol. 320, 2 May 1480; Jelle Koopmans, "The World of the Parisian Farce," in *New Approaches to European Theater of the Middles Ages: An Ontology*, ed. Barbara I. Gusick and Edelgard E. Dubruck (New York: Peter Lang, 2004), 143. The rivalry between the Collège de Guyenne students and the Basochiens of Bordeaux clearly had religious overtones by the late 1550s. See Kevin Gould, *Catholic Activism in South-West France, 1540–1570* (Ashgate: Aldershot, 2006), 18–33. Nevertheless, as late as 1565, some clerks of the Basoche were themselves Huguenots. BM Bordeaux MS 369, Savignac, "Extraits," 2:573–74 (10 Feb. 1565).
102. Gaullieur, *Histoire*, 258–60. Gaullieur relies for most of this account on records from the Archives Municipales de Bordeaux that were lost in a fire at the end of the nineteenth century.
103. Gaullieur, *Histoire*, 258–60; ADG 1 B 224, fols. 397v–398, 20 Feb. 1561.
104. BM Bordeaux MS 369, "Registres secrets de Parlement de Bordeaux," 20 Feb. 1561; ADG 1 B 226, fol. 321, 26 Feb. 1561.
105. ADG 1 B 229, fol. 330, 24 May 1561.

By the late 1550s, the freedom of both French students and Basochiens to use farce for satire was severely curtailed. That is not to say that all such theater was successfully repressed. Nevertheless, both groups were under close surveillance. Whereas other festive societies continued to perform unhindered during the 1520s through the 1550s, the cultural prominence of students and Basochiens necessitated their regulation. Censorship of Basochiens was tight and consistent, and they were directly under the thumb of the magistrates, who increasingly controlled access to the clerks' posts at the parlements. For students, the situation was more variable: at the provincial collèges, secular officials did not hesitate to curb any theater that was considered satirical; at the universities, the ambiguity of the students' legal status and the religious divisions among the faculty still allowed students a certain leeway to express their political and religious views on stage. In Paris, the university rector once again outlawed the performance of satirical farce in 1559; in 1579, Henry III (1574–89) included in his Edict of Blois a further warning against the seditious nature of student farce.[106] As religious and political tensions continued to intensify in France during the 1550s, both the parlements and the universities found that farce was no longer a desirable way of expressing their political concerns to the monarchy. Associated with youth, violence, slander, and dangerous religious ideas, farcical theater had finally become too inflammatory a medium to sanction any longer.

106. Petit de Julleville, *Comédiens*, 318; Du Boulay, *Historia*, 6:526.

4 *Farce during the Wars of Religion*

During the Renaissance, the citizens of Amiens reveled in farce. Profiting from the end of the Hundred Years' War, the success of the city's cloth industry, and continued royal military investment, Amiens residents chose to celebrate their prosperity with a newly lavish festive life. Farce playing was an integral element of these celebrations. In 1456, the urban elite marked a military victory over the Turks with a colorful festival, during which actors performed farces in the city streets. Other groups organized farcical performances on a regular basis: residents crowned a Maître des Farces and a Prince des Sots each year and apparently enjoyed the antics of law clerks who processed through the city at Carnival. Between 1450 and 1560, farcical theater was an accepted element of both secular civic ritual and Catholic festive life in Amiens, a manifestation of popular culture that was applauded by the city's elite and performed by its commoners.[1]

By the mid-sixteenth century, however, stirrings of social and religious unrest in Amiens began to undermine this symbiotic relationship between farce and civic culture. These developments started in the 1540s, when profits from the local cloth industry began to stagnate. Conflicts concerning the city's authority over the weavers' and wool combers' guilds exploded into riots. Amiens' socioeconomic difficulties were exacerbated in the 1550s by the arrival of Calvinist pastors, who attracted many disgruntled workers to the Reformed faith. Soon enough, just as city officials had feared, public gatherings began to coalesce into Protestant religious communities. In a city

---

1. Georges Lecocq, *Histoire du théâtre en Picardie, depuis son origine jusqu'à la fin du XVIe siècle* (Paris: Menu, 1880; reprint, Geneva: Slatkine, 1971), 138–42, 153–59; Ernest Noyelle, "Basoche et basochiens à Amiens au XVIe siècle," *Société des Antiquaires de Picardie* (1882): 33–34; Marie-Louise Pelus, "Amiens au XVIe siècle: De l'expansion à la rébellion," in *Histoire d'Amiens*, ed. Ronald Hubscher (Toulouse: Privat, 1986), 122; Isabelle Paresys, *Aux marges du royaume: Violence, justice et société en Picardie sous François 1er* (Paris: Publications de la Sorbonne, 1998), 234.

riddled with discontent, farce players' satirical jokes about licentious priests and corrupt magistrates began to seem less funny to city officials trying to maintain the status quo.[2]

Amiens officials reacted by censoring the theater and insisting that city officials vet all plays before they were performed. In 1555, a troupe dutifully followed this procedure only to find that the city council rejected all its plays but one, a morality play deemed to be "honest and not full of heresy."[3] The troupe's farces, which did not meet these standards, were explicitly banned from being performed anywhere in the city. Fearing such performances might spread dangerous ideas of Calvinist reform, the councilors throughout the next decade were to prohibit all actors from performing anything that touched on "the word of God."[4]

The city leaders of Amiens censored the theater both to prevent disruptions to public order and to keep the Catholic faith pure. These considerations even caused the city council to trump the authority of the province's military governor. During the summer of 1567, actors arrived in Amiens bearing letters issued to them by the provincial governor, Louis, the Prince de Condé, which granted them permission to perform farces. Condé, a peer and leading member of the Bourbon family who had publicly declared his Reformed faith, was the current military leader of French Huguenots. Under normal circumstances, a governor's endorsement of an acting troupe would sway authorities hesitant to allow actors into a city. Because he was a Calvinist, however, the recommendation of Condé was met with skepticism by the Amiens city council, which was at that time dominated by Catholic royalists. Ignoring the governor's letters, the council refused to allow the troupe to perform, citing a need to "prevent all quarrels and disputes that often occur at such meetings and all maladies that can occur in the heated nature of our times."[5] The council clearly associated farcical theater with violence. Local authorities were wary of any gathering of city residents, even if the meeting was not explicitly for religious purposes, assuming that the irreverent jokes that would make a Protestant sympathizer laugh might drive a good Catholic to blows. Amiens continued to uphold this policy of censoring the theater and banning farce for the next forty years, until the conclusion of the Wars of Religion in 1598. Farce playing had been transformed from a benign form of entertainment into a threatening cultural practice that city officials feared would contaminate the body social.[6]

2. Pelus, "Amiens au XVIe siècle," 102–3, 127–28; David Rosenberg, "Social Experience and Religious Choice: A Case Study, the Protestant Weavers and Woolcombers of Amiens in the Sixteenth Century," Ph.D. diss., Yale University, 1978, 145–80; Paresys, *Marges*, 261.
3. Quoted in Lecocq, *Histoire*, 143.
4. Ibid., 145.
5. Ibid., 147; Louis de Gouvenain, *Le théâtre à Dijon, 1422–1790* (Dijon: E. Joubard, 1888), 42–43; Pelus, "Amiens au XVIe siècle," 132–33.
6. Natalie Zemon Davis, "The Sacred and the Body Social in Sixteenth-Century Lyon," *Past and Present* 90 (1981): 40–70; Lecocq, *Histoire*, 144–48; Marie-Louise Pelus-Kaplan,

The experience of Amiens was not exceptional. Across France, particularly during the 1560s when religious violence was endemic, city officials and local magistrates reacted in a similar fashion, banning farce because it might spark riots in the cities. Yet even after 1572, when the violence within most cities had subsided, farcical theater failed to recover on a large scale. Urban officials remained suspicious and gradually defined comic theater, along with other practices such as raucous feasting and public dancing, as transgressive practices that good Catholics should avoid. For the most part, this suppression of amateur farcical performance took place in the cities and as a result of measures taken by city magistrates: it was urban officials not the king who took the lead in imposing a more narrow definition of propriety on the public stage. Both because they feared threats to public order and because their own religious sensibilities were changing, urban officials sought to regulate farcical performance—and popular festive culture more generally—much more strictly during the Wars of Religion than they had previously. Although formerly patrons of farce, after 1560 urban officials became its censors. This shift in urban elite attitudes occurred very much at the local level during a period of relatively weak royal authority. Whereas historians of France, focusing on seventeenth-century developments, have tended to emphasize the importance of political centralization on changing standards of public manners, attributing the decline of traditional popular culture to the new norm of civility that filtered down from the king's court, an examination of farce's decline demonstrates that the shift away from farcical revelry began at least a century earlier and for largely religious reasons.

The descent of the French state into religious and civil war during the second half of the sixteenth century had a decisive impact on the history of farcical performance. Lutheran ideas had been circulating in France for decades, but the arrival of pastors from Geneva after 1555 marked an important turning point in urban religious life. In many communities, the Huguenots quickly gathered 10 to 15 percent of city residents to their flock and presented a tangible threat to both the religious and political integrity of the French state. Indeed, during the first civil war (1562–63), Huguenots seized city halls in over two dozen major towns, including Lyon, Rouen, and Poitiers. Added to these religious tensions were economic conditions that did not improve during the 1560s: many cities suffered from rising grain prices, stagnating trade, and recurring bouts of the plague. Nevertheless, these developments need not have resulted in civil war had it not been for the weakness of the French monarchy. After Henry II's untimely and unexpected death in 1559, the crown was held by two of his young sons: first by the sickly Francis II, who died after a little more than a year in office,

"Amiens, ville ligueuse: Le sens d'une rébellion," *Revue du Nord* 78 (1996): 289–303; Annette Finley-Croswhite, *Henry IV and the Towns: The Pursuit of Legitimacy in French Urban Society* (Cambridge: Cambridge University Press, 1999), 23–46.

and then by his brother Charles IX, who was still a minor when he inherited the throne. Neither of these young kings could control court factions, and the crown's vacillating policies of accommodation with and military aggression against the Huguenots did not inspire confidence either among the nobility or the urban elites. Outright warfare between the French crown and the Huguenots erupted intermittently—in 1562–63, 1567–68, and 1568–70—but the unsatisfactory peace treaties that ended each of these military conflicts failed to resolve the question of the Huguenots' role in French society. As a result, local violence between Catholics and Huguenots only accelerated, contributing to the weakness of political authority at all levels.[7] During the Wars of Religion, the actions of various groups unhappy with the political situation were influenced by a traditional understanding of the body politic as an entity whose head could lead effectively only in consultation with the rest of the body. All those mobilized by this vision of what a state should be—Catholic priests impatient with the sluggish royal response to heresy, city officials frustrated by rising taxes during a period of economic contraction, and proud nobles alienated from the king's court—rebelled at various times during the next thirty years. The twin challenges of religious conflict and a weak monarchy left the various limbs to run amok, creating a prolonged crisis that ultimately caused a reevaluation of French political culture after 1598.

During this initial stage of open and endemic religious violence before 1572, farce playing was systematically suppressed throughout France. The instability caused by economic decline and intermittent warfare further contributed to the contraction of farcical theater during this period. Itinerant troupes found it more difficult to travel along war-torn roads and into volatile city centers. Both wartime circumstances and the new regulations imposed by local authorities prevented actors from performing their traditional repertoire. Depending on local conditions, French cities varied in their vigilance against farce during the 1550s. Nevertheless once war broke out in 1562, city officials interested in maintaining peace barred farce players—both Catholics and Huguenots—from performing in the city streets.

---

7. Denis Crouzet, *Les guerriers de Dieu: La violence au temps des troubles de religion*, 2 vols. (Seyssel: Champ Vallon, 1990); Philip Benedict, *Rouen during the Wars of Religion* (Cambridge: Cambridge University Press, 1981), 58–62, 111–22; Barbara B. Diefendorf, *Beneath the Cross: Catholics and Huguenots in Sixteenth-Century Paris* (Oxford: Oxford University Press, 1991), 49–106; James R. Farr, "Popular Religious Solidarity in Sixteenth-Century Dijon," *French Historical Studies* 14 (1985): 192–95; David Nicholls, "Protestants, Catholics and Magistrates in Tours, 1562–1572: The Making of a Catholic City during the Religious Wars," *French History* 8 (1994): 14–33; Penny Roberts, *A City in Conflict: Troyes during the French Wars of Religion* (Manchester: Manchester University Press, 1996), 101–11, 123–34, 142–55. Much of this work was inspired by Denis Richet's and Natalie Zemon Davis's work on this topic. Natalie Zemon Davis, "The Rites of Violence: Religious Riots in Sixteenth-Century France," *Past and Present* 59 (1973): 51–91, reprinted in *Society and Culture in Early Modern France* (Stanford: Stanford University Press, 1975), 152–87; Denis Richet, "Aspects socio-culturels des conflits religieux à Paris dans la seconde moitié du XVIe siècle," *Annales: Economies, Sociétés, Civilisations* 32 (1977): 764–89.

They were right to be wary. Some farces addressed religious questions directly and in ways that could easily have sparked violence. Although the vast majority of published farces extant today contain fairly innocuous social satire, we know from accusations of slander brought forward in royal law courts that farce players often ad-libbed, adding satirical jests to their script. By mocking human weaknesses and follies, farces had always dramatized the gap between people's behavior and Christian teaching, but by the mid-sixteenth century, with Calvinist preachers airing systematic critiques of Catholic dogma, such satire had become dangerous. Comic theater could even incite the faithful to violence, as a morality play published in the 1530s directly undertakes to do. This play, the *Farce of the School Teacher, the Mother, and the Three Students*, was billed by its publisher as a "joyous farce," but in fact it contains violent Catholic polemic against heretics and demonstrates the dangers of performance during a time of civic strife.[8]

The play opens conventionally enough, with a pompous teacher facing an empty classroom while extolling the virtues of his teaching methods. He is soon disturbed by a knocking at the door, at which he finds a curious mother eager to enter and see what her children are studying. The teacher is reluctant to allow her in since that would necessitate admitting that the students are not even present in the classroom. Although the teacher ostensibly welcomes her, saying "come in, if you want," he also physically blocks the doorway.[9] The mother persists and, after a brief tussle, she breaks through into the classroom. This comic opening, in which gender roles are reversed—the forceful mother, the ineffective and craven teacher—and the efficacy of Latin learning gently mocked, suggests that this play will probably follow a typical route. Audiences would expect rowdy student antics mocking the educational establishment. The play continues in the conventional way once the students arrive: they call to one another in pig Latin, parody grammar lessons, and sing a lighthearted song. After this musical interlude, however, the tone suddenly shifts to religious polemic. As expected, the young boys brag of their exploits outside the classroom, but these anecdotes are bloody and ruthless rather than comic. Specifically, they recount how they ran into a group of Lutherans in the streets and "shut them up."[10] The boys defend their actions on religious grounds, asserting that they are merely doing right by harassing sinful interlopers who do not observe Lent, honor the saints, or respect the word of God. The teacher, no longer the fool, is proud of having taught the boys these lessons of religious intolerance, and he applauds both the students' rhetoric and

---

8. Jonathan Beck, "De l'endoctrinement des enfants," in *Le théâtre et la cité dans l'Europe médiévale*, ed. Edelgard E. Dubruck and William C. McDonald (Stuttgart: H.-D. Hans, 1988), 471–74; "Farce du maistre d'escolle," in *Théâtre et propagande aux débuts de la Réforme: Six pièces polémiques du Recueil La Vallière: Textes établis d'après le MS BN 24341*, ed. Jonathan Beck (Geneva: Slatkine, 1986), 207–29.
9. "Farce du maistre d'escolle," 216.
10. Ibid., 219.

their efforts, as does the mother. Together they all agree that the only thing to be done with the Lutherans is to "burn them, without effigy," and at the end of the play they all set out together to do so.[11]

This play, though it is exceptional in its openly propagandist tone, nevertheless demonstrates the dangers of farce during the Wars of Religion. When students felt charged with a mission of religious persecution, traditional youth violence—fights, petty thievery, and carousing—could result in acts that undermined the very basis of religious and secular authority. This particular farce presents the students not at the margins of civil society, as they are usually depicted in farces, but at the very vanguard of civic engagement. The parallel the play makes between Catholicism and "our country" also challenges audience members to behave as good French subjects by undertaking the same mission of religious persecution. Had this play been performed in cities already divided by religious beliefs, it might well have driven normally peaceful city residents to violent action.

Farce was also targeted because of its association with traditional Catholic festivals. Farce playing was embedded in a Catholic festive tradition, a tradition that under the pressure of religious conflict had led to violence. During the 1560s, those times of the year when farce players usually gathered and performed—Carnival, May Day, Corpus Christi, saints' days—became moments that defined who was a conforming Catholic. Those families that failed to hang tapestries on their walls before Corpus Christi or who refused to honor a youth group's demands of wine on Carnival were taken to have demonstrated their break with the Catholic faith and, by extension, with the urban community as a whole. Consequently, during the first decades of the Wars of Religion, many religious riots took place during the traditional festive season of January through June, when Carnival insults tended to segue readily into violence among the different religious confessions. Unlike farce players who usually performed merely to chastise local officials or clergy rather than to undermine their authority, both Huguenot and Catholic rioters during the 1560s supplemented Carnival rituals with physical violence, so avid were they to eliminate spiritual contamination from their communities. Churches were ransacked, Catholic priests attacked and killed, Huguenot homes burnt to the ground. Much of the violence perpetuated by Huguenots occurred during their brief takeovers of city governments in 1562, when militants forced Catholic priests to eat excrement and to mock Catholic rituals. Among Catholics, confessional violence was usually triggered by defiant Huguenot worship, or it exploded during Catholic processions against heresy. Catholic violence was often led by self-appointed laypersons, sometimes by members of the local militia, and it involved the display and desecration of the bodies of murdered Huguenots during triumphal processions that imitated the rituals of judicial power. Both Catholic and

---

11. Ibid., 223.

Huguenot rioters used the symbolic language of traditional festive rituals as a medium through which to voice their fear and anger.[12]

Catholic festive societies were even sometimes physically attacked by fervent Huguenots. The Conards of Rouen suffered such violence not long after war broke out. During the late 1550s, the Parlement of Rouen issued several rulings aimed at preventing bawdy farce players from performing, including a ruling against the processions of the Conards.[13] Despite this charged religious atmosphere and a rapidly expanding Huguenot population, the festive confraternity decided to defy the law and perform as usual at Carnival in early 1562. During the procession, the Conards were confronted by a group of Huguenots who, "condemn[ing] such extravagances and deprivation," harassed and threw stones at the performers.[14] Even though the Conards had traditionally attacked clerical abuses and mocked licentious priests in its performances, the Huguenots recognized this Catholic confraternity as the enemy.

In general, Huguenots found the farces performed by festive societies to be a perfect illustration of the corruption of Catholic practice. They attacked Catholic rituals as dangerous distractions from a true understanding of Christ's message and deplored what they perceived to be the worldly excesses of Catholic festivals. In Calvinist theology, the Word of God and community solidarity replaced many of the trappings of traditional Catholic practice, including confraternities, images in churches, and the worship of the saints. The Geneva-trained pastors who brought the Calvinist message to France were particularly intolerant of such practices, and local Huguenot consistories attempted to eliminate them among their flock.[15] For the Huguenots

12. Crouzet, *Guerriers*, 1:320–410, 563–637; Davis, "Rites of Violence," passim; Diefendorf, *Beneath the Cross*, 49–106, 137–36, 160–75; Richet, "Aspects," 770–78. Not all riots that broke out during the Wars of Religion were religiously motivated. See Henry Heller, *Iron and Blood: Civil Wars in Sixteenth-Century France* (Montreal: McGill/Queen's University Press, 1991), 88–101; Emmanuel Le Roy Ladurie, *Carnival in Romans*, trans. Mary Feeney (New York: George Braziller, 1979), 35–59; Emmanuel Le Roy Ladurie, *The Peasants of Languedoc*, trans. John Day (Urbana: University of Illinois Press, 1976), 172–97; J. H. M. Salmon, "Peasant Revolt in Vivarais, 1575–1580," in *Renaissance and Revolt: Essays in the Intellectual and Social History of Early Modern France* (Cambridge: Cambridge University Press, 1987), 211–34.

13. Jacques Sireulde, *Le trésor immortel: Tiré de l'Écriture sainte*, ed. Charles de Beaurepaire (Rouen: Leon Gy, 1899), l–li.

14. Théodore de Bèze, *Histoire ecclésiastique des églises réformées au royaume de France*, ed. G. Baum, E. Cunitz, and R. Reuss (Paris: Fischbacher, 1883), 2:713; Benedict, *Rouen*, 53, 95–102.

15. Davis, "Sacred and the Body Social," 58–61; Luc Racaut, *Hatred in Print: Catholic Propaganda and Protestant Identity during the French Wars of Religion* (Aldershot: Ashgate, 2002), 33–35; Janine Garrisson, *Les protestants au XVIe siècle* (Paris: Fayard, 1988), 75–78; Robert Kingdon, "The Geneva Consistory in the Time of Calvin," in *Calvinism in Europe, 1540–1620*, ed. Andrew Pettegree, Alastair Duke, and Gillian Lewis (Cambridge: Cambridge University Press, 1994), 20–34. In practice, however, Huguenots borrowed traditional festive slurs and rituals to mock Catholics. See Crouzet, *Guerriers*, 1:670–700; Edward Muir, *Ritual in Early Modern Europe* (Cambridge: Cambridge University Press, 1997), 98–99.

in Rouen, a festive confraternity such as the Conards was yet another relic of traditional religion that needed to be purged from civic life. Their attack seems to have been effective: in the years immediately following the 1562 fracas, even after the Huguenots were ousted from political power in Rouen after the first civil war, there is no evidence of the Conards performing in the city.

The authority of most French city councils, royal law courts, and even military governors was too limited to prevent many of these riots from taking place. City officials did not have local police forces they could count on; indeed, it was often the leaders of the local militia or city guard who led Catholic rioters to attack their fellow city residents.[16] Although some local authorities tried to punish the perpetrators and to prevent inflammatory gatherings from occurring, city officials, faced with the religious hatred of the crowds, often found themselves torn between competing loyalties. Stopping riots was difficult and dangerous; eliminating farcical theater from civic culture was relatively easy. Decades of patronage and regulation preceding the wars left festive societies vulnerable to suppression. Since the outset of the sixteenth century, the societies had been in the habit of asking local authorities for a few livres to help pay for the expenses of mounting their plays. Usually these requests were granted, and the associations came to depend on such donations. In addition, because farce players were organized into long-standing confraternities and associations, they were easy to target. Beginning in the 1550s, city officials began to cut off funds, censor plays, and, in some cases, outlaw festive societies altogether.

One sign of the abrupt break in farcical performance is its publishing history. The publication of farces, which had been healthy until the 1540s, shut down just as religious tensions began to explode in many French cities. Although some plays published during the second half of the sixteenth century contained farcical scenes, the number of new farces dropped precipitously.[17] The actual practice of farce playing was, however, more subtly transformed than its publication history suggests. Although most city authorities turned against farce during the 1560s, some communities began to allow festive societies back onto the stage once local religious violence had subsided.

Not surprisingly, those farce players who were subject to the tightest regulation before 1560 were among the first to cease performing once the Wars of Religion broke out. Students at the provincial collèges, renowned for both their neoclassical and farcical performances during the first half of the century, increasingly fell silent. In many cities, this abandonment of the student stage reflected an overall contraction of Latin schooling: in many

16. Diefendorf, *Beneath the Cross*, 164–71.
17. Beck, *Théâtre et propagande*, 33–34; Donald Perret, *Old Comedy in the French Renaissance, 1576–1620* (Geneva: Droz, 1992).

towns, municipal collèges ceased offering classes, either because students stopped attending or because municipal authorities lacked the funds needed to keep the doors open. City councils that had previously invested considerable resources in establishing new institutions of learning were now focused on more pressing matters of defense, provisioning, and royal taxation. Alternatively, as we have seen in Bordeaux, city leaders often suspected the collège of harboring Calvinist sympathizers, and they discouraged students from performing plays that might arouse religious conflict. The murder of collège principal Barthélemy Aneau in Lyon in 1565 for his supposedly heretical views is an example of teachers' vulnerability to being attacked by devout but violent Catholics. Finally, some community leaders replaced the college faculties with Jesuit instructors, who were on principle hostile to farce.[18] The Jesuits, a vanguard of the Catholic reformation, sought to transform student plays into somber demonstrations of Latin rhetoric and Catholic piety. Even in Paris, where university students remained active in the cause of religious reform throughout the wars, student theatrical performances were less notorious than was the violence of student protests. Apart from two rulings against satirical farce, we know little about student performances during the Wars of Religion, a lack of evidence suggesting that farce had less influence on public opinion than earlier in the century.[19]

Another category of amateur farce players closely regulated before the 1560s was the Basoche, for whom the Wars of Religion period marked the end of farcical performance. Nevertheless, many Basoche groups survived and adapted to the changing circumstances of late sixteenth-century France. Pressure to change came from above: instead of offering the clerks patronage as they had done during the French Renaissance, the parlement magistrates now prevented them from expressing themselves on the public stage.

The magistrates in fact were in a difficult position, pulled in different directions by their complex mandate. As judges, they were responsible for adjudicating some heresy cases and thus seemed to many Catholics to be defenders of the faith. Yet as peacekeepers, the magistrates often disciplined Catholic rioters and outlawed traditional festivities. The parlements' legislative and political responsibilities, which included registering numerous peace treaties, none of which made either side happy, further compromised

---

18. Marie-Madeleine Compère, *Du collège au lycée (1500–1850): Généalogie de l'enseignement secondaire français* (Paris: Gallimard, 1985), 36–42; Georgette de Groër, Réforme et Contre-Réforme en France: Le Collège de la Trinité au XVIe siècle à Lyon (Paris: Publisud, 1995), 36–67, 138–39.

19. Michel Félibien, *Histoire de la ville de Paris* (Paris: G. Desprez et J. Desessartz, 1725), 4:765a (14 June 1554), 4:772b (May 1557); Pierre de L'Estoile, *Mémoires-journaux, 1574–1611*, ed. G. Brunet (Paris: Librairie des Bibliophiles, 1875–99; reprint, Paris: Tallandier, 1982), 1:309 (Mar. 1579); César-Égasse Du Boulay, *Historia Universitatis Parisiensis* (Paris: Pierre de Bresche, 1673), 6:526; Louis Petit de Julleville, *Histoire du théâtre en France: Les comédiens en France au moyen âge* (Paris: Le Cerf, 1885), 318.

their authority with the local people and with the king. Overall, the religious wars forced the parlements, particularly in the provinces, to intervene in the daily workings of local governance and challenge royal authority far more actively than they had previously done. Finally, religious divisions among the magistrates themselves prevented the parlements from developing consistent policies, as their leadership and membership fluctuated during periods of war and peace.[20]

The parlements' new and controversial political prominence made it more difficult for them to sanction farce, with its traditional mockery of clerical and secular authority figures. Contemporary authors, some eager to defend the parlements' assertiveness and others to criticize what they perceived to be the magistrates' meddling in religious or moral policies, began to accuse them of hypocrisy. Citing the magistrates' ambiguous religious loyalties, their habits of carousing among themselves, and their practice of accepting gifts from plaintiffs, reformers called on the magistrates to alter their own behavior to better reflect Catholic ideals. Under such pressure, some magistrates began to internalize this criticism and to urge their colleagues to avoid the "scandal" of associating too freely with the lower orders.[21] Their patronage of the Basoche was sacrificed in the magistrates' bid to conserve their authority and prestige during this period of war. In Rouen, Bordeaux, and Paris, all cities in which the Basoche had been actively patronized before 1560, the magistrates outlawed their farcical theater, although they allowed the Basoche to function as a professional association long afterward.[22] In other cities, the silence of the archival records suggests the same fate: in Lyon and Dijon we have evidence of Basoche performance in the early sixteenth century, followed by silence after 1560.[23] The fate of the Basoche in Paris illustrates this trend and helps to show why it occurred.

20. Diefendorf, *Beneath the Cross*, 70, 159–60, 167, 172; Finley-Croswhite, *Henry IV and the Towns*, 79; Jonathan K. Powis, "Order, Religion, and the Magistrates of a Provincial Parlement in Sixteenth-Century France," *Archiv für Reformationsgeschichte* 71 (1980): 184–88; Christopher W. Stocker, "The Parlement of Paris and Confessional Politics in the 1560s," *Proceedings of the Annual Meeting of the Western Society for French History* 15 (1988): 38–47; Linda L. Taber, "Religious Dissent within the Parlement of Paris in the Mid-Sixteenth Century: A Reassessment," *French Historical Studies* 16 (1990): 684–99.

21. Jonathan Dewald, *The Formation of a Provincial Nobility: The Magistrates of the Parlement of Rouen, 1499–1610* (Princeton: Princeton University Press, 1980), 60–65, 99–101; Colin Kaiser, "Les cours souveraines au XVIe siècle: Morale et Contre-Réforme," *Annales: Économies, Sociétés, Civilisations* 37 (1982): 20–27.

22. Raymond Lebègue, *Études sur le théâtre français* (Paris: Nizet, 1978), 2:92 (24 Feb. 1570); Archives Départementales (AD) Seine-Maritime (SM) 1 B 537, 24 Apr. 1551. The Rouen Basoche continued to plant maypoles and to act as a training association for the parlement clerks throughout the ancien régime. Archives Départementales Gironde (ADG) 1 B 224, fols. 397–98, 20 Feb. 1561; ADG 1 B 229, no. 330, 24 May 1561; ADG 1 B 277, no. 33, 5 Jan. 1565; ADG Arrêts du parlement, Jan. 1582, fol. 180, 17 Jan. 1582.

23. Jacques Rossiaud, "Prostitution, jeunesse et société dans les villes du Sud-Est au XVe siècle," *Annales: Économies, Sociétés, Civilisations* 31 (1976): 309; Jean Guéraud, *Chronique lyonnaise*

Although the magistrates of the Paris Parlement began censoring plays performed by the Basoche as early as the 1530s, they nevertheless continued to pay for its performances whenever they deemed the content of the plays to be appropriate. As late as 1549, the Basoche performed at the festivities after the Parisian royal entry of the new king, Henry II.[24] By the 1560s, with religious violence now endemic in the capital and their authority compromised in the face a radicalized Catholic population, the magistrates became more circumspect. In 1560, during the Carnival season immediately following the death of Henry II, the Basochiens were barred from performing. In addition, several *arrêts* point to the direct censorship of farcical theater during the period before the first civil war.[25] In January 1563, the Basochiens were given permission to perform only "modest plays" and were warned "not to add anything and to cross out that which had been cut from that play" or they would suffer a penalty.[26] Realizing that the magistrates were becoming less supportive, the Basochiens tried to trump their authority by turning to Charles IX. Unlike the magistrates, the king was not at all concerned about the content of the Basoche's performances. For several years in succession during the 1560s, he granted the Basoche letters patent establishing its privilege to perform farces each May and to be paid for this activity from the parlement's coffers.[27] Often absent from Paris and perhaps less concerned than the magistrates about threats to public order, Charles saw no harm in allowing the Basochiens to perform their amusing farces.

In the short term, the royal letters patent were useful for pressuring the magistrates to pay the Basoche's annual stipend. Every ruling concerning this stipend during the 1560s noted that the magistrates would pay the sum indicated because it had been "authorized . . . according to the letters patent of the king."[28] Previously, the Basoche's performance tradition and the magistrates' approval of the play had been sufficient for the release of funds. In 1568, however, the magistrates made the necessity of these letters patent explicit when they withheld payment for a full year, and only when the Basochiens produced that year's letters patent did they relent and disburse the requested sum. Not surprisingly, after 1568 there is no further evidence that the magistrates paid for the Basoche's theatrical performances. It is clear that obtaining royal letters patent was a bid to force reluctant magistrates to continue their patronage of farce. The Basochiens quickly

de Jean Guéraud, 1536–1562, ed. Jean Tricou (Lyon: Audin, 1929), 43, 52; Bibliothèque Municipale (BM) Bordeaux (B) MS 369, Savignac, "Extraits des registres secrets du Parlement de Bordeaux," 2:573–74 (10 Feb. 1565).
24. Archives Nationales (AN) x1a 1565, fol. 18, 9 May 1549.
25. AN x1a 1592, fol. 213, 9 Jan. 1560; AN x1a 1599, fol. 348, 5 Jan. 1562.
26. AN x1a 1604, fol. 136, 4 Jan. 1563.
27. AN x1a 1585, fol. 520a, 15 June 1557.
28. AN x1a 1609, fols. 223–23a, 2 June 1564. See also AN U*2057, Le Nain, "Registres du Parlement," fol. 318 (6 June 1565).

discovered, however, that even the king's official sanction was insufficient: only with the active support of the parlement magistrates was the association likely to survive.

The magistrates' new discipline of the Basoche was not limited to the content of its theatrical performances. During the 1560s, they issued rulings undermining the Basoche's claimed privileges to discipline its own members, chastised Basochiens who wore swords to court, and curbed the association's Carnival procession. In 1571, the magistrates even stripped the Basoche of its long-standing privilege to raise a maypole "for not only this year . . . but all the future."[29] This ban was lifted in 1578, but during the intervening decade the Basochiens' reputation in Paris as flamboyant comic performers quickly faded. Court poets no longer sang the praises of their youthful antics, nor did memoir writers note the success of their performances. Even Pierre L'Estoile, whose memoirs are one of the most detailed sources for this period, fails to mention the Basoche in his descriptions of Parisian life. It is not that L'Estoile is above such considerations: he describes at length the machinations of an Italian theatrical troupe, remarks on the shameful personal lives of parlement officials, and transcribes contemporary satirical pamphlets. In 1577, he notes that Henry III (1574–89) had a group of rambunctious students imprisoned for aping the mannerisms of his court favorites. Fifty years earlier, Parisian memoir writers assumed that the Basoche was involved in such antics; by the 1570s, however, the idea does not seem to have crossed L'Estoile's mind.[30]

The Basochiens' increasingly rare theatrical performances gradually shifted from farce to less scandalous genres. Sensitive to the magistrates' concerns about decency, the clerks began performing comedies and tragedies, plays much less likely to contain bawdy and irreverent jokes than did the traditional repertoire. A ruling of June 1582 also imposed new restrictions on the Basoche players, who were expected to perform their plays before the solicitor general each year to establish that there was "nothing in [these plays] against religion, the king, and the state of the realm" before they were granted permission to act them publicly; this permission was now granted on a case-by-case basis and only once a year.[31] Finally, the Basochiens were limited to performing in the Grande Salle of the parlement before the members of the court. No mention is made, as in rulings during the first half of the sixteenth century, of the Basoche performing in public

29. AN x1a 1632, fol. 57, 8 May 1571. See also AN x1a 1623, fols. 175–75a, 18 June 1568; AN x1a 1659, fol. 303, 28 May 1578; AN x1a 1628, fol. 249a, 11 Jan. 1570; AN x1a 1654, fols. 222a–23, 22 Jan. 1577. Harold C. Gardiner, *Mysteries' End: An Investigation of the Last Days of the Medieval Religious Stage* (New Haven: Yale University Press, 1946), 85.

30. AN x1a 1659, fol. 303, 28 May 1578; L'Estoile, *Mémoires-journaux*, 1:179–80, 192–93, 201–2, 309, 2:7.

31. AN x1a 1675, fol. 269, 12 June 1582. See also AN x1a 1675, fol. 309, 20 June 1582.

venues in the city for the pleasure of a broader public. Although the Basoche of the Paris Parlement nominally continued putting on plays until the early 1580s, the previously rowdy and sometimes satirical side of Basoche humor had been abandoned.

In the years that followed, the Basoche formally ceded its performance rights in return for securing a permanent professional status at the court. In 1583 and 1586, after decades of advocating for such privileges, Basoche leaders gained the magistrates' approval of statutes that codified privileges the clerks had accrued through legal cases during the last half-century. These statutes detailed procedures for electing Basoche officials, regulating the structure of the association, and determining its formal membership. Although the Basoche leaders did not acquire all the privileges they sought, the magistrates affirmed, among other privileges, the clerks' right to parade bearing a maypole each spring and their officials' authority to fine any clerk who missed the procession.[32] By the 1580s, the Basoche of the Paris Parlement was transformed from a festive society into a corporation focused on defending its members' more narrowly professional interests. When, in 1588, the city of Paris rebelled against the king, the Basoche remained loyal to the rump parlement: far from contributing to the disorder and rebellion of the 1589–93 period, the Basochiens refrained from performing satire and kept their heads down. Job security and survival during a time of troubles rated more highly with the clerks than did rowdy processions.[33]

Student and Basoche associations were not the only groups whose farcical humor was silenced during the 1560s. Throughout France, city authorities ceased patronizing and began prohibiting farcical performance at a time when street theater so often seemed to lead to religious riots. This urban violence reached a climax in the summer of 1572 during the notorious Saint Bartholomew's Day massacres. In August of that year, a royal wedding between the king's sister Marguerite and the Huguenot king Henry of Navarre was staged in Paris in the hopes of forging alliances between Catholic and Huguenots. What had been planned in the spirit of toleration ended, however, with a bloodbath. Galvanized by a plot to murder the Huguenot leaders, Catholic residents of the city went on a rampage, slaughtering Huguenots for three days. In the weeks and months that followed, Catholics in several other French cities staged copycat massacres: between August and October 1572, it is estimated that between 4,000 and 10,000 Huguenots were killed by their Catholic neighbors. The massacres sparked a fourth civil war, which ended the following year just as indecisively as the previous conflicts had. In the wake of the massacres, however,

32. AN x1a 1680, 14 May 1583; *Recueil des statuts, ordonnances, reiglements, antiquitez, prérogatives, et prééminences du royaume de la Bazoche* (Paris: C. Besongne, 1654), 9–19.
33. Sara Beam, "The Basoche and the Bourgeoisie Seconde: Careerists at the Paris Parlement during the League," *French History* 17 (2003): 383–86.

large numbers of Huguenots abjured or fled, and the Huguenot population in most French cities outside of the south rapidly declined. As a result, most French cities emerged after 1572 as either solidly Catholic or solidly Huguenot. Despite the continuation of intermittent warfare in parts of the country, there was less and less reason for endemic conflict among residents within a city's walls.[34] Nevertheless, theatrical performances in many towns and cities continued to be closely regulated or censored. This persistence suggests that more was at stake in theatrical regulation than maintaining peace between Catholics and Huguenots. Changing religious sensibilities, particularly among the urban elites, also had an important role to play in the suppression of farcical performance.

Recent research has shown that lay Catholic practice was reshaped by the trauma of the Wars of Religion. This shift toward a more austere, less colorful form of Catholicism was not merely a passing phenomenon driven by the arrival of a preacher into town but a gradual and measurable transformation of French religious practice, particularly in the cities among the urban elites. Because many festive societies were in some form or another religious confraternities, a new, more reserved kind of piety brought about a new attitude to farce. Groups like the Conards and the Confrérie de la Passion were official confraternities, and most Basoche associations celebrated the feast day of Saint Nicholas or Saint Yves as part of their annual activities. Other confraternities, even if they did not regularly perform whole plays, contributed comic and sometimes satirical performances to royal entry ceremonies and other civic celebrations. Farcical theater, broadly defined, traditionally had been integral to confraternal piety. It was thus inevitable that as confraternities changed in response to the theological and social challenges of Wars of Religion period, so too did farcical theater.

By the time war broke out in France in 1562, French Catholics had been faced with the dangers of heresy for over forty years. Protestant reform movements challenged Catholic religious practice on several levels. Theologically, Protestants stressed the importance of faith over good works in the individual's search for salvation, whereas the Catholic Church insisted on the necessity of good works as well, and on the efficacy of the sacraments. These doctrinal differences threatened many elements of traditional Catholic practice. Good works such as pilgrimages, frequent witnessing of

34. Philip Benedict, "The Saint Bartholomew's Massacres in the Provinces," *Historical Journal* 21 (1978): 205–25; Jean-Louis Bourgeon, *Charles IX devant la Saint-Barthélemy* (Geneva: Droz, 1995); Denis Crouzet, *La nuit de la Saint-Barthélemy: Un rêve perdu de la Renaissance* (Paris: Fayard, 1994); Barbara B. Diefendorf, "La Saint-Barthélemy et la bourgeoisie parisienne," *Histoire, Économie et Société* 17 (1998): 341–52; David Rosenberg, "Les registres paroissiaux et les incidences de la réaction à la Saint-Barthélemy à Amiens," *Revue du Nord* 70 (1988): 502; N. M. Sutherland, *The Massacre of St. Bartholomew and the European Conflict, 1559–1572* (London: Macmillan, 1973).

the Mass, and the celebration of saints' days all came under attack by the Huguenots, who deemed them unnecessary and even heretical. The official Catholic response to these attacks was the doctrinally conservative Council of Trent, which met between 1545 and 1563. Although the Tridentine decrees rejected all Protestant theology, they nevertheless sought to curb certain local variations and elements of paganism that had been introduced into Catholic practice over the centuries. Gallican forces resisted the formal implementation of the Tridentine decrees in France, but their existence evoked a unique French Catholic response to the challenges of Protestantism. Historians of the church now acknowledge that many of the seeds of the French Counter-Reformation or Catholic Reformation were sown during this period of religious strife and political decentralization.[35]

Under the pressure of the Protestant critique, Catholic reformers began to encourage lay believers and clergy to return to the core elements of devotional practice and belief. By midcentury, Jesuits, Franciscans, and other popular Catholic preachers urged their brethren to abandon Carnival frivolities, and devotional manuals encouraged laypersons to focus on the Eucharist rather than on traditional Marian worship and communal celebrations.[36] Catholics were also quick to take the fight to the enemy. Huguenots accused Catholics of excess—empty rituals, corrupt immoral clergy, and a casual mixing of the sacred and the profane—but Catholics promptly reversed these charges, accusing the Reformed religion of sinful sensuality: singing psalms in mixed company, for example, or engaging in sexual misconduct during their prayer meetings. Drinking, dancing, and feasting together, activities that Catholic priests had tolerated a century earlier, were

---

35. Marc Venard, "Catholicism and Resistance to the Reformation in France, 1555–1585," in *Reformation, Revolt and Civil War in France and the Netherlands, 1555–1585*, ed. Philip Benedict (Amsterdam: Royal Netherlands Academy of Arts and Science, 1999), 133–48. For distinctly French responses to the Reformation, see Thierry Wanegffelen, *Une difficile fidélité: Catholiques malgré le concile en France XVIe–XVIIe siècles* (Paris: Presses Universitaires de France, 1999); Megan Armstrong, *The Politics of Piety: Franciscan Preachers during the Wars of Religion, 1560–1600* (Rochester: University of Rochester Press, 2004); Barbara B. Diefendorf, *From Penitence to Charity: Pious Women and the Catholic Reformation in Paris* (Oxford: Oxford University Press, 2004); Ann W. Ramsey, *Liturgy, Politics and Salvation: The Catholic League in Paris and the Nature of Catholic Reform, 1540–1630* (Rochester: Rochester University Press, 1999); Virginia Reinburg, "Liturgy and the Laity in Late Medieval and Reformation France," *Sixteenth Century Journal* 23 (1992): 526–47.

36. A. N. Galpern, *The Religions of the People in Sixteenth-Century Champagne* (Cambridge, Mass.: Harvard University Press, 1976), 108–9; Virginia Reinburg, "Hearing Lay People's Prayer," in *Culture and Identity in Early Modern Europe (1500–1800): Essays in Honor of Natalie Zemon Davis*, ed. Barbara B. Diefendorf and Carla Hesse (Ann Arbor: University of Michigan Press, 1993), 31–34; Marc Venard, "Une réforme gallicane? Le projet du concile national de 1551," *Revue d'Histoire de l'Église de France* 67 (1981): 201–25; Marc Venard, "La crise des confréries en France au XVIe siècle," in *Populations et cultures: Études réunies en l'honneur de François Lebrun*, ed. Alain Croix, Michel Lagrée, and Jean Quéniart (Rennes: Université de Rennes, 1989), 398–400; Catherine Vincent, *Les confréries médiévales dans le royaume de France: XIIIe–XVe siècle* (Paris: A. Michel, 1994), 140–44, 170–78.

now demonized as a mark of the Huguenot enemy.[37] In reinventing these practices as Huguenot sins, Catholics had to confront their existence among the faithful. Although the purging of pagan elements from French Catholicism was a process that took several centuries, the threat of Protestantism certainly pushed the Catholic clergy and city officials to try to regularize and purify lay practice, particularly that of the lay confraternities.

Secular authorities reinforced the Catholic Church's campaign by attempting to curb confraternal excess. In 1539, Francis I issued a blanket decree outlawing all "professional confraternities," that is, organizations such as the Basoche that were both workplace associations and lay religious groups.[38] The king's action, directed at professional associations of laborers, was taken in response to labor disputes in Lyon and Paris, but it affected purely religious associations as well. In the short term, the king's edict was soon circumvented by groups that purchased exemptions from the law, but royal assaults against confraternities were renewed during the middle decades of the century: comprehensive ordinances forbidding confraternities from gathering and conducting their affairs were issued in 1558, 1559, 1561, 1566, 1567, 1577, and 1580.[39] These royal edicts, whose very frequency demonstrates their uneven enforcement, repeatedly focus on the potential of confraternities to foment dissension and riot. Beginning in the 1560s, local magistrates in vehemently Catholic cities, including Toulouse, Lyon, and Dijon, reinforced these edicts with local rulings prohibiting dancing and drinking at confraternal feasts.[40]

By the 1560s, as a result of these ecclesiastical and secular assaults, many traditional confraternities had lost much of their popular support. In cities like Troyes and Limoges, where lists of confraternity membership are extant, these documents demonstrate a significant drop in membership during the Wars of Religion. The Limoges Confrérie de Notre-Dame la Joyeuse,

37. Davis, "Rites of Violence," 157–59; G. Wylie Sypher, "Faisant ce qu'il leur vient à plaisir: The Image of Protestantism in French Catholic Polemic on the Eve of the Religious Wars," *Sixteenth Century Journal* 11 (1980): 59–84.

38. Quoted in Émile Coornaert, *Les corporations en France avant 1789* (Paris: Gallimard, 1941), 119–20; Marc Venard, "Les confréries en France au XVIe siècle et dans la première moitié du XVIIe siècle," in *Société, culture, vie religieuse au XVIe et XVIIe siècles*, ed. Yves-Marie Bercé (Paris: Presses de l'Université de Paris-Sorbonne, 1995), 50–51.

39. Antoine Fontanon, *Les edicts et ordonnances des roys de France depuis S. Loys iusques a presens* (Paris: I. De Puys, 1580), 1:508 (9 May 1539), 1:865 (July 1559), 1:867 (5 Feb 1561), 1:868 (July 1566), 1:639 (25 May 1567), 2:1113 (3 Sept. 1577), 1:657 (29 Nov. 1577), 2:1129 (26 Dec. 1580).

40. Archives Municipales Dijon (AMD) B 198, fol. 103v, 13 Feb. 1561; AMD B 205, fol. 35v, 13 July 1568; AMD B 208, fols. 73–76v, 1571; AMD B 210, fols. 107–8, 1573. James R. Farr, *Hands of Honor: Artisans and Their World in Dijon, 1550–1650* (Ithaca: Cornell University Press, 1988), 248–51; Prosper Cabasse, *Essais historiques sur le Parlement de Provence, depuis son origine jusqu'à sa suppression, 1501–1790* (Paris: A. Pihan Delaforest, 1826), 1:174 (12 Dec. 1559); Michel Cassan, "Villes et cultures au XVIe et XVIIe siècles," in Bercé, *Société,*

for example, had played a vital role in festive life during the first decades of the sixteenth century. This lay association, whose members were artisans and minor officials, had held three feasts each year and hired numerous musicians to enliven the dancing that followed their processions. By the 1550s, however, its ranks were reduced by a third—from 118 members in 1539 to 88 in 1557—and continued to decline to a low of 47 members in 1591. In other cities, the number of registered confraternities also shrank rapidly. Whereas the archbishop of Rouen registered 1,200 confraternities during the second half of the fifteenth century, he registered only 53 between 1560 and 1610.[41] Many confraternities that had performed satirical plays during the Renaissance quietly died out or lost much of their membership.

In their place, new, more solemnly pious confraternities sprang up under the sponsorship of the urban secular and ecclesiastical elite. Beginning in the 1560s, confraternities of the Holy Sacrament were established in many French cities. Their special mission was to defend the Host, the consecrated bread that Catholics believed was the Body of Christ, and their members often organized special masses and processions in its honor. Members were urged to confess their sins and to attend mass several times a year, as recommended by the Council of Trent. Although the new-style confraternities still celebrated with food and drink, their statutes devoted far less attention, and their coffers fewer resources, to the association's feasts. Such changes conformed to the wishes of many Catholic reformers, who advocated a more disciplined and private sort of Catholic piety. The social standing of these new confraternities was also much less mixed than that of the traditional medieval confraternities. Whereas older associations had often crossed social boundaries and helped to establish important social links of godparentage between the classes, many reformed Catholic confraternities drew their membership more exclusively from the educated elite. By the seventeenth century, the Confraternities of the Holy Sacrament were agents of social discipline and

culture, vie religieuse, 37–38; Philip T. Hoffman, *Church and Community in the Diocese of Lyon, 1500–1789* (New Haven: Yale University Press, 1984), 41, 87; Isabelle Paresys, "L'ordre en jeu: Les autorités face aux passions ludiques des lillois (1400–1668)," *Revue du Nord* 69 (1987): 541, 551; Nicole Pellegrin, *Les bachelleries: Organisations et fêtes de la jeunesse dans le Centre-Ouest, XVe–XVIIIe siècles* (Poitiers: Société des Antiquaires de l'Ouest, 1982), 57–60, 277–279. Regarding the uneven nature of the French monarchy's efforts to promote religious reform, see Alain Tallon, *Conscience nationale et sentiment religieux en France au XVIe siècle* (Paris: Presses Universitaires de France, 2002).
41. Michel Cassan, "Les multiples visages des confréries de dévotion: L'exemple de Limoges au XVIe siècle," *Annales du Midi* 99 (1987): 38–44; Davis, "Sacred and the Body Social," 51; Galpern, *Religions,* 103–6, 188–91; Hoffman, *Church and Community,* 28–30; David Nicholls, "Inertia and Reform in the Pre-Tridentine French Church: The Response to Protestantism in the Diocese of Rouen, 1520–1562," *Journal of Ecclesiastical History* 32 (1981): 189; Roberts, *City in Conflict,* 164; Venard, "Confréries en France," 52; Ramsey, *Liturgy,* 101–3.

moral cleansing in the cities.[42] Needless to say, these associations did not perform bawdy farces in the city's public squares. Nor were their members as likely to patronize or attend farcical performances in their spare time.[43]

Many confraternities that had previously performed farce found that the only way to survive during the Wars of Religion was to purge their public activities of the scandalous and satirical. In Aix, where the parlement had been particularly vigilant in its attack on heresy, three festive societies—the Basoche, the Prince d'Amour (Prince of Love), and the Abbé de Jeunesse (Youth Abbey)—emerged in the late sixteenth century as central players in the local Corpus Christi festival. This festival, which first became popular during the fourteenth century as a way to celebrate the corporeal relationship of the faithful with the body of Christ, had traditionally included farce and comic floats in its ritual vocabulary. By the 1570s, however, such elements were openly discouraged in Aix, and the Basoche's principal role was to process through the city streets bearing eight large white candles "to honor God and the Court."[44] The Basoche's adaption to a more rigorous Catholic practice extended to its traditional maypole plantings. Although Corpus Christi usually fell in June, it was only on the Saturday after Corpus Christi that the king of the Basoche was allowed to plant maypoles at several prominent locations throughout the city. The magistrates' reform of Corpus Christi was not without its setbacks: in 1584, the Parlement of Aix found it necessary to chastise several players for taking a more lighthearted approach to the festival than the magistrates deemed appropriate.[45] Nevertheless,

42. Andrew E. Barnes, "Religious Anxiety and Devotional Change in Sixteenth-Century French Penitential Confraternities," *Sixteenth Century Journal* 19 (1988): 395, 402–4; Benedict, *Rouen*, 68–69; Robert R. Harding, "The Mobilization of Confraternities against the Reformation in France," *Sixteenth Century Journal* 11 (1980): 85–107; Hoffman, *Church and Community*, 38–40; Venard, "Crise des confréries," 400–402; Mack P. Holt, "Wine, Community and Reformation in Sixteenth-Century Burgundy," *Past and Present* 138 (1993): 58–93; Robert Muchembled, *L'invention de l'homme moderne: Sensibilités, moeurs et comportements collectifs sous l'ancien régime* (Paris: Fayard, 1988), 112–33, 145–47.

43. Bernard Chevalier, *Les bonnes villes de France du XIVe au XVIe siècle* (Paris: Aubier-Montaigne, 1982), 274–85; Raymond Lebègue, *La tragédie religieuse en France: Les débuts (1514–1573)* (Paris: Champion, 1929), 55–60; Louis Paris, *Le théâtre à Reims depuis les Romains jusqu'à nos jours* (Reims: F. Michaud, 1885), 17, 28–31, 51–52; Jean Tricou, "Les confréries joyeuses de Lyon au XVIe siècle et leur numismatique," *Revue Numismatique* 40 (1937): 302–7; Catherine Vincent, *Des charités bien ordonnées: Les confréries normandes de la fin du XIIIe siècle au début du XVIe siècle* (Paris: École Normale Supérieure, 1988), 253–57; Charles Mazouer, *Le théâtre français de la Renaissance* (Paris: Champion, 2002), 32.

44. Arrêt of 5 May 1580, as quoted in Aristide Joly, *Note sur Benoet du Lac: Ou le Théâtre et la bazoche à Aix, à la fin du XVIe siècle* (Lyon: Scheuring, 1862; reprint, Geneva: Slatkine, 1971), 94; Gaspard Grégoire, *Explication des cérémonies de la Fête-Dieu d'Aix-en-Provence* (Aix: David, 1777), passim; Gustave Lambert, *Histoire des guerres de religion en Provence, 1530–1598* (Toulon: J. Laurent, 1868; reprint, Lyon: Chantemerle, 1972), 1:34–83, 120–34, 2:88–89; Miri Rubin, *Corpus Christi: The Eucharist in Late Medieval Culture* (Cambridge: Cambridge University Press, 1991), 243–63; Michel Vovelle, *Les métamorphoses de la fête en Provence de 1750 à 1820* (Paris: Aubier, 1976), 70–71.

45. Grégoire, *Explication*, 201; Joly, *Note*, 79 (14 June 1585), 86 (1 June 1584).

these festive societies continued to play a visible and mostly docile role in the Corpus Christi celebrations to the end of the Old Regime.[46] Festive performance in Aix was increasingly contained within the context of strictly pious religious celebrations. Although the festive societies were not disbanded, they could no longer speak out against the Catholic Church and local political officials.

In Bordeaux, the most prominent festive society, the Basoche, was also forced to abandon farcical performance. At first, the Bordeaux Basoche's experience of the Wars of Religion mirrored that of their Parisian compatriots. Prevented after 1561 from performing farces publicly, the Basochiens continued to be called on to accompany the king from the city gates during royal entry ceremonies throughout the 1560s.[47] The magistrates commended the clerks for having honored the court at these events and throughout the 1570s issued rulings confirming the king of the Basoche's right to collect annual fees and to regulate the clerks' professional conduct.[48] The Bordeaux Basoche seemed destined, like those in Paris and Rouen, to become a professional corporation whose primary role was to secure solicitor posts for its members.

Suddenly, in January 1582, the Bordeaux Parlement magistrates outlawed the Basoche. An arrêt issued by the parlement specified that all clerks, whether they worked at the parlement or the *présidial* court, were to desist from referring to anyone as the king of the Basoche and to cease holding public celebrations in the city, not only this year but for all future years.[49] This abrupt rejection resulted from a violent altercation between the Basoche and

46. Joly, *Note*, 77 (7 May 1596), 78 (3 June 1583), 79 (14 June 1585), 82 (30 May 1584), 85 (31 May 1581). Yves-Marie Bercé, *Fête et révolte: Des mentalités populaires du XVIe au XVIIIe siècle* (Paris: Hachette, 1976), 41; Cabasse, *Essais historiques*, 2:139–40. Histories of the Parlement of Aix make no reference to the Basoche in the seventeenth and eighteenth centuries, testifying to the limited role that the clerks' association played in the cultural life of the city. See Donna Bohanan, *Old and New Nobility in Aix-en-Provence: Portrait of an Urban Elite* (Baton Rouge: Louisiana State University Press, 1992); Monique Cubells, *La Provence des Lumières: Les parlementaires d'Aix au XVIIIe siècle* (Paris: Maloine, 1984); Sharon Kettering, *Judicial Politics and Urban Revolt in Seventeenth-Century France: The Parlement of Aix, 1629–1659* (Princeton: Princeton University Press, 1978).
47. BM Bordeaux MS 369, Savignac, "Extraits," 2:573–74 (10 Feb. 1565), 2:576 (5 Mar. 1565); ADG 1 B 382, fol. 6, 9 Mar. 1574; ADG 1 B 382, fol. 81, 14 Mar. 1574; *The Royal Tour of France by Charles IX and Catherine de'Medici: Festivals and Entries, 1564–6*, ed. Victor E. Graham and W. McAllister Johnson (Toronto: University of Toronto Press, 1979), 281; Sireulde, *Trésor immortel*, xii.
48. ADG 1 B 210, fol. 345, 16 Feb. 1560; ADG 1 B 280, fol. 60, 6 Apr. 1565; ADG 1 B 382, fol. 81, 14 Mar. 1574; ADG 1 B 359, fol. 2, 2 June 1572. Although the Bordeaux Parlement magistrates persecuted heretics vigilantly, they also resisted efforts of Catholic radicals to control the city in 1562. See C.-B.-F. Boscheron des Portes, *Histoire du Parlement de Bordeaux, 1462–1790* (Bordeaux: Charles Lefebvre, 1877), 1:147–49, 153–59, 188, 215–16; L. Desgraves and F. Loirette, "Humanisme et réforme," in *Histoire de Bordeaux*, vol. 4, *Bordeaux de 1453 à 1715*, ed. Robert Boutruche (Bordeaux: Fédération Historique du Sud-Ouest, 1966), 243–50.
49. ADG "Arrêts du Parlement," Jan. 1582, fol. 180, 17 Jan. 1582; Jean de Gaufreteau, *Chronique bordeloise* (Bordeaux: Charles Lefebvre, 1877), 1:224.

local residents after the clerks' procession that year. It is not clear whether this fighting was religiously motivated or whether the Basochiens' procession had been unusually flamboyant or satirical. Altercations between the Basoche and other groups had occurred on several occasions before the Wars of Religion and had resulted only in the clerks' chastisement; even the 1561 incident between the Basoche and students at the Collège de Guyenne had only resulted in the suppression of the association for a matter of months. By the 1580s, however, such behavior warranted a harsher response.

The magistrates' ruling seems to have been obeyed. Even at the end of the Wars of Religion, the Bordeaux Basoche did not reconstitute itself. Instead, clerks working at the parlement founded a new association in 1610, a sacred confraternity formally approved by both the parlement magistrates and ecclesiastical officials. Like most post-Tridentine confraternities, the Confraternity of Clerks and Legal Practitioners replaced raucous feasts with more solemn activities: its principal celebration, still held on the first of May each year, was to gather and celebrate a holy mass in honor of Saint Philip and the apostle Saint John. The prominent sixteenth-century Basoche of Bordeaux, which had entertained kings and city residents with lavish processions and daring farces, had become a cultural anomaly in Bordeaux in a period of Catholic reform.[50]

In Paris too the magistrates of the parlement sought to impose the principles of Catholic reform on the general population, not only by suppressing Basoche performance but also by eliminating the traditionally pious practice of performing mystery plays. Long sensitized to the dangers of heresy and the possibility that theater would mislead the public, the magistrates finally outlawed mystery plays in November 1548. This arrêt was sparked by the request of the long-standing Confrérie de la Passion for permission to resume theatrical performances in the capital. The confrérie had had earlier brushes with the parlement magistrates: in 1540 and 1541, the parlement had attempted unsuccessfully to suppress mystery performances, and in 1545 it had forced the confraternity out of its indoor venue, which was then transformed into a home for the poor. Nevertheless, early in 1548, the confrérie had purchased a large building from the crown, part of the uninhabited Hôtel de Bourgogne, and was in the process of converting the structure into a permanent indoor theatrical venue, the first of its kind in Paris. To protect the group's financial interests, confrérie leaders hoped they could obtain a monopoly on theatrical performances in Paris, and they acquired letters patent to that effect from Henry II. The parlement magistrates, however, while

50. AM Bordeaux MS 565, "Statuts et règles de la Confrérie des clercs et praticiens suivans le Palais de cette Ville de Bourdeaux," in "Recherches sur les corporations et confréries d'arts et métiers de la Ville de Bordeaux au XVIIe et XVIIIe siècles," fol. 177c; BM Bordeaux MS 1024 "S'ensuivant les arrestz, tiltres, documentz et statutz concernant la frerie des clerqz de palais de Bourdeaulx," fols. 1–8; Pellegrin, *Bachelleries*, 117.

approving the monopoly in principle, rejected the confrérie's request that it be permitted to perform traditional mystery plays. Instead, they allowed the confrérie to perform only "other honest and lawful secular plays without offending or insulting any persons."[51] This ruling thus warns not only against religious theater of any kind but also against satire that might be interpreted as slander. In practice, the ruling meant the confrérie would need to shift its repertoire to historical plays popular at the time. Since the confrérie did not protest, the shift to secular genres may have already been occurring. During the remainder of the century, both the Parlement of Paris and the Châtelet supported the rights of the Confrérie de la Passion to organize secular theater performances as long as their performances did not interfere with religious services in the capital. Barring the occasional complaint about performances on Sunday or during Lent, the confrérie seems to have obeyed these strictures. Over the next few decades, the confrérie was essentially transformed from a confraternity into a group of theater proprietors who increasingly contracted out its space to professional actors.[52]

Although the Parlement of Paris's 1548 arrêt against mystery plays applied only to Paris, the ruling seemed to reflect a change in the elite's attitude toward traditional Catholic genres throughout France. Few major productions of mystery plays, which so often contained farcical interludes, were organized after midcentury. An incident in Bordeaux illustrates this gradual but profound shift in the urban elites' religious sensibilities and theatrical taste. In 1578, a group of devout Catholic carpenters organized a mystery play, the first such performance in several years. Unfortunately, the play was so poorly acted that it inspired not religious devotion but jeering laughter. Local Huguenots taunted the actors, accusing them of not having performed a mystery play at all but a farce. When this incident was brought to the attention of the Bordeaux Parlement, the magistrates reacted by outlawing all future mystery performances in the city.[53] The magistrates' response was not to the threat of violence or even of heresy, since the incident had not resulted in even a minor skirmish and the orthodoxy of the carpenters was not brought into question. Apparently they were simply embarrassed by the Huguenots' insulting criticism. Mystery plays, in vogue until the mid-sixteenth century, no longer reflected the piety of the urban elites and were no longer considered to be effective tools for religious instruction or celebration. Yet public religious instruction was clearly imperative during the Wars of Religion, and Catholic urban officials were well aware of the power of the theater. As a result, secular

51. AN x1a 1564, fol. 5, 17 Nov. 1548.
52. AN x1a 1557, fol. 462a, 14 Dec. 1557; AN x1a 1645, fol. 351, 6 Nov. 1574; AN x1a 1688, fol. 205, 6 Oct. 1584; Félibien, *Histoire*, 5:5b (20 Sept. 1577); AN Usuels, Madeleine Jurgens, "La musique au XVIe siècle: Actes concernant les musiciens dans les minutes du notaire," (Minutier Central III:51, 19 Sept. 1578); Eudore Soulié, *Recherches sur Molière et sa famille* (Paris: Hachette, 1863), 152 (22 Feb. 1578), 153 (22 Feb. 1583).
53. Gaufreteau, *Chronique*, 1:212–14.

urban officials began to ask religious orders, in particular the Jesuits, to grace the public stage with more decorous fare that better reflected the spirit of Catholic reform.

Ironically, the parlement magistrates' suppression of mystery plays inadvertently contributed to the increased prominence of commercial actors in Paris during the final decades of the sixteenth century. Although jongleurs had long been part of the theatrical landscape of French cities, they had traditionally met with more skepticism and hostility than local festive societies. Now the tide had turned in their favor, a trend that was aided by the patronage of the king's court. Often, however, the theatrical tastes of urban officials were at odds with those of the last Valois monarchs, who retained a sense of humor until the end.

The French monarchy's support for professional actors during the Wars of Religion was consistent with its long tradition of patronizing farce players. Court fools reigned at the courts of both Francis I and Henry II, and actors visited the court regularly during the first half of the sixteenth century.[54] With the emergence of professional acting troupes in Italy, Francis I and his son Henry II soon began soliciting their services. As early as 1530, Italian troupes contributed lively entertainment to important court celebrations such as royal entry ceremonies and marriages. These troupes presented a variety of different genres for the pleasure of the court, including pastoral plays and neoclassical comedies as well as commedia dell'arte plays—improvised comedies full of acrobatics and bawdy humor. The Valois court's interest in Italian actors was an extension of its cultural orientation toward things Italian, a culture acknowledged by some to be the pinnacle of refinement during the sixteenth century.[55] Although French kings began to outlaw confraternal feasts and festivities at the outset of the Wars of Religion, they continued to patronize Italian troupes at court.[56] Henry III was sufficiently enamored of these actors to write to Bellièvre: "I have never had more perfect pleasure than in seeing them [perform]."[57] Since the Italians' performances were unlikely to have contained any reference to the religious and political crisis currently engulfing France, French kings apparently saw no reason not to enjoy these light diversions.

54. Michel Rousse, "Le pouvoir royal et le théâtre des farces," in *Le pouvoir monarchique et ses supports idéologiques*, ed. Jean Dufournet, Adeline Fiorato, and Augustin Redondo (Paris: Sorbonne Nouvelle, 1990), 185–86.

55. Regarding the love–hate relationship between the French and the Italians, see Henry Heller, *Anti-Italianism in Sixteenth-Century France* (Toronto: University of Toronto Press, 2003); Margaret McGowan, *The Vision of Rome in Late Renaissance France* (New Haven: Yale University Press, 2001).

56. Armand Baschet, *Les comédiens italiens à la cour de France sous Charles IX, Henri III, Henri IV et Louis XIII* (Paris: Plon, 1882), 3–9, 73, 91–92; Jacqueline Boucher, *La cour de Henri III* (Rennes: Ouest-France, 1986) 104–19; Virginia Scott, *The Commedia dell'Arte in Paris, 1644–1697* (Charlottesville: University Press of Virginia, 1990), 122–52.

57. Quoted in Raymond Lebègue, "La comédie italienne en France au XVIe siècle," *Revue de Littérature Comparée* 24 (1950): 7.

Both Charles IX and his brother Henry III were such avid enthusiasts of commedia dell'arte fare that they actively supported the Italians' efforts to perform not only at court but also at Confrérie de la Passion's new Hôtel de Bourgogne theater. In 1571, Charles granted letters patent to an Italian troupe called Il Gelosi, which had been waiting for some time at court for permission to perform publicly. Despite its growing concerns about farce, the Parlement of Paris registered these letters without complaint, granting the Italians the right to act only "tragedies and comedies" rather than commedia dell'arte plays for two months. Six years later, the Italians again returned to Paris and again sought to perform at the Hôtel de Bourgogne. On this occasion, however, the magistrates objected strongly to the debauchery of the Italians' performances and refused to register the letters patent issued by the king. The parlement's condemnation did not dissuade either the company or the king. Henry III simply reissued his letters, which allowed the Italians to perform without the parlement's sanction throughout the autumn of 1577.[58] The last Valois kings' taste for Italian theater exemplifies the growing distance between the king's court and Paris city residents: at a time when fervent Catholic preachers urged the faithful to participate in penitential rituals, the king of France continued to organize Carnival revelries and burlesque theatrical performances for his courtiers' pleasure. By the late 1580s, this emerging cultural divide contributed to Henry III's loss of authority in Paris.[59]

The Parlement of Paris magistrates' vehement rejection of the Italian commedia dell'arte performances reflected their hardening attitude toward farcical performance generally. Throughout the 1560s, the magistrates had made efforts to prevent masking from occurring in the city. A decade later, they forbade even the Basochiens to perform farces.[60] The magistrates' objections to the Italian performers expressed not their concern about religious riots or political satire but their distaste for what they considered unseemly body language. In Paris the Italians would have had to rely on physical humor since most of their audience could not follow Italian dialogue. These gestures incensed the magistrates, who feared, according barrister Pierre L'Estoile, that the plays were nothing but "a school of debauchery for the youth of both sexes in the city of Paris." The players' lewd costumes and suggestive "pectoral movements" were immoral, regardless of whether the

58. Félibien, *Histoire*, 4:833b (15 Sept. 1571), 3:5b (20 Sept. 1577); AN x1a 1633, fol. 321, 15 Oct. 1571; Baschet, *Comédiens*, 38–50; L'Estoile, *Mémoires-journaux*, 1:179, 192.

59. Jean Boutier, Alain Dewerpe, and Daniel Nordman, *Un tour de France royal: Le voyage de Charles IX (1564–66)* (Paris: Aubier, 1984), 153–58; L'Estoile, *Mémoires-journaux*, 2:2, 106, 109, 113, 147–48, 182–83, 3:5, 122; Keith Cameron, *Henri III: A Maligned or Malignant King? Aspects of the Satirical Iconography of Henri de Valois* (Exeter: University of Exeter Press, 1978), 1–45; David Potter, "Kingship in the Wars of Religion: The Reputation of Henri III of France," *European History Quarterly* 25 (1995): 485–528.

60. AN x1a 1586, fol. 462a, 14 Dec. 1557; AN x1a 1613, fol. 42a, 11 May 1565; Félibien, *Histoire*, 4:752b (21 July 1551), 4:764b (14 Dec. 1553), 4:834 (3 June 1572).

performances were in any way satirical.[61] The magistrates were particularly scandalized by the presence on the stage of women, who were apparently exposing their bosoms more than was deemed respectable. Although the magistrates' response to the Italians is particularly strong, what makes it notable is their readiness to condemn a group that had already received the approbation of the king. Whereas only twenty years earlier parlement magistrates had patronized and applauded the bawdy antics of the Basoche, they now considered such behavior, even if it won royal approval, to be inherently reprehensible. Overall, for the parlement magistrates, the meaning of the word *scandalous* had changed. A term that they had previously used to describe explicit satire or violence when disciplining amateur performers at the outset of the sixteenth century was now employed for any performance that expressed sexuality and bodily desire.

By the last decades of the sixteenth century, Parisian theater life had thus been decisively transformed. Gone from the city streets were the raucous performances of the Basoche and other festive societies such as the Enfants-sans-Souci that had entertained nobles and commoners during the heyday of the Renaissance. Instead, the performers who now played at the Hôtel de Bourgogne were usually professional actors who relied on the admission charged at the door for their livelihood. Whereas fifty years earlier censorship of farce had been episodic and haphazard, theatrical performance was now increasingly dependent on the patronage of the king's court as well as the approval of the parlement magistrates. This combination of regulation and patronage had effectively shut down amateur festive societies in the capital.

In the provinces the situation was more varied, as might be expected in a country as diverse and as large as France. Whereas in many cities associations that performed farce were either suppressed or reformed, some Catholic-dominated cities sought to reestablish traditional festive practice after 1572. In Lyon, for example, the traditionally mocking *chevauchée d'asne* ritual was reinvented in the 1570s as a form of comic theater designed to entertain the elite; similarly, in Dijon, where a vehemently Catholic city council controlled the city throughout most of the Wars of Religion period, the Mère Folle festive society was still permitted to operate. In general, the groups that were allowed to continue to perform during the last two decades of the Wars of Religion were brought under the wing of secular officials, usually by the parlements. As long as performers tolerated censorship and were willing to reflect the political aims of the urban elite, some groups during the 1570s and 1580s were able to resume performing at Carnival.

In Rouen, the Conards enjoyed a resurgence after the endemic religious violence of the 1560s came to an end. Attacked by Huguenots in 1562 when they took over the city during the first civil war, the Conards had gone into

61. L'Estoile, *Mémoires-journaux*, 1:192.

abeyance during the remainder of that decade. Nevertheless, in late January of 1571, they took the initiative of requesting permission to perform once again. They appealed to the chief military official residing in Rouen, the sieur de Carrouges, who granted their request. With Carrouges's permission in hand, the Conards then proceeded to the Parlement of Rouen to assure that the decision be formally registered and published. The magistrates, adding that they had no objections to Carrouges's decision because there was no immediate threat to public order in the city, issued an arrêt permitting the Conards to proceed with their Carnival preparations. Rulings almost identical to this one, all of which mention the permission granted by Carrouges, were issued by the parlement again in 1572, 1573 (notably after the Saint Bartholomew's Day massacres), 1574, 1575, and then, after a lacuna of six years, in every year but one between 1581 and 1588. It is remarkable that Carrouges and the magistrates granted the Conards permission to perform in the face of the king's prohibition of confraternal processions and with the knowledge that such processions might well inflame the Huguenots' wrath.[62]

This long run of parlement arrêts is striking, demonstrating the extent to which traditional festive practice had been reshaped by the confessional violence of the previous decade. Before 1560, the Conards had performed virtually every year at Carnival. Although the actors had occasionally been chastised for slandering priests and magistrates, local authorities had made no effort to regulate the festive society systematically. But whereas before the outbreak of the religious wars the Conards' participation in civic life had been taken for granted, after 1571 it needed to be constantly reaffirmed by both Carrouges and the parlement. The disorderly behavior of the Conards, previously appreciated as a traditional element of Carnival, was increasingly read as politically and morally disruptive.

That the Conards sought the parlement's permission to perform is not surprising. The magistrates had long taken responsibility for keeping an eye on them and, more recently, had claimed jurisdiction over any theater performance that smacked of heresy.[63] Yet the Conards did not follow the obvious course and approach the parlement directly. Instead, its leaders turned to the city's military governor, a decision that broke with local tradition. Carrouges's permission is mentioned in each of the parlement rulings concerning the Conards during this period, an anomaly that suggests that the governor's support was crucial.

62. Archives Départementales Seine-Maritime (ADSM) 1 B 619, 3 Feb. 1571; ADSM 1 B 628, 1 Feb. 1572; ADSM 1 B 631, 10 Jan. 1573; ADSM 1 B 635, 27 Jan. 1574; ADSM 1 B 638, 18 Jan. 1575; ADSM 1 B 663, 10 Jan. 1581; ADSM 1 B 667, 24 Jan. 1582; ADSM 1 B 675, 24 Jan. 1584; ADSM 1 B 679, 23 Jan. 1585; ADSM 1 B 683, 15 Jan. 1586; ADSM 1 B 689, 17 Jan. 1587; ADSM 1 B 694, 13 Feb. 1588.
63. ADSM 1 B 567, 25 Oct. 1556; ADSM 1 B 447, 20 May 1536.

The Conards probably turned to Carrouges for support because the confraternity feared a renewal of Huguenot violence and sought the protection of someone who had the means to provide it. In Carrouges, they found the right man for the job. Taneguy Le Veneur, sieur de Carrouges, was first appointed to a military role in Rouen in 1564, at the height of Catholic/Huguenot tensions in the city. As the chief deputy of Normandy's military governor and later appointed governor of Rouen, he emerged as the royal official directly responsible for maintaining public order in Rouen for the next quarter century. Except when he left the city on a tour of duty, Carrouges held the keys to the city gates, an honor and responsibility forfeited by the historically weak Rouen city council. These keys established his authority over the city's guard, the body of residents who patrolled the city in times of crisis, and over the city's three companies of professional military men. Born into a minor Norman noble family that had risen in the king's service, Carrouges actively upheld the king's policies and, as a result, intervened to diffuse a number of violent conflicts between Catholics and Huguenots during the 1560s. By disarming the local population, enforcing rigorous curfews, and strengthening the professional military, he rapidly earned a reputation for keeping the peace. Though a royal official, Carrouges also received a pension from the Guise family, whose leading members strongly disapproved of the crown's concessions to the Huguenots. The Guise had a large client base in Rouen, and Carrouges's association with this powerful family, though it complicates our understanding of his loyalty to the crown, only enhanced his authority in the city.[64] With Carrouges's support behind them, the Conards could be confident that they would be able to perform unmolested.

In early 1571, when the Conards first presented its request to perform, Carrouges had good reason to be optimistic that Rouen would be spared further religious riots.[65] During the previous summer, the third civil war had ended and Huguenots had begun to reestablish themselves in the city. Nevertheless, during that autumn no further violence had occurred between the two confessional groups. In this new atmosphere of peace and renewed tolerance, Carrouges may have seen the Conards' Carnival procession as a means to revive civic culture. The specific conditions that he and the parlement imposed on the Conards suggest that they also sought to reform a previously unruly Carnival tradition. The rulings set very clear limits on

64. Benedict, *Rouen*, 117–18, 120, 171; Stuart Carroll, *Noble Power during the French Wars of Religion: The Guise Affinity and the Catholic Cause in Normandy* (Cambridge: Cambridge University Press, 1998), 83–84, 124, 144–49, 196; *Deux chroniques de Rouen: 1er des origines à 1554; 2ème de 1559 à 1569*, ed. A. Héron (Rouen: Lestringant, 1900), 306, 332, 341–42.
65. Ironically, a religious riot did break out in Rouen in March 1571, though it was not associated with Carnival celebrations. See Jehan de La Fosse, *Les "mémoires" d'un curé de Paris (1557–1590): Au temps des guerres de religion*, ed. Marc Venard (Geneva: Droz, 2004), 100.

what the Conards were allowed to do. Although they did not censor the plays directly, they prohibited the players from roaming the city streets after ten o'clock at night and from gathering together in private homes after the procession. These measures ensured that the Conards remained in the public eye and demarcated precisely when the celebration came to an end. The Conards were also granted a monopoly over all festive activities at Carnival, a privilege that the confraternity had previously claimed as its own in burlesque poems and petitions. By granting the right to dress up in costumes, make festive music, and publicly parade through the city streets to a single festive society, Carrouges and the magistrates were presumably hoping to limit the activity to the members of just the one group and make sure that the audience in the street remained passive spectators. In the short term, the gamble was successful. The Conards performed in early February 1571, and Carnival turned to Lent with no blood being shed in the Rouen city streets.[66] These performances continued to be approved for the next several years, even after the Saint Bartholomew's Day massacre in Rouen in September 1572, during which three hundred to four hundred Huguenots were killed. As in many cities, this bloodletting in large measure resolved local religious tensions in favor of the Catholic majority. The Huguenots were so terrorized by the massacres that many of them either fled the city or converted. By late 1573, the Huguenot population in the city had shrunk to a community of some 1,500 individuals, a shadow of its former self.[67] As a result, by the mid-1570s, it seemed unlikely that Carnival mockery would spark religious violence. Rouen had reestablished its Catholic character, and bringing back a sanitized Carnival festival was part of the city's return to a semblance of normality.

By the early 1580s, however, the Conards faced a new threat, the self-righteous wrath of fervent Catholics. In Rouen, as in many French cities, Jesuit and mendicant preachers as well as newly formed penitential confraternities mobilized large groups of city residents to gather and profess their faith in the city streets.[68] They appealed to God to relieve them of the Huguenot scourge, but they were equally hostile to fellow Catholics, whom they considered lax or insufficiently repentant. After 1584, this new Catholic militancy converged with a political crisis. Henry III, king since the death of his brother Charles IX in 1574, had been a disappointment to Catholic radicals. Although Henry had proven himself on the battlefield against the

66. ADSM 1 B 619, 3 Feb. 1571; Dylan Reid, "Carnival in Rouen: A History of the Abbaye des Conards," *Sixteenth Century Journal* 32 (2001): 1046–47.
67. Benedict, "Massacres," 208–11; Benedict, *Rouen*, 126–29, 151–53; Gayle K. Brunelle, *The New World Merchants of Rouen, 1559–1630* (Kirksville, Mo.: Sixteenth Century Journal Publishers, 1991), 147–59; Robert Langlois d'Estaintot, *La Saint-Barthélemy à Rouen* (Rouen: Métérie, 1877), 19, 30.
68. Benedict, *Rouen*, 167–75; Carroll, *Noble Power*, 200–210.

Huguenots in his youth, once he took the throne he seemed reluctant to eliminate the Huguenots from the realm. Henry was a demonstrative Catholic who joined penitential processions in Paris, but his seemingly licentious lifestyle at court left many Catholics frustrated and angry. The question of Henry's commitment to the Catholic cause became more urgent in 1584 when Henry's heir, his youngest brother the Duke of Alençon, unexpectedly died. This situation left a Huguenot, Henry of Navarre, as the most obvious heir to the throne. Catholic militants urged Henry III to disown his heretical cousin, but the king prevaricated in the hopes that Henry of Navarre would convert back to Catholicism. The king's apparent indecisiveness sparked the resurgence of a Catholic opposition movement called the Holy League, a volatile alliance of Catholic preachers, frustrated municipal residents, and nobles led by the Guise family. In Rouen, both Catholic preachers and the Guise worked to foment a growing dissatisfaction with royal religious policy. The Guise family's efforts indeed met with such success that Carrouges reported as early as 1585 to Henry III that the "greater part" of Rouen's populace sympathized with the League.[69] Over the next few years, Carrouges continued to send reports to the king, but he did not break with the Guise and remained relatively passive in the face of the growing opposition to the king in Rouen.[70] Nevertheless, Carrouges seems to have been unwilling to participate actively in a political movement that challenged the authority of the king. Like many other men in power whom we now identify as belonging to the *politique* faction during the 1580s and 1590s, Carrouges apparently believed that religious or political reform in France had to take place within the context of obedience to the crown.[71]

The Conards evidently shared Carrouges's assessment of the political situation. Seeing no contradiction between celebrating Carnival and fighting heresy, the Conards persisted with their processional traditions and performed each year during the 1580s, even though their traditional festive fare seemed increasingly out of place in the polarized religious and political context of this pious decade. Every year, Carrouges supported their performances. Some powerful religious leaders in Rouen doubted, however, whether the Conards' Carnival antics deserved the sanction of the city's elite. The Conards' own actions during the 1580s only reinforced such misgivings. In December 1586, the Conards made the audacious decision to publish a collection of verse and buffoonery. This publication, titled *Triumph of the Abbey of the Conards*, contained innocuous bawdy verse composed by recent members of the group. More remarkably, it also reprinted an

69. Quoted in Benedict, *Rouen*, 171. See also Mark Greengrass, "The 'Sainte Union' in the Provinces: The Case of Toulouse," *Sixteenth Century Journal* 14 (1983): 493.
70. Benedict, *Rouen*, 68, 196, 200–201; Carroll, *Noble Power*, 202–6, 229–32.
71. Edmond M. Beame, "The 'Politiques' and the Historians," *Journal of the History of Ideas* 54 (1993): 355–79; J. H. M. Salmon, *Society in Crisis: France in the Sixteenth Century* (London: Ernest Benn, 1975), 234–73.

account of a 1541 procession, during which the Conards had held a mock tribunal, appointed a gluttonous cardinal, read from Rabelais, and performed a farce that mocked both secular and ecclesiastical authorities.[72] The Conards' motivations for republishing the 1541 pamphlet may have been innocent, but their gesture was ill timed. During that winter, the city faced food shortages, and contemporaries recounted scenes of skeletal figures dying in the city streets. In this context, the Conards' jokes seemed out of place, even blasphemous, and their form of Catholic piety incompatible with the dominant eschatology of the day. That spring during Lent, a canon at the Rouen cathedral preached against the Conards' excesses and followed up his sermon by registering a formal complaint with the parlement. This time the magistrates did not defend the Conards and issued a ruling stripping the association of its privileges: the confraternity was no longer allowed to elect an abbot or to publish pamphlets, and it was forced to rename itself the House of Sobriety.[73]

But the so-called House of Sobriety remained unchastened. Before the Carnival of 1588, the association again appealed to the parlement and to Carrouges, insisting on its right to perform "farces and merriment."[74] Interestingly, they gave permission for the Carnival performance, a decision that suggests they were only lukewarm enforcers of the Conards' newfound sobriety. Once again, the Conards performed in a charged atmosphere. Political support for Henry III in Rouen was fragile: the Guise and their allies were on the move, gathering funds and forces just outside the city walls. Within Rouen, the Duke of Guise was celebrated in pamphlets and commemorative medals as the military hero of the Catholic cause. Twisting these themes to their own ends, the members of the House of Sobriety employed political allegory during their procession. On one of their floats, the performers depicted a tableau vivant of three or four finely dressed men fighting over a royal scepter—a tableau interpreted by a contemporary witness of the procession as alluding to the ambition of the Guise to usurp royal authority.[75] Conservative in their fidelity to a traditional theatrical genre, the Conards also proved in 1588 to be conservative in their politics, choosing not to break with the king. Their longtime supporter, Carrouges, was soon to make a similar choice.

The sentiments of many Rouen residents did not lie with the Conards. Although Carrouges managed to keep Rouen loyal to the king throughout 1588, he could not contain the people's outrage when Henry III had the

---

72. *Triomphe de l'abbaye de Conards avec une notice sur les fêtes des fous* (Rouen, 1587; reprint, Paris: Librairie des Bibliophiles, 1874), 1, 3, 12.
73. Benedict, *Rouen*, 173–74; A. Floquet, "Histoire des Conards de Rouen," *Bibliothèque de l'École des Chartes* 1 (1839–40): 118.
74. ADSM 1 B 694, 13 Feb. 1588; Reid, "Carnival in Rouen," 1048–49.
75. Carroll, *Noble Power*, 207–8; Floquet, "Histoire des Conards," 119. For a similar mockery of the Guise in Tours, see Crouzet, *Guerriers*, 1:337.

Guise leaders assassinated that December. A few months later, a religious procession led by the League escalated into a violent rebellion, and the governor was forced to surrender the city's keys to the radical Catholic party. Under the new regime, the so-called House of Sobriety was suppressed.[76]

The defeat of the Conards and of Carrouges signals the failure of the Catholic moderate or *politique* position in 1589. The habit of obedience to the crown, though it had withstood the rising tide of Catholic radicalism, finally broke under the pressure of Henry's encroachment upon local privileges, his failure to defeat heresy, and his rash murder of the Guise. Although this overt connection between the Conards, Carrouges, and a royalist politic is a story unique to Rouen, the fate of traditional festivities throughout France followed a similar trajectory during the Wars of Religion. Whereas both Catholics and Protestants had in the 1560s used traditional festive rituals as an opportunity for religious violence, twenty years later Carnival itself was antithetical to the intense, eschatological piety of many Catholics. Rather, penitential processions emerged as a truly radical popular form of political expression during the 1580s. In cities like Paris and Rouen, where the League had a large measure of popular support, it was penitential piety, not the subversive satire of farce, that inspired the people to rebel against the king and helped to bring the Holy League to power during the 1589–93 period.

The Wars of Religion period, in short, marked a fundamental turning point in the history of farcical theater in France. Fearing that festive societies' performances might spark religious riots and undercut the Catholic faith, city officials throughout France outlawed farce in the 1560s. This abrupt break in a long tradition of comic performance condemned many amateur festive societies to oblivion. Although a handful survived, the back of the French amateur farce-playing tradition was broken. Instead, professional actors were to emerge as the primary performers of farce in the decades to come.

The intensified repression and censorship of the decades of the Wars of Religion deprived young men, particularly those belonging to the couche moyenne, of an important means to voice their concerns about the way that power was wielded in their communities. Before 1560, noble, bourgeois, and artisan youths had used farce as a public medium to point out and condemn local corruption. During the prolonged crisis of the second half of the sixteenth century, however, their political satire was silenced. Such a development is not surprising: any community at war is more concerned

---

76. Carroll, *Noble Power*, 212–15; Robert Langlois d'Estaintot, *La Ligue en Normandie, 1588–94* (Paris: Aubry, 1862), 7–10. The Conards regrouped briefly at the end of the Wars of Religion and performed until 1609, after which the association seems to have died out of its own accord. By the late 1620s, the Rouen Parlement outlawed all Carnival festivities but made no special mention of the Conards. ADSM 1 B 710, 20 Dec. 1594; ADSM 1 B 727, 20 Dec. 1597; ADSM 1 B 797, 3 Feb. 1609; ADSM 1 B 927, 21 Feb. 1626.

with a crushing tax burden and local violence than with maintaining festive privileges, particularly those that question authority. Often, with war's end, such traditions reassert themselves. Indeed, many popular cultural practices that went underground during the Wars of Religion, such as popular dancing and civic bonfires, were subsequently reestablished. Nor, of course, did farce die out after the Wars of Religion. Nevertheless, the tradition of amateur farce playing that had allowed the theater to take such a prominent role in civic life did not resume after 1600. This tradition had been dependent on the urban elites' tolerance and patronage, which did not on the whole survive. With the demise of these amateur associations, farce was transformed from an integral element of festive life into an exclusively commercial form of entertainment, and its role in civic culture changed for good.

Urban authorities' suppression of farce was driven first by fear and later by distaste. Both responses emerged out of the religious conflicts of this period. City officials rightly feared that farce might be used to promote radical religious violence, whether Catholic or Huguenot, and in the interests of maintaining public order they did their best to prevent this from occurring. Later, during the 1570s and 1580s, their own commitments to Catholic reform cemented their misgivings about farce as an inherently scandalous and unseemly genre. These concerns about the theater fomenting religious and moral sedition were apparently less pressing for the Valois kings, who, detached, perhaps, from the realities of urban violence, made no effort to purge the stage of farce. Indeed, the monarchy's patronage of the Confrérie de la Passion and Italian commedia dell'arte troupes hindered rather than aided city officials' efforts to cleanse the urban stage of scandal.

5 *Professional Farceurs in Paris,*
1600–1630

After 1600, farce enjoyed a temporary resurgence in Paris. When amateur actors exited the public stages of the capital, professional farceurs rushed in to replace them. Most of these actors performed at the Hôtel de Bourgogne, the indoor theater venue owned by the well-established Confrérie de la Passion. Unlike Renaissance farceurs, these performers were professionals: acting was their livelihood, and they tailored their performances to attract the largest possible audience. These professional troupes performed a variety of secular plays—histories and tragedies as well as farces—in front of paying audiences of elite Parisians. Only in the 1620s, when the tastes of these noble and educated theatergoers began to change, did professional actors eliminate or downplay the sexually explicit farces that until then had been their bread and butter.

Even during their heyday of the 1610s, however, professional farceurs had much less freedom to be satirical than had the amateur actors of the Renaissance. Unlike members of festive societies, who had been respectable artisans and even noblemen, professional actors were socially marginal and perceived as morally suspect by most French urban officials. As a result, securing the patronage and approval of the monarchy was imperative to their success: without the open approbation and intermittent patronage of Henry IV and Louis XIII, professional farceurs could not have succeeded on the Parisian stages of the early seventeenth century. The price of this success, however, was the removal of political and religious satire from their performances. Professional farceurs were too dependent on the monarchy to challenge royal policies openly. As a result, the lighthearted but pointed mockery of city officials and local bishops found in many Renaissance performances disappeared from the theatrical repertoire. The farceurs' sanitizing of farce and securing of royal approval were so successful that in

1630 Louis XIII forced the Confrérie de la Passion to rent the Hôtel de Bourgogne theater to their troupe indefinitely. Far from repudiating farce, French kings enjoyed its bawdy humor much longer than did most Parisian theatergoers.

Several groups of farce players were notorious in the capital during the first decades of the seventeenth century. Although most performed at the Hôtel de Bourgogne, street and fairground performers were also common-place. The best known of these outdoor performers was Tabarin, whose real name was Antoine Girard, and his brother the "Docteur Mondor." Beginning in 1618 and continuing through the 1620s, these brothers often set up a temporary stage near the Pont Neuf to entertain the passing crowds and to sell medicinal potions. The bridge and the area adjoining it to the Île de la Cité were an ideal location for such a show. Unlike late medieval bridges, the Pont Neuf, constructed during the reign of Henry IV, was built without houses or other structures along its sides. Because Tabarin's stage was visible from both sides of the river, passersby could see when he was performing and wander up, a pastime mentioned in pamphlets and memoirs of the day.[1] Tabarin's performances were a mixed bag: the brothers hawked their wares, but they also amused the crowd with comic dialogue, a combi-nation of commerce and entertainment that was commonplace at the time.[2] After Tabarin's marriage to Victoria Bianca, she joined the brothers on stage under the name Francisquine, and their repertoire expanded to include tra-ditional battle-between-the-sexes farces. Unlike most performers in Paris, Tabarin never performed at the Hôtel de Bourgogne theater, probably to avoid its high rent.[3]

---

1. Jean-Pierre Babelon, "Les derniers Valois et Henri IV à Paris," in *Paris et ses rois* (Paris: Paris-Musées, 1987), 85; La Paulmier, "Mondor et Tabarin, seigneurs féodaux," *Mémoires de la Société de l'Histoire de Paris et de l'Île-de-France* 10 (1883): 179–90; Émile Magne, *Le plaisant Abbé de Boisrobert, fondateur de l'Académie française, 1592–1662* (Paris: Mercure de France, 1909), 50n1; *La pourmenade du pré aux clercs* (1622); Gédéon Tallemant des Réaux, *Les historiettes*, ed. M. de Monmerqué and Paulin Paris (Paris: J. Techener, 1858), 7:534; Thomas Platter, as quoted in William L. Wiley, *The Early Public Theatre in France* (Cambridge, Mass.: Harvard University Press, 1960), 70.

2. Auguste Jal, *Dictionnaire critique de biographie et d'histoire* (Paris: Plon, 1872), 878; Archives Municipales Dijon (AMD) B 287, fol. 216v, 29 Nov. 1649; AMD B 294, fol. 32v, 28 June 1655. See also *Les fantaisies du farceur Tabarin*, ed. Yves Giraud (Paris: Pensée Univer-selle, 1976); Geneviève Serreau and David Esrig, *Tabarin* (Paris: Plasma, 1981).

3. Tabarin's immunity from the Confrérie de la Passion's monopoly was likely the result of royal patronage. He performed before Louis XIII at court and claimed that the Châtelet had granted him special permission to perform wherever he pleased in Paris. Bibliothèque Natio-nale (BN) MS fonds 500 Colbert, vol. 92, fol. 201v; BN MS fonds 500 Colbert, vol. 94, fol. 295; *La response du sieur Tabarin au livre intitulé "La tromperie des charlatans descouverte"* (Paris: Sylvestre Moreau, 1619); Jean de Gorris, *Discours de l'origine, des moeurs, fraudes et impostures des ciarlatans, avec leur descouverte, . . . par I. D. P. M. O. D. R.* (Paris: Denis Langlois, 1622); *Harangue faicte au charlatan de la place d'Aufine, à la descente de son théâtre* (Paris, [1620–22]).

FIGURE 5. Tabarin on stage, 1622. (Source: Bibliothèque Nationale de France, Réserve Y2–2825)

The professional lives of another trio of farceurs emerge more clearly from the historical record. Robert Guérin, Hugues Guéru, and Henri Le Grand—more commonly known by their stage names Gros Guillaume, Gaultier Garguille, and Turlupin, respectively—formed a long-lasting and popular association that entertained Paris audiences between 1600 through the early 1630s. Although they did not begin their careers as farce players, by the mid-1610s their renown was based on the short comic plays with which they closed each evening's performance.

Throughout most of their careers, this trio of farceurs performed at the Confrérie de la Passion's Hôtel de Bourgogne theater, which the association had built in 1548. This theater was a unique performing venue, the only public theater at this time in France.[4] The building itself was just over 33 meters long and 13½ meters wide, filling a large rectangular plot in the heart of Paris on the rue Mauconseil. The stage, probably 13 meters wide and 14 meters deep, was much larger than the temporary stages on which actors usually performed. Surrounding it in a U formation were nineteen elevated boxes, seven on either side of the building and five at the end, each of which could accommodate four to six individuals; these were often reserved for Confrérie de la Passion members or courtiers.[5] Although most of these boxes did not face the stage and thus did not provide an unobstructed view, those in the boxes could at least be seated during the performance. The rest of the audience was relegated to the parterre, the wide-open space in front of the stage some 19 meters long and 13 meters wide. The men who bought these cheaper tickets stood throughout the performance, a standard practice in Parisian public theaters until the late eighteenth century. Food sellers roamed among the audience members, offering refreshment during the performance, further contributing to a lively and somewhat raucous atmosphere. At full capacity, the Hôtel probably accommodated one hundred spectators in the boxes and one thousand in the parterre below.[6] The fact that the confrérie's theater was enclosed allowed the theater season to be significantly prolonged. During the long and dark winter months, Parisian troupes were more likely to persuade audiences to remain for a two- to three-hour program if they could guarantee some

4. A Lyon merchant founded a professional theater in 1539, but it soon failed. Claudius Brouchoud, *Les origines du théâtre de Lyon* (Lyon: Scheuring, 1865), 22–24.

5. David V. Illingworth, "Documents inédits et nouvelles précisions sur le théâtre de l'Hôtel de Bourgogne d'après des documents du XVIIIe siècle," *Revue d'Histoire du Théâtre* 22 (1970): 125–32; D.-H. Roy, "La scène de l'Hôtel de Bourgogne," *Revue d'Histoire du Théâtre* 14 (1962): 227–35; André Villiers, "L'ouverture de la scène à l'Hôtel de Bourgogne," *Revue d'Histoire du Théâtre* 22 (1970): 133–41.

6. S. Wilma Deierkauf-Holsboer, *Le théâtre de l'Hôtel de Bourgogne* (Paris: Nizet, 1968), 1:114; Wiley, *Early Public Theatre*, 211–12. See also Jeffrey S. Ravel, *The Contested Parterre: Public Theater and French Political Culture, 1680–1791* (Ithaca: Cornell University Press, 1999).

protection from the wind and rain. Performances were held in the afternoon, and although there is no direct evidence that theaters were heated, body heat and the oil lamps that lit the stage provided some measure of warmth.[7] Professional troupes took advantage of the Hôtel's relative comfort to provide entertainment several times a week throughout the winter season. This marks a significant departure from the practice in the sixteenth century, when amateur festive societies performed only on festival days and usually did so outdoors.

Gros Guillaume and his fellow farceurs spent part of their early careers working under the actor Valleran Le Conte, whose skills and good taste were celebrated by contemporaries.[8] Despite his strong reputation, however, Le Conte had trouble paying his rent at the Hôtel de Bourgogne. Although he was able to secure contracts at the theater every year between 1606 and 1612, his debts mounted. By 1612, having forfeited a long rental contract with the Confrérie de la Passion, he was forced to sell his extensive collection of costumes to settle them. Le Conte's career as a troupe leader continued after this debacle, but he rarely performed in Paris after 1612.[9] When he left the city, many of his fellow actors formed a new troupe under Guérin.

Unlike Le Conte, the trio of farceurs could well afford to use the Hôtel de Bourgogne. During the trio's heyday, between 1615 and 1620, the confrérie raised the rent from 200 to 240 livres per month, but they seem to have had no difficulty accommodating the increase.[10] The secret of the troupe's success may have been its tendency to sign on for short contracts. Whereas Le Conte repeatedly contracted the Hôtel de Bourgogne for periods as long as six months, the farceurs usually rented the theater for a month or two at a time. Shorter contracts allowed them to take their act to another city when public attention waned or, even more desirably, to the king's court when it left Paris for the season. As early as 1613, some "French actors," probably members of Guérin's troupe who were by this time calling themselves the *comédiens du roi*, performed before Louis XIII

7. Nicolas de La Mare, *Traité de la police, où l'on trouvera l'histoire de son établissement, les fonctions et les prérogatives de ses magistrats* (Paris: J. et P. Cot, 1705), 3:440; *Journal de Jean Héroard*, ed. Madeleine Foisil and Pierre Chaunu (Paris: Fayard, 1989), 1576 (14 Feb. 1609).

8. Archives Nationales Minutier Central (AN MC) X:9, 7 Apr. 1609; AN MC X:14, 29 July 1610; Deierkauf-Holsboer, *Hôtel de Bourgogne*, 1:179–91.

9. Jan Fransen, *Les comédiens français en Hollande au XVIIe et au XVIIIe siècle* (Paris: Champion, 1925), 16–17; Jean de Gaufreteau, *Chronique bordeloise* (Bordeaux: Charles Lefebvre, 1877), 1:306–7; Georges Mongrédien, *Dictionnaire biographique des comédiens français du XVIIe siècle* (Paris: CNRS, 1961), 162–63.

10. AN MC X:28, 1 Oct. 1615, 28 Nov. 1615; AN MC X:30, 28 Sept. 1616; AN MC X:44, 31 Aug. 1621; Jan Fransen, "Documents inédits sur l'Hôtel de Bourgogne," *Revue d'Histoire Littéraire de la France* 34 (1927): 353.

at court.[11] Although the *comédiens du roi* performed a mixed repertoire, it was their farcical performances that earned them notoriety. Contemporary engravings of the trio depict them in their grotesque glory. Gros Guillaume, in particular, was represented as a striking figure: dressed in a long tunic that he belted twice to emphasize the large size of his belly, he was said to resemble a barrel of wine filled to the brim.[12]

The farces performed by the Hôtel de Bourgogne trio and Tabarin clearly drew on the long-standing French farcical tradition, but their repertoire was nevertheless particularly attuned to the tastes of early seventeenth-century audiences. Bawdy jokes had just as much appeal as they had had a century earlier, but the scope of humor had narrowed: early seventeenth-century farces were less satirical than those of the Renaissance.

Like the farces of the Renaissance, early seventeenth-century farces were one-act plays that revolved around a small cast of characters and a simple plot line. The comedy was derived from the foibles of human nature, particularly selfish desires and bodily urges, which usually triumphed at the end of the play. Often the play centered on a ruse: a husband tricking his wife, a servant robbing his master, or a child thwarting the intentions of his parent. In *Pleasant and Entertaining Farce*, aging Gros Guillaume leaves his young daughter Florentine with his servant Turlupin to protect her chastity while he embarks on a long voyage to the Indies.[13] Although Turlupin is tempted to seduce Florentine himself, her affections lie elsewhere. By the end of the play, Gros Guillaume returns home, horrified to discover that Florentine has defied his wishes and is betrothed to marry a young lover. Fighting among all characters then ensues as the play ends. With the exception of Gros Guillaume's traveling to the Indies, the play is very similar to dozens of Renaissance farces, with just the same kind of humor. Physical violence was still commonplace on the Paris stage, and explicit sexual references were presumably not offensive to the audience.

Early seventeenth-century farces still represented the human individual as an open, porous body inextricably linked to the physical world. In the opening scene of one of Tabarin's farces, Piphagne, an elderly Italian lover, discusses with his servant Tabarin his plans to marry a young woman. Taking advantage of Piphagne's ignorance of French, Tabarin engages in two

---

11. Although we cannot be absolutely certain that the actors who performed before the king in 1613 and 1614 were Guérin's troupe, it seems likely, given that they dominated the Paris stage at the time and were by this time calling themselves the *comédiens du roi*. Gros Guillaume did perform before the king at Blois in 1618. Eudore Soulié, *Recherches sur Molière et sa famille* (Paris: Hachette, 1863), 157 (16 Jan. 1613); "Dons de Henri IV et de Louis XIII à leurs 'comédiens italiens' et 'comédiens françois' (1603–1623)," *Archives Historiques* 2 (1889–91): 282. See Magne, *Plaisant Abbé*, 49.

12. Wiley, *Early Public Theatre*, 66.

13. "Farce plaisante et recreative," in *Farces du Grand Siècle: De Tabarin à Molière, farces et petites comédies du XVIIe siècle*, ed. Charles Mazouer (Paris: Librairie Générale Française, 1992), 91–104.

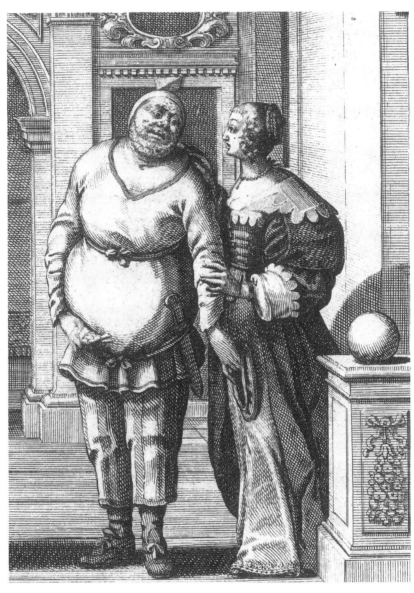

FIGURE 6. Gros Guillaume, in a detail from Abraham Bosse, *L'Hôtel de Bourgogne*, 1633–34. (Source: Bibliothèque Nationale de France, Réserve ED–30a)

levels of conversation, one quasi-respectful concerning the arrangements for the marriage and another addressed to the audience, in which he vents his true feelings. About Piphagne and his prospects as a lover, Tabarin minces no words. He compares the older man's sighs of passion to purified liquid farts and wonders whether Piphagne is enough of a man to satisfy his new wife, noting that "the clock no longer keeps time because the tip of the needle is worn out and the weights lie very low."[14] While apparently serving his master efficiently and with respect, Tabarin subjects him to a stream of sexual and scatological mockery that undermines his authority.

Tabarin does not exempt himself from his wry musings. Noting Piphagne's overwhelming sexual desires, he complains of his own physical compulsions and difficulties. Informing the audience that "it has been eight days that I haven't had an excremental encounter," he also laments that his hunger is starting to overwhelm him.[15] His eagerness to plan the wedding feast is clearly linked to his own interest in eating and drinking his fill at the celebration. Tabarin does not hesitate to characterize his own urges in the same terms as he does his master's: he genially hopes they may both satisfy their desires. In fact, Tabarin's greed for food and drink, which parallels his master's lust for his young bride, lands him in trouble. Thinking he has got a bargain from a meat seller when he purchases two huge sacks of meat, Tabarin opens them at the feast only to discover that the sacks contain two angry men, who had in turn been tricked by the meat seller. Like the farces of the Renaissance, early seventeenth-century comic fare embraces the grotesque in order to affirm the basic humanity of all the characters. Everyone craves food and sex; everyone must visit the outhouse; and finally everyone grows old and dies. These natural processes of physical need and deterioration are not as repressed as they would be later in the seventeenth century, when the demands of civility took hold in polite French society.

Without attendance records or even an account of theater ticket receipts, we cannot easily determine who laughed at these farces. Nevertheless, the evidence suggests that the audience at the Hôtel de Bourgogne consisted not of day laborers but of literate bourgeois and even aristocratic Parisians. Whereas memoir writers and apologists for the neoclassical theater after 1630 characterized theatergoers in the earlier period as crude louts, there is no direct evidence that the poorest Parisians attended this theater at the beginning of the seventeenth century.[16] Unlike farce players' performances during the sixteenth century, which had occurred at traditional festivals, performances at the Hôtel de Bourgogne took place on market days, when artisans and merchants would be busy selling their wares. The cost of attendance, which the Châtelet determined should be five sous for entry to the parterre

14. "Farce," 78.
15. Ibid., 75.
16. Maurice Magendie, *La politesse mondaine et les théories de l'honnêteté en France au XVIIe siècle, de 1600 à 1660* (Paris: Felix Alcan, 1926), 27, 106.

and ten sous for box seats, would have been prohibitively expensive for a common laborer; a man working in the construction industry would have had to sacrifice half his daily wages just for standing room in the parterre.[17] In addition, police rulings about rowdy crowds outside of the theater do not mention poor or working people in the throng. Instead, they focus on the disorderly behavior of military men, lackeys, and students, who seem to have predominated in the parterre. If the working poor had been an important element of these crowds, their presence would probably have been mentioned in these documents. Traditionally, Parisian authorities had objected to theater performances on the grounds that they distracted the poor from religious services and encouraged them to spend money they did not have.[18] Such complaints, while commonplace a hundred years earlier, are rarely mentioned in police rulings of the early seventeenth century.

Although the lowest classes, whose members might seem to us those most receptive to farce, were probably not represented among these audiences, the highest classes, whose members might have been expected to demand something more refined, were there in strength. Evidence from contemporary memoirs demonstrates that literate bourgeois and aristocratic men did attend Hôtel de Bourgogne performances. Parisian lawyer Pierre de L'Estoile attended a 1607 farcical performance in the presence of Henry IV, an anecdote that demonstrates that at least some Parisian men of the law had overcome their scruples about the scandalous nature of the theater by the early seventeenth century. In addition, Louis XIII's physician Héroard notes several occasions when the young king attended farcical performances at the Hôtel de Bourgogne during the 1610s. Other socially prominent memoir writers, including the abbot of Marolles, reminisce in some detail about performances they attended as students in Paris and recall the professional farce players as particularly enjoyable.[19] On the basis of such evidence, it seems reasonable to conclude that theatrical troupes geared their performances to the tastes of these educated bourgeois and aristocratic men, an audience that until approximately 1625 enjoyed crude farce at least as much as neoclassical tragedy.

Despite these plays' similarities with Renaissance farce, which also featured ribald comedy and attracted audiences from the French elite, there was an important difference: unlike earlier farces, these early seventeenth-century plays

17. Micheline Baulant, "Le salaire des ouvriers du bâtiment à Paris de 1400 à 1726," *Annales: Économies, Sociétés, Civilisations* 26 (1971): 483; La Mare, *Traité*, 3:440 (12 Nov. 1609); John Lough, *Paris Theatre Audiences in the Seventeenth and Eighteenth Centuries* (Oxford: Oxford University Press, 1957), 9–23, 43–44.

18. In contrast, sixteenth-century rulings issued by the Parlement of Paris explicitly mention the common people as members of the Confrérie de la Passion's audiences. See AN x1a 4914, fols. 80–82, 9 Dec. 1541; AN U*2062, Le Nain, "Registres du Parlement," fol. 27 (15 Sept. 1571); Lough, *Paris Theatre Audiences*, 11–22.

19. Pierre de L'Estoile, *Mémoires-journaux, 1574–1611*, ed. G. Brunet (Paris: Librairie des Bibliophiles, 1875–99; reprint, Paris: Taillander, 1982), 8:271–73; Lough, *Paris Theatre Audiences*, 43–44; Wiley, *Early Public Theatre*, 54–55.

were largely devoid of satirical content. There is little reference to social hierarchy in the dialogue and songs of the plays, apart from the distinction between master and servant, and there is no depiction of the judicial or religious authorities who often populated the farces, sotties, and morality plays performed by Renaissance amateurs. In the seventeenth-century plays, most of the characters are of vaguely artisan or peasant stock. The humor tends to hinge on one's place in the life cycle rather than on one's status in the social hierarchy: the clever daughter deceives the foolish father, the vengeful wife tricks her cuckolding husband, or the lusty young man makes a fool of himself in search of sex. Although some class differences do persist in these plays, rarely do we see a noble or a bishop, and certainly not an identifiable individual, mocked on the stage. Bawdy humor and social satire of the more generic kind persisted, but professional actors were much less critical of political and religious authority than their Renaissance predecessors were.

Some of these changes can be attributed to the prominence of Italian commedia dell'arte actors, who often performed both in Paris and at the king's court.[20] Whereas traditional French farce was acted by amateurs and linked to the church calendar and to Carnival, the theater that emerged in Italy during the sixteenth century was largely secular. These professional Italian troupes performed a variety of genres, including neoclassical plays, but when they traveled to France, where public audiences could not understand their spoken dialogue, they increasingly relied on the improvisational and physical aspects of their repertoire. Since the plays themselves were not published until much later, little is known for certain about the content of the commedia dell'arte repertoire, but the basic structure of the plays can be determined. Most performances alternated between comic interludes involving dancing, acrobatics, and crude humor, and dramatic narrative, in which the young lovers declare their passion and try to overcome the obstacles in the path to romantic union. Unlike plays performed by French festive societies during the Renaissance, which often referred to contemporary political events, commedia dell'arte plays performed in France seem to have contained little if any explicit satire.[21] The principal Italian element incorporated into seventeenth-century French farces seems to have been the love story. In Tabarin's farces, the lover is always from Italy and often speaks of his romantic passion in Italian. These speeches, accompanied by dramatic gestures of longing and lovesickness, would have been easily understood by French audiences and probably were enhanced by the ridiculous posturing of the actor playing the lover. The character of the Captain was also a new addition to French farce. When the Gros Guillaume

20. Mazouer, introduction to *Farces*, 12–13; Bernard Faivre, *Répertoire des farces françaises: Des origines à Tabarin* (Paris: Imprimerie Nationale, 1993), 439–47.
21. Virginia Scott, *The Commedia dell'Arte in Paris, 1644–1697* (Charlottesville: University Press of Virginia, 1990), 122–52; Gustave Attinger, *L'esprit de la Commedia dell'arte dans le théâtre français* (Paris: Société d'Histoire du Théâtre, 1950), 101–9.

character sets off to the Indies, he is following a long-standing plotline of commedia dell'arte rare in the French comic tradition.

No doubt another factor that made the professional Parisian farceurs avoid satire was their marginal social status. The Catholic Church disapproved of professional players and defined actors as outsiders who could contaminate the body social. Although there is evidence that actors signed formal acts of association with one another as early as the sixteenth century, such associations were granted no particular legal status.[22] Unlike most trades, actors were granted no privilege to practice their profession, and there was no formal apprenticeship system regulated by the monarchy. Nor does it seem that acting troupes in France enjoyed much support from aristocratic patrons during the sixteenth century, as they sometimes did in England and in Italy.[23] In theory, anyone who wished to could set himself up as the leader of an acting troupe; his success hinged only on the troupe's ability to entertain the crowds. Unlike Renaissance festive societies, which were exclusively male associations, most early seventeenth-century acting troupes had at least one woman performing on the stage, which contributed to the scandalous reputation accorded professional players.[24] Whereas many Renaissance actors belonged to confraternities with a long history of performance and service in the community, professional acting troupes usually formed and dispersed in less than a decade, and their transience contributed to their social marginalization.

Professional actors thus had a hard time until the monarchy reached out a helping hand. Although professional acting troupes were not new, their numbers only began to increase when French kings began encouraging them to perform at the Parisian Hôtel de Bourgogne theater during the last decades of the sixteenth century. Whereas in neighboring countries—notably in England, Spain, and Italy—professional actors had been the norm at a much earlier date, the vitality of amateur festive societies had discouraged the development of acting as a profession in France. During the Renaissance, French urban officials and notables were more likely to become honorary members of a festive society like the Mère Folle than they were to offer their patronage to a troupe of traveling players. Only after 1560, when most festive societies ceased to perform, did professional troupes begin to

22. Zbigniew Wilski, "La situation sociale des acteurs en Europe du XVIe au XVIIIe siècle," *Revue d'Histoire du Théâtre* 41 (1989): 411–21; *Recueil d'actes notariés relatifs à l'histoire de Paris et ses environs*, ed. Ernest Coyecque (Paris: Imprimerie Nationale, 1905), 1:580–98; Deierkauf-Holsboer, *Hôtel de Bourgogne*, 1:170–71, 180–81, 185–86.
23. Maurice Descotes, *Histoire de la critique dramatique en France* (Tubingen: Narr, 1980), 18–21; Harold C. Gardiner, *Mysteries' End: An Investigation of the Last Days of the Medieval Religious Stage* (New Haven: Yale University Press, 1946), 91.
24. AN MC XV:17 (1 Dec. 1607); AN MC XV:19 (4 Aug. 1612); AN MC XV:30 (28 Sept. 1616). Soulié, *Recherches*, 155 (13 Mar. 1610). Regarding the controversial nature of female performance, see Mlle. de Beaulieu, *La première atteinte contre ceux qui accusent les comédies* (Paris: Jean Richer, 1603).

fill the vacuum. Even then, and up to the first decades of the seventeenth century, most acting troupes lacked aristocratic patrons, and actors probably expected that local authorities would allow them to perform only for a few weeks each year. Once their repertoire was exhausted, the fair closed, or the building they rented was needed for some other purpose, the troupe would move on to another venue or another city. Except in Paris, where a single capacious theater existed, professional actors had to set up temporary stages in marketplaces, at fairgrounds, or in *jeux de paume*—indoor tennis courts that were often the site of gambling and carousing.

As they had been in the sixteenth century, provincial officials remained wary of professional troupes and often treated them more harshly than existing festive societies. In Rouen, where the Conards had resumed performing at Carnival at the beginning of the seventeenth century, the local parlement repeatedly issued warnings against professional actors. In 1598, the magistrates forbade a troupe of English actors to perform; twenty years later, they forced a troupe that had already set up its stage and indebted itself to local merchants to leave the city immediately.[25] In Toulouse, where the Basoche still roamed the streets on festival days and aristocrats staged elaborate Carnival festivities in their *hôtels*, the local parlement was also remarkably hostile to itinerant acting troupes. As late as the 1620s, the Toulouse magistrates prohibited professional troupes from performing on festival days and exiled several from the city.[26] In 1609, the Clermont-Ferrand city council was similarly appalled to discover that an acting troupe had set up a stage and was sounding a drum to announce its performances. Despite the fact that the *lieutenant-général* had approved the performance, the city council quickly intervened, challenged the actors, and summarily banished them from the city.[27] Although professional actors often performed, unbeknown to city officials, in French provincial cities, when such activities were reported, the magistrates often took the high moral ground against them. Parisians tended to be more tolerant of professional actors by 1600, but they did not necessarily want them in their neighborhoods. Residents often complained to the police about illegal goings-on outside of theaters. In 1633 a group of powerful Parisians went even further: alleging that the

25. Édouard-Hippolyte Gosselin, *Recherches sur les origines et l'histoire du théâtre à Rouen* (Rouen: Cagniard, 1868), 65–66.
26. Archives Départementales (AD) Haute-Garonne (HG) B 396, fol. 70, 5 May 1620; ADHG B 485, fol. 291, 18 May 1628; ADHG B 522, fol. 189, July 1632. That aristocrats nevertheless continued to celebrate Carnival at quasi-private festivities, see Robert A. Schneider, *Public Life in Toulouse, 1463–1789: From Municipal Republic to Cosmopolitan City* (Ithaca: Cornell University Press, 1989), 136–47.
27. André Bossuat, "Le théâtre à Clermont-Ferrand," *Revue d'Histoire du Théâtre* 13 (1961): 117–18. References to similar conflicts between local authorities concerning professional actors can be found in Arnauld Detcheverry, *Histoire des théâtres de Bordeaux, depuis leur origine dans cette ville jusqu'à nos jours* (Bordeaux: J. Delmas, 1860), 8–9; Louis de Gouvenain, *Le théâtre à Dijon, 1422–1790* (Dijon: E. Joubard, 1888), 47–52.

presence of professional actors was ruining the neighborhood, they successfully closed a theater located on their crowded city street.

The street in question was the rue Michel le Conte, a short block located
between the rue du Temple and the rue Saint Martin on the edge of the fash-
ionable Temple district of Paris. Situated at the northeastern boundary of the
city and bordered by a relatively undeveloped stretch of swampland to the
east, the Temple and Marais districts of Paris were to witness extraordinary
urban development during the seventeenth century. Aristocrats and wealthy
officers of the royal courts bought tracts of land in this area and built themselves luxurious private *hôtels* on the large lots.[28] Rue Michel le Conte was
no exception. On this short street there lived a number of royal officers,
including the widow of François des Cartes, *conseiller du roy*, whose "large
house" was adjacent to that of Jehan du Guc and Monsieur de la Croix, both
of whom were magistrates at the Chambre des Comptes. Not everyone who
owned property on the street was of such exalted status: Michel le Conte was
also home to more humble merchants and housed the site of a *jeu de paume*,
where gambling had been taking place since the early seventeenth century.[29]
Long tolerated by its neighbors despite occasional brushes with the law, the
jeu de paume became a source of controversy only when a professional acting troupe rented the premises for two years, with a contract approved by
Paris police officials. In a complaint brought before the police, the inhabitants of rue Michel le Conte, self-described as "several persons of quality, and
officers at the sovereign courts," questioned whether it was wise to allow
the troupe to rent the theater.[30] They argued that their street was too narrow and busy to accommodate the additional business that the actors would
bring to the jeu de paume. Their primary concerns, however, were for their
own safety. They insisted that the actors and the crowds that gathered before
each performance made it dangerous for local inhabitants to return home
at night. Finally, as evidence of the actors' fundamental depravity and lack
of Christian decorum, the plaintiffs complained that these actors continued
to perform "comedies and farces even during this sacred time of Lent."[31]
Although performing during Lent was normal practice in Paris by the 1630s,
this element of the actors' behavior was emphasized as being particularly
intolerable. The residents' arguments were apparently persuasive, and the
chief police officer quickly suspended the troupe's contract.

---

28. Robert Descimon, "Paris on the Eve of Saint Bartholomew: Taxation, Privilege and Social
Geography," in *Cities and Social Change in Early Modern France*, ed. Philip Benedict (London:
Unwin Hyman, 1989), 93–95; Orest Ranum, *Paris in the Age of Absolutism* (Bloomington:
Indiana University Press, 1968), 83–85.
29. AN x2b 1181, 22 Sept. 1611; AN MC XX:166, fols. 566–67, 15 Dec. 1625; AN MC
XIII:20, 14 Aug. 1634; AN MC XIII:20, 4 Sept. 1611; AN MC III:491, 23 Aug. 1611.
30. AN x1a 2063, fol. 517, 22 Mar. 1633.
31. Ibid. For performances in Paris during Lent, see AN MC X:4, 12 Feb. 1607; AN MC X:12,
3 Feb. 1610; AN MC X:28, 28 Nov. 1615.

Its fate on this occasion exemplifies the difficulties that professional actors faced in comparison with their amateur predecessors. As magistrates at the Chambre des Comptes and the parlement, the men who objected to the professional acting troupe in 1633 were of precisely the same professional and social class as the patrons of the Basoche fifty years earlier. Even in the early seventeenth century, it is likely that they or their relatives occasionally attended the public theater. Notably, the plaintiffs in the 1633 Michel le Conte case did not complain about the content of the theatrical performances themselves; they simply had no wish to live next to a professional theater, though they had put up with a jeu de paume for some decades. It seems there was something specific about the activities of itinerant professional actors, who had no permanent ties to the neighborhood, that offended the Parisian urban elite's sensibilities.

The vulnerability of professional actors in France highlights the central role that the monarchy played in the development of the theater. Together Valois and Bourbon monarchs—their direct patronage of professional troupes, and the permission they granted to the Confrérie de la Passion to build and maintain a commercial theater in the capital—laid the foundations for the establishment of a modern secular theater tradition in France. Until 1630, theater performance in Paris was nevertheless supervised in a relatively old-fashioned and reactive manner that reflected the transitional nature of monarchical authority during this period. Only loosely regulated by the local police at the Châtelet, the Confrérie de la Passion, and temporary royal appointees, the Parisian theater evolved into a relatively dynamic and competitive arena. At any one time, several troupes performed in the city and competed with one another for audience share. Despite their misgivings about living among professional actors, elite Parisians flocked to the theater and voted with their feet. Until at least 1620, what they wanted were apparently bawdy farces.

The French kings' primary contribution to the theater was to attract professional troupes to court. In comparison to city officials, French kings were far less concerned about the theater corrupting morals or threatening public order. This open and even enthusiastic attitude toward the theater, including farce, continued throughout the Wars of Religion and well into the seventeenth century. French actors regularly amused the court during the Renaissance, and beginning in the mid-sixteenth century, French kings had been active in recruiting commedia dell'arte troupes from Italy.[32] Henry IV often invited both Italian and French farce players to entertain him during his years in the wilderness as leader of the rebel Huguenots, and he continued to do so when he gained control of Paris as the newly Catholic king of France.[33]

32. Armand Baschet, *Les comédiens italiens à la cour de France sous Charles IX, Henri III, Henri IV et Louis XIII* (Paris: Plon, 1882), 157–58, 299–300, 313, 321.
33. Ibid., 85–87.

His wife Marie de Medici and son Louis XIII maintained this tradition. Even then, the indigenous performers were rarely compensated at the same level as the Italians. In December 1618, while a trio of performers from the Hôtel de Bourgogne were paid a mere eighty livres "for several comedies they performed by our commandment and for our pleasure and recreation," well-known farceur Tabarin received six hundred livres.[34] During a similar stay at court, an Italian troupe was offered double Tabarin's sum. Of course, the court's interest in the theater was not limited to farce and commedia dell'arte. Members of the king or queen's entourage often performed French tragedies, and Louis XIII also attended pious neoclassical plays performed at the Jesuit Collège de Clermont. Ballet productions—series of tableaux linked by song and dance—were also popular at court during the 1610s and 1620s.[35] Royal interest in the ballet and neoclassical genres continued in the decades that followed. What is notable about court theater in this period, however, is the comfortable inclusion of traditional comic genres in the entertainment cycle. The preponderance of Italian commedia dell'arte troupes and French farce players among the professionals summoned by the king through the mid-1620s demonstrates that he continued to find physical humor and raucous jokes entertaining. His willingness to bring farceurs to court probably helped them to attract Parisian audiences and to secure contracts at the Hôtel de Bourgogne theater. Considering the king's appreciation of theater, it is not surprising that professional actors flourished in Paris decades before provincial urban elites were willing to tolerate them on a regular basis.

Louis XIII's enthusiasm for farce lasted longer than that of his noble subjects. Whereas some aristocrats living in Paris began to repudiate the traditional comic repertoire during the 1620s, the king continued to patronize the farceurs of the Hôtel de Bourgogne, approving, for example, Gaultier Garguille's decision to publish a collection of songs in 1631. In the preface to the collection, Gaultier Garguille admits that since he has become too old to present his songs with his usual energy on stage, he wants as many readers as possible to see them in print. He concludes, however, by reminding anyone unsatisfied with the pallid printed version that "you could come see the living personage, either at the Louvre or at our everyday theater."[36] For all his apparent modesty about the deterioration of his acting skills, Gaultier Garguille does not hesitate to note that the king is still entertained by his repertoire.

34. BN MS fonds 500 Colbert, vol. 94, fols. 235, 255v. See also BN MS fonds 500 Colbert, vol. 92, fols. 201v, 214; BN MS fonds 500 Colbert, vol. 94, fol. 295; "Dons de Henry IV," 281–84.
35. *Journal de Jean Héroard*, 1940 (2 Aug. 1611), 2078 (11 Dec. 1612), 2085 (6 Jan. 1613), 2230 (3 Sept. 1614), 2273 (4 Mar. 1615), 2311 (2 Sept. 1615); Margaret M. McGowan, *L'art du ballet de cour en France (1581–1643)* (Paris: CNRS, 1963), 85.
36. *Chansons de Gaultier Garguille*, ed. Édouard Fournier (Paris: P. Jannet, 1858), 4.

Adding greatly to the prestige of Gaultier Garguille's collection, Louis XIII provided a signed letter issued by his council on March 4, 1631. In addition to the usual restrictions and privileges granted for the publication of an original work—the publisher was to have exclusive publication rights for ten years—Louis also affirms Gaultier Garguille's reasons for choosing to publish.

> Our dear and well loved Hugues Guéru, alias Fléchelles, one of our regular co-medians, brought to our attention that having composed a little book entitled *The New Songs of Gaultier Garguille*, he wanted to bring it to light and have it printed, but fears that someone besides he who is charged with printing it might make a counterfeit of it and might add some other songs more dissolute than his own, if he had not, by this [order], from ourselves been provided with our necessary permission.[37]

In addition to establishing that the king has a personal and affectionate rela-tionship with the farce player, this letter represents Gaultier Garguille's mo-tivations in an honorable light. The king refers to Guéru as Fléchelles—the stage name the actor used when performing neoclassical repertoire—and apparently respects Guéru's concern about counterfeit editions. As a final distinction, Louis makes it known that he wishes two copies of the songs to be added to his own personal library. Although these comments are cer-tainly somewhat ironical—it would be difficult, for example, to find songs more dissolute than Gaultier Garguille's—Louis's support does seem to have been based on sincere appreciation of the actor's talents.

In fact, Gaultier Garguille's songs are fully as crude as those in any farce of his day. In a song about the sexual adventures of a young girl, Garguille creates suspense and interest by playing on puns. The opening lines seem to refer to a young girl's talent for domestic sewing, which keeps her busily engaged at home when her father departs for market.

> Mon compère a une fille
> Qui coud, qui brode et qui fille[38]
> [My comrade has a daughter
> Who sews, who embroiders and who spins]

While her father is absent, the girl quickly becomes involved in less in-nocent pursuits with her neighbor Gilles: no sooner has he departed than she is found using her manual dexterity to excellent effect on Gilles's penis. Gaultier Garguille is playing on the double meaning of *coud*, either "sewing" or "shoulder"; *brode*, either "embroidery" or "haunch"; and *fille*, referring

37. Ibid., 9.
38. Ibid., 13.

at first to the thread with which the girl sews and later to Gilles's ejaculation. The song concludes

> Elle a tant dressé sa quille
> Qu'il luy a faict une fille
> Ha! qu'il est heureux qui coud![39]
> [She had so erected his staff
> That he made her into a whore
> Ha! that he is happy who sews!]

Songs like this one are in no way remarkable and fit comfortably into the Paris of 1631: they belong to a well-established bawdy tradition.[40] Gaultier Garguille's exceptional decision to publish his songs in a collected volume no doubt simply reflected his particularly privileged relationship with the king. Since Louis XIII, well into the 1630s, was supporting the broadest kind of sexually explicit humor, it is clear that when Parisian audiences began to turn away from farce in the mid-1620s it was not because the king's court was pressuring them to do so.

Despite Louis XIII's enthusiasm, however, the farceurs' heyday did not last long. Over time, as Parisian elites became more culturally assertive, the prestige of the king's patronage was no longer sufficient to guarantee their continued success. New ideals of *civilité* and *honnêteté* circulating in the capital eventually lured elite Parisian audiences away from farce. Most theater historians argue that the monarchy, specifically Cardinal Richelieu, the king's first minister after 1624, forced the farceurs off the stage in the 1630s.[41] Richelieu was alert to the possibilities of harnessing culture, particularly the emerging culture of the salon, to the centralizing state. In his patronage of the theater and creation of the Académie Française, Richelieu exploited the new emphasis on purity of language and polite manners to dignify and exalt the French monarchy—a scheme that left no room for vulgar farce.[42] Nevertheless, despite the importance of Richelieu's cultural policies, the new, much tighter

---

39. Ibid., 15.
40. K. van Orden, "Sexual Discourse in the Parisian Chanson: A Libidinous Aviary," *Journal of the American Musicological Society* 48 (1995): 1–41; Magendie, *Politesse mondaine*, 108.
41. Antoine Adam, *Histoire de la littérature française au XVIIe siècle* (Paris: Domat-Montchrestien, 1948), 1:466–68; Georges Couton, "Richelieu et le théâtre," in *Richelieu et la culture: Actes du colloque international en Sorbonne (19–20 novembre 1985)*, ed. Roland Mousnier (Paris: CNRS, 1987), 79–81; Maurice Descotes, *Le public de théâtre et son histoire* (Paris: CNRS, 1964), 91–92; Timothy Murray, *Theatrical Legitimation: Allegories of Genius in Seventeenth-Century England and France* (New York: Oxford University Press, 1987), 112–30; Wiley, *Early Public Theatre*, 262–80.
42. Georges Couton, *Richelieu et le théâtre* (Lyon: Presses Universitaires de Lyon, 1986), 7–13; Hélène Merlin, *Public et littérature en France au XVIIe siècle* (Paris: Belles Lettres, 1994), 153–91; Descotes, *Histoire de la critique*, 31–50; Dominique Bertrand, *Dire le rire à l'âge classique: Représenter pour mieux contrôler* (Aix-en-Provence: Publications de l'Université de Provence, 1995), 120–26.

regulations governing the theater did not originate with Richelieu, nor did they come about in an effort to celebrate absolute monarchical authority. A close examination of actors' contracts and theater regulation between 1600 and 1630 reveals instead that market forces pressured the farceurs to change their repertoire. By the mid-1620s, professional actors had to adapt to the new fashion for neoclassical plays or risk being eclipsed by other troupes.

Continued royal enjoyment of farce seems at odds with other political and cultural developments of the early seventeenth century. Since Norbert Elias identified a link between the rise of a new more restrained set of manners called *civilité* and the development of the French absolutist state, historians have sought to trace the origins of these developments before 1661. Certainly both Henry IV and Louis XIII pursued centralizing political policies that included a reinvention of political rituals to emphasize the absolute authority of the Bourbon monarchy. Yet neither Henry nor Louis seemed to see professional theater as possibly serving the same purpose, that is, enhancing the authority of the king. At a time when they devoted considerable resources to rebuilding parts of Paris, neither king ever contributed to the upkeep of the Hôtel de Bourgogne theater building.[43] Nor did they see it as their responsibility to provide professional troupes with permanent pensions: actors were paid for their services and then put out to pasture to fend for themselves in the competitive world of the Parisian stage. Diplomatic correspondence reveals that Henry IV, who was well known for his tolerance of the satirical, censored the performances of professional actors on only two occasions during his reign: once, in 1602, at the request of the queen of England, who was offended by a depiction of herself in Montchrestien's *The Scottish Queen*; and again, possibly in 1604, while he was in mourning after the death of his sister Catherine of Bourbon. Louis XIII, as far as we know, never intervened directly to shape the content of a theatrical performance.[44] The first Bourbon monarchs, like their predecessors, were relatively unconcerned about the moral content of the theater. Unlike French urban officials who had been willing and increasingly able to censor undesirable theatrical performances from the time of the Wars of Religion, French kings for the most part did not deign to become directly involved in theatrical censorship. As long as overt satire of the monarchy and its officials was avoided, they were content to enjoy bawdy humor both at court and on the public stage. The idea that such humor might in itself compromise their authority in some way seems to have been foreign to both Henry IV and Louis XIII.

43. Hilary Ballon, *The Paris of Henry IV: Architecture and Urbanism* (Cambridge, Mass.: MIT Press, 1991), 1–13; Ranum, *Paris*, 68–82.
44. Alfred Soman, "Press, Pulpit and Censorship in France before Richelieu," *Proceedings of the American Philosophical Society* 120 (1976): 444, 450, 461–63; Alfred Soman, "The Theatre, Diplomacy and Censorship in the Reign of Henry IV," *Bibliothèque d'Humanisme et Renaissance* 35 (1973): 273–88.

Instead, both kings relied on a variety of indirect mechanisms to supervise the theater in Paris. Both the Confrérie de la Passion, whose main concerns were defending its monopoly and keeping the Hôtel de Bourgogne profitable, and the Parisian police at the Châtelet, whose job it was to maintain public order in the city streets, kept an eye on the doings of professional actors. Together, the Confrérie de la Passion and the Châtelet imposed a loose juridical form of regulation on the theater that nevertheless allowed for some competition. Theatrical regulation during 1600–1630 was thus in transition from the reactive policies of the Renaissance, when kings and city officials punished festive societies mildly even after a complaint of slander, and the direct supervision and sustained financial support granted to the Parisian theater in the post-1630 period. Although the system in this interim period was relatively flexible, farce players and other actors were less free to speak their minds than they had been during the Renaissance, and certainly far less so than pamphlet writers of the day. Increasingly, the satire that was pushed off the stage found its way into print.

The Confrérie de la Passion's commercial focus—its interest in profit and loss rather than in culture, religion, or political commentary—was the cornerstone of early seventeenth-century Parisian theater regulation. This association of bourgeois Parisians, founded as a lay religious association in 1402, was a confraternity in name only by the early seventeenth century. Beginning in 1548, when the Parlement of Paris granted the association a monopoly on all secular theatrical productions in Paris, the confrérie gradually transformed itself into a commercial venture. Annual accounts and a detailed inventory compiled in 1639 demonstrate that very few of the confrérie's personnel or financial resources were directed toward those religious activities traditionally associated with confraternities. Although the officers of the association continued to pay a small sum to the Église de la Trinité each year, there is no evidence of other kinds of expenditures—payments to sick members, funeral masses, or even the purchase of devotional candles—that distinguish seventeenth-century confraternities from other kinds of corporations.[45] The confrérie owned several commercial buildings, but the bulk of its income was drawn from the Hôtel de Bourgogne theater. Extensive financial negotiations between the current masters and the retired masters regarding the pilfering of funds emphasize the large amounts of money at stake. In 1607, the confrérie's retired masters accused those currently in

45. AN MC X:16, 28 Mar. 1611; AN MC XXXV:373b, Mar. 1639, "Inventaire de la Confrérie de la Passion"; BN MS fonds Joly de Fleury, 214:2124, "Comptes of the Confrérie de la Passion 1656–57"; *Inventaire sommaire des archives hospitalières antérieures à 1790*, ed. Michel Moring (Paris: Grandremy et Henon, 1886), 245–67. The Confrérie de la Passion's accounts demonstrate that thousands of livres each year were passing through its coffers by the 1630s. In comparison, even the most wealthy sixteenth-century confraternities rarely had an annual budget that exceeded a few hundred livres. See Catherine Vincent, *Les confréries médiévales dans le royaume de France: XIII–XVe siècle* (Paris: Albin Michel, 1994), 152–53.

charge of lining their pockets with the theater's rental income and insisted that the current masters contribute some five hundred livres to the collective pool, a considerable sum equivalent to more than two months' rent of the theater. Apparently guilty of the charges, the miscreants surrendered without further debate. Significant expenditures related to the theater, including major repairs and innumerable legal cases to pursue defaulting tenants, also demonstrate that the theater dominated the Confrérie de la Passion masters' time and attention.[46] Maximizing their profits and defending their theatrical monopoly were the main concerns during these first decades of the seventeenth century.

Beginning around 1600, the confrérie was able to rent the Hôtel de Bourgogne to professional troupes several months of every year. Tenants usually reserved blocks of time ranging from as little as two weeks to as much as six months. During the term of the contract, they probably performed only two or three days a week, usually on Wednesday, Saturday, and Sunday.[47] Aside from paying their rent, the troupes had little contact with the theater's owners. A troupe provided its own costumes, props, and all other necessary supplies. Some contracts also made the troupe responsible for repairs to the theater, a stipulation referring no doubt to adjustments the troupe might have made to the stage to accommodate its scenery rather than to major construction, which we know that the confrérie undertook at its own expense.[48]

These contracts demonstrate that the confrérie was far less interested in a troupe's repertoire than in maximizing its own income from the theater. In only one contract of the forty-three that remain from the 1600–1625 period did the confrérie stipulate a particular repertoire. In 1600, after one troupe failed to honor its commitment to perform, the confrérie agreed to rent the theater to the farce player Robert Guérin, but insisted that his actors continue performing "the scenes that are left to perform from the *Tale of Valentin and Ourson* and any other plays and comedies that the said supervisor and masters want and would be pleased to have performed."[49] Guérin's troupe was presumably to pick up where the others had left off: the confrérie's concern about the repertoire seems to have been motivated by a desire not to disappoint a loyal clientele who were already following an unfinished series. In no later contracts, either with the farce players or with other troupes that

46. AN MC X:5, 10 May 1607; AN MC X:7, 24 Oct. 1607; AN MC X:16, 28 Mar. 1611; BN MS fonds Joly de Fleury, 214:2124.
47. S. Wilma Deierkauf-Holsboer, *Vie d'Alexandre Hardy, poète du roi, 1572–1632* (Paris: Nizet, 1972), 205; *Journal de Jean Héroard*, 1573 (7 Feb. 1609), 1576 (14 Feb. 1609), 1954 (21 Sept. 1611), 2254 (14 Dec. 1614); Lough, *Paris Theatre Audiences*, 29; AN MC X:1, 6 Feb. 1606.
48. AN MC XXXV:377 (Apr. 1640), 22 Apr. 1610; AN MC XXXV:377 (Apr. 1640), 25 May 1598; AN MC X:30, 5 July 1616; Deierkauf-Holsboer, *Hôtel de Bourgogne*, 1:185.
49. AN MC XXXV:377 (May 1640), 30 Oct. 1600.

visited the capital, were such detailed instructions included. A few contracts mentioned that the performances should be "restrained and decent,"[50] but most merely stipulated that this particular troupe and no other should perform "plays and comedies."[51] As long as the players remained within vague bounds of propriety, the confrérie had no interest in interfering with their repertoire. When we consider the scatological and sexually explicit content of some early seventeenth-century farces, the confrérie's conception of decency was quite liberal.

Although every king from Henry II through Louis XIV affirmed the confrérie's privileges to run the Hôtel de Bourgogne and recognized its claim to hold a monopoly on all performance in Paris, neither Valois nor Bourbon monarchs hesitated to undermine the confrérie's autonomy when it was convenient to do so. The most common tactic was to assign some of the income from the Hôtel de Bourgogne's revenue to a favored client. Ever since the Hôtel de Bourgogne's foundation in the mid-sixteenth century, this kind of royal interference had plagued the confrérie. Individuals and associations, including the Basoche of the Paris Parlement and members of the king's entourage, claimed at various times that the king had granted them the income from one of the seventeen stage boxes in the Hôtel de Bourgogne. Both Jean Dubois, a valet of the king's chamber, and Nicolas Guéru, a gardener at the Louvre, fought the confrérie for years in court during the early seventeenth century before they were able to collect proceeds from their boxes.[52] Nicolas Joubert, otherwise known as Sir Angoulevent, a court buffoon and pamphleteer, also claimed the income from one of the boxes, battling the confrérie in cases that went as high as the parlement and that resulted in a bitter exchange of printed pamphlets.[53] Most notable

---

50. AN MC X:2, 8 Apr. 1606.

51. AN MC XXXV:377 (June 1640), 17 Oct. 1613. Deierkauf-Holsboer, *Vie d'Alexandre Hardy*, 142; Raymond Lebègue, "Le répertoire de la troupe de Talmy," in *Études sur le théâtre français* (Paris: Nizet, 1977), 1:253–69.

52. *Recueil des principaux titres concernant l'acquisition de la propriété des masure et place où a été bâtie la maison appelée vulgairement l'Hôtel de Bourgogne* (Paris, 1632) 26; *Recueil des statuts, ordonnances, reiglements, antiquitez, prerogatives, et prééminences du royaume de la Bazoche* (Paris: C. Besongne, 1654), 13; *Inventaire sommaire des archives hospitalières*, 267; AN MC XXXV:373b, Mar. 1639, fols. 39–40; Soulié, *Recherches*, 154 (11 Aug. 1604), 158 (14 Feb. 1624).

53. *Plaidoyé sur la principauté des sots, avec l'arrest de la Cour intervenu sur iceluy* (Paris: David Douceur, 1608), 1, 18–19; *La guirlande et responce d'Angoulevent, à l'Archipöete des pois pillez* (Paris: Hubert Velut, 1603); *Journal de Jean Héroard*, 468 (14 Jan. 1604), 1109 (16 Nov. 1606), 1113 (22 Nov. 1606), 1587 (14 Mar. 1609), 1960 (12 Oct. 1611); AN x1a 1820, fol. 269, 19 July 1609; AN MC XXXV:373b, Mar. 1639, fol. 39; AN MC VIII:562, fol. 162, 12 Sept. 1603; AN MC VII:566, fol. 303, 9 Mar. 1605; AN MC VIII:566, fol. 377, 26 Mar. 1605. Although some scholars have argued that Angoulevent was the leader of the Basoche or a revitalized Enfants-sans-Souci, I have found no evidence to support these claims. See Adolphe Fabre, *Les clercs du palais: Recherches historiques sur les bazoches des parlements et sociétés dramatiques des bazochiens et Enfants sans Souci* (Lyon: Scheuring, 1875), 260–70; Maurice Lever, *Le sceptre et la marotte: Histoire des fous de cour* (Paris: Fayard, 1983), 281–91. Contracts between the confrérie and actors that acknowledge Angoulevent's claim include AN MC X:6, 6 Aug. 1607; AN MC X:10, 1 July 1609; AN MC X:28, 1 Oct. 1615; AN MC X:44, 31 Aug. 1621.

were the claims made by Jacques Fonteny. Beginning in 1610, Fonteny, a secretary for the Duchess of Barr, insisted that Louis XIII had granted him not only the rights to income from one of the theater boxes but also the title of Inspector of Actors. The confrérie took him to court to challenge both claims but nevertheless set aside income for Fonteny's box in most contracts after 1610.[54] There is no evidence, however, that Fonteny ever imposed regulations on professional troupes or interfered with the confrérie's business methods. Finally, after resisting his claims for over a decade, the confrérie welcomed Fonteny's membership in the association in 1621. In all these cases, the confrérie eventually had to concede a portion of its income to the king's favorites. Notably, the king never intervened directly to secure the box for his client. Despite having caused the problem himself by apportioning out some of the confrérie's income to court favorites, Louis let them fight their own battles and allowed the judicial system to work out the details for itself. The effect of his interference was, however, to keep the confrérie aware of its dependence on royal favor. Louis was also able to place some reliable men within the organization itself.

The second institution at the heart of theatrical regulation was the Châtelet, the "police force" of Paris. Nominally headed by an aristocratic provost, the Châtelet was overseen by his two deputies, the *lieutenants civil* and *criminel*, members of the urban elite, who in turn were aided by forty-eight commissioners and by a battery of lawyers, notaries, and part-time deputies. The Châtelet's responsibilities were extensive, from setting the price of bread and regulating street cleaning to deciding who could bear arms within the city. Nevertheless, because its manpower was relatively limited, its approach to peacekeeping was often reactive and dependent on residents' complaints.[55] During the early seventeenth century, its supervision of the theater was sparked by the confrérie's various law suits as well as by complaints made by neighbors about disturbances to public order.

The Parlement of Paris, interestingly, had very little to do with theatrical regulation during these transitional decades. Whereas sixteenth-century parlement magistrates regularly issued arrêts concerning the Basoche, the Confrérie de la Passion, and student performers, by the beginning of the seventeenth century they rarely did so. The parlement's last recorded effort to censor amateur actors occurred in 1594 during a particularly sensitive moment of Henry IV's reign. Although Henry had converted to Catholicism

54. AN MC XXXV:377, 22 Apr. 1610, 17 Oct. 1613, 8 Apr. 1614; AN MC X:44, 23 July 1621; AN MC X:55, 25 Jan. 1625; AN MC X:60, 11 Dec. 1626; Deierkauf-Holsboer, *Hôtel de Bourgogne*, 1:72–74.
55. Jean-Pierre Babelon, *Nouvelle histoire de Paris: Paris au XVIe siècle* (Paris: Hachette, 1986), 271–76; Barbara B. Diefendorf, *Beneath the Cross: Catholics and Huguenots in Sixteenth-Century Paris* (Oxford: Oxford University Press, 1991), 23–24; Paolo Piasenza, "Juges, lieutenants de police et bourgeois à Paris aux XVIIe et XVIIIe siècles," *Annales: Économies, Sociétés, Civilisations* 45 (1990): 1189–92.

the previous year and on those grounds had been welcomed in Paris as the rightful king of France, he was still officially excommunicated until August 1595. Hearing that students at the university were about to perform a play that might undermine Henry's fragile hold on authority by referring to the sincerity of his Catholic faith, the parlement magistrates forbade its public performance. The author of the play, a regent at the university named Louis Leger, was briefly imprisoned and all copies of the play destroyed. Significantly this is the last reference to a potentially controversial theatrical performance at the University of Paris.[56] Although student theater continued in Paris throughout the seventeenth century, politically quiescent neoclassical performances at the Jesuit collège gradually came to predominate. The absence from the historical record of references either to satirical student performances or to parlement regulation of the theater by the early seventeenth century indicates to what extent the theatrical world of Paris had been transformed. Festive societies no longer performed in the city streets, and theatrical regulation had been rendered mundane enough that the lower court at the Châtelet was able to handle most issues.[57]

During these first decades of the seventeenth century, the Châtelet placed restrictions on the confrérie's freedom of action but also helped it to maximize profits. In 1597, when the confrérie obtained a renewal of its privileges from Henry IV, the lieutenant civil at the Châtelet ruled that the confrérie's monopoly undermined other Parisians' privileges to practice their trades with accustomed liberty. As a result, he decided that traveling theatrical troupes would be permitted to perform at the Foire Saint-Germain, an annual fair on the outskirts of Paris that generally lasted two to three weeks each year. To compensate the confrérie for the loss of business, however, each troupe was to pay the association two *escus* every year that they performed.[58] As the years passed, the original ruling was amended to extend itinerant troupes' privileges further. By the 1610s, the Châtelet allowed troupes to perform anywhere they chose as long as they paid dues to the confrérie, set at 60 sous per day.[59] According to this ruling, the maximum amount a troupe would owe the confrérie each month would have been only 90 livres, a sum considerably less than the 200 livres usually charged for renting the Hôtel itself. This loophole was welcomed by troupes that could not or did not wish to secure the Hôtel de Bourgogne stage. We know

56. Soman, "Theatre, " 277–78.
57. This shift was not absolute. Châtelet officials were also involved in theatrical censorship during the Renaissance. See Soman, "Theatre," 276n8; Théodore de Bèze, *Histoire ecclésiastique des églises réformées au royaume de France* (Lille: Leleux, 1841), 1:8; James K. Farge, *Orthodoxy and Reform in Early Modern France: The Faculty of Theology of Paris, 1500–1543* (Leiden: Brill, 1985), 203–4.
58. La Mare, *Traité*, 3:440 (5 Feb. 1596); Léon Roulland, "La Foire Saint-Germain sous les règnes de Charles IX, de Henri III et de Henri IV," *Mémoires de la Société de Paris et de l'Île-de-France* 3 (1876): 192–218; Wiley, *Early Public Theatre*, 125–30.
59. Soulié, *Recherches*, 155 (10 and 15 Mar. 1610), 157 (1 Feb. 1619).

actors took advantage of this new freedom, since the confrérie often found it necessary to bring legal cases against actors who abused the terms of the regulation. During the spring of 1610, since the Hôtel de Bourgogne was already rented to another troupe, an actor named Claude Husson and his companions set up a stage at the Foire Saint-Germain without informing the confrérie or paying the requisite fee. The confrérie promptly brought this matter to the attention of the Châtelet, which ruled that Husson must pay the amount he owed.[60] Although we do not know whether these financial obligations were met, the case illustrates the ways in which the Châtelet helped develop a workable compromise between the financial demands of the confrérie's monopoly and the reality that more than one theatrical venue was needed in Paris, by then a city of some 250,000 residents.

The Châtelet also sought to maintain order near and in the Hôtel de Bourgogne. As early as 1596, acting on complaints brought by the theater's neighbors, the Châtelet forbade individuals who threw "stones, dirt and other things, that could provoke trouble among the people" to gather near the Hôtel de Bourgogne while performances were in progress.[61] A few years later, the Châtelet permitted the confrérie to erect barriers "in front of the door and entrance to the said Hôtel, to prevent the pressure of people when the show begins."[62] When in 1609 the Hôtel's neighbors complained about the late hours kept by the theater audiences, presumably fearing nighttime disorder and thievery, the Châtelet ordered winter performances to begin promptly at two o'clock and end by four thirty. Héroard's account of Louis XIII's comings and goings indicates that such strict hours were in fact rarely observed, but it seems that most performances at the Hôtel de Bourgogne did finish by eight o'clock in the evening.[63]

The Châtelet did not have sufficient resources, however, to keep track of the content of theatrical performances or maintain order within the theater itself. A 1609 conflict involving an Italian acting troupe reveals the limited nature of police control in early seventeenth-century Paris. One day that March, an Italian actor named Battistino was collecting receipts at the door when "a French *gentilhomme* belonging to a great house, closely related to Monsieur le grand Ecuyer," handed him a whistle rather than the ten sous required for entrance to the boxes.[64] Since theatergoers often blew whistles when they were displeased with a performance, the gentilhomme's gift was

---

60. AN MC XXXV:373b, Mar. 1639, fols. 35–37 (9 Dec. 1614, 2 Jan. 1615). For similar conflicts between the Paris Confrérie de la Passion and professional actors, see Soulié, *Recherches*, 154–57.
61. La Mare, *Traité*, 3:440 (5 Feb. 1596).
62. Soulié, *Recherches*, 154 (6 Oct. 1599), 153 (12 Apr. 1597), 155 (4 Feb. 1611), 158 (3 Sept. 1624).
63. La Mare, *Traité*, 3:440 (12 Nov. 1609); *Journal de Jean Héroard*, 1576 (14 Feb. 1609).
64. As quoted in Baschet, *Comédiens italiens*, 169–70; Pierre Mélèse, *Le théâtre et le public à Paris sous Louis XIV, 1659–1715* (Paris: Droz, 1934), 218–20.

an unambiguous insult. Battistino confronted the gentilhomme, who replied that "I paid you with the coinage that you deserve," a response that so infuriated the actor that he punched the gentilhomme in the nose.[65] Swords were drawn, and the actor saved himself only by fleeing the theater and barricading his home. According to a witness, who reported these events in detail to the Duke of Mantua, the incident evoked no interference from local authorities. Not only were there no Châtelet officials near the theater during the performance, but for days afterward Battistino feared leaving his home because the police had failed to protect him from the gentilhomme's threats of revenge. Only with the return of the king to Paris a few days later did the gentilhomme relent under the king's chastisement. The Italian actors, as the special guests of the French king, could expect a measure of royal protection. Other acting troupes, however, would probably have preferred the presence of a few Châtelet officials near the Hôtel to ensure that their receipts were safely collected. This absence of direct police supervision can be contrasted to the presence of Châtelet officers in the parterre of the Comédie Française by the end of the seventeenth century.[66] Whereas Henry IV and his son preferred to rely on informal methods to control violence at the theater, Louis XIV funded the Parisian police well enough to ensure that a permanent regulatory presence at the theater was possible. After 1661, maintaining public order and controlling scandal, at least in those parts of the city where nobles and respectable bourgeois might be seen, became more of a priority for the French state.

Perhaps because of this incident, the Châtelet made some effort after 1609 to regulate the theater more thoroughly. Acting on a complaint by a member of the king's council, the lieutenant civil made a number of specific recommendations about the internal workings of the theater and ordered local commissioners to report back to ensure the actors' and the confrérie's compliance.[67] These new regulations reiterated the Châtelet's concern that theatrical performances end before dark but also stipulated that the inside of the theater be better lit, specifically that the boxes, galleries, and the parterre be illuminated with lanterns or candles throughout the performance. The Châtelet set ticket prices at ten sous for boxes and five sous for the parterre; any divergence from these norms was to be approved by the lieutenant civil himself.

After 1609, the Châtelet also attempted to impose a regular regime of censorship on all performances at the Hôtel de Bourgogne. In a ruling published that year, the lieutenant civil insisted that all actors be prohibited "from performing any comedies or farces, about which they did not inform the *procureur du roy*, and unless their roster or register be signed by ourself."[68] This edict could have resulted in the systematic regulation of

65. Baschet, *Comédiens italiens*, 170.
66. Ravel, *Contested Parterre*, 86–95.
67. La Mare, *Traité*, 3:440 (12 Nov. 1609).
68. Ibid.

theatrical performance in the capital, but there is little indication that it was enforced. The Châtelet did not have adequate manpower to supervise the content of every performance in Paris. This was to be a persistent problem for the regulation of both the theater and the publishing industry in Paris until the middle decades of the seventeenth century.[69] Between 1609 and 1614, most rental contracts between troupes and the confrérie nevertheless set aside a box for the lieutenant civil, who no doubt appreciated both the income and the status of being able to attend the theater whenever he wished.[70] Notably, no further rulings were issued by the Châtelet to regulate theatrical practice for the next decade, and after 1614 contracts make no reference to a box reserved for any Châtelet official. The lieutenant civil's halfhearted attempts to supervise the inner workings of the Hôtel de Bourgogne seem to have come to naught.

That the Châtelet's regulation of the theater continued to be haphazard in nature is suggested by an incident in 1624. On October 4, the current actors at the Hôtel affixed a poster of that day's performances. Seeing it, the commissioner Bachelier reported to his superiors that the Prince of Orange's troupe was to perform a scandalous work titled *Great Mockery of Thieves, Wine-sellers, the Bourgeoisie, the Police Commissioner and the Tavern-Keeper* and claimed it would be "greatly detrimental to the public and in mockery of justice and in contempt of the officers and charges of the said commissioners, who are the representatives of the police."[71] The lieutenant civil responded by ordering that the actors be brought immediately to the Châtelet for further questioning and then imprisoned. He also warned the confrérie not to open its doors to the troupe in the future or allow it to perform any play, under threat of a fine of 1,200 livres.

The process by which the Châtelet determined the actors' repertoire is revealing. The local commissioner apparently had no idea that an objectionable play was being planned until the day of the performance, which suggests that he did not have a list of the troupe's repertoire or, if he did, that it was not unusual for actual performances to diverge from it. The case also suggests that the interest of the Châtelet in theatrical censorship was distinctly limited: apparently the lieutenant civil wanted to stop the performance only because the play mocked Châtelet officials specifically. Ridicule of street criers and tavern keepers—familiar themes in contemporary farces and burlesque pamphlets—would presumably not have made the judges blink. Bawdy farce was not the issue here, only direct political satire of the censors themselves. Here we see Châtelet officials responding to farce very much as city officials had

69. Soman, "Press," 453–57.
70. AN MC X:13, 22 Apr. 1610; AN MC X:16, 24 Mar. 1611; AN MC X:19, 4 Aug. 1612; AN MC XXXV:377, 17 Oct. 1613; AN MC XXXV:377, 8 Apr. 1614.
71. As quoted in Émile Campardon, *Les comédiens du roi de la troupe française pendant les deux derniers siècles* (Paris: Champion, 1879), 278.

done a hundred years' earlier. Concerned primarily with public order and the honor of their corporate body, they lashed out only when their personal interests were threatened. Nevertheless, even this somewhat haphazard regulation of professional troupes seems to have been effective. The combination of the Châtelet's supervision and the confrérie's eagerness to collect rent from all players kept most professional actors registered with Parisian authorities. These watchful eyes did not prevent the farceurs from making bawdy jokes, but it did keep political and religious satire off the stage.

Much of this satire found its way instead into the printed pamphlets of the day. Print was even more difficult than theater for the monarchy to regulate, and as a result, a vibrant culture of political satire emerged in Paris during the first decades of the seventeenth century. Whereas the plays acted and then published by Tabarin and the trio at the Hôtel de Bourgogne theater were relatively tame and did not contain political satire, pamphlets written in the name of these performers were often overtly critical of contemporary social norms and political figures. Because pamphlet publishing was less tightly regulated than theater and was not tied to a particular corporate structure like the confrérie, it was easier to publish satire with impunity than it was to perform it on the public stage.

Pamphlet writing was a largely unregulated business during the ancien régime. Until 1618, there was no mechanism for systematically censoring printed matter, and unlike book production, which did eventually tighten as the century progressed, pamphlet publishing remained notoriously difficult to control. As a result, we cannot know for certain who wrote these short, cheaply produced tracts. Most pamphlets appeared anonymously and with no indication of the place of publication. Such information did not have to be revealed since pamphlets were usually published without a *privilège du roy*, a copyright issued by the king. Because of the large number of publisher-printers in Paris at the beginning of the seventeenth century, authors probably had little difficulty finding a press willing to print their views. Although the pamphlets attributed to notable farceurs could have been written by the actors themselves, they were probably penned by the educated men who wrote most of the pamphlets published in Paris at this time: the secretaries of aristocrats and power brokers in the French capital. During the contested regency of Marie de Medici (1610–17) in particular, pamphlet writing was one means to demonstrate an author's loyalty to a specific faction at court.[72] Although the pamphlet was printed anonymously, those in the know were often aware of the author's identity.

Because pamphlet writers had no desire to make their identities public, they often pretended to be writing in the name of fictional characters, which

72. Hubert Carrier, *Les Mazarinades: La presse de la Fronde (1648–1653)* (Geneva: Droz, 1989–91), 2:3–40, 77–86, 105–12; Alain Viala, *Naissance de l'écrivain: Sociologie de la littérature à l'âge classique* (Paris: Minuit, 1985), 59–66; Hélène Duccini, *Faire voir, faire croire: L'opinion publique sous Louis XIII* (Seyssel: Champ Vallon, 2003), 35–54.

also conveyed a sense of agency and authority. As early as the 1580s, short satirical pamphlets appeared in France mocking their authors' adversaries in the voice of the common man.[73] After the unexpected death of Henry IV in 1610, a similar pamphlet war erupted. Although many of these pamphlets were written from a royalist perspective, writers who opposed the queen also placed their arguments in the mouths of fictional characters, who often were men of the lower classes. Jacques Bonhomme, a frank peasant who expressed his crude but remarkably well-informed opinions on political developments, was a familiar figure in these harangues and dialogues.[74] Indeed, Bonhomme and the other humble characters, who often advocated particular political policies, functioned like Common Fool (Sotte Commune) had in Renaissance farces. Such Everyman characters, though often themselves the object of satire, were spokesmen for the public good by dramatizing the king's responsibility to consult with his subjects, even the most humble. As men of indeterminate social standing well known in the capital, the farce players could represent the common man as effectively as could generic peasants: comic performers who spoke with broad humor, they harked back to the subversive license of Carnival.

Although they are not written in conventional theatrical genres, some farce-player pamphlets replicate the themes common in sixteenth-century French farce by celebrating the cathartic misrule of Carnival. Some are mock almanacs in which farce players make predictions for each month of the coming year. Not surprisingly, Tabarin predicts that this March will be famous for copulation and that September will be a month of wine drinking more boisterous than any experienced for several years.[75] Several pamphlets depict the final farewells of a farce player to the city of Paris, his adventures in hell after his death, or the actor's defense of Carnival against Lenten self-control.[76] These pamphlets, both those written in the name of farce players

73. Duccini, *Faire voir*, 50–51, 267–317; Hubert Carrier, "Pour un définition du pamphlet," in *Le pamphlet en France au XVIe siècle* (Paris: École Normale Superière de Jeunes Filles, 1983), 123–36; J. H. M. Salmon, "French Satire in the Late Sixteenth Century," in *Renaissance and Revolt: Essays in the Intellectual and Social History of Early Modern France* (Cambridge: Cambridge University Press, 1987), 73–97.
74. Lever, *Sceptre et la marotte*, 254–81; Henri-Jean Martin, *Livre, pouvoirs et société au XVIIe siècle (1598–1701)* (Geneva: Droz, 1969), 1:268–71; Jeffrey K. Sawyer, *Printed Poison: Pamphlet Propaganda, Faction Politics, and the Public Sphere in Early Seventeenth-Century France* (Berkeley: University of California Press, 1990), 89–95.
75. *L'almanach prophétique du Sieur Tabarin pour l'année 1623* (Paris: R. Bretet, 1622); *Raillerie de Gros Guillaume sur les affaires de ce temps, 1623*; *La réponce de Guérin à Maitre Guillaume et les réjouissances des Dieux sur les heureuses alliances de France et d'Espagne* (Paris: Jean Millot et Jean de Bordeaulx, 1612).
76. *L'adieu de Tabarin au peuple de Paris* (Paris: P. Rocolet, 1622); *Le retour du brave Turlupin de l'autre monde* (Paris, 1637); *Les bignets du Gros Guillaume envoyez à Turlupin et à Gaultier-Garguille pour leur mardy-gras par le sieur Tripotin* (Paris, 1615). See also *Les arrests admirables et authentiques du Sieur Tabarin, prononcez en la place Dauphine le 14 jour de ce présent mois* (Paris: Lucas Joffu, 1623); Tabarin, *Bon jour et bon an: A Messieurs le Cornards de Paris, et de Lyon* (Lyon, 1620).

and other types of burlesque songs and poems, were published in growing numbers during the seventeenth century. Bought for a few deniers from a traveling salesman by a parlement magistrate or a young bourgeois student, such pamphlets were, like the actors' performances, primarily a form of light entertainment.[77]

Other farce-player pamphlets ventured into the realm of more topical satire by ridiculing particular French social types. In *The Stroll along the Pré aux Clercs*, a gentilhomme tells of wandering the Paris streets one evening to catch Tabarin's latest performance and muses about the absurdities of Parisian society: the pretensions of bourgeois officers, the corruption of the Jesuits, and the fallibility of the aristocracy. The pamphlet *The Ballet of Turlupin* presents a series of racy tales about apothecaries, lawyers, and their clerks. Turlupin tells these tales, including one about a solicitor's clerk who seduces a young woman in the back room of a boot maker's shop, in some detail, leaving few physical details to the imagination.[78]

A small number of these pamphlets comment directly on contemporary political developments. One written in the name of Bruscambille, an actor at the Hôtel de Bourgogne and the "author" of several editions of comic prologues, mocks court society with a playful comparison between the life of the courtier and that of the actor. Eager to establish his credibility as political commentator, Bruscambille begins by asking who is more the fool: he or his audience? Noting that he is paid to be a fool and that at the end of the evening he leaves the theater with "some money in my purse," whereas "you, when the Tragedy is played out, one will throw you from high to low," he concludes that courtiers could learn from his example.[79] Becoming more specific, Bruscambille goes on to launch an invective against an unnamed favorite of the queen mother's, whom he compares to the ambitious Icarus and even to Lucifer, warning him that, like the sun and God himself, King Louis is quick to punish those who deceive him. We do not know the identity of this unnamed favorite. The pamphlet, published in 1619, perhaps during the negotiations between Louis and his mother after her escape from Blois, might refer to a member of her entourage or even to the rising star, Armand Jean du Plessis, later to become first minister Cardinal Richelieu. More likely, however, this pamphlet is a reprint of a satire against the queen mother's notorious favorite Concini, whom the king had had killed

---

77. Carrier, *Presse*, 1:434–39; Henri-Jean Martin, Anne-Marie Lecocq, with H. Carrier and A. Sauvy, *Livres et lecteurs à Grenoble: Les registres du libraire Nicolas (1645–1668)* (Geneva: Droz, 1977).

78. *Le ballet de Turlupin representé à Gentilly, devant les Letières du Bois de Vincennes* (Nyort, n.d.); *La pourmenade du pré aux clercs* (1622).

79. *Peripatetiques, resolutions et remonstrances sententieuses du Docteur Bruscambille aux perturbateurs de l'Estat* (Paris: Va du Cul, Gouverneur des Singes, 1619); Alan Howe, "Bruscambille, qui était-il?," *XVIIe Siècle* 38 (1986): 390–96; Christian Jouhaud, *Mazarinades: La Fronde des mots* (Paris: Aubier, 1985), 32.

two years earlier.[80] In another pamphlet, *Advertisement of Sieur Bruscambille on the Voyage to Spain*, the author presents a reasoned and thoughtful analysis of the king's 1615 marriage to the young Spanish princess.[81] Bruscambille presents himself as a political outsider concerned about the French monarchy's international reputation, which had been weakened by political challenges to Marie de Medici's regency. He voices legitimate concerns about the regent's decision to solidify France's alliance with Spain and worries about Protestant dissent within France. The pamphlet ends, however, on an optimistic note by claiming confidence in the young king's ability to make choices that will secure France's future. Bruscambille's explicit criticism of current royal policy is more reminiscent of the political commentary found in Renaissance farces than of the jokes performed at the Hôtel de Bourgogne in his day.[82]

By the early seventeenth century, such ideas were expressed in pamphlets rather than on the public stage, mainly because the theater was much more closely regulated than publishing. Although the monarchy did not systematically censor plays performed on Parisian stages, theater regulation was nevertheless tight enough that no farce player would dare to engage, in a public performance, with issues such as the debates of the Estates General of 1614 or the king's marriage. This gap between innocuous theater and satirical pamphleteering widened during the remainder of the ancien régime. As it became more and more difficult to challenge the king directly on stage, consumers sought out burlesque texts that tackled political questions. Although censorship eventually pushed the printing of such pamphlets outside of France, burlesque and even pornographic print satire continued to find its way back into the country.[83] Even the relatively innocuous publications of the farceurs had a long shelf life. New editions of some of Tabarin's dialogues and Bruscambille's monologues continued to be issued throughout the seventeenth century, long after their bawdy performances were deemed too risqué for polite society.[84] The comedy of the farceurs was increasingly savored alone or in the company of friends rather than at the public theater.

---

80. Hélène Duccini, "Une 'campagne de presse' sous Louis XIII: L'affaire Concini (1614–17)," in *Histoire sociale, sensibilités collectives et mentalités: Mélanges Robert Mandrou* (Paris: Presses Universitaires de France, 1985), 291–301; *L'ombre du marquis d'Ancre . . . le tout recueilli par un secrétaire de la Faveur, disciple de Tabarin* (1620).
81. *Advertissement du sieur Bruscambille sur le voyage d'Espagne* (1615). See also *Le discours de Bruscambille, avec la description de Conchini Conchino* (Paris: Antoine Chapenois, 1617); *Response de Gaultier Garguille aux révélations fantastiques de maitre Guillaume.*
82. Soman, "Press," 457–61.
83. Peter Burke, *The Fabrication of Louis XIV* (New Haven: Yale University Press, 1992), 135–47; Joseph Klaits, *Printed Propaganda under Louis XIV: Absolute Monarchy and Public Opinion* (Princeton: Princeton University Press, 1976), 44–57; Robert Darnton, *The Forbidden Best-Sellers of Pre-Revolutionary France* (New York: Norton, 1995), 3–21.
84. *Recueil général des oeuvres et fantasies de Tabarin* (Rouen: L. De Mesnil, 1664); Paul Lacombe, *Bibliographie parisiene: Tableaux des moeurs (1600–1800)* (Paris: Rouquette, 1887). At least one Mazarinade evoked the farceurs of the 1610s. See *Metamorphose Mazarine ou changement grotesque de Mazarin en Tabarin* (Paris: Julien Rambau, 1651).

Although literate Parisians continued to enjoy burlesque pamphlets, by the mid-1620s they increasingly sought more refined fare on the public stage. Unlike Louis XIII, who continued to be entertained by farceurs at court, Parisian audiences attending the Hôtel de Bourgogne and other public stages had a change of heart. Theatergoers gradually spurned the aging farceurs in favor of new troupes that performed a predominantly neoclassical repertoire. The Confrérie de la Passion and the Châtelet regulated the repertoire of professional troupes only in a haphazard fashion, so it was the pressure of the market rather than the coercion of the state that eventually drove the farceurs off the stage. Elite Parisian tastes were changing not in response to changes at the king's court but rather in response to other cultural developments, in particular to the new ideals of *honnêteté* and *civilité*, developed in and exemplified by the nascent salons of Paris.

During the first decades of the seventeenth century, aristocratic social circles in Paris began self-consciously to articulate a new and what they considered more fitting code of manners. Literate and wealthy members of the Parisian nobility began to meet informally to discuss literature and life in a more refined context than they found at court. Contemptuous of the lack of cultural sophistication of Henry and his son, aristocratic women such as the Marchioness of Rambouillet and the Duchess of Rohan entertained authors Malherbe, Balsac, and Voiture whose ambition was to purify French poetry of medieval corruptions. At informal meetings at their homes—their salons—these women encouraged the development of a more decorous style of conversation between the sexes and a more self-conscious appreciation of the French language. Models for such social interaction could be found in sixteenth-century Italian texts such as Castiglione's *Book of the Courtier*, in which nobles are advised to wear their humanist learning lightly and pair their good horsemanship with a nonchalant grace on the dance floor. Deploring the crass behavior of French military men—including, implicitly, the warrior king Henry IV—the emerging *salonières* championed mores and manners that would distinguish noble from commoner. By the 1630s, the terms that were used by Parisian authors, from letter writers to playwrights, to describe this new ideal of refined cultivation were *honnêteté* and *civilité*.[85]

Simultaneously, a rash of French-language civility manuals was appearing in France. These texts sought to instruct the novice or the educated bourgeois in the ways of the court and the salons, defining and codifying some of the practices current in Paris polite society. These texts reached a much

---

85. Although later in the seventeenth century this pairing became more controversial as authors began to question whether these two qualities were compatible, they were used interchangeably earlier in the century. Magendie, *Politesse mondaine*, 120–48; Emmanuel Bury, *Littérature et politesse: L'invention de l'honnête homme (1580–1750)* (Paris: Presses Universitaires de France, 1996), 83–94, 111–16.

wider audience than did the salons, which were limited to those individuals the hostess deemed worthy. Urban elites—city councilors, parlement magistrates, and all those who aspired to be as cultivated as the nobility even if they did not enjoy their legal status—bought and read these texts. Although the ideals of *honnêteté* and *civilité* were by no means ubiquitous or lacking in detractors, more self-consciously refined ideals of behavior began now to be articulated and practiced.[86] Champions of civility increasingly preferred theater that reflected these new ideals, and this shift in theatrical taste had a direct impact on the careers of Gaultier Garguille, Gros Guillaume, and Turlupin, the long-standing comédiens du roi.

By the early 1620s, more and more professional acting troupes were making the trip to Paris to perform either before the king or the growing public audiences. Greek, Spanish, and Italian, as well as a number of French troupes, occupied the stages during this period. As a result, competition for access to the Hôtel de Bourgogne theater, by far the largest venue in the city, was becoming stiff. The trio of Gaultier Garguille, Gros Guillaume, and Turlupin had predominated at the confrérie's theater during the late 1610s, but they could not always secure that stage after 1620. In 1621, for example, the trio was trumped by a troupe of Italian actors celebrated at the king's court, so the three were forced to perform at a local jeu de paume. We know this because a few months later the trio refused to pay the confrérie the fee they owed them under the 1597 ruling (for using a theater other than the Hôtel de Bourgogne for their performance).[87] Despite their desire to perform at the Hôtel, the comédiens du roi increasingly came to resent the confrérie's fickle renting policies and began to question the very principle of its monopoly.

Although the trio returned to the Hôtel de Bourgogne stage the following autumn, Gaultier Garguille and his comrades were soon faced with more formidable threats from two French-speaking troupes led by actors Charles Le Noir and Montdory, whose neoclassical repertoire was attracting enthusiastic responses from audiences both in aristocratic private homes and at the public theater.[88] In October 1625, given the opportunity to choose between

---

86. Roger Chartier, *Lectures et lecteurs dans la France d'ancien régime* (Paris: Seuil, 1987), 45–64; Robert Muchembled, *L'invention de l'homme moderne: Sensibilités, moeurs et comportements collectifs sous l'ancien régime* (Paris: Fayard, 1988), 140–52, 243–50; Jorge Arditi, *A Genealogy of Manners: Transformations of Social Relations in France and England from the Fourteenth to the Eighteenth Century* (Chicago: University of Chicago Press, 1998), 122–54; Norbert Elias, *The Civilizing Process: Sociogenetic and Psychogenetic Investigations*, trans. Edmund Jephcott, ed. Eric Dunning, Johan Goudsblom, and Stephen Mennell (Oxford: Blackwell, 2000), 80–87.

87. AN MC XXXV:373b, Mar. 1639, fol. 32 (16 Feb. 1622). AN MC X:44, 31 Aug. 1621; AN MC X:45, 16 Oct. 1621.

88. AN MC X:48, 4 Oct. 1622; AN MC X:49, 17 Feb. 1623. To juxtapose the farce-playing trio with these other two Parisian troupes in the early 1620s is somewhat artificial. Membership in the two new troupes was fluid; there is even evidence of Le Noir and Montdory performing together in 1622. See AN MC X:47, 14 July 1622, 10 Aug. 1622; AN MC X:51, 23 Dec. 1623; AN MC X:53, 10 Apr. 1624; AN MC X:54, 27 Aug. 1624.

the farce-playing trio and Le Noir's troupe, the confrérie chose to rent to Le Noir. The trio, outraged, went to court, arguing that they were the official comédiens du roi and as such should have automatic access to Paris's premier public stage. Parisian magistrates disagreed, however, and ruled in favor of the confrérie, upholding its privilege to contract with whichever troupe it chose. Adding insult to injury, the magistrates forbade the comédiens du roi to perform anywhere near the Hôtel de Bourgogne while Le Noir's troupe was in residence.[89]

These new French-speaking troupes were an altogether more serious threat to the farceurs than the Italians had been.[90] Unlike the Italians—who also performed a kind of farce, commedia dell'arte plays full of physical and sexual humor—Le Noir's and Montdory's troupes won the applause of Parisians for their grace and refinement. As early as 1618 the Duchess of Rohan noted the arrival of Le Noir's troupe with favorable reviews. She remarked that the actors were "excellent comedians . . . they are very circumspect, and careful of their language, not only in front of us but also in the city according to what I am told."[91] This passage indicates that although the duchess had not attended performances at the Hôtel de Bourgogne, Le Noir had probably graced her salon with a short performance of his repertoire. The troupe leader Montdory in particular was praised for his stage demeanor: the author Balsac remarked in a personal letter that "the sounds of [Montdory's] voice supported by the dignities of his gestures ennobles the most commonplace and banal conceptions."[92] Contemporary audiences valued the troupes' restrained style and their attempt to elevate the aesthetic tenor of the theater. They felt this refinement worth commenting on because it contrasted so sharply with the performances of the farce players.

During the remainder of the 1620s the comédiens du roi, rather than quietly ceding the stage to their rivals, decided instead to try to adapt to theatergoers' changing tastes. Deferring to the public's new sense of decorum, men who had spent most of their careers as Gros Guillaume, Gaultier Garguille, and Turlupin reinvented themselves as tragic actors. After 1625, in both their contracts with the Confrérie de la Passion and their petitions to the king, the trio now referred to themselves not only by their Christian names but also by noble stage names that reflected their altered personae on the public stage. Gaultier Garguille became Fléchelles; Turlupin became Belleville; Gros Guillaume became La Fleur.[93] The troupe also added a promising young actor to their roster and a neoclassical playwright to their team. The actor was Pierre Le Messier, a young man who soon attracted compli-

89. Soulié, *Recherches*, 158–59 (3, 13, and 14 Aug. 1625); Deierkauf-Holsboer, *Hôtel de Bourgogne*, 1:126–27.
90. Baschet, *Comédiens italiens*, 328–36.
91. Duchess of Rohan, as quoted in Fransen, *Comédiens français*, 52–53.
92. Balsac, as quoted in Wiley, *Early Public Theatre*, 103.
93. AN MC X:61, 2 Sept. 1627; *Recueil des principaux tiltres*, 57.

ments both for his own acting skills and for those of his wife. The playwright was Alexandre Hardy. Hardy, now an elderly man, had been a member of Valleran Le Conte's acting troupe, which had gone bankrupt in Paris two decades earlier. Years of performing in the provinces and the Netherlands had refined Hardy's playwriting skills.[94] The king's comedians performed over a dozen of his later tragedies and tragicomedies, as well as tragicomedies and comedies by younger playwrights. Notably, none of the over seventy plays mentioned in the troupe's repertoire during this period was a new farce. Although it is likely that the troupe still ended the evening's performance with a short comic play, there is no evidence that the group purchased the rights to or built scenery for any new farces after 1620. Evidently, the troupe's professional success no longer depended on its performance of farce but rather on its ability to compete with other professional actors performing a neoclassical repertoire.[95]

The neoclassical plays performed by the king's comedians in the 1620s, though decried by later generations as unrefined, were far less explicit about bodily needs and desires than were the farces that Parisians had applauded a decade earlier.[96] These plays were tragedies, comedies, or tragicomedies written in a loose Alexandrine verse. Although most were five-act plays concerning individuals of high estate and were based on tales from classical myth or history, few of them adhered to the rules of classical drama that later playwrights like Corneille and Racine were expected to uphold. French neoclassical plays of the 1610s and 1620s were in fact more like medieval drama, in which events occurred out of sequence and the conclusion was often resolved by an act of God. Most importantly, these early neoclassical plays did not always conform to the more ambiguous criteria of propriety and verisimilitude that later critics would use to condemn them.[97] The most famous of these early tragedies performed by the comédiens du roi was Théophile de Viau's *Pyrame*, first published in 1621. De Viau, an impoverished aristocrat, was a well-known libertine poet who later died in prison for having edited a volume of bawdy love poetry—a personal history that reveals, in melodramatic terms, the risks of offending society's new sense of decorum. His only surviving full-length tragedy, based on Ovid's tale of the doomed love affair between Pyramus and Thisbe, celebrated the power of

94. AN MC X:55, 25 Jan. 1625; AN MC X:59, 29 Aug. 1626. See Deierkauf-Holsboer, *Vie d'Alexandre Hardy*, 75–108.

95. Deierkauf-Holsboer, *Hôtel de Bourgogne*, 1:155–67; Laurent Mahelot, *Le mémoire de Mahelot, Laurent, et d'autres décorateurs de l'Hôtel de Bourgogne et de la Comédie-française au XVIIe siècle* (Paris: Champion, 1920), 70–72; Julie Stone Peters, *Theatre of the Book, 1480–1880: Print, Text, and Performance in Europe* (Oxford: Oxford University Press, 2000), 33–36.

96. Descotes, *Histoire de la critique*, 21–50; Raymond Lebègue, "Le moyen âge dans le théâtre françois du XVIIe siècle: Thèmes et survivances," *XVIIe Siècle* 29 (1977): 31–42.

97. René Bray, *La formation de la doctrine classique en France* (Paris: Nizet, 1957), 191–288.

passionate love. Although later generations considered the play to be too violent—a murder takes place on stage—and its verse too self-conscious, in its day it was considered sufficiently respectable to be performed by young noblewomen at the Hôtel de Rambouillet salon in the mid-1620s.[98] By this period, aristocratic and bourgeois audiences were already more interested in these playwrights' attempts at poetic refinement and morally elevating drama than they were in the bawdy farces that had dominated the Parisian stage only a few years earlier.

Having altered their repertoire to meet the taste of the times, the comédiens du roi continued to compete with Le Noir's and Montdory's troupes for contracts with the Confrérie de la Passion. Frustrated by their lack of access to the Hôtel de Bourgogne, however, Guérin and his companions once again turned to the law courts to challenge the right of the Confrérie de la Passion to rent to whomever it pleased. They evidently hoped that by undermining the confrérie's monopoly, they might return to prominence on the Parisian stage. Not discouraged by their earlier failure to convince Parisian judges of their right to rent the Hôtel de Bourgogne, in the late 1620s the comédiens du roi brought two more cases against the confrérie. In 1629 they took their complaints before the Chambre des Comptes, the highest financial court in France, making the rather farfetched claim that the confrérie was not the rightful owner of the Hôtel de Bourgogne theater and therefore should not hold any monopoly over theatrical performance in the capital. In early November 1629, after months of delay, the confrérie finally produced documents that demonstrated both its ownership of the theater and the legal basis of its monopoly, and the Chambre des Comptes ruled in the association's favor.[99]

At this point, Louis XIII entered the game, defending the interests of his dear friend Gaultier Garguille/Fléchelles against the monopoly of the confrérie. Within a month of hearing of the Chambre des Comptes' ruling, Louis overturned it. Although the king conceded that the confrérie owned the theater, he nevertheless concluded that its members were abusing their privileges in denying the comédiens du roi access to the Hôtel de Bourgogne stage. Louis therefore insisted that these comedians must be allowed to "perform for the time and duration of three years in the Hôtel de Bourgogne theater . . . in return for the sum of two thousand four hundred

98. Émile Magne, *Voiture et les origines de l'Hôtel de Rambouillet, 1597–1635* (Paris: Mercure de France, 1911), 146–48; Joan DeJean, *The Reinvention of Obscenity: Sex, Lies, and Tabloids in Early Modern France* (Chicago: University of Chicago Press, 2002), 29–51; Antoine Adam, *Théophile de Viau et la libre pensée française en 1620* (Paris: Droz, 1935); Gaston H. Hall, *Richelieu's Desmarets and the Century of Louis XIV* (Oxford: Clarendon Press, 1990), 64–70; François Parfaict and Claude Parfaict, *Histoire du théâtre françois depuis son origine jusqu'à présent* (Paris: P. G. Le Mercier, 1745), 4:269–80; Jacques Scherer, *La dramaturgie classique en France* (Paris: Nizet, 1950), 376–77, 411–17.
99. *Recueil des principaux tiltres*, 57–63 (12 and 26 Oct. 1629, 7 Nov. 1629).

livres of rent per year," renewable in perpetuity.[100] This ruling marks a decisive moment in Parisian theatrical administration: for the first time since the confrérie's monopoly was granted in the sixteenth century, the king had intervened directly in the endless conflicts between professional actors and the confrérie. Not only did this ruling establish the Hôtel de Bourgogne as the permanent venue of the comédiens du roi, but it also set the rent that the confrérie was allowed to charge the actors, thereby stripping the association of most of its fiscal autonomy. The confrérie leaders were sufficiently outraged by the king's ruling that they refused to let the troupe enter the theater until a court order compelled them to do so.

The significance of the December 1629 ruling was not only that the comédiens du roi had permanent access to the Hôtel but also that control of theater regulation had shifted to the monarch. Up to this point, the professional theater in Paris had not been managed by the king's council or court administrators but rather by the terms of the confrérie's monopoly, the statutes of which were enforced by judges at the Châtelet. Beginning in 1630, however, the theater's management became much more centralized. When, during the 1630s, the comédiens du roi failed to pay their rent to the confrérie, Cardinal Richelieu shored up the troupe's finances, thereby initiating what was to become a tradition of paying out an annual disbursement to the main Parisian troupes—a tradition that was to last throughout the ancien régime.[101] The importance of this shift, for my argument, is its date: the king took over administration of the Parisian theater only in 1630, several years *after* the farce players had already changed their names and personae and adapted their repertoire to the new demand for more sophisticated neoclassical fare. And it was the actors, hoping to escape the confrérie's fickle renting policy, who explicitly requested that the king take control of Parisian theatrical administration. The change in theatrical taste preceded the court's involvement and was initiated by Parisian theatergoers, who were more interested in the noble gestures of Montdory than in the farceurs' familiar comic repertoire.

Despite the 1629 triumph of the comédiens du roi over the Confrérie de la Passion, the actors and the theater owners continued to wrestle publicly during the early 1630s. The comédiens du roi still hoped they could dislodge the confrérie from the Hôtel de Bourgogne entirely, and the confrérie was not yet ready to accept its new role as mere landlords. As a result, the confrérie published a long pamphlet in 1632 that detailed its legal claims to the theater, its monopoly over theatrical production, and the financial insolvency of the comédiens du roi. In addition, the confrérie sued a Parisian publisher

100. Soulié, *Recherches*, 161 (29 Dec. 1629); AN MC XXXV:373b, Mar. 1639, fols. 44a–45.
101. Couton, "Richelieu et le théâtre," 80; Hall, *Richelieu's Desmarets*, 131–52; Théophraste Renaudot, *Recueil des gazettes nouvelles . . . 1634* (Paris: Bureau d'Adresse, 1635), 564; Wiley, *Early Public Theatre*, 272.

who printed pamphlets in the actors' defense.[102] The comédiens du roi, who were by this time led by the younger Pierre Le Messier, responded by further distancing themselves from their past identities as farce players. In one of these pamphlets, *Complaint to the King and the Nobles of His Council for the Abrogation of the Confrérie de la Passion in Favor of the Royal Troupe of Actors*, the actors sought to discredit the confrérie and to elevate the acting profession to a newly respectable professional status. Unlike pamphlets published in the farceurs' names during the 1610s, which represented them as irreverent outsiders, the 1631 pamphlet presents the royal actors as respectable, trained professionals engaged in a noble profession. Citing classical examples of the respect accorded actors in Roman times, the pamphlet argues that acting has always been necessary for the maintenance of states and empires. It stresses that actors' performances can "imperceptibly enhance the companionship and goodwill among men" by dramatizing exemplary conduct and manners and by rewarding good and punishing evil. They cite for particular praise the actors' "facility of pronunciation and movements of spirit and of good grace, which can serve as models" for the theater audience to emulate.[103] The comédiens du roi portrayed themselves in the same terms as had previously been used by defenders of Montdory's troupe, emphasizing the didactic purpose of the theater as an arbiter of good taste. Civility was now invoked even by socially marginal professional actors to justify their profession. The terms of the debate had shifted, and the heyday of the professional farceur was drawing to a close.

Professional farce players, though socially marginal, continued to flourish in the relatively unregulated world of the early seventeenth-century Parisian theater, their performances still enjoyed by the bourgeois and nobles who no longer allowed their sons to participate in amateur festive societies. But these professional actors had considerably less scope for satirizing figures of authority than amateur farceurs had had in the sixteenth century. As a result, farce playing turned from a form of political commentary into merely a form of entertainment. By the early decades of the seventeenth century, young men who wished to mock their elders and satirize political figures did so by writing slanderous pamphlets, which were readily published by anonymous Parisian printers. With the advent of the burlesque pamphlet, a genre that proliferated in the seventeenth and eighteenth centuries in France, much political satire left the public stage for the printed broadside.

By the mid-1620s, even these noncontentious farces ceased to attract Parisian theatergoers, and those troupes that performed refined neoclassical plays had begun to eclipse the farceurs, who relied on a traditional comic

---

102. *Recueil des principaux tiltres*, 71; AN MC XXXV:373b, Mar. 1639, fol. 42 (29 Apr. 1631).

103. Archives Assistance Publique de Paris, fonds Fosseyeux, 58, "Remonstrance au roy, et nosseigneurs de son conseil pour l'abrogation de la Confrairie de la Passion, en faveur de la troupe royale des comédiens."

repertoire. Aristocratic salons condemned the sexually explicit humor of the farce as vulgar and unworthy of elite patronage. This shift in theatrical taste owed nothing to the example of the king, who continued to enjoy burlesque court ballets and the songs of renowned farce players well into the 1630s. This is not to say that Cardinal Richelieu's patronage of the theater after 1635 was not of great significance to the emergence of neoclassical theater in France. Richelieu's interest did indeed enhance the prestige of the theater and encourage the creation of politicized, neoclassical tragedies designed to represent the triumphs of the Bourbon monarchy. What my analysis of the earlier period demonstrates, however, is that Richelieu's achievement was built on a cultural transformation that was already well under way.

6 Absolutism and the Marginalization of Festive Societies

With the end of the Wars of Religion, farce playing no longer threatened public order, and professional actors resumed performing sexually explicit plays on the Parisian stage. Why then did the amateur festive societies not reemerge, particularly in the provinces where professional acting troupes ventured only intermittently? The return of peace would seem to have presented an ideal environment for the resumption of traditional festive life. Such had certainly been the case at the conclusion of the Hundred Years' War, when festive societies profited from renewed political stability to enjoy unprecedented cultural prominence during the French Renaissance. Yet after 1600, amateur farce players failed to return to the stage either in Paris or in most provincial cities.[1]

Because most amateur festive societies had faded from view by the early seventeenth century, some historians of popular culture have attributed their demise to the emergence of the French absolutist state. The centralizing state, it is argued, sought to monopolize control over violence and found rowdy processions and performances increasingly intolerable.[2] Establishing a clear connection between state centralization and the suppression of festive culture is difficult, however. During the first half of the seventeenth century, French kings made little effort to outlaw popular culture. Additionally, the very urban magistrates who issued rulings condemning charivari,

---

1. Nicole Pellegrin, *Les bachelleries: Organisations et fêtes de la jeunesse dans le Centre-Ouest, XVe–XVIIIe siècles* (Poitiers: Société des Antiquaires de l'Ouest, 1982); Michel Vovelle, *Les métamorphoses de la fête en Provence de 1750 à 1820* (Paris: Aubier, 1976), 66–88; Robert Muchembled, *L'invention de l'homme moderne: Sensibilités, moeurs et comportements collectifs sous l'ancien régime* (Paris: Fayard, 1988), 272–73.

2. Robert Muchembled, *Popular Culture and Elite Culture in France, 1400–1750*, trans. Lydia Cochrane (Baton Rouge: Louisiana State University Press, 1985), 314–17; Edward Muir, *Ritual in Early Modern Europe* (Cambridge: Cambridge University Press, 1997), 104–9.

dancing, and farce were often at the same time actively resisting efforts at royal centralization.[3] Although state centralization played a role in the disappearance of amateur farcical theater, it was not direct royal intervention that brought about this change. Rather it was the king's active interference in the political life of French cities that encouraged urban elites to reorient their theatrical tastes and censor farce.

Disentangling the political and religious causes for cultural change in the early modern period is always challenging. Festive societies were ceasing to perform farce during the Wars of Religion, when local officials were suppressing religious festivals like Carnival and saints' feast days, a convergence that, I have argued, suggests a causal connection between the repudiation of farce and the development of reformed Catholicism. Without underplaying the importance of these religious developments, this chapter examines another factor affecting the decline of farce: the centralizing ambitions of the Bourbon monarchy, which encouraged urban elites to reconsider their support of festive societies. By examining three early seventeenth-century microhistories—the last decades of the Mère Folle of Dijon, the fate of the Basoche of the parlements, and the regulation of professional actors in the provinces—I argue that the collapse of festive societies was linked to the urban elites' efforts to reinvent themselves as government officials deserving of royal patronage. Whereas histories of seventeenth-century French politics have tended to locate the new cooperation between the nobility and the king at about 1650, my research suggests that urban elites were aligning with the monarchy to construct a new absolutist political culture at an even earlier date, and that their repudiation of farce is an index of their changing attitude.

Not all amateur festive societies died out during the Wars of Religion. A handful reemerged with the return to peace: the Conards of Rouen participated in Carnival celebrations until at least 1609, and the Basoche performed at Corpus Christi in Aix throughout the ancien régime.[4] Nevertheless, the role of festive societies in civic culture, with the exception of that of Mère Folle of Dijon, had fundamentally changed. Though they still sometimes participated in religious festivals, these groups of young bourgeois and

3. During the sixteenth century, when popular culture was linked to suppressing heresy, French kings issued numerous edicts outlawing confraternities. By the second half of the seventeenth century, decades after the last festive society ceased performing, the aims of the state and Church converged once again with regard to suppressing popular culture. See Muchembled, *Invention*, 187–234; Pellegrin, *Bachelleries*, 283–86; Philip F. Riley, *A Lust for Virtue: Louis XIV's Attack on Sin in Seventeenth-Century France* (Westport, Conn.: Greenwood Press, 2001).

4. Archives Départementales Seine-Maritime (ADSM) 1 B 710, 20 Dec. 1594; ADSM 1 B 727, 20 Dec. 1597; ADSM 1 B 797, 3 Feb. 1609; Michel Cassan, "Basoche et basochiens à Toulouse à l'époque moderne," *Annales du Midi* 94 (1982): 272–73; J. Lestrade, "Les gateaux de la Basoche," *Revue Historique de Toulouse* 2 (1915–19): 147–48; Jean Tricou, "Les confréries joyeuses de Lyon au XVIe siècle et leur numismatique," *Revue Numismatique* 40 (1937): 294, 296, 304, 306.

noble youths were no longer paid by the local city council to perform after peace treaties or royal entry ceremonies because the relationship between the monarchy and the cities was changing. Between 1598 and 1661, French provincial cities were transformed from relatively autonomous *bonnes villes*, many of which had rebelled against the crown during the Wars of Religion, into more docile political entities. As the urban elites became more dependent on the king, they ceased attempting to entertain him with bawdy farces.

In the aftermath of the religious wars, Henry IV and later his son Louis XIII were able to reassert monarchical authority with unprecedented effectiveness, particularly in the cities, a process that some historians refer to as the development of a new political system, absolutism.[5] Absolutism is a modern term invented by historians to try to encapsulate the political changes that took place in France between 1600 and 1700. Over the century, French kings centralized political power to an unprecedented degree, but there remained important limits on their authority, and political opposition to royal policies was never entirely quashed. Nevertheless, the political system that we call absolutism rested on the Bourbon monarchy's claim to hold absolute sovereignty and to be accountable only to God. During the height of Louis XIV's reign—roughly the 1660s to the 1690s—it became difficult to oppose the king or to suggest in public that he was anything less than what he claimed to be: God's emissary on earth. What I call the "discourse of absolutism" is a way of addressing the monarch that flatters and cajoles him by apparently accepting his view of himself and refrains from insisting on the traditional political privileges of the nobility or the city officials. During the last decades of the seventeenth century, members of the French elite—Louis's generals, his ministers, his judges, and even his urban officials—presented themselves publicly as being in agreement with the king in the hopes that he would grant them his favor. Although such favor could lead to a lucrative political appointment, a direct fiscal contribution, or the enhancement of social status, refusing to flatter Louis XIV in this way would result in banishment from court and abandonment by the king.[6] Regional and institutional studies have shown that both the traditional nobility and the leading officials of royal institutions, like

5. William Beik, *Absolutism and Society in Seventeenth-Century France: State Power and Provincial Aristocracy in Languedoc* (New York: Cambridge University Press, 1985); Fanny Cosandey and Robert Descimon, *L'absolutisme en France: Histoire et historiographie* (Paris: Seuil, 2002); James B. Collins, *The State in Early Modern France* (Cambridge: Cambridge University Press, 1995); Yves-Marie Bercé, *La naissance dramatique de l'absolutisme: 1598–1661* (Paris: Seuil, 1992); Richard Bonney, *The Limits of Absolutism in Ancien Régime France* (Aldershot: Variorum, 1995).

6. Alain Boureau, "Ritualité politique et modernité monarchique," in *L'état ou le roi: Les fondations de la modernité monarchique en France (XIVe–XVIIe siècles)*, ed. Neithard Bulst, Robert Descimon, and Alain Guerreau (Paris: Éditions de la Maison des Sciences de l'Homme, 1996), 9–25; Alain Guéry, "Le roi est dieu, le roi est dieu," in *L'état ou le roi*, 27–47.

the parlements and the regional estates, willingly participated in a restructuring of power after the Wars of Religion, a process that intensified after the constitutional crisis known as the Fronde (1648–53).[7] Recognizing that they could gain personally and win financial concessions for their locality by acceding to the Bourbon monarchy's absolutist aims, provincial elites cemented personal relationships of clientage with the king's ministers, sometimes compromising their provinces' autonomy in exchange for stability. Although the path to this new political consensus was by no means smooth, particularly during the first half of the seventeenth century, ultimately there emerged a more stable and harmonious relationship between the monarchy and the elites—a new relationship that was both shaped by and influenced changes in theatrical practice.

In the cities of France, some of the changes that ultimately led to absolutism were already well under way during the early decades of the seventeenth century. Profiting from the financial, political, and economic disarray in which the cities found themselves by the early 1590s, Henry generously granted amnesty to most royal and city officials in cities such as Paris, Dijon, and Rouen that had resisted his authority for several years after he claimed the throne in 1589. Nevertheless, he also took the opportunity to reform city charters and provincial privileges in his favor, capitalizing on local conflict to extend monarchical authority. His actions in Limoges, where he settled a 1602 tax revolt by limiting the city council's electorate and appointing many of its members himself, was typical of his practical approach. Although Henry's policy toward the cities was not systematic, he subverted the autonomy of provincial cities on several occasions, undermining election procedures, narrowing the mandate of city councils, and overriding appointments to local office unfavorable to royal interests. The intensification of these policies under Louis XIII during the 1630s, a period of warfare and fiscal crisis, signaled a tangible and permanent shift in the monarchy's claims to authority over urban France. Louis XIII and his first minister, Cardinal Richelieu, raised taxes rapidly during this period, undermining the autonomy of regional estates, city councils, and local tax officials. Such impositions often evoked protest, sometimes violent protest, but until the belated political crisis of the Fronde, no common cause brought the officials of different cities together. The first two Bourbon kings clearly intended to prevent the cities from ever again rebelling against the monarchy as they had during the Wars of Religion. Thus during the first half of the seventeenth

---

7. Albert N. Hamscher, *The Conseil Privé and the Parlements in the Age of Louis XIV: A Study in French Absolutism* (Philadelphia: American Philosophical Society, 1987); Sharon Kettering, *Patrons, Brokers and Clients in Seventeenth-Century France* (Oxford: Oxford University Press, 1986); Mark Potter, *Corps and Clienteles: Public Finance and Political Change in France, 1688–1715* (Aldershot: Ashgate, 2003); Guy Rowlands, *The Dynastic State and the Army under Louis XIV: Royal Service and Private Interest, 1661–1701* (Cambridge: Cambridge University Press, 2002).

century, the urban elites' traditional political privileges steadily eroded in favor of a centralizing state.[8]

These political developments dovetailed with long-term economic changes. Late medieval European cities, whose wealth was based on artisanal production and regional trade, were declining by the sixteenth century. In France, this economic restructuring was further exacerbated by decades of civil strife that disrupted trade routes and manufacturing. Important regional cities such as Rouen, Toulouse, and Lyon, prominent centers of trade, manufacture, and banking during the first half of the sixteenth century, saw many of their traditional sources of wealth stagnate. In Toulouse, pastel production for manufacturing textiles collapsed during the sixteenth century, leaving the city economically vulnerable.[9] Throughout the seventeenth century, a period of economic stagnation all over Europe, only cities that could reinvent themselves as administrative centers or political capitals tended to expand. French provincial centers such as Dijon or Rouen, already the loci of parlements and provincial estates, were in a good position to do so, but this shift required a new degree of cooperation with the monarchy.

These developments gradually altered the type of men who dominated local politics. By the early seventeenth century, the traditional merchant elite had been replaced on most French city councils by royal officials, whose administrative duties, linked to tax collecting and the judiciary, now produced much of these cities' wealth. The new elite expressed their wealth and status in various ways, for example, by building the gracious stone *hôtels* that often became the target of commoner anger during local tax revolts. The growing power of the Bourbon monarchy thus worked to the advantage of many urban elite families, whose wealth and prestige were linked to service as venal officers of the crown. The wealthiest of these families could exploit

---

8. S. Annette Finley-Croswhite, *Henry IV and the Towns: The Pursuit of Legitimacy in French Urban Society, 1589–1610* (Cambridge: Cambridge University Press, 1999); Michael P. Breen, "Legal Culture, Municipal Politics and Royal Absolutism in Seventeenth-Century France: The 'Avocats' of Dijon (1595–1715)," Ph.D. diss., Brown University, 2000; Hilary J. Bernstein, *Between Crown and Community: Politics and Civic Culture in Sixteenth-Century Poitiers* (Ithaca: Cornell University Press, 2004); Yann Lignereux, *Lyon et le roi: De la bonne ville à l'absolutisme municipal (1594–1654)* (Seyssel: Champ Vallon, 2003); William Beik, *Urban Protest in Seventeenth-Century France: The Culture of Retribution* (Cambridge: Cambridge University Press, 1997); Mack P. Holt, "Popular Political Culture and Mayoral Elections in Sixteenth-Century Dijon," in *Society and Institutions in Early Modern France*, ed. Mack P. Holt (Athens: University of Georgia Press, 1991), 98–116.

9. Jan De Vries, *European Urbanization, 1500–1800* (Cambridge, Mass.: Harvard University Press, 1984), 95–120, 253–58; Pierre Deyon, *Amiens, capitale provinciale: Étude sur la société urbaine au 17e siècle* (Paris: Mouton, 1967), 270–73; Barbara B. Diefendorf, *Paris City Councillors in the Sixteenth Century: The Politics of Patrimony* (Princeton: Princeton University Press, 1983), 51–53; Richard Gascon, *Grand commerce et vie urbaine au XVIe siècle: Lyon et ses marchands* (Paris: École Pratique des Hautes Études, 1971), 1:412; Frederick M. Irvine, "From Renaissance City to Ancien Régime Capital: Montpellier, c. 1500–c. 1600," in *Cities and Social Change in Early Modern France*, ed. Philip Benedict (London: Unwin Hyman, 1989), 111–18, 125–27.

centralization by advancing through the royal fiscal or judicial administration instead of, or in addition to, sitting on the local city council. Although balancing local interests with their obligations to royal service was not new for provincial urban officials, by the early decades of the seventeenth century the pull of the monarchy was steadily increasing.[10]

The discourse of absolutism altered the traditional notion of the body politic. In late medieval and Renaissance France, although kings often stressed the absolute nature of their authority and their sacred role as supreme judge, other members of the body politic, including the traditional nobility, the Parlement of Paris, the clergy, and provincial elites, were often ready to challenge this interpretation. Particularly during times of war, they insisted on their right to consult with the king and to oppose him if he seemed to be acting against the public good. French kings acknowledged the validity of their counsel by convoking frequent Estates General to obtain popular support for their policies.[11] During the sixteenth century, satirical farce often expressed this traditional understanding of the body politic. But beginning in the 1570s with the writings of Jean Bodin, who stressed the indivisibility of royal sovereignty, the king was increasingly represented in political ritual not only as the head of the body politic but also as the body's sole animator. Order, peace, and the public good depended on French subjects' obedience to the king, who had been divinely appointed to rule absolutely. The traditional privilege to offer consultation was replaced by humble supplication to an increasingly distant monarch. No Estates General were called after 1614, and by the late reign of Louis XIII, direct access to the king for the purpose of presenting complaints was often blocked by Cardinal Richelieu.[12]

10. Peter Burke, *Popular Culture in Early Modern Europe* (New York: Harper and Row, 1978), 270; Bernard Chevalier, *Les bonnes villes de France du XIVe au XVIe siècle* (Paris: Aubier-Montaigne, 1982), 129–49; Alexander Cowan, "Urban Elites in Early Modern Europe: An Endangered Species?" *Historical Research* 64 (1991): 121–37; George Huppert, *Les Bourgeois Gentilhommes: An Essay on the Definition of Elites in Renaissance France* (Chicago: University of Chicago Press, 1977), 34–46; Robert Schneider, *Public Life in Toulouse, 1463–1789: From Municipal Republic to Cosmopolitan City* (Ithaca: Cornell University Press, 1989), 167–87, 358–59; Judi Loach, "The Hôtel de Ville at Lyons: Civic Improvement and Its Meanings in Seventeenth-Century France," *Transactions of the Royal Historical Society* 13 (2003): 256–59.
11. Éric Gojosso, *Le concept de République en France (XVIe–XVIIIe siècle)* (Aix-en-Provence: Presses Universitaires d'Aix-Marseille, 1998), 60–69, 205–45; John Russell Major, *From Renaissance Monarchy to Absolute Monarchy: French Kings, Nobles and Estates* (Baltimore: Johns Hopkins University Press, 1994), 47–56; Hélène Merlin, *Public et littérature en France au XVIIe siècle* (Paris: Belles Lettres, 1994), 70–87.
12. Louis Marin, *Le portrait du roi* (Paris: Minuit, 1981); Jean-Marie Apostolidès, *Le prince sacrifié: Théâtre et politique au temps de Louis XIV* (Paris: Minuit, 1985); Peter Burke, *The Fabrication of Louis XIV* (New Haven: Yale University Press, 1992); Sara E. Melzer and Kathryn Norberg, eds., *From the Royal to the Republican Body: Incorporating the Political in Seventeenth- and Eighteenth-Century France* (Berkeley: University of California Press, 1988); Ralph E. Giesey, *Cérémonial et puissance souveraine: France, XVe–XVIIe siècles* (Paris: Colin, 1987).

The Bourbon monarchy sought to redefine its relationship to its subjects through political rituals that emphasized the absolute and unchanging authority of the monarchy, rituals that made manifest the changing balance of power. After 1610, royal entry ceremonies, funerals, and *lits de justice* deemphasized the king's role as judge and arbiter of traditional privileges, instead representing him as ruling by divine right.[13] This shift was epitomized by the smooth transfer of authority after Henry IV's assassination in 1610. Henry's son Louis XIII, instead of waiting to be recognized by his subjects after his father's funeral and at his own coronation—the standard way of marking a new king's succession—broke with tradition by holding a *lit de justice* at the Paris Parlement the day after his father's death to formalize his accession to power, even though he himself had not yet reached the age of majority. This unilateral royal act eliminated ambiguity or room for reciprocity.[14]

Under the Bourbons, the triumphant royal entry ceremony also evolved to express the monarchy's increasingly insistent claims to absolute authority. Traditionally, such ceremonies had allowed the urban elites to demonstrate their homage to the king while at the same time press the monarch for recognition of the city's privileges, such as exemptions from taxation and rights to self-rule. During the Renaissance, royal entries were reciprocal rituals during which the mutual obligations of city and monarch were formally articulated through exchanges of gifts and a procession through the city streets. Louis XIII continued to practice the traditional ritual of the royal entry until the 1620s, when a renewal of military conflict with the Huguenot minority necessitated frequent tours in the south and border regions. After this period and during the reign of his son Louis XIV, however, royal entry ceremonies were held less often.[15] Once the political autonomy of most French cities was undermined, affirming the loyalty of the cities through elaborate and expensive rituals became redundant. When Bourbon monarchs did venture forth to process triumphantly through the city streets, they were less interested in acknowledging corporate privileges and celebrating local culture than they had been a century earlier. Louis XIV's triumphal entry into Paris in 1660, for example, after his marriage to the Infanta of Spain, allowed no

13. Lawrence M. Bryant, *The King and the City in the Parisian Royal Entry Ceremony: Politics, Ritual, and Art in the Renaissance* (Geneva: Droz, 1986), 166–67, 207–14; Giesey, *Cérémonial*, 33–47, 49–66; Sarah Hanley, *The Lit de Justice of the Kings of France: Constitutional Ideology in Legend, Ritual and Discourse* (Princeton: Princeton University Press, 1983), 254–67.

14. Hamscher, *Conseil Privé*; A. Lloyd Moote, *The Revolt of the Judges: The Parlement of Paris and the Fronde, 1643–1652* (Princeton: Princeton University Press, 1972); John Peter Hurt, *The Parlement of Brittany in the Reign of Louis XIV* (Chapel Hill: University of North Carolina Press, 1969).

15. Marie-France Wagner and Daniel Vaillancourt, eds., *La roi dans la ville: Anthologie des entrées royales dans les villes de province (1615–1660)* (Paris: Champion, 2001).

room for the traditional expressions of corporate privilege: the focus was now exclusively on the glory of the monarch.[16]

Not surprisingly, in this context of contracting urban power and increasingly absolutist political ritual, urban magistrates and city councilors no longer allowed festive societies to accompany the king as he entered the city or to perform during the celebrations that followed. The reconstituted Basoche of Bordeaux, whose members had greeted the king and other visiting dignitaries at the city gates during the Renaissance, no longer undertook this duty after 1600.[17] In a city such as Lyon, where as late as the 1590s royal entries had included artisan confraternities performing comical and bawdy *chevauchées d'asne*, such processions took a more dignified tone at the turn of the century. Beginning in 1609, burlesque representatives from the different Lyon quartiers were no longer invited to participate.[18] Even in smaller centers such as Châlon-sur-Saône, the Enfants de la Ville—an umbrella association of festive societies that had participated in entry ceremonies throughout the sixteenth century—was also excluded from such events after the Wars of Religion. In 1598, in an attempt to reassert its traditional procession privileges, the Enfants of Chalon-sur-Saône stole a mule from the visiting cardinal of Florence during his entry, forcing the aging papal legate to return to his quarters on foot. As punishment, one of the leaders was imprisoned and another, the Prince of the Basoche, was compelled to apologize to the cardinal.[19] In general, festive societies that had often been integrated into royal entry ceremonies during the Renaissance were no longer tolerated by local officials. Except in Dijon, city councils no longer entertained the king or other royal officials with farcical theater. Although royal entry ceremonies as late as the 1620s celebrated not only the glory of the monarchy but also that of the city and its inhabitants, urban elites no longer sought to express these ideas through farce.[20] Such discretion demonstrates

---

16. Bryant, *King*, 207–24; Jean-Marie Apostolidès, "Entrée royale et idéologie urbaine au XVIIe siècle," *XVIIe Siècle* 53 (2001): 509–20; Abby E. Zanger, *Scenes from the Marriage of Louis XIV: Nuptial Fictions and the Making of Absolutist Power* (Stanford: Stanford University Press, 1997), 37–67.

17. Archives Départementales Gironde (ADG), 1 B 210, fol. 40, 29 Nov. 1559; ADG 1 B 382, fol. 81, 14 Mar. 1574; Bibliothèque Municipale (BM) Bordeaux MS 369, Savignac, "Extraits des registres secrets du Parlement de Bordeaux," 2:573–74 (10 Feb. 1565).

18. Tricou, "Confréries," 308. Although the Enfants de la Ville still participated in royal entries until 1622, their performances by that time no longer included burlesque or farcical elements. See *Entrées royales et fêtes populaires à Lyon du XVe au XVIIIe siècles* (Lyon: Bibliothèque de la Ville de Lyon, 1970), 50–56, 111–17.

19. Marcel Canat, *Recherches historiques sur la corporation des enfants de ville de Châlon-sur-Saône, dite Abbaye des enfants* (Châlon-sur-Saône: Montalan, 1849), 19–23; Tricou, "Confréries," 308.

20. Michael Breen, "Addressing 'la ville des dieux': Entry Ceremonies and Urban Audiences in Seventeenth-Century Dijon," *Journal of Social History* 37 (2004): 341–64; Daniel Vaillancourt, "La ville des entrées royales: Entre transfiguration et défiguration," *XVIIe Siècle* 53 (2001): 491–508; Marie-Claude Canova-Green, "Révolte et imaginaire: Le voyage de Louis XIII en Provence," *XVIIe Siècle* 53 (2001): 429–39.

not necessarily that they had capitulated to royal authority but that they had found other strategies, such as sending delegations to court and developing clientage relationships with royal officials, more effective for maintaining their hold over local affairs.[21] Although presenting themselves as humble servants to the king was of course a traditional form of compliment, the new language of obedience and subservience that came to predominate in seventeenth-century political discourse marks a rupture with the Renaissance. By the early decades of the seventeenth century, urban elites increasingly employed absolutist discourse to the exclusion of other means of addressing the monarch. The amateur farceurs who had traditionally enlivened the interludes in civic ritual held the stage no more; absolutist discourse left no room for the satire and frivolity of farce.

Although most French cities eliminated farce from civic ritual by the early seventeenth century, Dijon was an important exception. Located near the eastern border of France, Dijon was the capital of Burgundy, a province in which elites were able to hold onto local political power a few decades longer than were most areas of France. The Dijon city council's decision to patronize a highly visible and prestigious festive society was a symbol of this political confidence. Nevertheless, the gradual demise of the Mère Folle by the mid-seventeenth century also demonstrates how transgressive the display of unruly bodies had become now that French kings insisted on representing their authority as absolute.

The Mère Folle's survival was intimately linked to the status of Burgundy as a relatively autonomous province within the French state. During most of the fifteenth century, Dijon had not been subject to the French king's authority. Indeed in 1447 some textile workers performed an audacious farce in Dijon that mocked the French king, imagining that they had nothing to fear since at the time Dijon was in effect ruled by the Duke of Burgundy. Though, as it turned out, they were wrong—one of them spent a few days in prison as a result—their audacity illustrates their sense of the city's independence from royal authority. The duchy of Burgundy was fully reintegrated into France only after the death of the Duke of Burgundy in battle in 1477. During the Wars of Religion, Dijon once again proved to be remarkably resistant to royal authority. During the last phase of the civil wars, it emerged as a stronghold of Catholic resistance and one of the cities most consistently loyal to the Duke of Mayenne, the military leader of the Catholic League. Dijon only ceded to Henry IV in 1595, after Mayenne was finally defeated in battle. Despite the monarchy's threat to the contrary, the Burgundian elites were able to fend off Henry IV's and Louis XIII's attempts to undermine local control of taxation, defense, and municipal election

21. Breen, "Legal Culture," 306–35; Bernstein, *Crown*, 250–74; Guy Saupin, *Nantes au XVIIe siècle: Vie politique et société urbaine* (Rennes: Presses Universitaires de Rennes, 1996), 47–73, 109–21.

procedures in the immediate postwar period. The Dijon elite had every reason to believe that they would continue to enjoy a large measure of political autonomy under the new Bourbon regime.[22]

Like the Bourbon kings, the Dijon city council realized that political power was bolstered by ritual, and, perhaps in order to use popular culture for this purpose, the city council developed a close relationship with the Mère Folle. This traditional festive society had emerged in Dijon during the second half of the sixteenth century, performing bawdy and satirical farces and participating in royal entry ceremonies.[23] By the early seventeenth century, the association was several hundred strong as well as socially secure; probably most of its members were the sons of magistrates, lawyers, and prominent merchants. Certificates of admission to the Mère Folle demonstrate that the festive society had close ties not only to the urban officials but also to the local nobility and the ecclesiastical hierarchy, including the Count of Harcourt and the bishop of Langres. Even Henry de Bourbon, Prince of Condé, a prominent peer who would later become the military governor of Burgundy, joined the Mère Folle in 1626.[24] Although it is unlikely that these noble members actively participated in its performances, their association with the group added greatly to its prestige. In addition, many of the association's plays were written by prominent civic leaders such as Étienne Bréchillet and Pierre Malpoy, barristers and longtime members of the Dijon city council. In short, the Mère Folle had by 1600 been thoroughly co-opted by the establishment. Any danger that it might want to express the opinions of the common people or defy the official political line had long since been eliminated. Instead, the festive society was increasingly a mouthpiece through which the Dijon city council could demonstrate the vitality of Burgundian culture to the French crown and encourage public order within the city.[25]

The Mère Folle's close association with men of power in Dijon granted it unusual privileges to perform traditional genres at a time when local authorities actively tried to suppress popular culture. Like authorities in many other French cities, the Dijon city council, during the first decades of the

22. Breen, "Legal Culture," 167–228; Holt, "Popular Political Culture," 110–14.

23. Some historians have argued that the Mère Folle's performances originated centuries earlier, but all available evidence demonstrates that fifteenth- and early sixteenth-century Feast of Fools performances in Dijon were undertaken by groups of young priests. J. B. L. Du Tilliot, *Mémoires pour servir à l'histoire de la fête des fous qui se faisait autrefois dans plusieurs églises* (Lausanne: Marc-Michel Bousquet, 1751), 97–107; Jacques Heers, *Fêtes des fous et carnavals* (Paris: Fayard, 1983), 203–4; Maurice Lever, *Le sceptre et la marotte: Histoire des fous de cour* (Paris: Fayard, 1983), 83; Juliette Valcke, "Théâtre et spectacle chez la Mère Folle de Dijon (XVe–XVIe)," in *Les arts du spectacle dans la ville (1404–1721)*, ed. Marie-France Wagner and Claire Le Brun-Gouanvic (Paris: Champion, 2001), 66.

24. Du Tilliot, *Mémoires*, 115, 117–53.

25. Roger Chartier, "Discipline et invention: La fête," in *Lectures et lecteurs dans la France d'ancien régime* (Paris: Seuil, 1987), 30–31; Breen, "Addressing," 341–58.

seventeenth century, issued several rulings outlawing confraternities, traditional feasts, gaming, and dancing.[26] In contrast, we know from printed accounts of the association's performances that the Mère Folle was permitted to march through the city streets with relative license: on at least one occasion, the city council actually paid the group to perform after the wedding of a local dignitary.[27] The Mère Folle's intimate relationship with the Dijon city council differentiates it from most festive societies before the Wars of Religion, when regulation was haphazard and authorities reacted to slanderous performances after the fact. By the early seventeenth century, Mère Folle theater was a form of festive propaganda thoroughly sanctioned and controlled by the Dijon urban elite.

The Dijon city council's efforts to control political representations extended to print materials as well. Throughout the first half of the seventeenth century, the city council reacted vigorously whenever it felt that dangerous religious or political ideas were being circulated in books or in printed *affiches* posted on the city walls. The council attempted to regulate the Dijon publishing industry closely by granting privileges for particular books, including the accounts of Mère Folle performances.[28] Whereas in Lyon and Rouen festive societies often arranged to have their plays published without consulting local authorities, sometimes with controversial results, in Dijon the city council appointed a specific individual to undertake this task.[29] In 1608, Claude Guyot was named *imprimeur de la ville* of Dijon, apparently the first individual to hold this post. In return for printing whatever the city council requested without charge, Guyot was provided with free lodging in the city's collège and was exempted from the taille.[30] Why the city council chose to hire Guyot, who was an *imprimeur du roy* at Châlons-sur-Marne 200 kilometers away from Dijon, remains a mystery. There were at least two publishers already active in Dijon at that time. If the city council had wanted to hire a royalist, local publisher Jean des Planches would have been a more obvious choice. It is possible that Guyot was recommended to the

26. Rulings against masks, dancing, and charivari in Dijon during this period include Archives Municipales Dijon (AMD) B 238, fols. 103–4, 1 Sept. 1600; AMD B 239, fol. 163v, 15 Nov. 1601; AMD B 245, fols. 69v–70r, 17 July 1607; AMD B 282, fol. 230, 17 Feb. 1645; AMD B 286, fol. 200v, 26 Jan. 1649; AMD B 286, fol. 223, 15 Feb. 1649; AMD B 293, fol. 256, 19 Jan. 1655; AMD B 294, fol. 186v, 4 Feb. 1656; Bibliothèque Nationale (BN) MS coll. Dupuy, 630, fol. 86, 8 Aug. 1622; James R. Farr, *Hands of Honor: Artisans and Their World in Dijon, 1550–1650* (Ithaca: Cornell University Press, 1988), 248–51.

27. AMD B 252, fol. 171, 13 Jan. 1615; AMD B 253, fol. 73, 24 July 1615; AMD B 253, fol. 162, 10 Nov. 1615.

28. AMD B 198, fol. 30, 20 July 1560; AMD B 198, fol. 100, 3 Feb. 1561; AMD B 214, fol. 175, 3 May 1578; AMD B 231, fol. 167, 10 May 1594; AMD B 246, fol. 201, 23 Feb. 1609; AMD B 280, fol. 128, 19 Sept. 1642; AMD G 46, Aug. 1609.

29. *Entrées royales*, 54–56; *Triomphe de l'abbaye des Conards avec une notice sur les fêtes des fous* (Rouen, 1587; reprint, Paris: Librairie des Bibliophiles, 1874).

30. AMD B 246, fol. 77, 29 July 1608; Michel Clément-Janin, *Les imprimeurs et les libraires dans la Côte-d'Or* (Dijon: Darantière, 1883), 3–10.

position by a nobleman whose lands bordered the two provinces or that the council thought Guyot, as an outsider, would be easier to control.[31] The aim in creating the post of official publisher for the city is, however, made clear by Guyot's contract: the council was attracted to Guyot's claims that he could establish in Dijon "a suitable printing house, comparable to those that are of the best reputation in the cities of Paris, Lyon, and others."[32] Also noted with appreciation was the full complement of typefaces and equipment that Guyot brought with him. The council's aims in hiring Guyot were strikingly ambitious for a relatively small city like Dijon, which had little more than 10,000 inhabitants at this date.

Guyot's tasks included printing the texts of the plays performed by the Mère Folle as well as other official political documents issued by the city council. In doing so, he helped to proclaim the political confidence of the Dijon urban elite to a literate audience that might have extended outside the city walls. On at least one occasion, Guyot went even further and defended local Burgundian interests by publishing a pamphlet that criticized royal policy. The pamphlet in question, written by a member of the Dijon city council, condemned Henry IV's plan to demolish a local military stronghold—a plan the city council had been opposing for several years. Although the council later chastised Guyot for his audacity, they did not fine him or remove him from his post, a mildness of reprimand that suggests the council was divided about the wisdom of the pamphlet's publication.[33] Guyot's position as imprimeur de la ville was an ambiguous one, not unlike that of the Renaissance farce players. Although he was sometimes rapped on the knuckles when he pressed the case of Burgundian autonomy too far, his post as official printer of the city encouraged him to promote local culture and local political concerns over those of the Bourbon monarchy. In Dijon, as in Paris during the first decades of the seventeenth century, such explicitly critical material was

---

31. Regarding the town Châlons-sur-Marne as a royalist stronghold during the last phase of the religious wars, see G. Hérelle, *La Réfome et la Ligue en Champagne* (Paris: Champion, 1887), 2:283–92; Mark W. Konnert, *Civic Agendas and Religious Passion: Châlons-sur-Marne during the French Wars of Religion, 1560–1594* (Kirksville, Mo.: Sixteenth Century Journal Publishers, 1997), 145–61. Examples of Guyot's early royalist pamphlets include *Remonstrance à Monseigneur le duc de Lorraine pour le retirer de la Ligue* (Châlons-sur-Marne: Claude Guyot, 1589); Charles de Navieres, *Chant triomphal de la céleste victoire donnée au Roy tres chrestien pres d'Yvry* (Châlons-sur-Marne: Claude Guyot, 1590). The Dijon city council had suspected Jean des Planches's father of being a Huguenot and was perhaps reluctant to appoint his son as imprimeur de la ville. AMD B 231, fols. 150v–51, 22 Mar. 1594; AMD B 231, fols. 159v–60, 15 Apr. 1594; Clément-Janin, *Imprimeurs*, 15–20. Regarding the close ties between the lower nobility of Burgundy and Champagne, see Laurent Bourquin, *Noblesse seconde et pouvoir en Champagne aux XVIe et XVIIe siècles* (Paris: Publications de la Sorbonne, 1994), 188; Gaston Roupnel, *La ville et la campagne au XVIIe siècle: Étude sur les populations du pays dijonnais* (Paris: Colin, 1955), 168.
32. AMD G 46, fol. 77, 26 July 1608; AMD G 46, 20 Aug. 1609.
33. AMD B 246, fol. 201, 23 Feb. 1609; Gabriel Peignot, *De la liberté de la presse à Dijon au commencement du XVIIe siècle* (Paris: Techner, 1836), 10.

increasingly to be found in printed pamphlets instead of on the stage. Despite efforts to regulate it closely, print was a medium that often allowed authors to escape punishment more easily than actors.

The Mère Folle's plays, performed in the city and published by Guyot as imprimeur de la ville, exemplified the balance between monarchical and local interests that the city council tried to achieve under the Bourbon kings, who proved increasingly deaf to the traditional discourse of reciprocal political obligations. The troupe generally performed at civic celebrations that marked important events such as the arrival of an important noble or a royal military victory. In 1601, the Mère Folle performed a series of short vignettes—two plays interspersed with songs, poems, and dancing—to mark the wondrous birth of the dauphin, the future Louis XIII.[34] Like most Mère Folle performances during the seventeenth century, this one used a mixture of genres. The first play was allegorical and drew on classical mythology: a series of elaborately dressed figures representing Uranus, Neptune, and the four continents—Asia, Africa, America, and Europe—all declare their homage to the young prince. In contrast to this largely static visual spectacle, the second play was a traditional sottie in which three local winegrowers comment on the affairs of the day in a heavily accented Burgundian dialect, deride the allegorical performance of the first play, and mock the nasal tone of the pure French of its characters. They also muse about the allegory's meaning, at first mistaking the names of the continents for local or nonsense names: they mishear "Amerique" as "Maire Etique" and take Neptune with his trident for a sergeant of the local militia. Their comments express their sense that Dijon is the center of their world, a message that undermines the overt displays of homage to royal authority that characterize the rest of the performance. In the end, however, after a third winegrower joins the discussion and explains the true meaning of the allegory, the trio prepare to feast in honor of the young prince.

This performance, lightheartedly mocking courtly affectation and valorizing traditional Burgundian culture, was typical of Mère Folle plays published by imprimeur de la ville Guyot in this period.[35] Unlike the Mère Folle's sixteenth-century performances, in which references to classical

---

34. *Genethliaque autrement triomphe sur la naissance de Monseigneur le Daufin, par l'Infanterie Dijonnoise le 27 décembre 1601* (Cisteaux: Jean Savine pour Pierre Grangier, 1602).

35. Étienne Tabouret, *Les escriagnes dijonnoises: Recueillies par le sieur des Accords* (Poitiers, 1610); *Description en vers bourguignons de l'ordre tenu en l'Infanterie Dijonnoise pour la mascarade par elle representée à Monseigneur de Bellegarde* (Dijon: Jean des Planches, 1610); *La confirmation de la paix par l'Infanterie Dijonnoise* (Dijon: Claude Guyot, 1613); *Avant-exercice de l'infanterie dijonnoise, du XVI février 1614, sur l'heureux mariage du Roy* (Dijon: Claude Guyot, 1614); "Le reveil de Bontemps, 1623," in *Théâtre de l'Infanterie Dijonnoise*, ed. Joachim Durandeau (Dijon: Darantière, 1887); [Pierre Malpoy], *Le chariot de triomphe du roy représenté par l'infanterie dijonnoise, le dimanche 25 février 1629* (Dijon: Nicolas Sprinx, 1629); *La braverie ou réjouissance de 1630, pour la naissance de M. de Conty* (Dijon: Veuve Claude Guyot, 1630).

mythology and humanist poetry were integrated into the traditional sottie, these seventeenth-century productions were dominated by allegorical poetry written in contemporary and relatively standardized French. Dialogues among local winegrowers were now sandwiched in between more respectful, neoclassical pastorals, and the discourse of absolutism was given the last word. Nevertheless, by including any farcical elements at all, the Mère Folle's performances were exceptional by the 1620s.[36]

Events that unfolded after a Dijon tax revolt of 1630 demonstrate that including farce in civic celebrations had become a risky undertaking. This tax riot, known as the Lanturelu, had its origins in 1629. That summer, Louis XIII issued an edict that abolished the Estates of Burgundy, whose traditional privileges included assessing local taxes. Abolishing the estates was an explicitly centralizing move by the monarchy in that *pays d'états*, which Burgundy had been until that point, generally paid much lower taxes than did regions in which royal officials collected taxes directly. Not surprisingly, the estates and some members of the city council sought to combat this royal infringement of traditional privileges. Possibly they also spread rumors around the city that the king was planning to raise taxes. Possibly because of such rumors and because of the failure of city officials to appeal the king's decision, soon after Mardi Gras in early 1630 several dozen angry artisans and winegrowers marched to city hall to complain about royal taxes. The following morning, February 28, several hundred rebels, supposedly led by the "king" of Carnival, began looting the houses of royal financial officers. Only after several hours of looting and confusion did the local Dijon militia finally quell the violence.[37] During the months that followed, Louis XIII and the Estates of Burgundy negotiated a settlement typical of early seventeenth-century tax revolts: the Burgundian Estates made a large financial contribution to the king's coffers in return for the privilege of maintaining its traditional role as assessor of Burgundian taxes. Burgundy would remain a *pays d'états*, at least for the time being. Nevertheless, the king was unhappy with the Dijon city council because of its relatively slow response to the riot, and he punished its members directly by abrogating the city council's traditional election procedures and reducing the number of city councilors from twenty to six. He also turned against the Mère Folle. Citing the "disorder and debauchery that this group has produced and continues to produce on a regular basis against the good manners, peace and tranquility

---

36. Juliette Valcke, "La satire sociale dans le répertoire de la Mère Folle de Dijon," in *Carnival and the Carnivalesque: The Fool, the Reformer, the Wildman and others in Early Modern Theatre*, ed. Konrad Eisenbichler and Wim Hüsken (Amsterdam: Rodopi, 1999), 58–60; *Entrées royales*, 55–59.

37. Beik, *Urban Protest*, 126–33; Breen, "Legal Culture," 197–205; Farr, *Hands*, 203–10; Mack P. Holt, "Culture populaire et culture politique au XVIIe siècle: L'émeute de Lanturelu à Dijon en février 1630," *Histoire, Économie, Société* 16 (1997): 597–615.

of the city," Louis outlawed all future Mère Folle performances and ordered that the association be disbanded.[38]

Ironically, there is no direct evidence that members of the Mère Folle had in fact been involved in the revolt. Contemporaries testified that local winegrowers and artisans had been the ones who led and participated in the February violence. The Mère Folle may have impersonated such common people in its plays, but the actual members of the organization were sons of the city's elite. Louis, however, probably suspected the Dijon elite of spreading hostile rumors before the riot and of delaying the capture of the ringleaders. He was right to be suspicious, since relative passivity in the face of popular protest was a not uncommon means for local elites to convey to the monarchy the difficulty of imposing unpopular royal political innovations.[39] Although the responsibility for maintaining order fell to the Dijon militia, the city council had found it difficult that day to muster its membership, most of whom were artisans and merchants possibly sympathetic to the rioters. If the council had been truly determined to stop the looting, moreover, it could perhaps have sent the several-hundred-strong Mère Folle into the fray.[40] For the king, the city council's inaction signaled that his administrative reforms were being resisted by some of Dijon's elite. Louis's revision of the city council charter and his suppression of the Mère Folle sent a clear message that local officials' autonomy would be tolerated only if those officials demonstrated a proper respect for the structure of authority on which their very existence depended.

Nevertheless, Louis's reference to the Mère Folle as an example of "debauchery and disorder" suggests that there was something specific about these amateur farce players that offended his sense of propriety.[41] The bawdy and disrespectful tone of the Mère Folle's performances apparently registered as a challenge to royal authority in a way that it had not a century earlier, when French kings had regularly asked to be entertained by local festive societies. It is easy, however, to exaggerate Louis's distaste for the Mère Folle and to forget the give-and-take of seventeenth-century politics.

38. *Édit donné à Lyon qui abolit et abroge, sous de gros peines, la Compagnie de la Mère Folle de Dijon* (21 June 1630), as quoted in Du Tilliot, *Mémoires*, 182; AMD B 267, fol. 293, 30 July 1630.
39. Charles Févret, *De la sédition arrivée en la ville de Dijon le 28 février 1630, et jugement rendu par le Roy sur icelle* (Lyon: I. Barlet, 1630); Beik, *Urban Protest*; Yves-Marie Bercé, *Histoire des Croquants: Étude des soulèvements populaires au XVIIe siècle dans le sud-ouest de la France* (Geneva: Droz, 1974).
40. Although the militia had the responsibility for quelling the riot, the Mère Folle and other prominent festive societies were comprised of young men who usually processed with arms at Carnival and other civic festivals. On several occasions, the Basoche of the Paris Parlement either offered their military services during a riot or were warned against gathering with arms for fear that they might incite rebellion. Mathieu Molé, *Mémoires* (Paris: Renouard, 1857), 3:326; Du Tilliot, *Mémoires*, 115.
41. Du Tilliot, *Mémoires*, 182.

The following year, when the Dijon elite refused to join a rebellion led by the king's brother Gaston d'Orléans, the king, in May 1631, rewarded the city by restoring both the Mère Folle and the council's traditional privileges.[42] The Mère Folle rallied in the years that followed. Not only did the group perform before the new governor of Burgundy, the Prince of Condé, in autumn 1632, but it also presented plays after several other civic celebrations during the 1630s.[43] Like the Dijon city council, which resumed its usual activities after its reconstitution in 1631, the Mère Folle was not apparently so chastened by the king's reprimand that it altered the tone of its performances. On the contrary it continued to make clear that Dijon was a unique component of the body politic that deserved acknowledgment and respect from the French monarchy.[44]

By midcentury, however, elite tastes and political loyalties were in flux, even in traditionally independent-minded Burgundy. Although the Dijon city council experienced few open conflicts with the crown after the Lanturelu revolt, Louis XIII and later Louis XIV continued to pressure the urban elite to cede control over local affairs. In 1668, Louis XIV permanently reduced the personnel of the Dijon city council and usurped many of its powers. Cultural changes among the Dijon elite had preceded this formal political transformation, however, and signaled their realization that fighting for the province's political autonomy was a losing battle. In early 1665, the city council had decided to abolish the post of imprimeur de la ville. At a time when most political treatises of interest to the Dijon elite were being published in Paris, it seemed an extravagance to house and to pay a printer to represent Dijon's interests.[45] Analogously, as early as the 1640s, the Mère Folle had begun to perform less often at important civic celebrations. Instead, the council appointed students from the local Jesuit collège to perform after civic rituals, or it hired professional acting troupes to present the latest Parisian theatrical sensation. These actors eschewed the farce and sottie, and lauded the Bourbon monarchy without qualification in the course of their performances.[46] By the mid-seventeenth century, even

42. AMD B 268, fol. 242, 12 May 1631.
43. Valcke, "Théâtre et spectacle," 76–80.
44. [Bénigne Perard and Étienne Bréchillet], *Le retour de Bontemps: Dedié à Monseigneur le Prince [de Condé] . . . et representé à son entrée par l'Infanterie Dijonnoise, le dimanche troisième octobre 1632* (Dijon: Veuve Claude Guyot, 1632); [Étienne Bréchillet], *Resjouissance de l'infanterie dijonnoise, pour la venue de Monseigneur le duc d'Anguyen [Louis de Bourbon], le 25 février 1636* (Dijon: Veuve Claude Guyot, [1636]); [Étienne Bréchillet], *Rejouïssance de l'Infanterie Dijonnoise pour l'entrée de Monsieur le marquis de Tavannes, lieutenant du roi en Bourgogne* (Dijon: Claude Guyot, 1636); *Relation de ce qui s'est passé en la ville de Dijon pour l'heureuse naissance de Monseigneur le Dauphin* (Dijon: Pierre Palliot, 1638); Breen, "Addressing," 353–57.
45. AMD B 303, fol. 123, 16 Jan. 1665.
46. Politically quiescent ballets began to supplant the Mère Folle's sotties during civic celebrations as early as the 1620s. See *Ballet dansé à Dijon le XXIII janvier 1627, en l'honneur de Roi et de monseigneur Le Prince*; *Ballet dansé à Dijon devant monseigneur Le Prince, l'onzième février*

the traditionally independent-minded Dijon elite recognized that displaying outward compliance to the French monarchy would best serve their interests. Thus it was lack of interest and patronage within the city itself rather than direct royal intervention that led to the gradual eclipsing of the Mère Folle in seventeenth-century Dijon.

Limiting urban privileges was one way the king went about centralizing authority. Another was the regularization of venality. When the purchase of royal offices became standard practice, another group of former farceurs was radically affected: the clerks of the Basoche. Basoche theater had been shut down during the Wars of Religion, when parlement magistrates feared that Carnival plays could lead to sectarian violence. Many of the associations, notably in Paris, Rouen, Toulouse, Bordeaux, Aix, and Avignon, had survived the wars intact, but they had now become pious confraternities or professional corporations. Indeed, the Paris Basoche even made some efforts to erase the very memory of farcical theater from its corporate history. Although cultural developments, such as exposure to the ideal of civility, no doubt contributed to this transformation of the clerks' association, certain actions of the Bourbon monarchy, specifically its regulation of venality, also helped to silence Basoche theater after 1600. Like city officials in Dijon, legal officials working at the parlements of France were well aware that it was in their interest to cooperate with rather than resist the king's efforts to achieve political stability.

Already suppressed at most provincial parlements by the 1560s, Basoche theater seems to have survived longest in Paris. There, as late as the early 1580s, the clerks continued to perform before the parlement magistrates each May. By this time, however, the Basochiens were no longer acting out farces; the magistrates permitted only decorous and restrained comedies and tragedies to be staged at the Palais. Even this last vestige of the centuries-old Basoche theatrical tradition was eliminated soon afterward when the clerks' association in Paris finally made the transition from festive society to professional corporation. In 1586, the Paris Parlement magistrates approved formal statutes regulating the Basoche, statutes that made no reference to the clerks' tradition of farcical performance or even to their more recent practice of performing classical plays in the Grande Salle. Rather than insisting on its theatrical privileges, the Basoche cannily adapted to the changing theatrical environment of the capital. By the 1580s, amateur theatrical performance in Paris was largely a thing of the past: professional acting troupes dominated the city's stages, and most of the performances were organized by a single

---

1627. Jesuit students at the Dijon Collège de Godrans began performing plays at civic events in the 1620s and by the 1640s were doing so on an annual basis. See Charles François Muteau, *Les écoles et collèges en province depuis les temps les plus reculés jusqu'en 1789* (Dijon: Darantière, 1882), 455–56, 464–65, 476; Louis Desgraves, *Répertoire des programmes des pièces de théâtre jouées dans les collèges en France (1601–1700)* (Geneva: Droz, 1986), 52–53.

association, the Confrérie de la Passion, which claimed a monopoly on all theater profits in the capital. Instead of challenging the confrérie's rising star, the Basochiens convinced the magistrates to grant them the right to share in the confrérie's wealth. In its statutes, the Basoche acknowledged the confrérie's monopoly but claimed ownership of one stage-box in the confrérie's Hôtel de Bourgogne theater. The 1586 statutes establish the clerks' privilege to parade from the parlement to the theater each year during Carnival, bearing their "traditional banners and coat of arms," in order to claim their rightful place in their stage-box, a privilege they claimed as late as 1640.[47] Once actors and playwrights themselves, the Paris Basochiens had become by the final decades of the sixteenth century mere spectators and shareholders in the commercial theater. In return, they became an officially recognized corporate body whose primary responsibilities were to train and regulate all clerks working at the court.

Not all Basoche festive activity was suppressed: Basochiens still paraded through the streets to celebrate various saints' days and, in some cities, also raised a maypole each spring. In Paris, there is intermittent evidence that the parlement magistrates were willing to help pay for the annual maypole procession and celebration. In addition, Basochiens in Paris continued to act out mock legal cases both to amuse and instruct their fellow clerks.[48] The public performance of farce after royal entries and for the king's pleasure was, however, a practice the clerks had long since abandoned. At most parlements, Basochiens accepted these new limitations on their festive life with equanimity.[49] In Toulouse, where the Basoche had not been permitted to perform farces since the 1520s, however, the clerks sometimes pushed the bounds of seventeenth-century decorum. Like many Basoche associations in southern France, the Basoche of Toulouse was still permitted to participate in a religious festival, in this case the traditional Feast of Kings. Several arrêts from this period show that Basochiens sometimes wore masks and were

---

47. *Recueil des statuts, ordonnances, reiglements, antiquitez, prérogatives, et prééminences du Royaume de la Bazoche* (Paris: C. Besongne, 1654), 13, addendum; *Inventaire sommaire des archives hospitalières antérieures à 1790*, ed. Michel Moring (Paris: Imprimerie Nationale, 1886), 267.

48. During this period, the Basochiens usually performed their *causes grasses* at the Parlement of Paris. Given the long-standing hostility between the Basoche and the Confrérie de la Passion regarding the Basoche's claim to a loge, it seems doubtful that the masters of the confrérie would have allowed the clerks on stage. See *Recueil des statuts*, 9–12, 97 (5 June 1640), 143–48 (24 May 1621, 13 May 1634); AN x1a 8394, fol. 126a, 16 May 1665; *Arrêt de parlement portant règlement donné en faveur des clercs du palais, contre les officiers de la basoche, 26 février 1656; Ouverture des jours gras, ou l'Entretien carnaval*, ed. J. Lough (Oxford: Blackwell, 1957); *Arrêt du parlement qui fait défenses au prévôt de Paris de prendre connaissance de ce qui concerne la juridiction de la basoche, 17 février 1640*; Marie Bouhaïk-Gironès, "La Basoche et le théâtre comique: Identité sociale, pratiques et culture des clercs de justice (Paris, 1420–1550)," Ph.D. diss., University of Paris 7, 2004, 145.

49. I have found little complaint regarding Basoche activity in the archives of Paris, Rouen, or Bordeaux.

unruly during these events, behavior that resulted in reprimands from the magistrates.[50] Nevertheless, even the Toulouse Basoche did not dare perform satire on the stage. Although the magistrates in Toulouse had some difficulty curbing the festive enthusiasm of their clerks, that was clearly their intention. Parlement magistrates were willing to recognize the Basoche as a legitimate association and to accept that young men needed an outlet for their excess energies, but this limited tolerance was a far cry from the enthusiasm for Basoche farce during the society's heyday.

The magistrates' reservations about Basoche farce were shaped by their experience of the Wars of Religion. Nevertheless, these reservations persisted during the seventeenth century, partly because, as power became centralized around the king, doubt grew about the honesty and fairness of the system of justice. Much ink was spilled demanding judicial reform, and the issue became a major source of debate at the Estates General of 1614.[51] A major worry was the burgeoning authority of the royal judiciary, as more and more legal cases were diverted from seigniorial, ecclesiastical, and municipal jurisdictions to royal courts of law. Equally problematic for local city officials was that royal efforts to adjudicate conflicts of authority between the parlement and the city council tended to favor the parlement. Royal courts, and the parlements in particular, were seen as gaining authority in the provinces at the expense of local institutions.[52] As a result, qualifications for the judiciary and the propriety of their conduct as officers of the crown were subject to considerable public scrutiny.

Would-be reformers objected to venality, a practice that, though it had secured royal finances throughout the sixteenth century, was still a matter of controversy. French kings, though they repeatedly promised to reform or abandon venality altogether, nevertheless kept working to regularize the processes by which officers could purchase and hold their offices. One such effort was the *paulette*, a new tax introduced in 1603 that consolidated the legal standing of an office as a form of private property inalienable by the crown. Although parlement magistrate offices had been purchased from the crown since the mid-sixteenth century, the paulette—a tax that charged officeholders one-sixtieth of the office's value in return for the freedom to sell or bequeath it at will—enhanced the security and thus the

---

50. Archives Départementales de la Haute-Garonne (ADHG) B 141, fol. 368, 29 Dec. 1594; ADHG B 314, fol. 279, 18 Jan. 1613; ADHG B 447, fol. 503, 30 Dec. 1624; ADHG B 520, fol. 425, 25 May 1632.
51. Jeffery K. Sawyer, "Judicial Corruption and Legal Reform in Early Seventeenth-Century France," *Law and History Review* 6 (1988): 95–117; Yves-Marie Bercé, *The Birth of Absolutism: A History of France, 1598–1661*, trans. Richard Rex (New York: St. Martin's Press, 1992), 53–63.
52. Breen, "Legal Culture," 136–52, 176–94, 319–43; James B. Collins, *Classes, Estates, and Order in Early Modern Brittany* (Cambridge: Cambridge University Press, 1994), 135–39; Irvine, "Renaissance," 119–25; Robert A. Schneider, "Crown and Capitoulat: Municipal Government in Toulouse, 1500–1789," in *Cities and Social Change*, 199–206.

profitability of venal offices.[53] The paulette is taken to be a turning point in the foundation of absolutist power: whether historians consider absolutism to be a modern or a fundamentally feudal political system, they agree that it was a system founded on a venal bureaucracy. French subjects at the time also recognized the paulette as a turning point, and they were determined to resist it. During the 1610s in particular, some men of the law, nobles, and clergy protested venality on the grounds that it could only lead to a corruption of royal justice. Reformers accused the paulette tax of reducing magistrate appointments to mere commercial transactions and of producing law courts full of young, inexperienced magistrates unable to judge effectively. On the other hand, many magistrates were committed to the paulette because it helped to secure their status as nobles, a rank that was conferred on parlement magistrates only after three generations of service.[54]

The question of the paulette (and judicial corruption more generally) made parlement magistrates sensitive to questions of propriety during the first half of the seventeenth century. Toulouse magistrate Bernard de La Roche Flavin's treatise about parlement procedure, *Thirteen Books of the Parlements of France*, first published in 1617, was an important contribution to this debate about the professional role of magistrates and their social status. As a magistrate who had served at the Paris Parlement and more recently at the Parlement of Toulouse, La Roche Flavin urges his colleagues to prove their critics wrong. Much to the dismay of his colleagues, La Roche Flavin airs the dirty laundry of the judiciary in an effort to reform current practice, acknowledging the faults of his colleagues in the hopes of holding them to higher standards in an age when venality threatens to undermine the authority of the profession.[55] La Roche Flavin, for whom the magistrates' integrity is the very cornerstone of the French judicial system, urges that court procedure be regularized and that magistrates maintain their public dignity at all times. Warning of the dangers of appearing frivolous in the courtroom, he

---

53. Mark Cummings, "The Social Impact of the 'Paulette': The Case of the Parlement of Paris," *Canadian Journal of History* 15 (1980): 332–34; Sawyer, "Judicial Corruption"; Roland Mousnier, *La vénalité des offices sous Henri IV et Louis XIII* (Paris: Presses Universitaires de France, 1971), 251–89.
54. Donna Bohanan, *Old and New Nobility in Aix-en-Provence, 1600–1695: Portrait of an Urban Elite* (Baton Rouge: Louisiana State University Press, 1992), 20–27; Jonathan Dewald, *The Formation of a Provincial Nobility: The Magistrates of the Parlement of Rouen, 1499–1610* (Princeton: Princeton University Press, 1980), 54–68, 106–12; Huppert, *Bourgeois Gentilhommes*, 6–15; Ellery Schalk, *From Valor to Pedigree: Ideas of Nobility in France in the Sixteenth and Seventeenth Centuries* (Princeton: Princeton University Press, 1986), 145–73; Robert Descimon, "La haute noblesse parlementaire parisienne: La production d'une aristocratie d'état aux XVIe et XVIIe siècles," in *L'état et les aristocraties: France, Angleterre, Écosse*, ed. P. Contamine (Paris: Presses de l'École Normale Supérieure, 1989), 357–86; Moote, *Revolt*, 31–35; Mousnier, *Vénalité*, 647–63.
55. Carole Desplat, "Savoirs et déboires d'un juriste, Bernard de la Roche Flavin (1552–1627)," *Histoire, Économie, Société* 19 (2000): 173, 176–78.

enjoins parlement members to avoid all laughing or carousing.[56] Magistrates must set an exalted example for others not only at court but also during their leisure time, when some might be tempted to attend the theater: "According to our internal disciplinary regulations, it is prohibited for court officials to go see, or listen to buffoons and actors because of the dissolute actions, lascivious and scandalous speeches, that one sees there; in order that sovereign magistrates do not go spend the evening, and defile themselves among the ignorant and disrespectful people."[57] Whereas sixteenth-century parlement magistrates had openly patronized the Basoche and had defined as scandalous only those performances that referred directly to politics or religion, for La Roche Flavin no theatrical performance was worthy of a magistrate's attention. Even when the actors were mere buffoons who avoided satire, laughing publicly at their antics might, it seems, undermine the magistrates' authority among the people. La Roche Flavin's description of the Basoche is also telling: although he acknowledges that clerks had long ago performed bawdy farces, he cites only those parlement arrêts in which the magistrates chastised the clerks and emphasizes that the association is much changed in his own time.[58] Given the contempt with which he held professional actors, La Roche Flavin presumably thought that having the Basoche perform farces would fatally compromise the dignity of the parlement as a whole. La Roche Flavin's depiction of the ideal magistrate as a sober professional whose professional status precluded any association with common city residents certainly did not reflect the actual behavior of parlement magistrates during the first decades of the seventeenth century.[59] Nevertheless, attitudes like La Roche Flavin's help to explain why the magistrates did not encourage the Basochiens to resume their theatrical performances after 1600.

Some members of the Basoche agreed with La Roche Flavin that farcical theater was below the dignity of clerks who worked at the parlement. Eager to secure solicitors' offices for the clerks, those Basoche organizations that survived the religious wars—particularly in Rouen and Paris—downplayed their traditional role as festive entertainers and instead highlighted their function as the clerks' professional representatives. Whereas farcical theater had been useful to the clerks at an earlier period, enhancing their prestige, by the early seventeenth century their interests were better served by suppressing the history of their long-standing performance tradition.

Like those of the magistrates, the clerks' attitudes toward farce evolved in response to the crown's regularization of venality. Most members of the

56. Bernard de La Roche Flavin, *Treze livres des parlemens de France* (Bordeaux: Simon Millanges, 1617), 517.
57. Ibid., 541.
58. Ibid., 170–71.
59. Dewald, *Formation*, 54–58; Colin Kaiser, "Les cours souveraines au XVIe siècle: Morale et Contre-Réforme," *Annales: Économies, Sociétés, Civilisations* 37 (1982): 28; Schneider, *Public Life*, 188–219.

Basoche worked for solicitors (*procureurs*) and hoped, after their ten-year training as clerks, to become solicitors one day. Like barristers (*avocats*), solicitors were members of a liberal profession, in effect independent contractors who were registered at the courts where they did business. Transforming the post of solicitor at the parlement into a venal office, that is to say, a life-term appointment purchased from the crown, was the ultimate goal of the French monarchy. From the middle of the sixteenth century, solicitors staunchly resisted becoming venal officers, and this issue continued to be a source of conflict throughout the early seventeenth century. As early as 1586, King Henry III had made all solicitor posts venal except those at the Parlement of Paris, but the breakdown of royal authority in the years immediately afterward made this legislation unenforceable. After 1597, Henry IV achieved somewhat more success and converted provincial solicitors into venal officers. Parisian solicitors, however, held out until 1639, when Louis XIII finally won them over by decreeing that only three hundred solicitor offices would be available for purchase at the Parlement of Paris.[60] When solicitor offices became venal, clerks of the Parisian Basoche found that their access to promotion to solicitor was significantly impeded. Solicitors began selling their offices to the highest bidder, with a total disregard for parlement regulations, including the requirement of a ten-year clerkship.[61] In both Paris and Rouen, the Basoche, in response to this threat, carved out a role for itself as defender of the clerks' professional interests, insisting on rights of first refusal when solicitor offices came on the market. In 1648, the Rouen Basoche gained authority to regulate all subsidiary legal practitioners at the parlement and insisted that all Basochiens had a right to become solicitors if they had fulfilled the required ten-year training period. By the 1690s, solicitors in Rouen repeatedly complained that the Basoche, defying the solicitors' monopoly of their offices, were practicing as solicitors without licenses—complaints that demonstrate the vitality of the Basoche organization and its persistence in the face of a shrinking job market.[62] In Paris, the Basoche continued throughout the seventeenth century to wage an aggressive legal campaign against the solicitors' right to sell their offices at will. The stakes in this battle for solicitor posts were high since the financial and social well-being of whole families relied on a clerk's promotion. Extensive research on the bourgeoisie of Paris has demonstrated that families able to acquire royal offices during the late sixteenth and early seventeenth centuries, even relatively minor ones such as

60. Charles Bataillard, *Histoire des procureurs et des avoués, 1483–1816* (Paris: Hachette, 1882), 1:138, 154–64; Laure Koenig, *La communauté des procureurs au Parlement de Paris au XVIIe et XVIIIe siècles* (Cahors: Coueslant, 1937), 10–17.
61. Cummings, "Social Impact," 345.
62. ADSM 1 B 2291, 5 May 1618; ADSM 1 B 5457, 19 Aug. 1689; ADSM 1 B 5470, 5 May 1690; ADSM 5E 124.

solicitor posts, profited greatly from this association with the monarchy. On the other hand, those bourgeois families that failed to secure a place in the royal bureaucracy saw their political and economic status fall rapidly.[63] By the early seventeenth century, this stark social reality would have been very clear to the Basochiens, who were determined to press their case on a number of fronts, including the use of print to garner sympathy for their plight.

One means the Basochiens used to voice their complaints about changes to the clerks' profession was the bawdy pamphlet. The first of these pamphlets, *The Pont-Breton of the Solicitors, Dedicated to the Clerks of the Court*, published in Paris in 1624 and ostensibly written by a clerk working at the parlement, closely resembled in content, if not in form, sixteenth-century Basoche theatrical performances. This thirty-page pamphlet (and a sequel of the same length issued later that year) told scandalous tales of clerks who were beaten by solicitors, propositioned by their masters' wives, or otherwise victimized by the solicitors' authority. These anecdotes do not identify specific solicitors or clerks by name but, like sixteenth-century Basoche sotties, provide their street addresses, thereby allowing the reader to decide for himself "if these histories are true or fabricated."[64] A few years later, another self-identified clerk wrote a long pamphlet complaining of abuses suffered by clerks at the hands of the solicitors' wives—beating, seduction, bad cooking, skimpy wine rations—and characterizing the clerks as wronged by an abusive apprenticeship system, as victims whose only recourse was to play nasty tricks on their masters. This pamphlet, published in 1627 at a time when there were new rumors circulating that Paris Parlement solicitors might become venal officers, might have been a burlesque attempt to evoke sympathy for the clerks' cause. Instead, it seems only to have inspired an equally bawdy rejoinder, which claims to have been written by a solicitor's wife, a Madame Choiselet. She replies in kind, accusing the clerks of being lazy good-for-nothings who worked little and spent their nights in cabarets accumulating debts they could not pay. In these pamphlets, the clerks present themselves as wronged and mourn the days when the Basochiens roamed the streets of Paris freely and were well known for their satirical performances.[65]

63. Robert Descimon, "The 'Bourgeoisie Seconde': Social Differentiation in the Parisian Municipal Oligarchy in the Sixteenth Century, 1500–1610," *French History* 17 (2003): 388–424; Robert Descimon, "Conflits familiaux dans la robe parisienne aux XVIe et XVIIe siècles: Les paradoxes de la transmission du statut," *Cahiers d'Histoire* 45 (2000): 677–97; Robert Descimon, "Le corps de ville et les élections échevinales à Paris aux XVIe et XVIIe siècles: Codification coutumière et pratiques sociales," *Histoire, Économie, Société* 13 (1994): 507–30.
64. *Le Pont-Breton des procureurs, dedié aux clercs du palais* (1624), 4; *Suite du Pont-Breton des procureurs: Dedié aux clercs du palais* (Paris, 1624).
65. De Tournabons, *La misère des clercs des procureurs* (Paris: A. Robinot, 1627); *La response a la misere des clercs des procureurs ou l'innocence deffendue par Madame Choiselet* (Paris, 1627). For later pamphlets written in the name of the Basoche, see *Sentence burlesque* (1649); *Conseil salutaire au Cardinal Mazarin, gasconnade en vers burlesque dediée à Messieurs les*

The officers of the Paris Basoche took a very different approach to rectifying the clerks' vulnerable situation. Instead of playing on the traditions of Carnival, the officers presented a sober face to the literate Parisian public. In 1644, the Basochiens compiled a long pamphlet titled *Collection of Statutes, Ordinances, Rules, Antiquities, Prerogatives and Pre-eminences of the Kingdom of the Basoche* whose aim appears to have been to present the Basoche as a respectable corporation deserving of the legal right to purchase solicitor posts. The *Collection* included the 1586 Basoche statutes registered by the Paris Parlement and over thirty legal cases involving magistrate arbitration concerning the Basoche's authority to discipline clerks working at the court. The statutes and court cases, some of them dated as far back as the mid-sixteenth century, present the Basoche's authority in a positive light, emphasizing the clerks' utility to the smooth working of the court. Although a few cases refer in passing to traditional May processions, there is no mention at all of the Basoche's long tradition of being paid to perform farces for the magistrates' and the king's pleasure. Presumably, the Basoche's leaders thought such rulings would weaken its case, which depended on the organization presenting itself as an honorable corporation just as deserving of recognition as the professional association of the solicitors. Attempting to secure the right to purchase venal offices at the parlement, the Basoche leaders repressed their history of farcical performance, with the result that it was lost to the historical record for over two hundred years.

The Basoche's new reticence about its farcical tradition cannot be attributed to any change in the clerks' social status. Like clerks in the mid-sixteenth century, Basochiens of the Paris Parlement in the 1630s and 1640s usually married within their own social class and were unlikely to rise beyond the status of solicitor. Although the sums that changed hands at the Basochiens' weddings and the amounts that clerks paid to purchase a solicitor's post had increased since the mid-sixteenth century, these changes were the result of inflation and the high price charged for all parlement offices during the first half of the seventeenth century.[66] The clerks of the Basoche were still members of a relatively stable class of minor royal officials, a *bourgeoisie seconde*, whose members had finally concluded that achieving a place in the ranks of royal officialdom was worth some accommodation. Securing the rank of

---

officiers de la Basoche du Parlement de Paris (Paris: Veuve Marette, 1652); David Avrom Bell, "Lawyers and Politics in Eighteenth-Century Paris," Ph.D. diss., Princeton University, 1991, 68–71, 253, 415–16.

66. Archives Nationales Minutier Central (AN MC) VII:35, 9 Dec. 1646; AN MC CX:93, 17 June 1640; AN MC XII:46, 15 Jan. 1617; AN MC XIX:404, 5 June 1633. For clerks who purchase solicitor offices from their masters, see AN MC XVIII:134, fol. 665, 23 Nov. 1602 for 1,800 livres; AN MC XXIII:242, fol. 13, 7 Jan. 1611 for 3,600 livres; AN MC XXIII:254, 7 and 17 Jan. 1617 for 6,000 livres. This small sample suggests that the price of solicitor offices rose along with those of magistrate posts in the early seventeenth century. See Cummings, "Social Impact," 337–38.

solicitor at the parlement probably enabled Basochiens to secure a wealthier and more influential clientele than they otherwise would have done. Giving up farce seemed a small price to pay for such benefits. After decades of legal wrangling the Paris Basoche, at the beginning of the eighteenth century, finally obtained the right to purchase any solicitor office that did not pass directly to a son or nephew.[67] The Basochiens' efforts to reinvent themselves as sober professionals seemed to have paid off.

That is not to say that young clerks working at the parlements were never again chastised for being loud and unruly. During the eighteenth century, the Basoche at the Paris Parlement and at many other subsidiary courts enjoyed a resurgence, and once again contemporaries celebrated their elaborate maypole processions.[68] But all evidence suggests that during the seventeenth century the Basochiens were more circumspect. At a time when Cardinal Richelieu and then Louis XIV insisted on outward subservience to the monarchy, it was impolitic to draw attention to the Basochiens' rowdy past. Urban officials, from city councilors to the Basoche, could easily be excluded from royal favor, and they were well aware of what was at stake. The Basochiens did not want to be left out in the cold, and they sacrificed farce for the greater good of professional security.

The cultural reorientation of the urban elites and the bourgeoisie, which involved both the repudiation of festive societies and the active search for a more stable fiscal and professional relationship with the French monarchy, meant that they identified less with their native region and more with the tastes of the French nobility. The popularity of civility manuals that taught outsiders how to ape the manners of the Paris *salonières* testifies to this cultural reorientation. Equally important for the fate of festive theater was the urban elites' new tolerance for professional actors. Whereas during the first decades of the seventeenth century, provincial city councils often treated actors with disdain and sometimes exiled them from the city, by the 1640s increasingly they welcomed them without hesitation, in part because the actors' repertoire had shifted away from farce. Royal patronage of neoclassical theater was also crucial. By the 1640s, many of the troupes circulating through French provincial cities had secured the direct patronage of Louis XIII, Cardinal Richelieu, or a French peer and had already been well received in Paris. By midcentury, Paris had become an irresistible cultural magnet, and the provincial elites' desire to emulate the taste of court and capital city further doomed the provincial traditions of festival and farce.

---

67. Michel Félibien, *Histoire de la ville de Paris* (Paris: Chez G. Desprez et J. Desessertz, 1725), 4:444a–445b; *Arrêt du parlement qui reçoit l'opposition des officiers de la basoche à la réception d'Et. de Vaulx en la charge de procureur en la cour, 1645.*
68. Bell, "Lawyers," 75–77, 126–28; Koenig, *Communauté,* 101–6. For a list of eighteenth-century Basoche organizations outside of Paris, see Lucien Genty, *La Basoche notariale: Origines et histoire du XIVe siècle à nos jours* (Paris: Delamotte, 1888) 162–74.

By midcentury, an influx of traveling troupes suddenly appeared in the French provinces. City magistrates began permitting troupes to enter and set up temporary stages or perform in jeux de paume on a regular basis. In Rouen, troupes that had been barred from performing until the 1620s were making regular contributions to poor relief thirty years later.[69] Itinerant acting troupes of this kind made their way up and down the Garonne River to Bordeaux, Toulouse, and other communities along its banks. In 1643, the Toulouse city council fretted that a troupe of actors stationed in the city for over three months had unhappily been unable to perform because of the king's death—in marked contrast to the council's attitude toward commercial troupes twenty years earlier. Fortunately, the council noted, it could soon hire the actors to help celebrate the accession of the dauphin, a function that during the Renaissance would certainly have been undertaken by a local festive society.[70] Even in smaller centers—Avignon, Marseille, and Nantes—city archives demonstrate an expanding traffic of commercial troupes.[71] Although city officials were still sometimes wary of particular troupes whose repertoire they deemed to be suspect, they had come to realize that actors were a valuable source of revenue. In larger cities like Bordeaux, Rouen, and Lyon, itinerant troupes regularly paid the city's *hôpital* a tax for the privilege of performing: the sin of the theater had its uses and could be contained by a careful scrutiny of the plays each troupe proposed to perform.[72]

In Dijon, city council records reveal an elaborate system of regulation to manage commercial troupes by the 1640s: the council determined whether professional acting troupes could enter the city, monitored the troupes' repertoire, and issued rulings concerning the management of the theater building. Like the Mère Folle before them, most professional troupes that visited Dijon performed at the Tripot de la Poissonière, a gambling den that was easily converted to a theater by constructing a stage and distributing chairs to some of the spectators. Although the Dijon city council took no responsibility for maintenance of the Tripot, it ruled that the building's caretaker could only charge one sou for each chair he rented.[73] The city council also issued

69. Jules-Édouard Bouteiller, *Histoire complète et méthodique des théâtres de Rouen* (Rouen: Giroux et Renaux, 1860), 1:5–6.

70. Jean Robert, "Comédiens et bateleurs sur les rives de la Garonne au XVIIe siècle," *Revue d'Histoire du Théâtre* 11 (1959): 38.

71. Georges Mongrédien, *Dictionnaire biographique des comédiens français du XVIIe siècle* (Paris: CNRS, 1972), 214–22.

72. Bouteiller, *Histoire*, 1:4–5; Claudius Brouchoud, *Les origines du théâtre de Lyon* (Lyon: Scheuring, 1865), 59–66; Arnauld Detcheverry, *Histoire des théâtres de Bordeaux depuis leur origine dans cette ville jusqu'à nos jours* (Bordeaux: J. Delmas, 1860), 6–8; Charles Mazouer, *La vie théâtrale à Bordeaux des origines à nos jours*, vol. 1, *Des origines à 1789*, ed. Henri Lagrave (Paris: CNRS, 1985), 95–96.

73. AMD B 293, fol. 71v, 7 July 1654; AMD B 294, fol. 31, 25 June 1655.

rulings about the troupes' repertoire, the amount charged for admission, and the actors' contributions to poor relief. Those who defied these regulations risked punishment: in 1661, the city council imprisoned troupe members merely for replying with insolence when asked by a city councilor whether they had paid the requisite poor tax.[74]

By the mid-seventeenth century, the Dijon city council increasingly made a clear distinction between high- and lowbrow performers. The lowbrow actors were like the farceurs Tabarin and Gaultier Garguille, who had entertained Parisian crowds a few decades earlier. Such men, for example, Charles Beroin, "alias La Fleur, surgeon, distiller and eye doctor of the king," worked alone or with a partner, both providing entertainment and peddling medications from the stage. Their performances sometimes included comedies and ballets but more often consisted of novelties such as remarkable puppets or "fountains that he makes come out of his mouth, of diverse colors."[75] Although the prices that these lowbrow actors were allowed to charge their audiences—usually two sous—and the small fee they were expected to pay the city's *hôpital* indicate that the city council deemed their performances to be geared to a commoner audience, they were nevertheless barred from performing "farces," which suggests just how unsavory the genre was considered by this date.[76]

In contrast, acting troupes sponsored by members of the French aristocracy also began arriving in Dijon by mid-century. These troupes were allowed to charge their audiences considerably more—ten sous for repertoire plays and fifteen sous for new material—and were ordered to contribute substantively more to the local *hôpital*, sometimes as much as a hundred livres.[77] On some occasions, this poor tax took the form of a free performance of a play chosen by the city council from the troupe's repertoire. Overall, the city council was more concerned about the morality of these troupes' performances than it was about that of the medicine-selling buffoons. In 1649, the Dijon mayor himself vouched for a particular troupe by stating that he had "determined [it] to be excellent."[78] The city council judged a troupe's excellence on the basis of its repertoire, which the actors regularly submitted to the council for approval. A desirable repertoire was

74. AMD B 286, fol. 187, 12 Jan. 1649; AMD B 286, fol. 192, 15 Jan. 1649; AMD B 299, fol. 86v, 30 July 1660; AMD B 299, fol. 398, 14 June 1661.
75. AMD B 292, fol. 244, 7 May 1654; AMD B 292, fol. 240v, 7 May 1654. See also AMD B 287, fol. 216v, 29 Nov. 1649; AMD B 287, fol. 371v, 13 May 1650; AMD B 294, fol. 32v, 28 June 1655; AMD B 295, fol. 139v, Nov. 1656; AMD B 299, fol. 387, 31 May 1661.
76. AMD B 292, fol. 244, 7 May 1654; AMD B 366, fol. 62v, 2 Aug. 1667.
77. AMD B 265, fol. 104v, 13 Sept. 1627; AMD B 281, fol. 216, 22 Dec. 1643; AMD B 292, fol. 129v, 26 Aug. 1653; AMD B 292, fol. 205, 30 Jan. 1654; AMD B 293, fol. 68, 3 July 1654; AMD B 294, fol. 84, 23 Aug. 1655; AMD B 294, fol. 97v, 7 Sept. 1655; AMD B 295, fol. 283, 15 June 1657; AMD B 296, fol. 104, 23 Aug. 1657; AMD B 299, fol. 377, 24 May 1661.
78. AMD B 287, fol. 234, 17 Dec. 1649.

one that contained no "comedies, farces or anything scandalous, and no play that was not *dans la civilité* and honorable."[79]

These concerns were of some urgency since the city council members sometimes attended the commercial theater, occasionally reserving a row of seats for themselves.[80] A program of November 1662, advertising performances by the troupe of the Prince of Condé, suggests the kind of audience these actors were hoping to attract:

> The Comedians of his High and Most Serene Monseigneur le Prince:
> We cannot better convey the desire that we have to please all of fashionable society, of which each day we are honored by their presence, than by presenting today the 16th of November a magnificent production of the incomparable *Eudoxe* of M. de Scudéry. The virtue of this great princess is of such authority that she should serve as an example to all ladies and should oblige them to come to this performance, from which without a doubt they will come away with complete satisfaction. Following you will be presented with the comedy *The Imaginary Cuckold*, which will cost alone twenty sous.
> While waiting for the grand *Sertorius*. Performances will take place at the usual location at three o'clock sharp.[81]

By the early 1660s, urban elites in outposts as culturally remote as Dijon were actively engaged in demonstrating their culture and sophistication through the newly prestigious classical theater. The fact that this *affiche* was clearly directed at the women of Dijon is also remarkable: whereas professional acting troupes had traditionally performed at gaming and gambling dens, where women could not be seen unaccompanied, now theatrical performances were respectable enough to serve as cultural instruction even for the ladies of Dijon's elite.

The 1662 program illustrates the commercial troupes' desire to ape Parisian and court tastes. Many of the plays presented were by authors then popular in the capital. Corneille's *Sertorius* was the aging but still-respected playwright's latest tragedy, which had first been performed in Paris earlier that year. The presentation of a work by Madeleine de Scudéry, who today is best known for her novels but whose salon was at its height in the early 1660s, also demonstrates the Dijon audience's desire to profit from the latest Parisian literary trends.[82] Itinerant troupes typically performed lighter

79. AMD B 301, fol. 112, 6 Oct. 1662. Other rulings that mention the repertoire's modesty or the necessity to register plays with the city council include AMD B 286, fol. 173, 28 Dec. 1648; AMD B 292, fol. 244, 7 May 1654; AMD B 294, fol. 31, 25 June 1655; AMD B 298, fol. 382v, 28 May 1660; AMD B 299, fol. 332, 22 Mar. 1661; AMD B 303, fols. 126v–27, 23 Jan. 1665.
80. Louis de Gouvenain, *Le théâtre à Dijon, 1422–1790* (Dijon: E. Joubard, 1888), 69.
81. As quoted in Joachim Durandeau, *Aimé Piron ou la vie littéraire à Dijon pendant le XVIIe siècle* (Dijon: Librarie Nouvelle, 1888), 40–41.
82. Barbara Krajewska, *Du coeur à l'esprit: Mademoiselle de Scudéry et ses samedis* (Paris: Kimé, 1993), 16–21; Georges Mongrédien, *Madeleine de Scudéry et son salon, d'après des documents inédits* (Paris: Taillander, 1946), 163–77.

fare to finish off the afternoon's entertainment. The choice of Molière's *Imaginary Cuckold*, a very popular comedy first performed by the author in Paris two years earlier, is not surprising. Molière's earliest published comedies were little more than farces—short, one- or three-act pieces in which the humor derived from stereotypical depictions of social types. Yet even Molière's earliest plays were much less crude than Tabarin's performances during the 1620s, as innuendo gradually replaced the sexually explicit jokes of an earlier generation.[83] Although the French elite, from Louis XIV to a Dijon magistrate, still enjoyed a light comedy at the end of the evening's entertainment, the bounds of comic license had contracted.

In one sense, there was nothing new or remarkable about provincial elites' desire to imitate the literary innovations of the court. During the sixteenth century, they had already been eager to have royal entry ceremonies written and choreographed by courtiers. What had changed, however, was that they now rejected low humor as inappropriate to their station. Although a distinction between comedy and farce existed by the mid-sixteenth century, the festive societies' performances were still an accepted element of civic culture embraced by both the secular and the ecclesiastical elite. By the mid-seventeenth century, however, provincial urban elites increasingly distinguished between entertainments they considered worthy of their patronage and those they did not. Gradually, the prestige of professional troupes patronized by the king outweighed the attraction of local festive societies such as the Mère Folle, whose last plays were published in the 1640s. This transformation is particularly remarkable in a city like Dijon, which throughout the first decades of the seventeenth century had self-consciously resisted royal infringements on local political autonomy and sought to celebrate Burgundian culture. This refinement of theatrical taste was not imposed from above: no one forced the Dijon elite to attend the plays of Corneille and Molière. Yet slowly, inexorably, they shifted their attention from local farce to neoclassical entertainments. In doing so, they relegated farce to the realm of the lowbrow and chose instead for their amusement plays unlikely to contain unruly bodies or political satire.

The new insistence on civility in public theater performances was an indirect product of royal centralization. Actions taken by the king—the curbing of municipal autonomy, the formalizing of venality, and the patronage of the neoclassical theater after 1630—encouraged his subjects to cooperate with him rather than challenge his power. Increasingly, during their civic celebrations and political rituals, the provincial elites reflected back to the Bourbon monarchs the image that the monarchs sought to present of themselves in absolutist propaganda. That is not to say that urban elites were turned into mere political puppets during the first half of the seventeenth century. The

83. William D. Howarth, *Molière: A Playwright and His Audience* (Cambridge: Cambridge University Press, 1982), 97–106; Charles Mazouer, *Farces du Grand Siècle: De Tabarin à Molière, farces et petites comédies* (Paris: Librairie Générale Française, 1992), 371–74.

Fronde, which began at the Parlement of Paris in 1648 and quickly spread to the provinces, makes it clear that rebellion against the king was still possible. Nevertheless, with the exception of the rebellion in Bordeaux, most urban unrest was relatively brief and modest in its aims. French cities did not fight for a return to the relative municipal autonomy of the Renaissance. The late medieval vision of the body politic, with its emphasis on the king as the head of a body whose members had an active role to play in the political affairs of the nation, seems to have lost its resonance for the French urban leadership by the middle of the seventeenth century. The marginalization of farcical theater highlights that the shift toward public deference to the monarchy and civility took place, even in the provinces, as early as 1600. Although the demise of amateur farceurs did not immediately signal the advent of absolutist power, the gradual silencing of satirical theater and the cultural reorientation of urban elites toward Paris and the king's court did encourage the predominance of a single public discourse—the discourse of absolutism.

7 Jesuit Theater

CHRISTIAN CIVILITY AND ABSOLUTISM
ON THE CIVIC STAGE

In 1622, Louis XIII, accompanied by his wife and mother, visited the city of Lyon and was received with the pomp appropriate to his status. After the traditional royal entry ceremony, in which Louis was praised and given gifts by prominent citizens, he and his entourage were presented with three plays performed by students at Lyon's Jesuit collège. Whereas a century earlier, French royalty had been welcomed by festive societies performing bawdy *chevauchées d'asne*, now the king was presented with much less crude fare. Dressed in costumes of silk and silver thread, the Jesuit students sought to impress the royal party with the refinement of their acting and dancing skills. During one of several entertainments presented over a series of days, they performed a play titled *Philip Augustus, Conqueror of the Rebels* that explicitly compared the military exploits of this medieval French king with those of Louis XIII. The performance was punctuated by several scenes of dancing, ballets that provided amusement and heightened dramatic tension. In the opening scene, when the sorcerer Merlin warns that King Philip's enemies will soon defeat him in battle, six students dressed in military garb come onto the stage and begin dancing in what was supposed to be the Roman style to demonstrate the military prowess of the king's enemies. Later, once it becomes clear that Philip can defeat his foes, students dressed as the four winds dance with "irregular steps" and wild gestures to signify the disarray of these enemies.[1] At the play's conclusion, Philip enters Paris in triumph, accompanied by pastoral and allegorical characters who praise his military successes. Shepherds (representing his chief councilors), hunters (representing the nobility), satyrs, and nymphs dance and sing of the dawning of a new

---

1. *Réception de très-chrestien, très-juste, et très-victorieux monarque Louis XIII, roi de France et de Navarre* (Lyon: Jacques Roussin, 1623), 54.

golden age of peace. During this performance, the students present themselves to the king as graceful and obedient subjects of the crown, and their efforts are rewarded with applause.

This performance was more than an elegant display of physical prowess: it spoke a language of militant Catholicism, royal glory, and cultural sophistication.[2] The hero of the piece, thirteenth-century Philip Augustus, king of France, is presented as a man of action who responds to several crises—first, rebellions within his territory, and later the machinations of the king of England—with direct and decisive force. The published account of the ballet performance makes it clear that the audience was meant to draw an analogy between Philip's territorial expansion in the thirteenth century and Louis XIII's military successes four hundred years later. Unlike those of his medieval predecessor, Louis's military exploits were sparked by religious problems: his enemy was the Huguenots, who had been allowed, under the 1598 Edict of Nantes, to maintain military strongholds within the realm. These strongholds had been intended as a temporary measure to help reestablish peace in France, and by the time Louis XIII ousted his mother from her role as regent in the late 1610s, he had come to see them as an aberration. During the summer fighting seasons of 1620 and 1621, Louis had eliminated many of these strongholds, with the important exceptions of Montaubon and La Rochelle. At the moment when Louis witnessed the ballet in Lyon, in December 1622, it was unclear whether he would embark on another military campaign the following year or rather, as an some of his advisors suggested, attempt to isolate the Huguenots diplomatically. The ballet's celebration of Louis's predecessor Philip as a man of action who continued fighting until he had achieved complete dominance was an admonitory hint from the Jesuits that the king should continue fighting. Judging from Louis's enthusiastic appreciation of the students' performance, he welcomed this tactful exhortation from his provincial subjects: the Jesuits had demonstrated to their students and the local audience how a theatrical performance could be used to press for a political policy without offending the crown.

The 1622 Jesuit student performance highlights the changes that had taken place in civic ritual, theatrical taste, and political culture in a few short decades. Lyon, home to at least a dozen festive societies during the sixteenth century, had often entertained kings and visiting dignitaries with bawdy farces but now instead presented, for the king's pleasure, a new kind of pious and neoclassical entertainment. The last known public *chevauchée d'asne* performance in Lyon occurred as late as 1609, but it did not take place before the king. Lyon's festive societies gradually faded into the background of the city's cultural life during the early seventeenth century: although a

2. Daniel Vaillancourt, "La ville des entrées royales: Entre transfiguration et défiguration," *XVIIe Siècle* 53 (2001): 491–508; Margaret M. McGowan, "Les Jésuites à Avignon: Les fêtes au service de la propagande politique et religieuse," in *Les fêtes de la Renaissance*, ed. Jean Jacquot (Paris: CNRS, 1975) 3:153–71.

few members of the traditional Enfants de la Ville marched with Louis XIII into the city in 1622, any element of farce had long since been purged from their activities.[3] Instead, Jesuit students had replaced them on the civic stage and would continue to dominate it during the remainder of the seventeenth century. Although these students were of the same social status as the Enfants de la Ville and the Basoche, who had performed satirical farces during Lyon's Renaissance, they now used flattery rather than satire to communicate their opinions about royal policy. Instead of mocking human foibles as traditional farces had done, the 1622 Jesuit ballet sought to teach through the presentation of a worthy Christian example. King Philip makes the right choices, providing a model for his successor Louis. The glory of the monarchy is exalted, and there is no mention of the rights of the common people to voice their humble concerns, as occurred in some Renaissance farces. In this way, the 1622 Jesuit performance was not exceptional. Throughout the seventeenth century, Jesuit students performed plays that both encouraged Catholic activism in the face of heresy and shamelessly lauded the power, authority, and majesty of the French monarchy. Between 1598 and 1661, amateur theater continued to function as a form of political advice-giving, but flattery not ridicule was its operative mode. This shift both reflected and contributed to the new neoclassical aesthetic. It also reflected the ambitions of Bourbon monarchs and their ministers, who were increasingly insistent that the "discourse of absolutism" be maintained at all times.

Examining Jesuit theater is a particularly useful means for assessing changes in both theatrical tastes and provincial political culture, for it was very popular with the urban elites both in Paris and in the provinces. Everywhere that the Jesuits established a collège in France, they also performed plays that were paid for and applauded by local elites. Even more than professional acting troupes, who performed only occasionally outside Paris before 1650, Jesuit students replaced the festive societies of the Renaissance on the civic stage. Their productions thus can be assumed to have resonated not only with the king when he visited town but also with the city councilors, magistrates, and bourgeoisie, who regularly attended and paid for these student performances. Jesuit theater thus demonstrates that urban elites were by no means passive recipients of court culture. Even before the monarchy became actively involved in theatrical regulation in Paris in the 1630s, Jesuit performances in the provinces were reflecting a neoclassical and far more restrained theatrical aesthetic. The new style was a fit vehicle for a discourse of absolutism that attempted to shape policy through praise of the monarchy.

The Jesuits were in a good position to influence religious and political culture in the French provinces, particularly the culture of the urban elites,

3. Jean Tricou, "Les confréries joyeuses de Lyon au XVIe siècle et leur numismatique," *Revue Numismatique* 40 (1937): 307–8; *Entrées royales et fêtes populaires à Lyon du XVe au XVIIIe siècle* (Lyon: Bibliothèque de la Ville de Lyon, 1970), 54–59, 90–97, 116–17.

who had once been the patrons of farce. During the late sixteenth and seventeenth centuries, the Jesuits were very popular, in fact the most popular, teachers in France. Brought in to replace suspected Huguenot teachers at many provincial collèges, they quickly established themselves as committed educators, with a pedagogical program that sought to produce fluent speakers of classical Latin, refined gentlemen, and orthodox Catholics. Each of these aims shaped the kinds of theater that they had their students perform and helps to explain why urban elites concerned with orthodoxy and public order supported their efforts.

The emergence of hundreds of Jesuit collèges in France during the late sixteenth and early seventeenth centuries reflected both the particular nature of the order and the course of Catholic reform in France. The Jesuits, or the Society of Jesus, were founded by Ignatius Loyola in 1540 as an order prepared to travel the world in the service of Christ. Initially involved in a wide variety of ministries including itinerant preaching and caring for the sick, the Jesuits soon found their principal calling as teachers. Profiting from their own high level of education—all the founding members of the order were university educated, though not all of them were priests—the Jesuits soon began to found collèges in the hopes of training a new generation of Catholics steeped in an activist spirituality and orthodox theology.[4] The Jesuits' educational model appealed to French authorities increasingly concerned about the orthodoxy of education being offered at local collèges. As early as 1561, even Charles IX recognized the importance of winning the educational institutions over to the Catholic cause when he openly advocated enlisting their support to indoctrinate the young against heresy.[5] Although the Jesuits were by no means the only religious order to establish collèges in France during this period, they were by far the most successful when measured in terms of sheer numbers of students enrolled. Despite the French educational establishment's early resistance to them, the Jesuits were able to find wealthy patrons and establish a solid institutional foothold in several French cities.[6]

To offer free schooling, as they had done in their first institutions in Italy, the Jesuits needed to find wealthy patrons to underwrite each collège they

4. John W. O'Malley, *The First Jesuits* (Cambridge, Mass.: Harvard University Press, 1993), 91–127; Jennifer D. Selwyn, *A Paradise Inhabited by Devils: The Jesuits' Civilizing Mission in Early Modern Naples* (Aldershot: Ashgate, 2004), 55–94.

5. Bernard Chevalier, *Les bonnes villes de France du XIVe au XVIe siècle* (Paris: Aubier-Montaigne, 1982), 229–33; Marie-Madeleine Compère, *Du collège au lycée (1500–1850): Généalogie de l'enseignement secondaire français* (Paris: Gallimard, 1985), 38–39; George Huppert, *Public Schools in Renaissance France* (Chicago: University of Illinois Press, 1984), 104–15.

6. Capuchins and Oratorian collèges also opened during the sixteenth century. In the seventeenth century, many girls were serviced by the Ursulines religious order. Roger Chartier, Marie-Madeleine Compère, and Dominique Julia, *L'éducation en France du XVIe au XVIIIe siècle* (Paris: Société d'Édition d'Enseignement Supérieur, 1976), 159–202; Elizabeth Rapley, *The Dévotes: Women and Church in Seventeenth-Century France* (Montreal: McGill/Queen's University Press, 1990), 42–73. Institutional histories of the Jesuits in France include Pierre

214 | *Laughing Matters*

founded. During their first decades in France, much of this patronage was provided at the local rather than at the national level, as individuals and communities came to realize the value of the Jesuits' skills. In Tournon, as early as 1561, the cardinal in charge of the local university replaced the existing faculty with Jesuits. Similarly, despite a looming financial crisis, the strongly Catholic city council of Dijon provided the order with the means necessary to establish a Latin school in 1582 and did its utmost to sustain the order throughout the religious wars. Municipal archives demonstrate that many city councils provided the funds needed to establish and maintain Jesuit collèges in order to try to purge heresy from their cities and improve student discipline. In contrast, the Jesuits met with intransigent resistance from the clergy in the northern French city of Rouen. Despite popular reception to Jesuit preachers and the archbishop's endowment of two thousand livres to found a new collège, the mendicant orders that dominated education in Rouen successfully defended their monopoly in a lawsuit in 1570.[7] Clerics at the University of Paris were able to mount a similar campaign against the order, which did not prevent the Jesuits from founding the Collège de Clermont in 1564 but did keep the school outside of the university accreditation system. Despite such obstacles, by 1580 the Jesuits had opened nineteen collèges in France, some of which claimed to be instructing several hundred students.[8]

By 1593, after Henry IV's conversion to Catholicism and amid growing disillusionment with the Catholic League, the Jesuits realized that gaining royal support for their cause was of primary importance. As a religious order under the direct authority of the pope, the Jesuits were compelled to uphold the pope's excommunication of Henry, despite the king's rising popularity among French subjects. In early 1594, realizing the precariousness of their situation, the Jesuits requested and were granted special dispensation to offer their allegiance to the new king. The Jesuits' enemies were not, however, satisfied with the declaration of fealty and urged Henry to expel the Jesuits from France. In December 1594, these enemies found a convenient

Delattre, ed., *Les établissements des Jésuites en France depuis quatre siècles*, 4 vols. (Enghien: Institut Supérieur de Théologie, 1940–57); Henri Fouqueray, *Histoire de la Compagnie de Jésus en France*, 5 vols. (Paris: Picard, 1910–23); Édouard Piaget, *Histoire de l'établissement des Jésuites en France, 1540–1640* (Leiden: Brill, 1893).

7. Archives Municipales Dijon (AMD) B 227, fol. 118, 17 Oct. 1589; AMD B 231, fol. 109, 26 Nov. 1593; AMD B 231, fol. 160, 15 Apr. 1594; Charles de Robillard de Beaurepaire, *Recherches sur l'instruction publique dans le diocèse de Rouen avant 1789* (Evreux: Pierre Huet, 1872), 2:33–35; Marc Venard, "Y a-t-il une 'stratégie scolaire' des Jésuites en France au XVIe siècle," in *L'Université de Pont-à-Mousson et les problèmes de son temps* (Nancy: Université de Nancy, 1974), 78–80; Eric Nelson, *The Jesuits and the Monarchy: Catholic Reform and Political Authority in France, 1590–1615* (Aldershot: Ashgate, 2005), 124–27.

8. Chartier, Compère, and Julia, *Éducation en France*, 187; Fouqueray, *Histoire*, 2:186; Aristide Douarche, *L'Université de Paris et les Jésuites* (Paris: Hachette, 1888; reprint, Geneva: Slatkine, 1971).

excuse to act when a former Jesuit student tried to assassinate the king. In its concluding statement against the attempted murderer, the Paris Parlement banished the Jesuits from the realm. Although some regional parlements, such as Toulouse, refused to register this arrêt and many southern communities quietly defied the edict, many Jesuit schools had to close in 1595.[9]

By 1603, however, a financially solvent and confident Henry IV, eager to reestablish good relations with the papacy, allowed the Jesuits to return to France. Seeing the value of patronizing Catholic education, Henry shored up the Jesuits' finances and even helped them to establish new collèges, including the prestigious Collège Henri IV in La Flèche. Without Henry's, and later Louis XIII's, active patronage, the Jesuits would have been unable to reestablish themselves in France. Although their detractors began another campaign to vilify the order after Henry IV's assassination in 1610, the Jesuits survived and indeed flourished during the decades that followed. By the 1620s, members of the Jesuit order were prominent at the king's court, and Jesuit confessors continued to have the ear of the French monarch through the seventeenth century. The Jesuits were well aware that their privileged position was dependent on their close relationship with the crown, which they sought to reaffirm in every way they could, including the use of student theater. The urban elites of France, who themselves were being forced to renegotiate their relationship with a centralizing French monarchy during this period, learned important lessons from the order about how to manipulate public ritual to cement a good relationship with the crown.[10]

The Jesuit pedagogical system was a variation of the Parisian model developed during the first half of the sixteenth century.[11] The order's founder, Ignatius Loyola, and his followers, all former students at the University of Paris, adapted its humanistic curriculum that focused on the mastery of classical Latin language and literature. During the second half of the sixteenth century the Jesuits systematized their pedagogical approach, setting down in a detailed rule book, *Rules for Study*, the texts that were to be taught at each level and the specific tasks that a teacher was to accomplish during

9. Michel De Waele, "Pour la sauvegarde du roi et du royaume: L'expulsion des Jésuites à la fin des guerres de religion," *Canadian Journal of History* 29 (1994): 267–80; Michel Péronnet, "Les établissements des Jésuites dans le royaume de France à l'époque moderne," in *Les Jésuites parmi les hommes au XVIe et XVIIe siècles*, ed. G. Demerson, B. Dompnier, and A. Regond (Clermont-Ferrand: Université de Clermont-Ferrand II, 1987), 461–80; Nelson, *Jesuits*, 43–55.
10. Marc Fumaroli, *L'âge de l'éloquence: Rhétorique et res literaria de la Renaissance au seuil de l'époque classique*, 2nd ed. (Paris: Albin Michel, 1994), 233–46; A. Lynn Martin, *Henry III and the Jesuit Politicians* (Geneva: Droz, 1973), 208–23; Stéphane van Damme, *Le temple de sagesse: Savoirs, écrits et sociabilité urbaine (Lyon, XVIIe–XVIIIe siècle)* (Paris: EHESS, 2005), 123–53; Nelson, *Jesuits*, 57–96, 110–14.
11. Regarding Jesuit pedagogy, see André Collinot and Francine Mazière, eds., *L'exercice de la parole* (Paris: Cendre, 1987); *Ratio studiorum: Plan raisonné et institution des études dans la Compagnie de Jésus*, ed. Adrien Demoustier, Dominque Julia, and Marie-Madeleine Compère, trans. Léone Albrieux and Dolorès Pralon-Julia (Paris: Belin, 1997); François de Dainville,

each lesson.[12] The admissions records of a handful of Jesuit collèges suggest that this educational program was followed in practice: students moved progressively through the curriculum, usually satisfying the requirements of one class each year.[13] Thus the Jesuit curriculum served many of the same functions as did the traditional arts education that French students had been obtaining at either municipal collèges or at the well-established universities. In fact, they attracted a very similar group of students to their collèges.

The Jesuit *Rules for Study* stipulated that Jesuit teachers were to record attendance each year. Although the vast majority of these records have been lost, a handful of them remain in French archives. One such series documents the social status of students at the Collège de la Madeleine in Bordeaux during the mid-seventeenth century. For an eight-year period between 1644 and 1652, a complete admissions list exists for the Collège de la Madeleine.[14] This exhaustive inventory reveals that most of the students attending the Jesuit collège were drawn from the same social class that had performed farces in the city streets during the Renaissance.

Between 1644 and 1652, 1,082 students were admitted to the Collège de la Madeleine in Bordeaux. The admissions records indicate that an average of 135 new students enrolled per year and that there were probably several hundred students studying at the collège each year in the 1640s. Nonresidents were a sizable minority of the student body, comprising slightly less than half the students who were admitted during this period.[15] During the years before the Fronde, nonresidents were on average seventeen years old, and they overwhelmingly enrolled in the logic class, which provided advanced studies not offered at smaller collèges. Local boys, in contrast, began their studies in the lower classes: the average Bordeaux student enrolled at

Naissance de l'humanisme moderne: Les Jésuites et l'éducation de la société française (Paris: Beauchesne, 1940); J.-B. Herman, *La pédagogie des Jésuites au XVIe siècle* (Paris: Picard, 1914); Aldo Scaglione, ed., *The Liberal Arts and the Jesuit College System* (Philadelphia: John Benjamins, 1986); Georges Snyders, *La pédagogie en France aux XVIIe et XVIIIe siècles* (Paris: Presses Universitaires de France, 1965).

12. L. W. B. Brockliss, *French Higher Education in the Seventeenth and Eighteenth Centuries: A Cultural History* (Oxford: Clarendon Press, 1987), 117–19, 199–201; Stéphane van Damne, "Devenir enseignant de collège au XVIIe siècle: Itinéraires et expériences de formation des professeurs et régents jésuites de la province de Lyon," *Cahiers d'Histoire* 71 (1998): 37–54.

13. Dainville, *Éducation*, 110–14; Willem Frijhoff and Dominique Julia, *École et société dans la France d'ancien régime* (Paris: A. Colin, 1975), 50–61; Adrien Demoustier, "Des 'grandes écoles au collèges': Un aspect du rôle des Jésuites dans l'évolution scolaire du royaume de France au XVI siècle," in Demerson, Dompnier, and Regond, *Jésuites parmi les hommes*, 382; Dominique Julia, "Les institutions et les hommes," in *Histoire des universités en France*, ed. Jacques Verger (Paris: Privat, 1984), 142.

14. *Ratio studiorum*, item 261; Archives Départementales Gironde (ADG) H 3142, "Liber status classium collegii Burdegalensis societatis Jesu."

15. Resident to nonresident admission ratios by year are as follows: 1644–45, 55:90; 1645–46, 101:80; 1646–47, 26:38; 1647–48, 74:56; 1648–49, 100:68; 1649–50, 89:41; 1650–51, 73:68; 1651–52, 64:38. In 21 cases, residency was not indicated. Residents comprised 55 percent of students admitted during the 1644–52 period.

the age of eleven and began his studies in the sixth class, where he would be instructed in basic Latin grammar.[16] This pattern of differential enrollment suggests that nonresidents used the Collège de la Madeleine as a finishing school to complement an education begun at home or at another collège. Residents, on the other hand, sent their boys to the Jesuit collège as soon as they had learned to read and write.[17]

The Bordeaux admissions records show a consistent pattern of class distribution, based on a father's profession or social status. The sons of artisans and *laboureurs* (independent farmers) were a tiny minority of the students admitted to the Collège de la Madeleine, comprising less than 3 percent of the total. In contrast, about 8 percent of the students were noblemen's sons, a disproportionately high percentage relative to the region's demographics but in keeping with admissions patterns at other Jesuit collèges.[18] Merchants' sons made up 24 percent of the student population, and sons from families that listed themselves as bourgeois supplied another 12 percent. The sons of legal officials and liberal professionals were, however, the ones who flocked to the Jesuit collège in the greatest numbers. Sons of *avocats du roi*, magistrates, seneschal judges, doctors, and lawyers comprised 27 percent of the admitted students, the largest single category. If the *officier* members of the *bourgeoisie seconde* are included—solicitors, notaries, scribes, and tax collectors—the proportion of this group rises to almost 45 percent of the student body entering the Collège de la Madeleine during the 1640s and early 1650s. Although there was a considerable difference in wealth, power, and status between a magistrate and a notary, their sons were united in their need for Latin education to maintain their family's social and professional status.[19]

The length of time that students remained at collège assured that the sons of men of the law and liberal professionals dominated the student body at most Jesuit schools. Students at either end of the social spectrum attended a collège for the shortest number of years: noblemen's sons because they were called to military duty or allowed to accelerate through the academic program, and artisans' sons because they generally abandoned their education after mastering basic Latin grammar. In contrast, the sons of legal and tax officials remained for longer periods. A comparison of the Bordeaux data

16. In 1645–46, the average age at which residents enrolled was eleven, and most of them registered in the fifth or sixth class (88 percent). In the same year, the average age at which nonresidents were admitted was seventeen, and they registered in the highest classes, most often in the Logic class (46 percent). That year, 11.2 percent of the nonresidents were nobles' sons. See Frijhoff and Julia, *École et société*, 14.

17. Ibid., 45–46.

18. Ibid., 14.

19. Among resident students, the percentage of *officiers' sons* was slightly higher (50.1 percent).

with collège admissions records from Auch, Châlons-sur-Marne, and Troyes suggests that the pattern in Bordeaux was not an anomaly.[20] At the Jesuit collège in Auch at the beginning of the seventeenth century, 65 percent of senior legal officials' sons remained enrolled through the humanities class (four years altogether); in contrast, only 30 percent of students in other social categories studied at the collège that long.[21] Thus most boys who spent several years attending a Jesuit collège were drawn from the same social class as were those who had attended similar institutions a century earlier: they were urban officials' sons, who needed an education to get ahead. By the early seventeenth century, the university students and members of festive societies such as the Mère Folle or the Basoche, who had performed playful and satirical farces during the Renaissance, were increasingly attending Jesuit institutions, where they were encouraged to repudiate the students' traditionally licentious and carefree lifestyle.

Far more so than masters at French universities, the Jesuits injected a strong moral and spiritual element into the humanities curriculum, a priority that was reflected in their student theater. From the establishment of the order, the Jesuits saw themselves as missionaries actively engaged in society. Jesuit religious practice was founded on the *Spiritual Exercises*, a guide to spiritual renewal written by Ignatius Loyola. Progress through the *Spiritual Exercises*, in a four-week retreat that takes the individual systematically through a series of reflections to reach a deeper understanding of Christ's sacrifice for humanity, was often a conversion experience, which was then supposed to be manifested by the individual's actions in the world. For the Jesuits, it was not enough to be privately pious at home: inner piety had to be expressed in social action. The Jesuits asked laypersons to take personal responsibility for their faith and to practice constant self-discipline in order to avoid what the Jesuits considered to be the excesses of earlier Christian habits.[22] At the collèges, they insisted on a rigorous spiritual schedule: students were expected to undertake a monthly confession and to maintain regular attendance at sermons and mass. Although academic exams each year evaluated mastery of Latin, an informal assessment of moral character also contributed to the decision whether or not a boy would advance to the next class the following autumn.[23] This stress on the student's moral development differentiated Jesuit institutions from municipal collèges. The Jesuits would not teach classical authors whose texts they deemed to be

20. Marie-Madeleine Compère and Dominique Julia, *Les collèges français: XVIe–XVIIIe siècles* (Paris: CNRS, 1984), 1:151–52; Dainville, *Éducation*, 78–79.
21. Dainville, *Éducation*, 125; Frijhoff and Julia, *École et société*, 57–60.
22. O'Malley, *First Jesuits*, passim.
23. Philippe Ariès, *Centuries of Childhood: A Social History of Family Life*, trans. Robert Baldick (New York: Vintage, 1965), 171–73; P. Camille de Rochemonteix, *Un collège de Jésuites aux XVIIe et XVIIIe siècles: Le collège Henri IV de La Flèche* (Le Mans: Leguicheux, 1889), 4:202–5.

immoral, such as Terence or Plautus, and the *Rules for Study* warned students to abstain "absolutely from reading depraved and useless books."[24] In many ways, the Jesuits saw the collèges as launching pads for a much wider program of Catholic revitalization. Theater was to become one of the means through which the Jesuits were able to show the wider community both the Latin learning and the spiritual success they had achieved with their students.

The Jesuits were also very concerned with disciplining the body, both inside and outside the classroom. Physical discipline was thought to reflect and contribute to spiritual discipline, which was of course understood as the ultimate goal. The Jesuits themselves, though not all priests, adopted a priestly demeanor, dressing in black and behaving in public with conspicuous sobriety, but they realized that most of their students would not follow a religious calling. As a result, the Jesuits sought to reconcile the seemingly contradictory world of the devout with that of the salons.[25] In large measure, the Jesuits did so by infusing noble virtues of gallantry and social poise with Christian morality. Along with Latin grammar, some Jesuit collèges also offered dance and equestrian lessons to students who might aspire someday to visit the king's court. The Jesuits also employed the new genre of civility manuals in their classrooms. New editions of both Erasmus's *On Civility in Boys* and a French translation of Giovanni Della Casa's *Galateo* were produced for the Jesuits' use during the early seventeenth century.[26] In addition, another Italian text written, it seems, by a Jesuit instructor, titled *Decency in Conversation among Men*, was translated and published for students at the Pont-à-Mousson collège. This text, produced in both French and Latin to reach the widest possible audience, was possibly also used as a Latin tutorial in the classroom with younger students.[27] *Decency in Conversation* began with the fundamentals, which for the Jesuits involved learning how to behave during religious services, and from there continued on in much the same vein as other civility manuals of the day, enjoining the young men to walk gracefully in the streets and to avoid dipping their bread in the common pot after having eaten of it. These texts implicitly rejected the medieval alternation between times of fasting and times of feasting that had contributed to the vibrant festive tradition of the Renaissance. In the Jesuit system, the same bodily discipline was to be maintained at all times: the Christian gentleman was consistent both in his own deportment and in his respect for and deference to others. Although the Jesuits were not alone in their

---

24. *Ratio studiorum*, item 477. See also item 57.
25. Alain Couprie, "'Courtisanisme' et Christianisme au XVIIe siècle," *XVIIe Siècle* 33 (1981): 373–90.
26. Ariès, *Centuries*, 119, 290. Regarding the Jesuits' ambivalence about Erasmus, see O'Malley, *First Jesuits*, 262–64.
27. *De la bienséance de la conversation entre les hommes* (La Flèche: Sébastien Chappelet, 1618).

attempt to reconcile Christianity with courtly civility, their pedagogy was perhaps the most influential, affecting a wide swath of young boys, from merchants in the provinces to the sons of the French nobility.

The Jesuits expected secular authorities to enforce their standards of moral discipline. In 1610, the Bordeaux city council noted that the Jesuits had complained about students converging "at the cabaret and at cafés, which since this causes great debauchery and deprivation of manners, [the principal of the Jesuits] requests that this matter be attended to. On which it is deliberated that the principal will advise [the council] of the first incident of debauchery and of the students who are involved, so that the council can imprison them."[28] The council did not make this threat idly: later that year, it punished and jailed a handful of students who had dressed up as Jesuits and paraded with arms through the streets during May day celebrations. In both Bordeaux and Dijon, the city council repeatedly issued rulings that outlawed the election of "abbots" to lead the student "nations" and forbade students to carry arms in the city or visit local brothels.[29] In 1612 and 1625, the Bordeaux city council stiffly reprimanded students caught fistfighting at the Jesuit collège.[30] In Dijon, faced with fighting and vandalism within the collège, the parlement placed responsibility for correcting student behavior squarely on the city council, repeatedly urging the "mayor and chief prosecutor of this city to enforce the said principal's and teachers' authority, if they are requested to do so."[31] On occasion, the Dijon Parlement punished students for striking teachers or breaking school windows. The need to reissue these rulings throughout the seventeenth century demonstrates that this campaign of reform did not immediately change student behavior. Nevertheless, the Jesuits had successfully enlisted the city authorities' support in curtailing student violence and upholding more rigorous standards of public propriety.[32]

The Jesuits' efforts to discipline their students largely dovetailed with local authorities' efforts to contain public violence and to suppress festive practice during the early decades of the seventeenth century. In cities throughout France, there was during this period a second wave of local rulings against practices as varied as charivari, Maytime dancing, and drinking at cabarets. These initiatives seem in the short term to have had little impact on public

28. *Inventaire sommaire des registres de la jurade de Bordeaux (1520–1783)*, ed. Paul Courteault and Alfred Leroux (Bordeaux: F. Pech, 1909), 5:63.
29. Ibid., 5:63–66; Charles François Muteau, *Les écoles et collèges en province depuis les temps les plus reculés jusqu'en 1789* (Dijon: Darantière, 1882), 451–56.
30. *Inventaire sommaire . . . Bordeaux*, 5:65 (17 May 1629), 8:206 (8 March 1625).
31. Bibliothèque Municipale Dijon, MS 1500, Saverot, "Extraits des registres," fol. 51, 11 Jan. 1623; Muteau, *Écoles*, 462.
32. That student violence persisted through the seventeenth century is demonstrated by a number of studies. See J. P. Poussou, "L'agitation étudiante à Bordeaux sous l'ancien régime, spécialement au XVIIIe siècle," *Revue Historique de Bordeaux* 19 (1970): 79–92; Rochemonteix, *Collège*, 2:96–102.

behavior. In light of the Jesuits' educational reforms, however, they are significant, demonstrating, as a number of historians have argued, a new cooperation between the secular urban oligarchy and the local clergy to reform traditional festive practices.[33] At the same time, Jesuit education was instilling in the sons of urban notables and the *bourgeoisie seconde* an alternative model of honorable behavior that upheld rather than undermined both local and monarchical authority.

The Jesuits' efforts to reshape the moral lives of their students, though rigorous, were less thoroughgoing than those of other seventeenth-century French educators, most notably the Jansenists. At the Jansenist collège at Port-Royal, where relentless day-and-night supervision of a small student body was intended to establish complete moral control over body and soul, the ideals of Christian civility were still more systematically enforced.[34] Most Jesuit students were free of such supervision, since they either lived at home or boarded with local families, where neither their study time nor their personal behavior would be closely controlled. By 1650, the Jesuits had established dormitories only at their collèges in Paris, Pont-à-Mousson, and La Flèche, which suggests that monitoring their students' private moral lives was not their highest priority.[35] The tension between protecting their students from moral contamination and leaving them unsupervised outside school hours was never fully resolved by the Jesuits, and a similar tension between Christian purity and participation in the real world can be detected in the students' theatrical performances.

From the beginning, Jesuit educators used student theater for a variety of purposes. In Billom, where a contract to open a Jesuit collège was signed in November 1558, students were performing sacred dramas even before the first stone of the building was laid.[36] Evidence from memoirs, theatrical programs, and city council records demonstrates that the Jesuits had established a vibrant tradition of performance at all their French collèges by the end of the sixteenth century. Although celebrating the triumphs of the absolutist state became an important theme of Jesuit theater after 1620, during

33. Peter Burke, *Popular Culture in Early Modern Europe* (New York: Harper and Row, 1978), 207–34; Philip T. Hoffman, *Church and Community in the Diocese of Lyon, 1500–1789* (New Haven: Yale University Press, 1984), 73–90.

34. Snyders, *Pédagogie*, 44.

35. Only a minority of Jesuit students lived in dormitories located on the collège grounds. See Ariès, *Centuries of Childhood*, 275–80; Fouqueray, *Histoire*, 2:185; Rochemonteix, *Collège*, 2:58–60.

36. Delattre, *Établissements*, 1:703. Letter of Robert Claysson, as cited in A. Lynn Martin, *The Jesuit Mind: The Mentality of an Elite in Early Modern France* (Ithaca: Cornell University Press, 1988), 72. Jesuit theater was also enormously successful in central and southern Europe. See Ronnie Po-Chia Hsia, *Social Discipline in the Reformation: Central Europe, 1550–1750* (New York: Routledge, 1989), 94–100; Lucette Elyanne Roux, "Cent ans d'expérience théâtrale dans les collèges de la Compagnie de Jésus en Espagne," in *Dramaturgie et société: Rapports entre l'oeuvre théâtrale, son interprétation et son public au XVIe et XVIIe siècles*, ed. Jean Jacquot, Élie Konigson and Marcel Oddon (Paris: CNRS, 1967), 3:479–520.

the first fifty years of the Jesuits' time in France, they focused their energies on purging immoral elements and providing an appropriate reformed Catholic aesthetic. The *Rules for Study* outlined such a model for student performances: "The subject of these tragedies and comedies—which should only be in Latin and very rare—will be sacred and pious; there will be no interludes, if so Latin and decent, and no feminine characters or clothing will be introduced."[37] These guidelines call for a student theater in line with humanist and Tridentine ideals. Historians have found, however, that in practice Jesuit student performance rarely met these criteria. Often the desire to convert local residents, to entertain the king and local elites, and to display the students' cultivation led Jesuit performances in directions that contravened the principles laid out in the *Rules*.

Between 1555 and 1620, the Jesuits' theatrical strategies reflected both their insecurity as a struggling new religious order and their anxiety about Protestant heresy. Purifying and strengthening the Catholic faith were their primary goals. In the face of the threat of Huguenot heresy, founding collèges seemed to be an effective way to establish a foothold in a community, from which the Jesuits could then pursue these broader evangelical goals. As a result, the Jesuits in the beginning took every opportunity to reach out to all the city's residents: their students regularly participated in religious processions and performed sacred theater in public. Even without the institutional support of a collège, former Jesuit students, such as Bernard Bardon of Limoges, returned home to write an anti-Huguenot play performed by a local confraternity in 1596.[38] In the interests of what would now be called accessibility, collège teachers sometimes chose to perform traditional genres such as mystery plays rather than the classical genres stipulated in the *Rules*, and students were encouraged to perform in French if that would bring more people to confession.[39] Whereas after 1620 Jesuit student performances came to be presented in interior, often dedicated acting spaces and before an elite audience, during the sixteenth and early seventeenth centuries they usually took place in front of the school or in a public square. Hoping for large crowds, the Jesuits presented traditional theatrical genres couched in understandable imagery.

One theatrical genre that Jesuit educators refused to take advantage of was the farce, which they associated with disorder, ignorance, and archaic

37. *Ratio studiorum*, item 87.
38. Michel Cassan, *Le temps des guerres de religion: Le cas de Limousin (vers 1530–vers 1630)* (Paris: Publisud, 1996), 292–94; Martin, *Jesuit Mind*, 17–21.
39. Father Maggio as cited in Delattre, *Établissements*, 2:1516–17; Jean Houllon, rector of Rodez college, as quoted in Martin, *Jesuit Mind*, 69. The *Ratio studiorum* of 1591 encouraged regents to actively pursue the theater, as cited in Rochemonteix, *Collège*, 4:180. Jesuit student performances in French occurred in Lyon as early as 1574. See Georgette de Groër, *Réforme et Contre-Réforme en France: Le Collège de la Trinité au XVIe siècle à Lyon* (Paris: Publisud, 1995), 139.

social customs. Some Jesuits were even eager to abolish traditional Carnival festivities entirely. Emond Auger, a popular Jesuit preacher who helped establish the Jesuit collège in Lyon, claimed triumphantly, and as it turned out optimistically, that Carnival festivities had been successfully eradicated from the city in 1564. Similarly, in 1587, the prominent Father Maggio prohibited Jesuit students from participating in all Carnival activities.[40]

Nevertheless, most Jesuits realized that abolishing a festival as popular as Carnival was neither possible nor desirable. Instead, they found a way of co-opting it so as to eliminate its unruly and satirical elements. Lille's theatrical history demonstrates the efficacy of this moderate policy. During the first half of the sixteenth century, several well-established festive societies celebrated Carnival each year in Lille, usually with the city council's approval. Their performances—masked processions, tableaux vivants, short morality plays, and farces—entertained common people and the elite alike. Yet even before the Jesuits established a collège in Lille in 1592, these festive associations were on the wane. As early as the 1540s, the city council began issuing rulings against masking, processions, and unruly behavior, limitations that only intensified during the Wars of Religion period. During the 1590s, Jesuits helped to seal the fate of the city's traditional festive societies when they offered the city council their students' services at Carnival. Every year between 1592 and the 1620s, the Lille city council permitted and indeed paid Jesuit students to perform in February during the festive season.[41] The "comedies" they performed replaced the festive societies' bawdy farces with biblical stories and hagiography, including a *History of Saint Catherine*, the *Dialogue of Saint Nicholas*, and the *Escape from Egypt by the Children of Israel*.[42] Jesuits throughout France replicated this strategy, which occupied the students in pious activities even as it displaced more morally dangerous fare. Paradoxically, Carnival became one of the times during the year when Jesuit students were sure to perform.

As part of their campaign against farce, the Jesuits were also resolutely hostile to professional theatrical troupes, ruling firmly that their students "will not attend public spectacles, theatrical performances or public games."[43] They had two reasons for condemning commercial theater. First,

40. Martin W. Walsh, "The Condemnation of Carnival in the 'Jesuit Relations,'" *Michigan Academician* 15 (1982): 18; Father Maggio, as quoted in Fouqueray, *Histoire*, 2:201; Emond Auger, as quoted in Martin, *Jesuit Mind*, 77–78; Selwyn, *Paradise*, 216–17.
41. Ariès, *Centuries of Childhood*, 88–89; Valerie Delay, "Compagnies joyeuses, 'places,' et festivités à Lille au XVIe siècle," *Revue de Nord* 69 (1987): 503–14; Léon Lefebvre, *Fêtes lilloises du XIVe au XVIe siècle* (Lille: Lefebvre-Ducrocq, 1902); Léon Lefebvre, *Le théâtre des Jésuites et des Augustins dans leurs collèges de Lille du XVIe au XVIIIe siècle* (Nancy: Berger Levrault, 1907), 5–9.
42. Louis Desgraves, *Répertoire des programmes de théâtre jouées dans les collèges en France (1601–1700)* (Geneva: Droz, 1986), 52–53.
43. *Ratio studiorum*, item 478.

professional actors usually performed in places of ill repute such as jeux de paume, where students drank, fought, and harassed the actors.[44] Second, the actors were considered suspect both because they accepted money for portraying immoral characters and because their performances threatened to heighten the passions of their audiences. Like most seventeenth-century clerics, the Jesuits feared that contact with commercial actors and actresses might reorient their students' sensitive moral compasses.[45]

When local authorities did allow commercial actors to perform, Jesuit preachers protested vigorously. In a 1639 letter to a friend, the scholar Marin Mersenne remembers his Jesuit teachers' hostility to professional acting of all kinds:

> I remember when I was a student at La Flèche, the teacher having fulminated from the pulpit against these sorts of people, who were in town at the time, the next day the leader, who was named it seems to me Valeran, and who was most excellent in his art, mounted on his platform, contradicted everything that the teacher had said and proved the excellence of his art and that it was very useful and permitted with reason, by [citing] the Greek and Latin scholars etc. I did not hear [the actor's defense of his profession] because our teachers forbade us from going with the threat of being whipped.[46]

Valleran Le Conte, a well-known actor in Paris and Bordeaux who was well received at the king's court, apparently failed on this occasion to convince the Jesuits of the worthiness of his profession.[47] The Jesuits' intransigence was so well known that in 1607 another professional actor, Mathieu Lefebvre, challenged what he considered to be their hypocrisy. In a pamphlet titled *Prologue of La Porte*, written after the Jesuits prevented Lefebvre and his troupe from performing in the city of Bourges, the actor defends his profession with reference to Thomas Aquinas's support of the theater and the French monarchy's willingness to sanction it. Citing Henry IV's love of the theater, Lefebvre suggests that because the Jesuits reject commercial theater that they are not the loyal subjects that they claim to be—an insinuation not uncommon in anti-Jesuit propaganda at this time. Finally, Lefebvre questions why, if the Jesuits consider acting so villainous, they allow their own students to perform on stage. Precisely because Lefebvre's points are by no means original, his pamphlet demonstrates that the Jesuits' hostility

44. AM Bordeaux BB 51, fol. 60, 18 Jan. 1657; Jean Robert, "Comédiens et bateleurs sur les rives de la Garonne au XVIIe siècle," *Revue d'Histoire du Théâtre* 11 (1957): 37; Brockliss, *French Higher Education*, 100–101.

45. Jean Dubu, "L'Église catholique et la condamnation du théâtre en France," *Quaderni Francesi* (1970): 319–49; J. H. Phillips, "Le théâtre scolaire dans la querelle du théâtre au XVIIe siècle," *Revue d'Histoire du Théâtre* 35 (1983): 212–14.

46. Mersenne, as quoted in Raymond Lebègue, *Études sur le théâtre français* (Paris: Nizet, 1978), 2:165; André Rivet, *Instruction chrestienne touchant les spectacles publics des comédies et tragédies* (La Haye: T. Maire, 1639).

47. Jean de Gaufreteau, *Chronique bordeloise* (Bordeaux: Charles Lefebvre, 1877), 1:306–7.

to commercial theater was notorious at the beginning of the seventeenth century and that their efforts to reform civic culture were not universally applauded.[48]

An incident that occurred in Lyon during the summer of 1607 demonstrates the passions evoked by Jesuit theater in an age when theatrical tastes were rapidly evolving and when the Jesuits' own client relationship with the crown was still untested. Only a few years after their return from exile and the reestablishment of their collège in Lyon, the Jesuits performed the three-day-long *Play about the Last Judgment*, a traditional mystery play designed to inspire repentance and piety. A few weeks later they would read a slanderous account of the performance in a short pamphlet titled the *Fabulous Tale*.[49] This document accused the Jesuits of blasphemy and specifically of having performed a "ridiculous farce, a degrading performance" that mocked the pope and depicted God in a heretical fashion on the stage.[50] As just punishment for the Jesuits' sins, claimed the pamphleteer, on the third day of the performance a thunderstorm struck near the collège, killing some of the participants. These deaths were clearly God's punishment for having impersonated God and Lucifer on stage, a claim that might have seemed not implausible to Lyon city residents at the turn of the seventeenth century.[51] The pamphleteer evidently hoped to raise fears that the Jesuits' return to Lyon invited God's direct intervention in its earthly affairs.

This pamphlet was only one of dozens against the Jesuits printed in the decade following their return to France in 1603 and reveals how fragile was their standing in France at the time. Their enemies at the University of Paris and at the Paris Parlement hoped that such attacks might force the Jesuits to abandon France once and for all. We know that the 1607 pamphlet describing the Jesuit theatrical performance was widely read and distributed: the Parisian memoir writer Pierre de L'Estoile notes that he received a copy of *Fabulous Tale* that autumn. So frequent was slander of this

---

48. Pierre de L'Estoile, *Mémoires-journaux, 1574–1611*, ed. G. Brunet (Paris: Librairie des Bibliophiles, 1875–79; reprint, Paris: Taillander, 1982), 8:348, 9:50. For evidence of Lefebvre's travels throughout France, see Georges Mongrédien, *Dictionnaire biographique des comédiens français du XVIIe siècle* (Paris: CNRS, 1972), 103; "Prologue de La Porte," reprinted in Hippolyte Boyer, *L'ancien théâtre à Bourges: Le théâtre du collège* (Bourges: H. Sire, 1892), 14–20.

49. Charles Ledré, "Théâtre et 'exercices publics' dans les collèges lyonnais du XVIe au XVIIIe siècle," *Bulletin de la Société Littéraire, Historique, et Archéologique de Lyon* 16 (1940–44): 6.

50. André de Gaule, *Conviction veritable du recit fabuleux divulgué touchant la representation exhibée en face de toute la ville de Lyon au Collège de la Compagnie de Jésus, le 7 d'août, 1607* (Lyon: Abraham Cloquemin, 1607), 6. For a Parisian League procession of 1590 that was denigrated in analogous terms, see Ann W. Ramsey, *Liturgy, Politics, and Salvation: The Catholic League in Paris and the Nature of Catholic Reform* (Rochester, N.Y.: University of Rochester Press, 1999), 79–80.

51. *Conviction veritable*, 12; Natalie Zemon Davis, "The Sacred and the Body Social in Lyon," *Past and Present* 90 (1981): 55–56.

kind against the Jesuits that he dedicated to them a special file titled "Jesuit mockeries." Several accounts of the 1607 performance were also printed in England.[52] Catholics and Protestants alike were eager to get at the Jesuits by maligning their student theater.

Feeling compelled to respond to these slanderous accusations, a Lyon city resident named André De Gaule wrote a reply to the *Fabulous Tale* that defended the Jesuits' theatrical performance and the order's religious mission more generally. De Gaule insists that the Jesuit students performed not a "farce" at all but a "devout" series of allegorical tableaux that were well received by a large and penitent audience.[53] The slander presented in the *Fabulous Tale*, De Gaule concludes, could only have been the work of the Jesuits' most dire enemy, the Huguenots, who "hated the Jesuits to death."[54] He ends his discourse with a long discussion of the Huguenots' false teachings and their mistaken doctrine that all theatrical performance is fundamentally immoral. Both the original performance and De Gaule's defense reflect the tense religious atmosphere in which the Jesuits performed during the Wars of Religion and the opening decades of the seventeenth century. Although the Huguenots had failed to convert the monarchy, they remained dangerous: a small but vocal minority with powerful foreign allies.[55]

The Jesuits' history in Lyon was long and peppered with conflict. As early as 1565, the Lyon city council invited them to found a collège, but they were later expelled from the city under a cloud of suspicion in the 1590s. Upon their return in 1603, the Jesuits quickly secured the support of the city council and received a generous pension from the king himself. Their new collège flourished, and they quickly reestablished a large base: by 1604, the Jesuits in Lyon claimed to be instructing nine hundred students. Within a few years, finding that they could no longer accommodate the student population in the buildings allocated for their use, the Jesuits requested to relocate to what was then an empty lot near the central Place des Terreaux. Although the city council and the military governor of Lyon supported the move, the local Huguenot community wanted to buy the same piece of land for a church and lobbied the king, who rejected the Jesuits' proposal. The Jesuits' problem had still not been solved by the summer of 1607. Attacking Jesuit theater may have been an easy means to undermine the Jesuits' popularity among Lyon city residents at a moment when Henry's patronage was anything but secure.[56]

52. L'Estoile, *Mémoires*, 8:348–53.
53. *Conviction veritable*, 6.
54. Ibid., 20.
55. Lebègue, *Études*, 1:202–5.
56. De Groër, *Réforme*, 154–67, 183–201; Delattre, *Établissements*, 2:1504, 1518, 1521–23; Richard Gascon, *Grand commerce et vie urbaine au XVIe siècle: Lyon et ses marchands* (Paris: École Pratique des Hautes Études, 1971), 2:511–15; Hoffman, *Church and Community*, 38;

In the end, the Jesuits were able to build their new collège in Lyon and maintain their ties with Henry IV and his successors, but the 1607 controversy revealed that the Jesuits' attitude toward the two theatrical genres they cared about was viewed as doubly archaic. Hostile to farce and to the growing numbers of professional troupes that visited cities like Lyon by the early seventeenth century, the Jesuits seemed unnecessarily strict in their attitude toward harmless comic entertainment. At the same time, by staging mystery plays, a genre that had not been performed in Paris since the mid-sixteenth century, they presented themselves as culturally behind the times. Perhaps in response to the 1607 controversy, the Jesuits by the 1620s had stopped performing traditional mystery plays and shifted to the neoclassical theatrical genres originally dictated by the *Rules for Study*. The order began to couch its Christian message in gentler neoclassical terms—unlike those of the allegorical warfare between absolute good and evil as presented in earlier Jesuit theater—and to compose plays that met contemporary secular criteria for tragedy. Their neoclassical fare featured the Alexandrine line, the five-act structure, the unities of time and place, and what was known in literary discussion in the 1630s and 1640s as *bienséance*, the avoidance of violent acts on stage.[57] So closely did the Jesuits imitate the kinds of plays being performed at Parisian theaters that they even abandoned the *Rules'* precepts regarding the depiction of women and the use of the French language in their student performances.

The Jesuits' production of *Adonias* in 1648 illustrates the way Christian-themed collège theater was conforming to secular literary fashions by the mid-seventeenth century.[58] Performed in Paris at the Jesuits' well-established and prestigious Collège de Clermont, this play dramatizes a story from the Old Testament. Adonias, who as King David's eldest living son expects to inherit the throne of Israel, is passed over in favor of his younger half brother Solomon. When his father dies, Adonias, fearing that Solomon will kill him to secure the throne, flees to the temple. Solomon has no such intentions, however, and the two brothers are quickly reconciled. Soon afterward, Adonias tests Solomon's generosity by seeking to marry Abishag, the beautiful young virgin who had nursed King David before his death. Fearing that Adonias is trying to strengthen his claim to the throne by marrying, in effect, his father's widow, Solomon has Adonias killed.

Judi Loach, "The Hôtel de Ville at Lyons: Civic Improvement and Its Meanings in Seventeenth-Century France," *Transactions of the Royal Historical Society* 13 (2003): 262–72; Nelson, *Jesuits*, 114–18.

57. Maurice Descotes, *Histoire de la critique dramatique en France* (Paris: Narr, 1982), 24–28.

58. *Regi christianissimo agonothetae munificentissimo Adonias: Tragoedia dabitur in theatrum Claromontanum Societatis Jesu* (Paris, 1648); Gustave Dupont-Ferrier, *Du Collège de Clermont au Lycée Louis-le-Grand* (Paris: Boccard, 1921), 1:289.

The elaborate poster advertising this performance, which included illustrations and a detailed plot summary, demonstrates that this play fully adhered to contemporary neoclassical rules for tragedy. Illustrations of students dressed in both male and female costumes and represented in contemplative and graceful postures suggest that the Jesuit performance will be a refined form of entertainment designed for audiences who enjoy the professional troupes at the Hôtel de Bourgogne. Unlike early Jesuit productions, *Adonias*, though thoroughly Christian in its message, is neoclassical in its form, resembling contemporary French tragedies. The play is divided into scenes and acts; it dramatizes a single action and takes place in a single day and in a single location; its focus is narrow, with the dramatic tension deriving from the central characters' psychological and moral dilemmas— Solomon's decision to have Adonias killed is presented as a difficult but necessary act with tragic repercussions. *Adonias* is also notable for its *bienséance*: whereas in earlier Jesuit plays God's judgment and the torments of Hell are portrayed violently and concretely, in *Adonias* the main character's death is not depicted; all the audience sees is Adonias's corpse, which is brought on stage in the last scene for Abishag to grieve over. Abishag herself, though a young, nubile woman, is presented as an active individual with a voice of her own who is allowed to express her passion for Adonias, if only at the moment when she mourns for him. For a Parisian theatergoer, the Jesuits' performance would have seemed a delicate treatment of a tragic Old Testament tale that conformed to contemporary standards of the commercial neoclassical theater.

Although the seventeenth-century Jesuit theatrical repertoire is vast, the order's plays address a relatively narrow and homogeneous set of religious themes. The dramas depict either tragic stories of heresy or heroic tales of faith and Christian justice. These plays, which present the optimistic theology of the Jesuits and stress the importance of public virtue and the individual's ability to triumph over sin, dramatize the same theological messages that were presented in the Jesuits' public sermons.[59] Judging from the hundreds of theater programs that remain today, the Jesuits drew from a number of sources for their story lines: the Old Testament, ancient history, classical mythology, and contemporary religious and political events. As the century wore on, the narratives dramatized in these plays tended to be more secular, except in smaller towns, where hagiography and overt anti-Protestant polemic still were to be found on the stage. A series of performances in Dijon demonstrates the variety of topics addressed by the Jesuits: in 1640, students performed a tragedy titled *Nobunaga*, drawn from recent Japanese history, in which missionaries' efforts to convert the local population end in disaster;

59. Brendan Thomas Scott, "Jesuit Theater in Paris, 1660–1740," Ph.D. diss., Princeton University, 1993, 184–89; André Stegmann, "Le rôle des Jésuites dans la dramaturgie française du début du XVIIe siècle," in Jacquot, Konigson, and Oddon, *Dramaturgie et société*, 2:448–51.

FIGURE 7. Jesuit students performing Act 4 of the tragedy *Adonias*. Detail from theater program of *Regi christianissimo agonothetae munificentissimo Adonias*, Paris, 1648. (Source: Bibliothèque Nationale de France, Réserve YF-2614)

the following year, the Jesuits presented a comedy about the wrongheaded religious practices of the Calvinists; in 1648, the Prince of Condé's military triumphs were explored in a tragedy titled *Lyderix*, ostensibly about a seventh-century Burgundian prince; and in 1649 the students put on a tragicomedy titled *Vulfran, or Christian Theology Victorious over Infidelity*.[60]

The range of literary genres embraced by the Jesuits reflects both their training as humanists and their interest in contemporary literary developments. The first generation of Jesuits, educated in mid-sixteenth-century Paris at the height of humanist influence, embraced classical theatrical genres as long as they were purged of pagan spirituality and immoral references; indeed in Dijon, before the Jesuits' exile in 1595, the order's library even contained a copy of Terence's *Comedies*, though no doubt for the inspiration of the instructor who wrote the plays rather than for the students themselves. Members of the order were always interested in literary issues: both Father Donati and Father Galluzzi wrote literary treatises in French, studies that contributed to the definition of neoclassical tragedy during the 1630s when it was being debated in Paris literary circles.[61]

Although the direct impact of these theoretical works outside the classroom is difficult to assess, enough of their former students became secular playwrights to suggest that the teachers' approach to literature influenced the pupils' own adult writing. Among the first generation of French neoclassical playwrights in the 1630s, both Pierre Corneille and Jean Rotrou had attended Jesuit collège in their youth, and some of their later plays—Corneille's *Sertorius*, for example—may well have been based on earlier Jesuit productions. By midcentury, some Jesuit scholars certainly enjoyed the commercial theater: Father de la Rue, writing to his friend Corneille, notes that "thanks to you, the license of the stage has been restrained; good taste has replaced it and the theater offers an innocent pleasure, music to even the most severe ears."[62] De la Rue's admiration suggests that Jesuit educators may well have encouraged their students to read Corneille's plays. During the eighteenth century, when Jesuit theater reached its most *mondain*, Jesuit

---

60. Dainville, *Éducation*, 504–5; Desgraves, *Répertoire*, 52–53; Jacques Hennequin, "Théâtre et société dans les pièces du collège au XVIIe siècle (1641–71)," in Jacquot, Konigson, and Oddon, *Dramaturgie et société*, 2:459.

61. Father Donati, *L'art poétique* (1630); Father Galluzzi, *Restitution de l'ancienne tragédie* (1631); Marylin Perrin, "Aux origines d'une bibliothèque: Les livres des Jésuites de Dijon en 1595," Dijon Technical University, 1982; Compère, *Collège au lycée*, 76–77. French Jesuit authors also wrote many of the most important treatises on dance of the ancien régime period. Judith Rock, *Terpsichore at Louis-le-Grand: Baroque Dance on a Jesuit Stage in Paris* (St. Louis, Mo.: Institute of Jesuit Sources, 1996), 17–18.

62. Father de la Rue, as quoted in Ernest Boysse, *Le théâtre des Jésuites* (Paris: H. Vaton, 1880; reprint, Geneva: Slatkine, 1970), 93; Joseph de Jouvancy, *De la manière d'apprendre et d'enseigner. De ratione discendi et docendi*, trans. H. Ferté (Paris: Hachette, 1892), 53; Charles Brand, "Corneille et les Jésuites: Un poème inédit," *XVIIe Siècle* 53 (2001): 545–49; Lebègue, *Études*, 2:80; Stegmann, "Rôle," 2:452–54.

students even performed adaptations of Molière's and Corneille's plays before public audiences.[63]

The growing importance of interludes in Jesuit productions, particularly the dominance of the ballet, suggests that the Jesuits were taking their cue not only from public commercial theater but also from cultural fashions at the king's court. Although neoclassical tragedies and comedies had achieved some prestige by the 1640s, writing plays was still considered a less noble pursuit than writing poetry. If pressed to contribute to a theatrical production for an important marriage or royal entry, court poets from Ronsard to Malherbe wrote not neoclassical plays but poems to accompany a ballet.[64] During the sixteenth and early seventeenth century, it was the poetry in the ballet that was its most significant element, but by the 1620s it had evolved into a genre that highlighted ever more complicated dance steps that were nevertheless possible for skilled amateurs to execute. Some court ballets were lewd and playful confections performed at Carnival: professional actors and members of the court put on satirical ballets that mocked the court as well as various Parisian estates. There is a notorious engraving of Louis XIV as a young man performing in one of these ballets, but even the somber Louis XIII actively participated in elaborate ballet productions during his youth in the 1610s and 1620s. Ballet was the quintessential court dance: it was assumed that commoners uninstructed in the ways of the court would not possess the skill or beauty to master the art.[65]

The Jesuits adapted this courtly genre to reflect the ideals of Christian civility, abandoning the playful satirical side of the ballet and instead seeking to demonstrate their students' good taste and physical prowess.[66] Training in music was a traditional component of French parish schools, and the Jesuits adapted it to the collège curriculum. During the sixteenth century, Father Maggio urged that the students' musical performances be limited to singing solemn or sacred songs to mark Christian holidays, but in the seventeenth

---

63. Brockliss, *French Higher Education*, 169–70.
64. Margaret M. McGowan, *L'art du ballet de cour en France (1581–1643)* (Paris: CNRS, 1963), 49; Christopher Smith, ed., "Part One: 1550–1630," in *French Theatre in the Neo-Classical Era, 1550–1789*, ed. William D. Howarth (Cambridge: Cambridge University Press, 1997), 91–99; Frances Amelia Yates, *The French Academies of the Sixteenth Century* (London: Warburg Institute, 1947; reprint, London: Routledge, 1988), 236–74.
65. Victor Fournel, *Les contemporains de Molière* (Paris: Firmin Didot, 1863–67; reprint, Geneva: Slatkine, 1967), 2:177–85; William L. Wiley, *The Early Public Theatre in France* (Cambridge, Mass.: Harvard University Press, 1960), 302n7; Maurice Magendie, *La politesse mondaine et les théories de l'honnêteté en France au XVIIe siècle, de 1600 à 1660* (Paris: Felix Alcan, 1925), 79–84.
66. These precepts were codified by the Jesuits in the early eighteenth century. See Angelica Goodden, *Actio and Persuasion: Dramatic Performance in Eighteenth-Century France* (Oxford: Clarendon Press, 1986), 113–14. See also Robert Lowe, "Les représentations en musique dans les collèges de Paris et de province (1632–1757)," *Revue d'Histoire du Théâtre* 15 (1963): 119–26; Pierre Guillot, *Les Jésuites et la musique: le collège de la Trinité à Lyon, 1565–1762* (Liège: Margada, 1991). Rock, *Terpsichore*, passim.

century music was gradually integrated into the students' theatrical performances, and several collèges employed musicians and dance masters.[67] Unlike sixteenth-century festive societies, whose performances and processions often included bawdy and suggestive dancing, the Jesuits made sure that all dance, even movements characterizing vulgar or drunken figures, conformed to the ideals of Christian civility. Father Le Jay tells students that if they portray joy on the stage, "then the dance should be lively and nimble, . . . the feet, in their repeated jumps, should seem to hardly touch the earth . . . . if you have cause to appear like fools or drunkards, . . . the turmoil, the incoherence of their gestures and their steps [should] express the distress of their minds."[68] Unlike the comic dramatization of gluttony and selfishness in sixteenth-century farces, which seems to have involved a joyful sense of release, Jesuit dance sought to represent spiritual states that were clearly moralized. For the Jesuits the ballet was the very antithesis of farce. Far from celebrating the grotesque and earthy sides of human nature, the ballet enabled students to demonstrate what they had learned from their civility manuals. Whereas farce played on the impossibility of consistent Christian obedience and the fluidity of personal identity, which is always being subverted by bodily needs and appetites, ballet sought to capture permanent moral truths through the graceful movement of the human body. In so doing, the theater developed by the Jesuits demonstrated for the audience both the moral purity and the cultural sophistication of their students.[69]

The introduction of musical interludes into a neoclassical play was not unique to Jesuit performance. A performance involving several genres was commonplace in this period, when an afternoon's entertainment traditionally ended with a light comedy or farce. Although the Jesuits avoided farce, they did perform comedies, musical interludes, and eventually operas. By the mid-seventeenth century, such interludes might not only begin and end Jesuit performances but also mark the divisions between the acts of a single play. In 1642, to give an elaborate example, students of the Collège de Clermont, the Jesuit collège in Paris, performed two intertwined plays for Louis XIII: a Latin tragedy called *Ungodliness Subdued: Valens, Emperor of the Orient, Tragedy* and a second piece, *Royal Action*, which was seemingly unrelated to the story of the emperor but whose individual acts alternated with those of the tragedy.[70] In the first play, Valens, emperor of Rome in the late fourth century, refuses to renounce his heretical understanding of Christianity and is punished for his sins through military defeat and the breakdown of the empire; in the allegorical interlude—the *Royal Action* part of the performance—two

---

67. Lefebvre, *Théâtre des Jésuites*, 3; Rochemonteix, *Collège*, 4:187–89.
68. Father le Jay, as quoted in Boysse, *Théâtre*, 52–53.
69. Rock, *Terpsichore*, 13–27.
70. *L'impieté domptée, Valens empereur d'Orient, tragedie pour la distribution des prix que le Roy a fondez a perpetuité dans le College de Clermont, août 1642.*

pagan gods debate the virtues of Louis XIII. These two story lines seem at first to be arbitrarily juxtaposed. In the second act of *Valens*, the merciless emperor decides to kill his enemy's son and refuses his own son's appeal to become a true Christian; in the second act of *Royal Action*, which directly follows these gruesome and regrettable events, Mars and Apollo debate whether it is possible for a single monarch to be great both at war and in the arts. Apollo is skeptical that such qualities could be found in one man, but Mars decides to offer his service to the "first among the world's monarchs," Louis XIII.[71] In the final scene of the tragedy, Valens dies unrepentant as his empire breaks apart under the pressure of invading Visigoths. In the final scene of the *Action*, Apollo is convinced of the French king's virtue, and the two gods decide to visit the king, who happens at this moment to be attending a performance at the Collège de Clermont. The two plays at first seem to have little in common, but by the end of the performance the parallels would have been obvious.

This double-bill performance in 1642 was not unusual, serving both to disseminate the Jesuits' theological ideas and to engage in the political deference expected by Louis XIII as absolute monarch. The tragic story line illustrated some of the main principles of Jesuit theology and provided a cautionary tale to those who might wander from the true faith. In particular, Valens's tragic decision to turn away from the Christianity of the Catholic Church illustrated the importance of free will in Jesuit theology, one of its central tenets: with the help of God's grace, an individual could overcome the vulnerability to sin through good actions and prayer. Many heroes of Jesuit dramas were individuals whose choice whether or not to embrace Christianity is shown to have had a profound impact on their lives and the lives of those around them. Valens was nominally a Christian, but he adhered to a particular interpretation of Christ's divinity called Arianism, often shorthand for Protestantism in Jesuit theatricals.[72] Confronted with right teaching, Valens fails to realize his error, and his tragic end is a warning that such a failure of intellectual self-examination can result in disaster. Catholic audiences would have recognized Valens's example as an invitation to ensure their own salvation by renewing their faith and guarding vigilantly against theological error.[73]

In contrast, the *Royal Action*, which is a typical interlude in a Jesuit play, illustrates how the Jesuits strengthened their relationship to the monarchy through outright, shameless flattery. Louis XIII, skilled in arts and war alike and worthy of being served by the gods, is certainly above the criticism of mere mortals. Such interludes often use historical or mythological themes to glorify the arrival of a dignitary, the birth of a dauphin, or a

71. Ibid., 6.
72. Rock, *Terpsichore*, 142–43.
73. Scott, "Jesuit Theater," 161–68.

recent military triumph. Though the allegory is not always as transparent as the 1642 *Action*, the relevance of the stage action to contemporary events is often clarified for the audience by the printed theater program.[74] In the 1642 performance the contrast between Valens the heretic and the heroic Catholic monarch is implied rather than stated—the audience was no doubt expected to know that unlike Valens, Louis XIII was known to guarantee his orthodoxy and his personal religious engagement by keeping a Jesuit as his personal confessor—but many other Jesuit plays are more explicit. In the 1622 ballet produced in Lyon and described at the beginning of this chapter and in Jesuit plays from the early 1680s urging Louis XIV to abrogate the terms of the Edict of Nantes, the Jesuits made it clear that the French monarch must be an orthodox Catholic in order to rule by divine right. Not only for the Jesuits but also indeed for most political theorists of the seventeenth century, the legitimacy and authority of the French monarch were inseparable from his devotion to Roman Catholicism: the Bourbon monarchy was consistently celebrated in explicitly Catholic terms. What the Jesuits' plays reveal is how broadly this new conception of the monarchy had already penetrated among the urban bourgeoisie by the 1630s and 1640s. Through their student theater, the Jesuits disseminated an absolutist rhetoric about the Catholic Bourbon monarchy to a wide segment of the educated French elite, and they used this rhetoric to defend a militant Catholic agenda.

By the middle of the seventeenth century, Jesuit theater evolved toward increasingly secular themes and plots. Not only were Jesuit tragedies less obviously models of Christian teaching, but Latin tragedy itself, once the cornerstone of an evening's performance, was gradually being supplemented, interrupted, or replaced by secular comedies and interludes in French.[75] Both the Jesuits and their rivals noted this change with dismay. Whereas during the Wars of Religion, Huguenots and secular authorities alike were suspicious of collège theater, by the mid-seventeenth century few public commentators questioned the value of student theater as an educational tool. The Jesuits' critics were, however, quick to accuse the order's students of performing in too worldly a style. In Reims, where the university and the Jesuit collège were at odds concerning the Jesuits' incorporation into the university, its rectors twice complained about Jesuit student theater, protesting in 1617 and 1631 that Jesuit theatrical performances were too profane and had maligned members of the university.[76] Jansenist writers accused the Jesuits of having brought commercial actors

---

74. H. M. C. Purkis, "Quelques observations sur les intermèdes dans le théâtre des Jésuites en France," *Revue d'Histoire du Théâtre* 18 (1966): 190–91; Rock, *Terpsichore*, 31.
75. Dainville, *Éducation*, 506–17; Purkis, "Quelques observations," 182–98.
76. E. Cauly, *Histoire du collège des Bons-Enfants de l'Université de Reims, depuis son origine jusqu'à ses récentes transformations* (Reims: F. Michaud, 1885), 317–28; Delattre, *Établissements*, 4:297, 317.

to the Collège de Clermont to instruct students rehearsing a performance. Other prominent theologians, such as Bossuet, deplored the money wasted on costumes and props at the expense of moral teaching.[77] Although all these critics had self-serving reasons for undermining the Jesuits, throughout the seventeenth century members of the order echoed such concerns in private letters and in annual reports. In 1683, the Jesuit father Jouvancy publicly revealed such concerns in his educational handbook *On the Method of Learning and Teaching*.[78] Jouvancy deplored the elaborate sets, expensive costumes, and excessive energies that were devoted to the theater in many of France's Jesuit collèges and warned against the common practice of allowing students to represent female characters on the stage. Yet despite such criticisms, student theater became an increasingly important element of the Jesuit curriculum during the eighteenth century, by which time humanities and rhetoric students were spending several months preparing for each performance.

Urban elites were enthusiastic enough about Jesuit theater to give it considerable financial support. The court gazetteer Loret noted in his *Historical Muse* that Louis XIV and over seven thousand other spectators attended the summer courtyard production of *Gasto Fuxensis* at the Collège de Clermont in 1655. Jesuit theater had achieved such fame that audience members in Paris sometimes even paid admission.[79] Urban elites in the provinces also invested in Jesuit theater. During the first half of the seventeenth century, several provincial collèges, including those at Bordeaux, Dijon, La Flèche, Pont-à-Mousson, Rouen, and Reims, constructed a *salle d'action* for theatrical performances within the collège buildings. Although during the summer performers could use the school's enclosed courtyard, during the winter the *salles d'action* provided a more convenient, not to say prestigious, acting space. In Rouen, where the theater's dimensions were some 25 meters by 5 meters, the room could accommodate an audience of over a hundred. Even in smaller towns like Tulle and Hesdin, audiences during the 1620s sometimes numbered in the hundreds. City councils sometimes helped defray the cost of these expensive buildings: in Avignon, the council, after debating the issue, concluded that a gracious collège building would enhance the city's prestige. Even in cities where no new theater hall was constructed, Jesuit theater performance by the 1620s no longer took place on the street: a classroom, the chapel, or even a château would instead be appropriated for

77. Dupont-Ferrier, *Collège*, 1:298; Phillips, "Théâtre scolaire," 202–3, 221–13.
78. Jouvancy, *Manière*, 54–58; Dupont-Ferrier, *Collège*, 1:298.
79. *La muse historique, ou recueil des Lettres en vers, contenant les nouvelles du temps, écrites à Son Altesse Mlle de Longueville, par le sieur Loret: 4 mai 1650–28 mars 1665* (Paris: C. Chenault, 1658), Aug. 21, 1655; C. J. Gossip, "Le décor du théâtre au collège des Jésuites à Paris au XVIIe siècle," *Revue d'Histoire du Théâtre* 33 (1981): 28, 37; John Lough, *Paris Theatre Audiences in the Seventeenth and Eighteenth Centuries* (Oxford: Oxford University Press, 1957), 82.

the afternoon's performance.[80] The move away from open-air performances to elaborate indoor venues demonstrates that the Jesuits' aims for student theater had changed over the decades: they were less interested in converting the masses to purified Tridentine Catholicism than in flattering the elite parents of their students.

Along with the new *salles d'action*, Jesuit theater now required expensive and elaborate sets and costumes. Particularly for the ballet performances, frequent changes of scenes—from the emperor's palace to a scene of pastoral bliss—required complex machines. In 1659, when the students of Bordeaux's Collège de la Madeleine performed the ballet *The Olive of Peace* before Louis XIV, the stage set consisted of five arcades, each depicting a cardinal virtue: Religion, Justice, Prudence, Clemency, and Force. Over these arcades hung a balustrade garnished with friezes and emblems. The students' costumes, financed by their parents, could sometimes cost as much as twenty livres, a substantial sum considering that a single afternoon's performance sometimes required as many as two hundred different costumes.[81] By the mid-seventeenth century, Jesuit student performances did less to inspire common city residents to attend confession than they did to demonstrate to urban notables the compatibility between Christian faith and royal office.

In allowing this transformation to take place, Jesuit teachers were not carelessly flouting the order's rules but following through with other aspects of their pedagogy. Specifically, the Jesuits' development of emulation as a central element of their educational program encouraged the students to perform elaborate politically engaged interludes rather than dry neoclassical morality tales. The Jesuits sought to show the local elites, who paid for the collèges and whose sons attended them, that their investment had paid off: their offspring had been turned into not only solid Catholics who could speak and read classical Latin but also sophisticated young men who could perform a ballet as well as a courtier. Producing visibly cultivated sons was a way for the elite in provincial cities, where so many of these students were educated, to erase the social distance between themselves and the king's court. Jesuit theater provided a highly visible stage on which to display this cultivation. It was also, however, a form of imitation that provided much less opportunity for the expression of local culture and local political concerns than had the festivities of the Renaissance.

Emulation was a key principle of all humanist educational theory, but it had a particular resonance for Jesuit educators. The humanist system

---

80. Cauly, *Histoire*, 337; Dainville, *Éducation*, 482, 484–85; Gossip, "Décor," 30–31; Charles Mazouer, *La vie théâtrale à Bordeaux des origines à nos jours*, vol. 1, *Des origines à 1789*, ed. Henri Lagrave (Paris: CNRS, 1985), 81.

81. Dupont-Ferrier, *Collège*, 1:297; Fouqueray, *Histoire*, 3:336–38; Rochemonteix, *Collège*, 4:195. The tragedy *Duus Ludovicus* (Reims, 1641) required 117 different roles, and the interlude required another 86. See Hennequin, "Théâtre," 2:461, fol. 11.

of education encouraged students to learn from the example of classical authors, emulating—that is, imitating, learning from, and ultimately bettering—the classics. Sixteenth-century collège and university instructors across western Europe encouraged their students to imitate classical style, rhetoric, and tropes, and to use these skills in their own compositions and later in their public lives.[82] Emulation was also considered an important element in specifically Christian education, a way of encouraging students to seek spiritual perfection. Jesuit educators had accordingly always used emulation as a pedagogical tool in their classrooms. In monthly recitals and debates conducted in the great hall, rhetoric and humanities students recited poems or debated an assigned passage of text. These exercises were presented for the benefit of the younger students, and the topics were chosen to encourage them to seek a greater perfection in God. Classical texts mediated by advanced students were thus intended to inspire the younger boys to moral rectitude and Christian devotion.[83]

Emulation as practiced by the Jesuits was both public and competitive. Although daily classroom debates usually took place while the teacher was busy correcting written assignments, the monthly recitals and the practice of posting students' poems on the classroom walls make clear that imitating the classics also involved bettering one's peers. At end of the year, students sat examinations in Latin and Greek, which were graded blind by both the teachers and a prominent outsider and then ranked, and prizes were awarded to the top students in each class. The award ceremonies were elaborate affairs, held at the end of the school year in August before a large audience, and the event brought the best students—the students whose example would presumably inspire their peers—to the attention of the collège and the civic community.[84] Because the local elite usually paid for the prizes, they were invited, and these ceremonies evolved into major civic celebrations. By the beginning of the seventeenth century, student theatrical productions became a regular element of these prize-giving ceremonies.

The point of this kind of publicity was to demonstrate the merits of the Jesuits' students to the wider community. Merit, like honor, was a quality

82. Anthony Grafton and Lisa Jardine, *From Humanism to the Humanities: Education and the Liberal Arts in Fifteenth- and Sixteenth-Century Europe* (London: Duckworth, 1986), 1–28; Howard Weinbrott, "'An Ambition to Excel': The Aesthetics of Emulation in the Seventeenth and Eighteenth Centuries," *Huntington Library Quarterly* 48 (1985): 121–39. See also Ann Moss, *Printed Commonplace-Books and the Structure of Renaissance Thought* (Oxford: Clarendon Press, 1996).
83. Compère, *Collège au lycée*, 83; Dupont-Ferrier, *Collège*, 1:284. The Jesuit practice of emulation was rejected by the Jansenists at their Port-Royal collège. See Snyders, *Pédagogie*, 53; *Ratio studiorum*, item 85; François Lebrun, "Un aspect de la pédagogie jésuite: Contrôle des connaissances et examens d'après la 'Ratio Studiorum,'" in Demerson, Dompnier, and Regond, *Jésuites parmi les hommes*, 385–94.
84. *Ratio studiorum*, item 319, 322; Ernest Gaullieur, *Histoire du Collège de Guyenne* (Paris: Sandoz et Fischbacher, 1874), 416–17; Desgraves, *Répertoire*, 35, 70.

that had traditionally been imparted by blood, not by education. The traditional French nobility assumed that only they possessed those qualities necessary for public service to the king. The possibility that others might be worthy of such a calling was a matter hotly debated during this period, when nonnoble *officiers* were taking on more royal commissions as administrators and tax collectors. For families hoping to advance their sons' careers in royal administration, a collège education was not only a necessary prerequisite for further studies in law but also a way of demonstrating the student's mastery of cultural capital—a familiarity with high culture and modern ideas of public comportment—that had previously been acquired only through exposure at the king's court.[85] Through public display of their students' literary cultivation and good manners, the Jesuits demonstrated that their students were of sufficient moral, cultural, and social standing to be worthy of public service. Honorable theatrical performance for members of the urban elite no longer involved participation in arms-bearing processions that demonstrated the city's corporate privileges in bawdy farces. By the mid-seventeenth century, what needed to be cultivated in young men was a discourse of subservience to monarchical authority as well as the bodily self-discipline and grace that civility manuals had made clear were expected of successful courtiers.[86] Such behaviors were propagated by the Jesuits and assimilated by the urban elites in an effort to minimize their distance from political power. For the Jesuits, their students' theatrical performances helped to deflect the criticism of those who still questioned the order's allegiance to the French crown; for provincial urban elites, most of whom had not achieved even nominal noble status, participation in such events demonstrated their achievement of the cultural if not the legal status of the traditional nobility.

Understanding these motivations makes clear why the Jesuits' student theater so consistently broke the *Rules*. Jesuit educators were certainly interested in creating better Christians and in protecting their students from the corruption of cabarets, gaming, and theatergoing. But they also needed to expose them in a public arena in order to demonstrate, to the local elite and to the king, the excellence of the products their system was turning out.

85. Pierre Bourdieu, *Distinction: A Social Critique of the Judgment of Taste*, trans. Richard Nice (New York: Routledge and Kegan Paul, 1984), 70–73; Jonathan Dewald, *Aristocratic Experience and the Origins of Modern Culture: France, 1570–1715* (Berkeley: University of California Press, 1993), 79–94; Nira Kaplan, "A Changing Culture of Merit: French Competitive Examinations and the Politics of Selection, 1750–1820," Ph.D. diss., Columbia University, 1999, 26–39; Mark Motley, *Becoming a French Aristocrat: The Education of the Court Nobility, 1580–1715* (Princeton: Princeton University Press, 1990), 96–112, 209–11; Ellery Schalk, *From Valor to Pedigree: Ideas of Nobility in France in the Sixteenth and Seventeenth Centuries* (Princeton: Princeton University Press, 1986), 174–201; Jay M. Smith, *The Culture of Merit: Nobility, Royal Service, and the Making of Absolute Monarchy in France, 1600–1789* (Ann Arbor: University of Michigan Press, 1996), 164–80; Snyders, *Pédagogie*, 146.

86. Orest Ranum, "Courtesy, Absolutism, and the Rise of the French State, 1630–1660," *Journal of Modern History* 52 (1980):448–51.

Local elites approved this social program, as indicated by their willing-ness to attend Jesuit performances even when the king was not visiting. By the 1620s, Jesuit student performances were occurring with increasing frequency not only in Paris but also in major provincial cities. Although in 1630 Father Vitelleschi complained about the growing number of per-formances and urged principals to limit them to twice a year, by midcen-tury provincial theater programs suggest that three or four performances a year was the norm.[87] Performances regularly took place at Carnival and at the August prize-givings, but Jesuit students also acted at special civic and religious events, much as festive societies had done a century earlier. In Bordeaux, as early as 1612, Jesuit students at the Collège de la Madeleine performed before a "multitude of the nobility" a short play about the de-sired marriage of the young king, Louis XIII, to the Princess Anne, daughter of the king of Spain; in 1615, when the king himself visited the city, the students presented a series of tableaux vivants in his honor; in 1622, they marked Loyola's canonization with a weeklong series of events that culmi-nated in the performance of a tragicomedy recounting his life story. Louis XIII's triumphs over the Huguenots at La Rochelle, the birth of his first son, the future Louis XIV, and the funerals of local dignitaries were other important events celebrated by Jesuit student performances all over France. Both because city councilors requested the actors' services and because the Jesuits were eager to demonstrate their loyalty to the Bourbon monarchy through their students' grace and learning, they seized these opportunities to participate in civic ceremonial.[88]

From a form of Christian propaganda designed to stem the threat of her-esy, Jesuit student theater evolved into a form of entertainment that demon-strated the students' cultural sophistication while convincing audiences that Christianity was compatible with civility. For the pleasure and instruction of the king and urban elites alike, Jesuit plays articulated on the civic stage a new vision of the French body politic: salvation was in the hands of the monarch, and glory was the destiny of French kings who realized the au-thority that God had granted to them. Actively embraced by city councils throughout France as a welcome alternative to traditional festive societies, Jesuit theater symbolized the urban elites' new self-conscious identification with Parisian theatrical trends as well as their enthusiastic participation in the discourse of absolutism increasingly demanded by the monarchy. Con-firming the king's sense of his own omnipotence, Jesuit theater encouraged the convergence between Louis XIV's version of absolute rule and religious intolerance later in his reign.

87. Father Vitelleschi, as cited in Dainville, *Éducation*, 504; Desgraves, *Répertoire*, 63–64, 72, 137; Rochemonteix, *Collège*, 4:184.
88. Mazouer, *Vie théâtrale*, 1:81–85; *Les Champs Elyziens, ou la réception du roy Louys XIII au collège de Bourdeaus de la Companie de Jésus, le huictième de novembre 1615* (Bordeaux: Simon Millanges, 1615).

It is difficult to say just how much the combination of Jesuit theater and a new kind of reformed Catholic piety contributed to the demise of satirical farce. They were admittedly not the only factors: though the Jesuits both contributed to and drew from the Parisian fashion for neoclassical tragedy, urban elites had other ways of learning about the rising prestige of this new genre: royal gazettes and published plays, for example. But their live experience of neoclassical tragedy would have been limited. Professional troupes performed only occasionally in French provincial cities in the seventeenth century; indeed, most provincial cities did not even build a dedicated public theater until the mid-eighteenth century—Toulouse in 1740, Bordeaux in 1738—and did not boast a permanent acting company until even later. It was amateur actors who performed in the provinces at Carnival and civic events, and by the early seventeenth century the amateur actors were Jesuit students.[89] The high visibility of these students, who performed three or four times each year in a provincial city, suggests that it was they who would have had the greatest impact on local theatrical taste and that it was probably their prestige that eventually did away with farce. The financial support of the urban notables, which had a century earlier gone to groups like the Basoche, now went to the Jesuits, through regular disbursements from the city council and contributions from the students' parents. Urban elites' patronage of Jesuit theater marks a fundamental change in their concept of public propriety, and this change helped lay the cultural foundation for the consolidation of absolutism as a discursive and a political system after 1661.

89. Lebègue, *Études*, 2:76; Mazouer, *Vie théâtrale*, 1:167; Robert Schneider, *Public Life in Toulouse, 1463–1789: From Municipal Republic to Cosmopolitan City* (Ithaca: Cornell University Press, 1989), 336. See also Max Fuchs, *La vie théâtrale en province au XVIII siècle* (Geneva: Droz, 1933), 19–34; *Entrées royales et fêtes populaires*, 192–98; Christiane Jeanselme, "Les représentations d'écoliers au Collège Royale Bourbon d'Aix-en-Provence," *Provence Historique* 40 (1990): 145.

Conclusion

Gédéon Tallemant des Réaux, a notorious Parisian gossip writing in the mid-1650s, did his best to pronounce the death of farce. In a discourse about Parisian theatrical developments after 1600, Tallemant des Réaux argued that crude farce players like Gaultier Garguille had been replaced by honorable actors, whose performances were noble exercises in elocution. Farce dominated the stage, he suggested, during a less civilized era, when "respectable women never attended" the theater, partly because the violent rabble in the parterre made it dangerous to do so.[1] Yet for all his celebration of the neoclassical theater, even Tallemant des Réaux had to admit that a very skilled farce player, like the popular actor Jodelet who performed at the Hôtel de Marais, could still attract a following: "Jodelet, for a naive joker, is a good actor; there is no longer any farce except at the Marais, where he is, and it is because of him that there is any at all."[2] Our chronicler also lets slip that Italian commedia dell'arte troupes had returned to the Parisian stage by the mid-1640s and were again entertaining theatergoers with their physical humor.

Farce exhibits a remarkable tenacity. As late as the mid-seventeenth century, Parisian audiences still enjoyed ending an evening at the theater with some slapstick humor. In 1658, only a few years after Tallemant des Réaux wrote his *Historiettes*, Molière and his troupe arrived in Paris to be received at Louis XIV's court. Although Molière tried to impress the king with his skills as a tragic actor, the king was unmoved until the troupe's final number,

---

1. Gédéon Tallemant des Réaux, *Les historiettes*, ed. M. de Monmerqué and Paulin Paris (Paris: J. Techener, 1858), 7:171; Dominique Bertrand, *Dire le rire à l'âge classique: Représenter pour mieux contrôler* (Aix-en-Provence: Publications de l'Université de Provence, 1995), 87–93, 240–50. Tallemant des Réaux's claims for farce's demise are based on a notorious comment in Scarron's *Roman comique* (1651) that farce was dead.
2. Tallemant des Réaux, *Historiettes*, 7:176.

a trifle pulled from its comic repertoire. The farce was new, it was funny, and Molière's Parisian career was launched. Like French kings before him, Louis XIV was an enthusiastic appreciator of farce and certainly did not lead the public away from the genre. For the next fourteen years, Molière competed for audience share with the tragic players at the Hôtel de Bourgogne and for much of this period shared a theater with the resident commedia dell'arte troupe. Although many of the plays for which we remember Molière are sophisticated comedies of ideas, throughout his career the troupe continued to perform his early farces both in the city and at court.[3] As a result, Molière's intellectual contemporaries never took him seriously as a playwright: poet and literary critic Nicolas Boileau decried the vulgarity of his comedy, and a 1670 painting titled *French and Italian Farceurs* portrayed him as the latest incarnation of a performance tradition established by actors like Gros Guillaume half a century earlier.[4] Contemporary reactions to Molière, who was celebrated as a performer and despised as a playwright, reveal the ambivalence of French elites toward farce by the second half of the seventeenth century.

Yet for all the supposed vulgarity and all his debts to both French farce and Italian commedia dell'arte, Molière's plays mark a turning point in French comedy. Stereotypically foppish courtiers and hypocritical priests populate many of these plays, but they do not dominate every scene. Characters develop, domineering fathers sometimes mend their ways, and at the play's conclusion, justice—often, to be sure, the king's justice—is finally served. Molière evokes the world of folly but usually contains it within a neoclassical structure.[5] His plays include physical and sexual humor, but their dialogue does not describe failed erections or excremental activities in the explicit detail that we find in earlier farces. By cleaning up farce a little

3. René Bray, *Molière, homme de théâtre* (Paris: Mercure de France, 1954), 8–10, 108, 247–53; C. E. J. Caldicott, "La cour, la ville et la province: Molière's Mixed Audiences," *Seventeenth-Century French Studies* 10 (1988): 72–87; Roger Chartier, *Forms and Meanings: Texts, Performances, and Audiences from Codex to Computer* (Philadelphia: University of Pennsylvania Press, 1995), 43–82; William D. Howarth, *Molière: A Playwright and His Audience* (Cambridge: Cambridge University Press, 1982), 40–47.

4. Maurice Descotes, *Molière et sa fortune littéraire* (Bordeaux: Ducros, 1970), 1–31; Georges Forestier, "Le classicisme de Molière ou la quête de reconnaissance littéraire," *L'Information Littéraire* 42 (1990): 17–20.

5. Davis Maskell, "Terence, Tabarin and Molière's 'Fouberies de Scapin,'" *French Studies* 56 (2002): 303–15; David Clarke, "'L'école des femmes': Plotting and Significance in a 'Machine à Rire,'" *Seventeenth-Century French Studies* 11 (1989): 119–35; Howarth, *Molière*, 87–105; Harold C. Knutson, "Molière et la satire contre la médecine: Hargne personnelle ou décision de métier?" *XVIIe Siècle* 43 (1991): 127–31; *Farces du Grand Siècle: De Tabarin à Molière, farces et petites comédies du XVIIe siècle*, ed. Charles Mazouer (Paris: Libraire Générale Française, 1992), 20–24; Mitchell Greenberg, *Baroque Bodies: Psychoanalysis and the Culture of French Absolutism* (Ithaca: Cornell University Press, 2001), 22–61; Bernadette Rey-Flaud, *Molière et la farce* (Geneva: Droz, 1996); Philip A. Wadsworth, *Molière and the Italian Theatrical Tradition* (Columbia, S.C.: French Literature Publications, 1977). Regarding Molière's turn from comedy to the *comédie-ballet* at the end of his career, see Bray, *Molière*, 201–2, 253–57; Gérard Defaux, *Molière, ou les métamorphoses du comique: De la comédie morale au triomphe de la folie* (Lexington, Ky.: French Forum, 1980), 289–301.

FIGURE 8. *French and Italian Farceurs*, 1670. Molière can be found at the far left. (Source: Bibliothèque Nationale de France 4-W-1835)

Jodelet   Turlupin   Zel'epben   Molomes   Gros Guillaume   Gauthier-Gargouille   polichinelle   Pantaton   Philippin.   Briguelle.   Trose

Guillot Corju

and folding it into a neoclassical tradition, Molière takes it one step farther away from its festive beginnings. Both Louis XIV's court fool and also a commercial playwright, Molière was writing for audiences who sought amusement not just at Carnival but throughout the calendar year. The theater had become a secular, commercial form of entertainment rather than a comic element in an otherwise solemn civic or religious festival. Unlike the plays put on by many Renaissance festive societies, which defied local magistrates' orders, mocked authorities, and often got away with it, *Tartuffe*, Molière's most satirical work, was censored by the king after only a single private performance and never reached the public stage in its original form.[6] Although Molière's plays are full of social satire, they rarely criticize royal policies or refer to specific political events. The kind of political and religious satire that pointed to identifiable individuals had left the French stage almost a century earlier.

Farce survived, however, as it always will. In every society, in every period, there are comedians who make rueful or mocking jokes about bodily urges and ridicule those in authority. What changes is the social status of those comedians and the contexts in which they are allowed to make such jokes. By the time of Tallemant des Réaux and Molière, French farceurs no longer dominated the stage as they had during the Renaissance. With the exception of Molière's farcelike comedies, no new farces were published in France during the second half of the seventeenth century. By the 1650s, the Basoche had turned into a full-fledged professional corporation that was trying to erase its performance history, and Jesuit collège students were performing neoclassical plays rather than farces for the pleasure of the urban elites and the aristocracy. Farce was not dead, but its place in French society would have been unrecognizable to an early sixteenth-century parlement magistrate or bourgeois. By the beginning of the seventeenth century, farce was put on only by professional actors of marginal social status, and a century later, it was seen only at fairgrounds and boulevard theaters, never at the premiere theaters of Paris.[7]

Farce's gradual exclusion from polite society signals a fundamental religious and political reorientation of French urban elites, the city councilors and urban magistrates who were at the forefront of this cultural transformation.

---

6. François de Dainville, "Les comédiens et le clergé: Une pièce au dossier de "'Tartuffe,'" *Revue d'Histoire du Théâtre* 4 (1948–49): 263–65; Howarth, *Molière*, 195–204; Joan DeJean, *The Reinvention of Obscenity: Sex, Lies, and Tabloids in Early Modern France* (Chicago: University of Chicago Press, 2002), 84–121. Indeed, the very lack of specificity in the satire of the published version of *Tartuffe* later made it an effective weapon in the political debates of the postrevolutionary period. See Sheryl Kroen, *Politics and Theater: The Crisis of Legitimacy in Restoration France, 1815–30* (Berkeley: University of California Press, 2000).

7. Michèle Root-Bernstein, *Boulevard Theater and Revolution in Eighteenth-Century Paris* (Ann Arbor: UMI Research Press, 1984); Robert M. Isherwood, *Farce and Fantasy: Popular Entertainment in Eighteenth-Century Paris* (New York: Oxford University Press, 1986).

During the Renaissance, city notables had been proud to celebrate Catholic festivals by paying a festive society to perform a farce that made fun of clergy and lay sinners alike. The reversals of authority and the sexually explicit nature of dialogue in the farce did not dismay such officials, who nevertheless considered themselves to be good Catholics. During the Wars of Religion, however, their attitude toward bawdy plays rapidly shifted, both because of concerns about public order and because of changes in their own religious sensibilities. Urban elites' identification with the Catholic Reformation caused them to distance themselves from farcical performance, which had become associated with unreformed and "pagan" ritual practices. By the end of the sixteenth century, city officials both in Paris and in the major provincial cities sought to eliminate traditional festive societies or convert them into more pious confraternities. Like urban officials all over Catholic Europe, French elites' religious scruples also informed their decision to invite Jesuit educators into their cities by the end of the sixteenth century. The Jesuits, with their emphasis on religious orthodoxy, classroom order, and civility, taught the urban youth who had once performed farce that in order to be good subjects of the French king they needed to demonstrate grace and deference at all times. The demise of amateur festive societies after 1600 signaled the withdrawal of urban elites from popular culture and makes clear how important a role was played in that process by specifically religious developments. Civility and Christianity were far more closely linked than has previously been recognized.

Changes in theatrical censorship and patronage both reflected and contributed to the gradual consolidation of absolutism in France. During the Renaissance, farcical theater profited from the divided nature of political authority. Although the king was thought of as the head of the body politic, Renaissance French subjects did not interpret this to mean that he held absolute authority in all realms of public life. *Bonnes villes*, jealous of their right to run local affairs with minimal interference, sometimes used farce to send a critical political message to greedy royal tax officials. Farce playing thus contributed to the formation of public opinion and was a political act tolerated and even patronized by urban notables. As their traditional political privileges were increasingly undermined by the Bourbon monarchy after 1600, however, city officials became more wary of irritating the king with audacious theatrical performances. At the same time, many of them—financial officials, parlement magistrates, and even clerks working at the law courts—began to identify with the absolutist state, in large measure because venality granted them financial security and sometimes even a chance to attain noble status.

The Jesuits taught urban elites that a better way to obtain royal favor was to use the discourse of absolutism to their advantage. By celebrating the divine and absolute nature of the French monarchy in their student performances, the Jesuits abandoned the irreverent satire of the farce even as they continued to use the theater as a means of pressing for particular political policies. The urban elites, whose sons attended the Jesuit collèges, signaled their willingness to flatter the monarchy when they commissioned Jesuit students to perform. It is not surprising that this urban notable class adopted the discourse of absolutism decades before the traditional French nobility. Because their power base had been the political autonomy and economic vibrancy of their provincial cities, urban elites were, by the outset of the seventeenth century, more vulnerable and more dependent on the king's favor than were the military nobility. Civility, a code of manners that at once distinguishes the elite from the rabble and demands subservience to the prince, was useful for ambitious urban officials who sought to profit from the consolidation of royal authority.

This repudiation of farce had a direct impact on the youth of the couche moyenne, who had most often performed farce during the Renaissance. These sons of minor royal officials, artisans, and merchants ceased to perform once funding and patronage dried up during the Wars of Religion. Nevertheless, many of them continued to participate in unlicensed popular celebrations, from charivari to bouts of drinking and fighting in the city streets. In fact, fighting at the commercial theaters became a notorious problem, one that city councils combated without success during the seventeenth century. Although such rowdy behavior continued to serve some of its usual social purposes, confirming young men's masculine bravado and allowing them to expose their neighbors' sexual transgressions, much of its traditional political function had been lost: critiques of local and national authority figures no longer played an important role in such antics during the remainder of the ancien régime.[8]

By the middle of the seventeenth century, the French absolutist body politic reigned triumphant. Louis XIV embodied the charismatic glory and the heroism required for absolutism to work: he was able to convince his subjects that obedience to the Sun King would result in prosperity for all. This was not, however, an illusion that could be sustained after his death. In the freer atmosphere of the eighteenth century, the period of the Enlightenment, and the development of a bourgeois public sphere, political and religious debate reemerged. The history of farce playing makes clear that far from silencing dissent, absolutism merely suppressed it for a time. Censorship, though it can shape political culture, is in the long run impossible to enforce, especially in a premodern state. Social and cultural dissent have a tendency

8. Yves-Marie Bercé, *Fête et révolte: Des mentalités populaires du XVIe au XVIIIe siècle: essai* (Paris: Hachette, 1976); J. P. Poussou, "L'agitation étudiante à Bordeaux sous l'ancien régime, spécialement au XVIIIe siècle," *Revue Historique de Bordeaux et du Département de la Gironde* 19 (1970): 79–92; Nicole Pellegrin, *Les bachelleries: Organisations et fêtes de la jeunesse dans le Centre-Ouest XVe–XVIIIe siècles* (Poitiers: Société des Antiquaires de l'Ouest, 1982); Michel Vovelle, *Les métamorphoses de la fête en Provence de 1750 à 1820* (Paris: Aubier, 1976).

to reemerge with a vengeance once the charismatic leader or the political crisis has passed. In France, the burlesque energy and the inversionary political paradigms of farce were picked up by printed pamphlets and acted out in popular bread and tax revolts.[9]

Nevertheless, absolutism had become a political model that other European kings sought to emulate by the early eighteenth century. Envious of the apparent invincibility of the French monarchy, rulers like Peter the Great of Russia and Frederick the Great of Prussia sought to adapt elements of French absolutism to help consolidate their political authority. The adoption of French language and culture was central to the diffusion of absolutist ideals. By the end of the eighteenth century, European cultural sophistication was defined by mastering the French language and imitating French manners. As a result, an understanding of how the French marginalized farce, which was in its heyday an important outlet for political opinion, had implications for states other than France. As the French exported their culture, their savoir faire, and their fashions, they also thereby inspired other elites—nobles in places as far away as Russia and Poland—to distance themselves from their fellow subjects, indeed, to feel themselves essentially superior to the peasants who worked the land. This sense of the cultural gap between upper and lower classes was to have a long history in Europe, inhibiting democracy and free political debate until the late nineteenth century. Insofar as it contributed to this gap in France, the eclipse of satirical farce was a cultural phenomenon that cast a long political shadow over the history of the West.

9. David Garrioch, *The Making of Revolutionary Paris* (Berkeley: University of California Press, 2002); Roger Chartier, *Les origines culturelles de la Révolution française* (Paris: Seuil, 1990); Robert Darnton, *The Forbidden Best-Sellers of Pre-Revolutionary France* (New York: Norton, 1995); Arlette Farge, *Dire et mal dire: L'opinion publique au XVIIIe siècle* (Paris: Seuil, 1992).

Bibliography

Archives Nationales (AN)

PARLEMENT RECORDS

U2000–U2112	Registres de Le Nain
x1a 1482–8393	Conseil records (1486–1663)
x1a 8345	Après-Dinés records
x1a 8356	
x1a 4906–18	Plaidoiries records
x1a 4947	
x1a 4953	
x1a 5073	

MINUTIER CENTRAL (AN MC)

XXXV:373bis	Inventaire of the Confrérie de la Passion
XXXV:377	Confrérie de la Passion documents
X:1–68	
CXXII:367	Documents concerning Parisian actors
XV:16–17	
VIII:562–66	Notary records concerning Nicolas Joubert
VIII:583	
XXIII:280	
XXIV:309	
CV:191	
III:472–91	Notary records concerning rue Michel le Conte
XIII:9	
XIII:20	
XX:166	
LXXII:153	
III:174	Documents concerning *procureurs*, *clercs des procureurs*, and *praticiens*
VI:6	
VII:35	

This bibliography includes archival and printed primary sources only. A full bibliography, including modern secondary works cited in the text, can be found on the Internet by way of the author.

VIII:68
VIII:66–74
XII:46
XIII:19
XVIII:5
XIX:404
LIX:2
CX:93
CXXII:1
CXXII:10

Bibliothèque Nationale (BN)

Coll. Dupuy, 231, fol. 33   letters patent of the Confrérie de la Passion issued
                                     in 1402
Coll. Dupuy, 630, fol. 86   Arrêt concerning actors in Dijon, 1622
Mélanges Colbert, 56, fol. 170v   Letter addressed to actors, ca. 1630
500 Colbert, 92, fol. 201   Documents concerning actors performing at
                                     court
———, 92, fol. 214   17th century actors
———, 94, fol. 235
———, 94, fol. 255
———, 94, fol. 295
———, 488, fol. 329   Burlesque poems about Parlement and Châtelet
———, 488, fol. 464   *Avocats*
———, 488, fol. 488
Coll. Joly de Fleury, 214, 2124   Accounts of the Confrérie de la Passion, 1656–57

Archives d'Assistance Publique de Paris

Fonds Hôpital de la Trinité, 4, fol. 8   Document concerning the Confrérie de la Passion
Fonds Fosseyeux, 58   Pamphlet demanding abrogation of Confrérie de
                                         la Passion, 1631

Archives Départementales Seine-Maritime (Rouen) (ADSM)

1 B 447–1071   Arrêts of the Parlement (1536–1648)
5 E 124   Documents concerning the Basoche
1 B 5470
1 B 5457

Archives Municipales de Rouen/Bibliothèque de Rouen

E 57   Compilations of Rouen Parlement arrêts
Y 137
Y 32
Coll. Leber 2452   Pamphlets of 17th-century farceurs

Archives Municipales de Dijon (AMD)

B 198–306   Deliberations of the Dijon city council (1560–
                                     1667)
G 39   Documents concerning the Basoche
G 46   Documents concerning Dijon printers

Archives Départementales de Gironde (Bordeaux) (ADG)

1 B 81–421   Arrêts of the Parlement (1532–94)
Arrêts 1582–94
H 3142   Collège de la Madeleine admission records (1644–52)

Archives Municipales de Bordeaux

MS 565, 176–78   Unpublished history of the Basoche
Fonds Delpit, MS 436

Bibliothèque de Bordeaux (BM Bordeaux)

MS 1024   Documents concerning the 17th-century confrérie of parlement
                   clerks
MS 369   Extracts from the Bordeaux Parlement's "Registres secrets"
MS 828/5   Unpublished history of Bordeaux

Archives Départementales de la Haute-Garonne (Toulouse) (ADHG)

2 Mi 165–206   Arrêts of the Parlement (1478–1526)
B 57–522   Arrêts of the Parlement (1564–1632)

Printed Sources

L'adieu de Tabarin au peuple de Paris. Paris: P. Rocolet, 1622.
Advertissement du Sieur de Bruscambille sur le voyage d'Espagne. 1615.
Advis de Gros Guillaume sur les affaires de ce temps. Paris, 1619.
L'almanach prophétique du Sieur Tabarin pour l'année 1623. Paris: R. Bretet, 1622.
Apologie de Guillot Gorju. Paris: Michel Blageart, 1634.
L'arrest d'amour donné sur le reiglement requis par les femmes à l'encontre de leurs marys: Par devant l'Abbé des Conards. Paris: Pierre Ménier, 1611.
Les arrests admirables et authentiques du Sieur Tabarin, prononcez en la place Dauphine le 14 jour de ce présent mois. Paris: Lucas Joffu, 1623.
Arrêt de parlement portant règlement donné en faveur des clercs du palais, contre les officiers de la basoche, 26 février 1656.
Arrêt du parlement qui fait défenses au prévôt de Paris de prendre connaissance de ce qui concerne la juridiction de la basoche, 17 février 1640.
Arrêt du parlement qui reçoit l'opposition des officiers de la basoche à la réception d'Et. de Vaulx en la charge de procureur en la cour, 1645.
Auton, Jean d'. *Chroniques de Louis XII.* 4 vols. Edited by René de Maulde La Clavière. Paris: Renouard, 1889–95.
Auvergne, Martial d'. *Les arrets d'amour, nouvellement imprimé.* Paris: Veuve Jean Ruelle, 1585.
Avant-exercice de l'infanterie dijonnoise, du XVI février, 1614, sur l'heureux mariage du Roy. Dijon: Claude Guyot, 1614.
Ballet dansé à Dijon devant monseigneur Le Prince, l'onzième février 1627.
Ballet dansé à Dijon le XXIII janvier 1627, en l'honneur du Roi et de monseigneur Le Prince.
Ballet des sciences et arts liberaux, dancé à Dijon à l'arrivée de Monseigneur le duc d'Anguyen [Louis de Bourbon]. Dijon: Veuve Claude Guyot, [1636].
Le ballet de Turlupin, représenté à Gentilly, devant les Letières du Bois de Vincennes. Nyort, n.d.

Ballet du bureau d'adresse dansé devant Monseigneur le Prince, par Monseigneur le duc d'Enghien le trentième décembre 1640. Dijon: Guy-Anne Guyot, [1641].

Ballets et mascarades de cour, de Henri III à Louis XIV (1581–1652). 6 vols. Edited by Paul Lacroix. Geneva: J. Gay, 1868.

Baude, Henri. *Dictz moraulx pour faire tapisserie.* Edited by Jean-Loup Lemaître. Paris: Diffusion de Boccard, 1988.

——. *Les vers de maître Henri Baude, poète du XVe siècle.* Edited by M. J. Quicherat. Paris: Aubry, 1856.

Beaulieu, Mlle. de. *La première atteinte contre ceux qui accusent les comédies.* Paris: Jean Richer, 1603.

Beauvoy, Jaques de. *L'anti mardi-gras, adressé généralement à toutes les villes de France.* Paris: Isaac Mesnier, 1620.

Bèze, Théodore de. *Histoire ecclésiastique des églises réformées au royaume de France.* Edited by G. Baum, E. Cunitz, and R. Reuss. Paris: Fischbacher, 1883.

Les bignets du Gros Guillaume envoyez à Turlupin et à Gaultier-Garguille, pour leur mardy-gras par le sieur Tripotin. Paris, 1615.

Bouchet, Jean. *Épistres morales et familières du Traverseur.* Edited by M. A. Screech. London: Jonson Reprint, 1969.

La braverie ou réjouissance de 1630, pour la naissance de M. de Conty. Dijon: Nicolas Sprinx, 1630.

[Bréchillet, Étienne], *Resjouissance de l'Infanterie Dijonnoise, pour la venue de Monseigneur le duc d'Anguyen [Louis de Bourbon], le 25 février 1636.* Dijon: Veuve Claude Guyot, [1636].

[Bréchillet, Étienne], *Rejouïssance de l'Infanterie Dijonnoise pour l'entrée de Monsieur le marquis de Tavannes, lieutenant du roi en Bourgogne.* Dijon: Claude Guyot, 1636.

Cest la deduction du sumptueux ordre plaisantz spectacles et magnifiques theatres dressés, et exhibes par les Citoiens de Rouen. Rouen: Robert le Hoy Robert, 1551.

Les Champs Elyziens, ou la réception du roy Louys XIII au collège de Bourdeaus de la Companie de Jésus, le huictième de novembre 1615. Bordeaux: Simon Millanges, 1615.

Chansons de Gaultier Garguille. Edited by Édouard Fournier. Paris: P. Jannet, 1858.

Les clercs du palais, la farce du cry de la bazoche. Edited by Adolphe Fabre. Vienna en Dauphiné: Savigné, 1882.

Collection des meilleurs dissertations, notices et traités particuliers relatifs à l'histoire de France. 20 vols. Edited by J. M. C. Leber. Paris: Dentu, 1838.

Collection des ordonnances des rois de France: Catalogue des actes de François Ier. 10 vols. Paris: Imprimerie Nationale, 1887–1908.

Collerye, Roger de. *Oeuvres.* Edited by Charles d'Héricault. Paris: P. Jannet, 1855.

La confirmation de la paix par l'Infanterie Dijonnoise. Dijon: Claude Guyot, 1613.

Conseil salutaire au Cardinal Mazarin, gasconnade en vers burlesques dediée à Messieurs les officiers de la Basoche du Parlement de Paris. Paris: Veuve Marette, 1652.

Coquillart, Guillaume. *Oeuvres suivies d'oeuvres attribuées à l'auteur.* Edited by M. J. Freeman. Geneva: Droz, 1975.

Correspondance des réformateurs dans les pays de langue française. 9 vols. Edited by A. L. Herminjard. Geneva: H. Georg, 1886.

Crevier, Jean-Baptiste-Louis. *Histoire de l'Université de Paris, depuis son origine jusqu'en l'année 1600.* Paris: Desaint et Saillant, 1761.

De Gaule, André. *Conviction veritable du recit fabuleux divulgué touchant la representation exhibée en face de toute la ville de Lyon au Collège de la Compagnie de Jésus, le 7 d'août, 1607.* Lyon: Abraham Cloquemin, 1607.

De la bienséance de la conversation entre les hommes. La Flèche: Sébastien Chappelet, 1618.

Della Casa, Giovanni. *Le galatée, premièrement composé en italien par I. de La Case et depuis mis en français, latin et espagnol par divers auteurs.* Geneva: Jean de Tournes, 1598.

Description en vers bourguignons de l'ordre tenu en l'Infanterie Dijonnoise pour la mascarade par elle representée à Monseigneur de Bellegarde. Dijon: Jean des Planches, 1610.

De Tournabons. *La misère des clercs des procureurs.* Paris: A. Robinot, 1627.

Deux chroniques de Rouen: 1er des origines à 1544; 2ème de 1559 à 1569. Edited by A. Héron. Rouen: Lestringant, 1900.

Deux moralités de la fin du moyen âge et du temps des Guerres de Religion. Edited by Jean-Claude Aubailly and Bruno Roy. Geneva: Droz, 1990.

Le discours de Bruscambille, avec la description de Conchini Conchino. Paris: Antoine Chapenois, 1617.

Documents du Minutier central concernant l'histoire de la musique (1600–1650). 2 vols. Edited by Madeleine Jurgens. Paris: Documentation Française, 1974.

Du Boulay, César-Égasse. *Historia Universitatis Parisiensis.* 3 vols. Paris: Pierre de Bresche, 1665–73.

Du Tilliot, J. B. L. *Mémoires pour servir à l'histoire de la fête des fous qui se faisait autrefois dans plusieurs églises.* Lausanne: Marc-Michel Bousquet, 1751.

Entrées et réjouissances dans la ville de Dijon. Dijon: Darantière, 1885.

Entrées royales et fêtes populaires à Lyon du XVe au XVIIIe siècles. Lyon: Bibliothèque de la ville de Lyon, 1970.

The Entry of Henri II into Paris, 16 June 1549. Edited by I. D. McFarlane. Binghamton, N.Y.: Center for Medieval and Early Renaissance Studies, 1982.

Facécieuses paradoxes de Bruscambille et autres discours comiques. Rouen: T. Maillard, 1615.

La farce des Théologastres. Edited by Claude Longeon. Geneva: Droz, 1989.

Farces du grand siècle: De Tabarin à Molière, farces et petites comédies du XVIIe siècle. Edited by Charles Mazouer. Paris: Libraire Générale Française, 1992.

Farin, François. *Histoire de la ville de Rouen.* 3 vols. Rouen: J. Hérault, 1668.

Félibien, Michel. *Histoire de la ville de Paris.* Paris: G. Desprez et J. Desessartz, 1725.

Févret, Charles. *De la sédition arrivée en la ville de Dijon le 28 février 1630, et jugement rendu par le Roy sur icelle.* Lyon: I. Barlet, 1630.

Fontanon, Antoine. *Les édicts et ordonnances des Roys de France depvis S. Loys jusques à present.* Paris: Du Puys, 1580.

Gaufreteau, Jean de. *Chronique bordeloise.* 2 vols. Bordeaux: Charles Lefebvre, 1877.

Genethliaque autrement triomphe sur la naissance de Monseigneur le Daufin, par l'Infanterie Dijonnoise le 27 décembre 1601: Dedié à Monseigneur le duc de Biron. Cisteaux: Jean Savine pour Pierre Grangier, 1602.

Gorris, Jean de. *Discours de l'origine, des moeurs, fraudes et impostures des ciarlatans, avec leur descouverte, . . . par I. D. P. M. O. D. R.* Paris: Denis Langlois, 1622.

Gouberville, Gilles de. *Le journal du sire de Gouberville.* Edited by Alexandre Tollemer, Eugène Robillard de Beaurepaire, Auguste de Blangy, and Madeleine Foisil. Bricqueboscq: Champs, 1993.

Grégoire, Gaspard. *Explication des cérémonies de la Fête-Dieu d'Aix-en-Provence.* Aix: David, 1777.

Gringore, Pierre. *Oeuvres complètes de Gringore.* Edited by Charles d'Héricault and A. Montaiglon. Paris: P. Jannet, 1858–77.

Guéraud, Jean. *La chronique lyonnaise de Jean Guéraud, 1536–1562.* Edited by Jean Tricou. Lyon: Audin, 1929.

La guirlande et response d'Angoulevent à l'Archipöete des pois pillez. Paris: Hubert Velut, 1603.

Harangue de Turlupin le soufreteux. 1615.

Harangue du Sieur Mistanguet, parent de Bruscambille, pour la défense des droicts du mardy gras. Paris, 1615.

Harangue faicte au charlatan de la place d'Aufine, à la descente de son théâtre. Paris, [1620–22].

Histoire de l'art au XVIe siècle, 1540–1600. Edited by Catherine Grodecki. Paris: Archives Nationales, 1986.

L'impieté domptée, Valens empereur d'Orient, tragedie pour la distribution des prix que le Roy a fondez a perpetuité dans le College de Clermont, août 1642.

Inventaire des archives communales de la ville de Toulouse antérieures à 1790. Edited by E. Roschach. Toulouse: E. Privat, 1891.

Inventaire des registres des insinuations du Châtelet de Paris, règnes de François Ier et de Henri II. Edited by Émile Campardon and Alexandre Tuetey. Paris: Imprimerie Nationale, 1906.

Inventaires après décès (1483–1547). Edited by Madeleine Jurgens. Paris: Archives Nationales, 1982.

Inventaire sommaire des archives communales antérieures à 1790, Rouen. Edited by Charles de Robillard de Beaurepaire. Rouen: Le Cerf, 1887.

Inventaire sommaire des archives hospitalières antérieures à 1790. Edited by Michel Moring. Paris: Grandremy et Henon, 1886.

Inventaire sommaire des registres de la jurade de Bordeaux (1520–1783). Edited by Paul Courteault and Alfred Leroux. Bordeaux: F. Pech, 1896–1947.

The Jesuites Play at Lyons in France as It Was There Presented. London: Nathaniell Butter, 1607.

Joubert, Laurent. *Traité du ris: Contenant son essance, ses causes, et mervelheus effais.* Paris: Nicolas Chesneau, 1579.

Journal de Jean Héroard. Edited by Madeleine Foisil and Pierre Chaunu. Paris: Fayard, 1989.

Journal d'Olivier Lefèvre d'Ormesson et extraits des mémoires d'André Lefèvre d'Ormesson. Edited by M. Chéruel. Paris: Imprimerie Impériale, 1860.

Journal d'un bourgeois de Paris sous le règne de François 1er (1515–1536). Edited by Ludovic Lalanne. Paris: Renouard, 1854.

Jouvancy, Joseph de. *De la manière d'apprendre et d'enseigner: De ratione discendi et docendi.* Translated by H. Ferté. Paris: Hachette, 1892.

La Mare, Nicolas de. *Traité de la police, où l'on trouvera l'histoire de son établissement, les fonctions et les prérogatives de ses magistrats.* 4 vols. Paris: J. et P. Cot, 1705–38.

Larivey, Pierre de. *Les comédies facetieuses de P. de l'A., Champenois: À l'imitation des anciens grecs, latins et modernes italiens.* Rouen: Raphael Du Petit Val, 1611.

La Roche Flavin, Bernard de. *Treze livres des parlemens de France.* Bordeaux: Simon Millanges, 1617.

Lesnauderie, Pierre Lemonnier de. *La farce de Pates-Ouaintes: Pièce satyrique représentée par les écoliers de l'Université de Caen, au carnaval de 1492.* Edited by T. Bonnin. Evreux: Jules Ancelle, 1843.

L'Estoile, Pierre de. *Mémoires-journaux, 1574–1611.* 12 vols. Edited by G. Brunet. Paris: Librairie des Bibliophiles, 1875–99. Reprint; Paris: Tallandier, 1982.

Liber nationis provinciae Provinciarum: Journal des étudiants provençaux à l'Université de Toulouse (1558–1630). Edited by Marie-Madeleine Mouflard. La-Roche-Sur-Yon: Imprimerie Centrale de l'Ouest, 1965.

Le magnifique et royal ballet dansé à Lyon, en la présence des deux reines, sous le nom de l'Aurore et Céphale. Paris, 1622.

Malingré, Claude. *Les antiquitez de la ville de Paris.* Paris: Pierre Rocolet, 1640.

[Malpoy, Pierre.] *Le chariot de triomphe du roy représenté par l'infanterie dijonnoise, le dimanche 25 février 1629.* Dijon: Nicolas Sprinx, 1629.

———. *Entrée de . . . Henri de Bourbon, prince de Condé, . . . en la ville de Dijon, le trentième du mois de septembre mil six cens trente-deux.* Dijon: Veuve Claude Guyot, 1632.

[———.] *Resjouissance de l'Infanterie Dijonnoise, pour la naissance de Monsieur le Prince de Conty [Antoine de Bourbon].* Dijon: Veuve Claude Guyot, 1630.

Marot, Clément. *Oeuvres poétiques.* 2 vols. Edited by Gérard Defaux. Paris: Classiques Garnier, 1990.

Le mémoire de Mahelot, Laurent, et d'autres décorateurs de l'hôtel de Bourgogne et de la Comédie-Française au XVIIe siècle. Edited by Henry Carrington Lancaster. Paris: Champion, 1920.

Mémoires du maréchal de Florange, dit le Jeune Adventureux. 2 vols. Edited by Robert Goubaux and P.-André Lemoisne. Paris: Renouard, 1913–24.

Metamorphose Mazarine ou changement grotesque de Mazarin en Tabarin. Paris: Julien Rambau, 1651.

Métivier, Jean de. *Chronique du Parlement de Bordeaux, 1462–1566.* 2 vols. Bordeaux: Arthur de Brezetz et Jules Delpit, 1886–87.

Miraulmont, Pierre de. *Les mémoires de Pierre de Miraulmont sur l'origine et institution des cours souveraines.* Paris: Chevalier, 1612.

Molé, Mathieu. *Mémoires.* Paris: Renouard, 1855.

Montaigne, Michel de. *Les essais de Michel de Montaigne, publiés d'après l'exemplaire de Bordeaux.* Edited by Fortunat Strowski. Bordeaux: F. Pech, 1906.

La muse historique, ou recueil des Lettres en vers, contenant les nouvelles du temps, écrites à Son Altesse Mlle de Longueville, par le sieur Loret: 4 mai 1650–28 mars 1665. Paris: C. Chenault, 1658.

Navarre, Marguerite de. *Heptaméron.* Edited by Renja Salminen. Geneva: Droz, 1999.

Navieres, Charles de. *Chant triomphal de la céleste victoire donnée au Roy très chrestien près d'Yvry.* Châlons-sur-Marne: Claude Guyot, 1590.

Noirot, Claude. *L'origine des masques, mommeries, bernez et revennez ès jours gras des Caresmeprenant.* Lengres: Jehan Chauvetet, 1609.

Les nouvelles et plaisantes imaginations de Bruscambille. Paris: François Huby, 1612.

L'ombre du marquis d'Ancre à la France . . . le tout recueilli par un secrétaire de la Faveur, disciple de Tabarin. (1620).

Ouverture des jours gras, ou l'Entretien carnaval. Edited by J. Lough. Oxford: Blackwell, 1957.

Parfaict, François, and Claude Parfaict. *Histoire du théâtre françois depuis son origine jusqu'à présent.* Paris: P. G. Le Mercier, 1745–49.

Pasquier, Étienne. *Les recherches de la France.* Edited by Marie-Madeleine Fragonard and François Roudaut. Paris: Champion, 1996.

[Perard, Bénigne, and Étienne Bréchillet]. *Le retour de Bontemps: Dedié à Monseigneur le Prince [de Condé], gouverneur et lieutenant general de sa majesté . . . et representé à son entree par l'Infanterie Dijonnoise, le dimanche troisième octobre 1632.* Dijon: Veuve Claude Guyot, [1632].

Peripatetiques, resolutions et remonstrances sententieuses du docteur Bruscambille aux perturbateurs de l'Estat. Paris: Va du Cul Gouverneur des Singes, 1619.

Petit de Julleville, Louis. *Histoire du théâtre en France: Répertoire du théâtre comique en France au moyen âge.* Paris: Le Cerf, 1886.

Pisan, Christine de. *Le livre du corps de policie.* Edited by Angus J. Kennedy. Paris: Champion, 1998.

Plaidoyé sur la principauté des sots, avec l'arrest de la Cour intervenu sur iceluy. Paris: David Douceur, 1608.

Le Pont-Breton des procureurs, dedié aux clercs du Palais. 1624.

La pourmenade du pré aux clercs. 1622.

Prédictions grotesques et recreatives du docteur Bruscambille pour l'année 1619, où, souz motz couverts est traicté des choses de ces temps. Paris, 1618.

Querelle de Marot et Sagon. Edited by Paul Lacombe and Émile Picot. Rouen: Albert Lainé, 1920.

Rabelais, François. *Le tiers livre des faicts et dicts héroiques du bon Pantagruel.* Edited by Jean Plattard. Paris: Société des Belles Lettres, 1948.

Raillerie de Gros Guillaume sur les affaires de ce temps. 1623.

Ratio studiorum: Plan raisonné et institution des études dans la Compagnie de Jésus. Edited by Adrien Demoustier, Dominque Julia, and Marie-Madeleine Compère. Translated by Léone Albrieux and Dolorès Pralon-Julia. Paris: Belin, 1997.

Réception de très-chrestien, très-juste, et très-victorieux monarque Louis XIII, roi de France et de Navarre. Lyon: Jacques Roussin, 1623.

Recueil d'actes notariés relatifs à l'histoire de Paris et ses environs au XVIe siècle. 2 vols. Edited by Ernest Coyecque. Paris: Imprimerie Nationale, 1905–23.

Recueil de farces (1450–1550). Edited by André Tissier. Geneva: Droz, 1986–2000.

Recueil de farces, moralités et sermons joyeux. 4 vols. Edited by Antoine-Jean-Victor Le Roux de Lincy. Paris: Techener, 1831–38.

Recueil des plus excellents ballets de ce temps. Paris: Toussainct du Bray, 1612.

Recueil des poésies françoises des XVe et XVIe siècles. 13 vols. Edited by Anatole de Montaiglon. Paris: Daffis, 1878.

Recueil des principaux titres concernant l'acquisition de la propriété des masure et place où a été bâtie la maison appelée vulgairement l'Hôtel de Bourgogne. Paris, 1632.

Recueil des statuts, ordonnances, reiglements, antiquitez, prérogatives, et prééminences du royaume de la Bazoche. Paris: C. Besongne, 1654.

Recueil général des oeuvres et fantasies de Tabarin. Rouen: L. De Mesnil, 1664.

Recueil général des sotties. 3 vols. Edited by Émile Picot. Paris: Firmin Didot, 1902.

Recueil Trepperel. Edited by Eugénie Droz. Geneva: Slatkine, 1966.

Regi christianissimo agonothetae munificentissimo Adonias: Tragoedia dabitur in theatrum Claromontanum Societatis Jesu. Paris, 1648.

Registres des délibérations du bureau de la ville de Paris. 15 vols. Edited by François Bonnardot, Alexandre Tuetey, Paul Guérin, and Léon Le Grand. Paris: Imprimerie Nationale, 1883–1921.

Relation de ce qui s'est passé en la ville de Dijon pour l'heureuse naissance de Monseigneur le Dauphin. Dijon: Pierre Palliot, 1638.

Remonstrance à Monseigneur le duc de Lorraine pour le retirer de la Ligue. Châlons-sur-Marne: Claude Guyot, 1589.

Renaudot, Théophraste. *Recueil des gazettes nouvelles . . . 1634.* Paris: Bureau d'Adresse, 1635.

La réponse de Guérin à Maitre Guillaume et les réjouissances des Dieux sur les heureuses alliances de France et d'Espagne. Paris: Jean Millot et Jean de Bordeaulx, 1612.

La response a la misere des clercs des procureurs ou l'innocence deffendue par Madame Choiselet. Paris, 1627.

Response de Gaultier Garguille aux révélations fantastiques de maistre Guillaume.

La response du sieur Tabarin au livre intitulé "La tromperie des charlatans descouverte." Paris: Sylvestre Moreau, 1619.

Le retour du brave Turlupin de l'autre monde. Paris, 1637.

Rithmes du seigneur d'Engoulevent sur les affaires de la Ligue: Extraites de la Satyre Menippee. Lyon, 1594.

Rivet, André. *Instruction chrestienne touchant les spectacles publics des comédies et tragédies.* La Haye: T. Maire, 1639.

The Royal Tour of France by Charles IX and Catherine de'Medici: Festivals and Entries, 1564–66. Edited by Victor E. Graham and W. McAllister Johnson. Toronto: University of Toronto Press, 1979.

La ruine de la chicane; ou la misère des advocats, procureurs, greffiers, notaires, huissiers, clercs, praticiens et autres, et de leurs femmes. Paris, 1649.

Salisbury, Jean of. *The Statesman's Book of John of Salisbury.* Translated by John Dickinson. New York: Russell and Russell, 1963.

Savaron, Jean de. *Traitté contre les masques.* Paris: Adrien Périer, 1611.

Scudéry, Georges de. *L'apologie du théâtre.* Paris: Augustin Courbé, 1639.

Sentence burlesque. 1649.

Sireulde, Jacques. *Le trésor immortel: Tiré de l'Ecriture sainte.* Edited by Charles de Beaurepaire. Rouen: Leon Gy, 1899.

Six farces normandes du Recueil La Vallière. Edited by Emmanuel Philipot. Rennes: Plihon, 1939.

Solemnité de la canonization de Sainct Ignace de Loyola fondateur de la Compagnie de Jésus, et de S. François Xavier de la mesme Compagnie, faicte à Bordeaux. Bordeaux: Jacques Millanges, 1622.

Suite du Pont-Breton des procureurs: Dedié aux clercs du palais. Paris, 1624.

Tabarin. *Bon jour et bon an: A Messieurs le Cornards de Paris, et de Lyon.* Lyon, 1620.

Tabouret, Étienne. *Les escriagnes dijonnoises: Recueillies par le sieur des Accords.* Poitiers, 1610.

Taillepied, Noel. *Recueil des antiquitez et singularitez de la ville de Rouen, avec un progrez des choses memorables y advenues depuis sa fondation jusques à present. par. F. N. T.* Rouen: Martine Le Mesgissier, 1610.

Tallemant des Réaux, Gédéon. *Les historiettes.* 9 vols. Edited by M. de Monmerqué and Paulin Paris. Paris: J. Techener, 1854.

Théâtre de l'Infanterie Dijonnoise. 2 vols. Edited by Joachim Durandeau. Dijon: Darantière, 1887.

Théâtre et propagande aux débuts de la Réforme: Six pièces polémiques du Recueil La Vallière: Textes établis d'après le MS BN 24341. Edited by Jonathan Back. Geneva: Slatkine, 1986.

Théâtre royal du Persée françois ouvert à l'arrivée de sa Majesté dans le collège de la Compagnie de Jesus à Toulouse. Toulouse, 1622.

Theodoricus, tragédie à representer par la jeunesse du Collège de la Societé de Jesus à Malines le 11 septembre 1618. Malines: Henri Iaey, 1618.

La tragi-comedie des enfans de Turlupin malhereus de nature: Où l'on void les fortunes dudit Turlupin, le mariage d'entre luy et la boulonnoise, et autres mille plaisantes joyeusetez qui trompent la morne Oisiveté. Rouen: Abraham Cousturier, [1612].

Triomphe de l'abbaye des Conards avec une notice sur la fête des fous. Rouen, 1587. Reprint; Paris: Librairie des Bibliophiles, 1874.

Trois farces du Recueil de Londres. Edited by Emmanuel Philipot. Rennes: Plihon, 1931.

Vers composés pour les enfants de la Mère-Folle de Dijon vers la fin du XVIe siècle. Edited by Luc Verhaeghe. Dijon: Bibliothèque Municipale, 1995.

Victoire de Phebus François contre le Python de ce temps, tragedie. Rouen, 1617.

Index

Note: Page numbers with an *f* indicate figures.

This index includes references to authors of secondary source books to guide you to relevant footnotes.